WORKING WOMEN AND THEIR RIGHTS IN THE WORKPLACE

This wonderful book brings together the best traditions of international human rights law and law and society scholarship to illuminate a topic of great importance. It is a major contribution to the ongoing struggle for full recognition of the rights of working women, in Libya and across the globe.

Luke McNamara, University of Wollongong, Australia

To my devoted Mother and Father who taught me to dream

Working Women and their Rights in the Workplace

International Human Rights and Its Impact on Libyan Law

NAEIMA FARAJ A.A. AL-HADAD
University of Bahrain, Bahrain

Routledge
Taylor & Francis Group
LONDON AND NEW YORK

First published 2015 by Ashgate Publishing

2 Park Square, Milton Park, Abingdon, Oxfordshire OX14 4RN
52 Vanderbilt Avenue, New York, NY 10017

Routledge is an imprint of the Taylor & Francis Group, an informa business

First issued in paperback 2020

British Library Cataloguing in Publication Data
A catalogue record for this book is available from the British Library

Library of Congress Cataloging-in-Publication Data
Al-Hadad, Naeima Faraj A.A., author.
Working women and their rights in the workplace : international human rights and its impact on Libyan law / by Naeima Faraj A.A. Al-Hadad.
pages cm
Includes bibliographical references and index.
Based on author's thesis (doctoral – University of Wollongong), 2011.
ISBN 978-1-4724-4499-8 (hardback)
1. Women – Employment – Law and legislation – Libya. 2. Labor laws and legislation, International.
3. International and municipal law – Libya. I. Title.
KSP1424.A949 2015
344.61201'4 – dc23

2014029250

ISBN 978-1-4724-4499-8 (hbk)
ISBN 978-0-367-59957-7 (pbk)

Contents

List of Abbreviations

C3	Maternity Protection Convention 1919
C103	Maternity Protection Convention (Revised) 1952
C111	Discrimination (Employment and Occupation) Convention
C183	Maternity Protection Convention 2000
CEACR	Committee of Experts on the Application of Conventions and Recommendations
CEDAW	Convention on the Elimination of All Forms of Discrimination against Women
CESCR	Committee on Economic, Social and Cultural Rights
CRC	Convention on the Rights of the Child
DEDAW	Declaration on the Elimination of Discrimination against Women
EEO	Equal Employment Opportunity
GGCHR	Great Green Charter of Human Rights
GP Cttee	General People's Committee
GPC	General People's Congress
HREOC	Human Rights and Equal Opportunity Commission (Australia)
ICCPR	International Covenant on Civil and Political Rights
ICESCR	International Covenant on Economic, Social and Cultural Rights
ICERD	International Convention on the Elimination of All Forms of Racial Discrimination
ILC	International Labour Conference
ILO	International Labour Organization
LYD	Libyan dinar
MMR	Maternal Mortality Rate
NGO	Non-Governmental Organisation
OAU	Organisation of African Unity
OECD	Organisation for Economic Cooperation and Development
OHCHR	Office of the United Nations High Commissioner for Human Rights
UDHR	Universal Declaration of Human Rights
UN	United Nations
UNDP	United Nations Development Programme
UNDRC	United Nations Declaration of the Rights of the Child
UNECA	United Nations Economic Commission for Africa
UNESCO	United Nations Educational, Scientific and Cultural Organization
UNHCR	United Nations High Commissioner for Refugees
UNICEF	United Nations International Children's Emergency Fund
VCLT	Vienna Convention on the Law of Treaties
WHA	World Health Assembly
WHO	World Health Organization

Glossary of Arabic Terms

Jamahiriya	State of masses
Kafalah	Islamic system of adoption
Qur'ān	The holy book of Islam revealed by Allah to the Prophet Muhammad (PBUH); contains the divine message that Muslims believe to be unaltered since its revelation
Shar' iah	Islamic law
Sunnah	The traditions of the prophet Muhammad (PBUH)
Wali	A benefactor, companion, protector, governor; the legal guardian of a minor, woman or incapacitated person
Wilaya	Guardianship

Note on Transliteration

Below is the McGill University Institute of Islamic Studies' transliteration system of Arabic words and names which was used in this volume.

b = ب	z = ز	f = ف
t = ت	s = س	q = ق
th = ث	sh = ش	k = ك
j = ج	s{ = ص	l = ل
h{ = ح	d{ = ض	m = م
kh = خ	t{ = ط	n = ن
d = د	z{ = ظ	h = ه
dh = ذ	‘ = ع	w = و
r = ر	gh = غ	y = ي

Short: a = ´ ; i = ; u = ʼ
Long: a< = ا ; i> = ي ; ū = و
Diphthong: ay = ا ي ; aw = ا و

Acknowledgements

This journey to publication has been a rollercoaster ride, long and full of ups and downs but in the end worth the screams of terror and long restless nights.

There have been so many people who have made this ride easier at times, who have reminded me of how close I was to the end, and who have sat with me, at times in the same chair, and experienced it all with me. I would like to acknowledge these people.

My sincerest gratitude goes to my parents, for without them I would not have dared endeavour to go on such a ride. It is through their encouragement and hopes that I started to dream and believe I could do it, and so began this journey.

However, I would not have continued on this long and winding yet rewarding path if it were not for my supervisor and Dean of the Faculty of Law, Luke McNamara. It is through his support and words of encouragement that I continued. English being my second language was a barrier, but he did not allow it to be. Even when we were on completely different continents, he still encouraged me and supported me when times were hard, and so thank you for your support and patience.

Another absolutely fundamental person who has not only helped me but really made it possible for me to finish this journey is Elaine Newby. She is passionate about what she does and puts her whole mind and heart into it, looking not only at grammar or punctuation but also offering advice on English expression and alerting the writer to possible misinterpretations. So thank you for your support, help and understanding, for your assistance with the task that was set before me. I could not have done it without you.

Also Maha Elhage, thank you. Thank you for your patience and time. Thank you for helping me during the translation of the interview transcripts. Thank you for being a true friend and neighbour.

Also I would like to thank the University of Wollongong, especially the Faculty of Law. The staff were amazing, kind and supportive, and made me feel at home – a true family. Thanks also to the library staff, especially Elizabeth White, who encouraged me in my research activities and helped me with footnotes. I would also like to express my sincere gratitude to my fellow researchers, particularly Thanh (the note wizard) and Mai Hanh, for coming to my aid when technology was not my best friend. Thank you for answering all my questions even though you had your own deadlines, and thank you for all the cookies.

I am also very grateful to my sponsor, Dr Omran Zwed, for his understanding and financial support; and to Dr Amal Obeidi for her guidance during the long and tiring data collection period. Dr Zaineb Zahrie, another amazing woman who was just as excited and passionate about this research, and who was there guiding me and blowing me away with all her ideas, thank you. Also Dr Cassandra Sharp, I thank for all her time and professional advice.

Also to all my friends, a million thanks. A big thank you goes to Jamila Arrish and her husband Abdelrazeg Bashasha. Thank you guys for stealing away my children for a couple of days; thank you for supporting me and helping me in every way possible; and thank you for being there for me and my family during times of hardship. Ruveda Ozturk, thank you. You have really helped me and been there for me every time I emailed you – and that was often Also to my wonderful sister-in-law, Ilham Hbaci, many thanks.

I thank my family: my wonderful husband, Ali, for his support, especially in the demanding time of the ESL course; and our daughter Hager and sons Aimen and Anas. Thank you for believing in me; thank you for pretending to love your father's cooking; and thank you for knowing how to deal with me and my emotional heights. I hope you are as inspired as I have been by you.

Last but definitely not least, I would like to thank Ashgate Publishing for giving me this wonderful opportunity to share my years of research with the world. I hope this book makes a difference to the lives of many.

Chapter 1

Introduction

This volume explores the relationship between the rights of women at work and their rights as mothers. It considers how these two sets of rights, as protected under international human rights law, can and should be recognised and promoted within the Libyan legal system. It examines the theoretical and practical operation of relevant Libyan laws in the context of the standards set by international human rights law, including the *Convention on the Elimination of All Forms of Discrimination against Women* (CEDAW) and the *Convention on the Rights of the Child* (CRC) as well as the International Labour Organization (ILO) conventions, in particular the three Maternity Protection Conventions and the *Discrimination* (*Employment and Occupation*) *Convention* (C111).

Libya is a country on the horizon of a new era; it seeks change for the better. This study is the first in its field to bring to light the injustice Libyan women encounter in society from a legal perspective. A new approach has been adopted, unique in its style, to assess, explore and address the struggle working mothers, particularly those in Libya, face. Libya was the chosen focus as it is a country which has signed and agreed to many International conventions and is a party in a number of international organisations; however, it does not implement these laws. The struggle between theory and practice of law in Libya is evident. In Libya, prevailing cultural stereotypes and traditional views of women make it very clear that the 'best' (most acceptable) place for women is their homes, and that the most significant role women can play is inside the home not outside it.

This study assesses the adequacy of existing Libyan laws and, where warranted, recommends amendments and reforms to ensure the protection of both sets of rights. This volume aims to facilitate the enjoyment by working women of their rights as both independent workers and as mothers, without requiring a choice of one role over the other.

Libyan employment laws in relation to working mothers are examined, as are the steps that have been taken within the Libyan legal system to prevent discrimination and to encourage participation. How and why participation continues to be limited is also examined.

Research undertaken included a review of primary and secondary materials on relevant international human rights law in order to determine what is expected of States parties in regard to respecting work rights and motherhood rights (including maternity leave).

A 'qualitative research approach' was used to conduct the study and collect the research data, as it is claimed that data collected using this method can provide rich and in-depth understanding of the area under investigation. The semi-structured interview, a form of qualitative research method, was selected for use. It is defined as a flexible type of interview in which the interviewer begins with a number of defined questions but includes open-ended questions which promote a broader range of responses than those anticipated, enabling a researcher to take advantage of relevant material that is disclosed. Material collected is then analysed, in this instance, to provide a view of the contemporary experience of Libyan women, particularly as it relates to the intersection of pregnancy and motherhood with their working lives.

The study documented in this volume attempts to make radical and practical contributions to the current Libyan legal regime. It is hoped that its findings and recommendations can lead to the improvement of employment and other legislation, especially where it relates to maternity leave and other issues affecting the lives of working mothers. In this way, the study will make a contribution to the scholarly literature in this area of human rights norms, and also offer some practical steps to strengthen Libyan laws and regulations in this field as they relate to working women's rights. These changes will benefit Libyan women and provide them with ways to possess and enjoy their rights both as mothers and as independent working women who can play an effective role in broader Libyan society. If implemented, the changes put forward will have a positive effect on the Libyan economy, including an increase in women's participation rates in the workforce that will achieve the country's desired goal of increased national productivity and also raise the standard of living for many families.

Background

Employment laws have been introduced over many years and in diverse countries to provide better conditions in the workplace. Equal employment opportunity (EEO) remains a highly debated topic in many socio-economic, political and educational forums both at local and international levels. Within this context, working women are seeking positive changes to workplace policies in order to minimise discrimination in industries, services and organisations, both in government and the private sector.

The term 'equal employment opportunity' can be defined as every person having fair access to, and opportunities in, the workplace, including obtaining and retaining employment, and having access to training and promotion regardless of gender, race, colour, religion, age or status. In Australia, for example:

> It is unlawful to discriminate in recruitment and offers of employment, as well as the actual terms and conditions of employment, access to promotion and training and dismissal or any other detriment.[1]

The project undertaken by the author and referred to in this volume explores the relationship between the rights of women at work and their rights as mothers, and considers how these two sets of rights, as protected under international human rights law, can and should be recognised and promoted within the Libyan legal system.

Although this publication is predominantly about the situation prevailing during the era before the Revolution of 17 February 2011, it is particularly relevant as Libya formulates a new pathway in the twenty-first century. The situation remains, understandably, somewhat in flux as a new era dawns in Libya, one which may (or may not) see further progress in areas critical to women being able to enjoy their rights both as mothers and as workplace participants. The author hopes that her work will make a positive contribution to the legislative framework and also in regard to implementation so as to reduce the 'gap' between the law and practice and make the enjoyment of the above rights possible.

---

1 Human Rights and Equal Opportunity Commission (Australia), *Federal Discrimination Law* (HREOC, 2008) 20.

Overview of Libyan Society

Libya[2] is the fourth largest country in Africa by area and the 17th largest in the world.[3] In 2010, it had a population of approximately 6.5 million.[4] On an economic note, although agriculture is constrained by the country's extensive deserts, Libya's economy is boosted by its role as the world's 11th largest oil producer.[5]

Libya is a North African country which – until the events of early 2011 – had been governed under what was rather euphemistically termed a 'socialist democratic system' since the late Muammar Gaddafi seized power from King Idris in a seemingly bloodless military coup in September 1969, less than 20 years after the country had gained independence.[6] Welcomed initially by many as representative of a new Arab nationalism and independence from pro-western political and economic policies, the new regime appeared to advance the nation in terms of per capita income, education, housing, longevity and infant and maternal mortality rates (MMR), as well as women's rights in terms of education, labour force participation and other matters. However, this was achieved in a rather idiosyncratic and dictatorial manner, and in circumstances not conducive to overall human rights and the progress of peace. As in many socialist states, dissent came to be repressed and press freedoms strictly curtailed in a still essentially paternalistic state that more resembled a military dictatorship than 'popular socialism' despite the introduction of the General People's Congress.[7]

---

2 *Al-Jamahiriya al-arabia al-Libya al-shabbia al-Ishtieryiakiah al-Ozmah* is the official name of Libya. In this volume, it will be referred to as 'Libya'. After the Revolution of 17 February 2011, the official name is now simply 'Libya'. The name 'Libya' is of ancient derivation. It was initially applied to a single Berber tribe by the Ancient Egyptians, and later used by the Greeks to indicate those persons living in North Africa and their lands: Library of Congress Federal Research Division, *Country Profile: Libya* (Library of Congress, 2005) 1.

3 United Nations, Economic and Social Affairs, United Nations Statistics Division *Demographic Yearbook 2003* <http://unstats.un.org/unsd/demographic/products/dyb/2000-round.htm>; Central Intelligence Agency (CIA), *The World Factbook* (2010) <https://www.cia.gov/library/publications/the-world-factbook/geos/ly.html>.

4 Or 6,461,454: (CIA), *The World Factbook: Population* (2010) <http://www.nationsencyclopedia.com/WorldStats/CIA-World-Factbook-Population.html>. However, this number has been affected by the recent unrest which has seen over 500,000 (including approximately 125,000 Libyans) flee the country at least temporarily: UNHCR, *Lack of Funds Threatening UNHCR's Work in Libya, Neighbouring Countries* (9 June 2011) <http://www.unhcr.org/4da81fcd9.html>.

5 Adel Abdulhamid Mashat et al, 'The Social Role of Accountings: Views and Perceptions of the Accounting Community in Libya towards Corporate' (Paper presented at Social Responsibility Research, Leeds, 4–6 September 2005) 2.

6 This was the unrealistic term used to define the dictatorship existing during the Gaddafi era, prior to the Revolution of 17 February 2011. See also Al Jazeera, *Profile: Muammar Gaddafi* (22 August 2011) <http://www.aljazeera.com/indepth/2011/02/201122117565923629.html>.

7 For example, the concept of elections was early rejected by Muammar Gaddafi as 'the people … [lack] a degree of consciousness where they could have free elections': Muammar Gaddafi cited in Ruth First, *Libya: The Elusive Revolution* (Penguin, 1972) [Pt III], republished in 2012, 128. See also 103–9, 110–18, 120–28, 133. See <http://www.ruthfirstpapers.org.uk>. The introduction of the General People's Congress did not reduce the overall extent of his control, as he continued to try to shape the country's development.

Although Libya was clearly aiming at some new type of Islamic socialist state (at 138). the twin fears were Islamic ultra-radicalism and pro-western reactionism: at 133–5. The text of the *Great Green Charter* reflects concerns about religious extremism and sectarianism while simultaneously claiming to uphold judgements made by society which were based on 'sacred law, religion and custom, the terms of which are

By far the vast majority of Libyan citizens are of the Arab Nation, as could be previously inferred from the country's name but not so easily from the current title of simply 'Libya'.[8] The official language is Arabic (spoken by the vast majority and the common language of the country, though some dialectical variations exist),[9] and Islam remains the formal religion of the state. Religious freedom is protected in accordance with the customs and laws of the country. The family is the cornerstone of society, and it is the unit where religion, morality and patriotism are founded and practised. Social harmony within the community is regarded as the foundation of unity.

Every Libyan citizen who is able to work, whether male or female, has the right and duty to work,[10] and it is considered an honour to be working for the country. Some people are specifically chosen to be employed in public service, and the goal of all public servants is to serve the nation to the best of their ability.[11] It is worth noting that the public sector comprises the larger part of the employment sector, as can be expected in what had for long been a socialist state. A smaller proportion of the population is privately employed.

Libya has had a long association with supranational bodies. It is a member of the League of Arab States, which it joined in 1953 – the first country to do so after the formation of the League in 1945, when it had seven founding members.[12] The question of its independence (from its

---

stable, unchangeable and for which there can be no substitute': *Great Green Charter of Human Rights in the Jamahiriya Era 1988* (Libya) art 10.

Those unsympathetic to Gaddafi's regime (or believed to be) could find themselves imprisoned by the secret police (First: at 138) as a 'cultural revolution' was implemented during those early years. In later years, repression could be 'firm'. For example, the ruthless execution of almost 1,300 prisoners in a single day after rioting erupted over conditions in the Abu Salim Prison (Tripoli) in 1996, where those killed included academics and others who had simply got 'on the wrong side' of the secret police: Portia Walker, '10,000 Still Missing in Gaddafi's Killing Fields' *Independent* (UK) 1 July 2012 <http://www.independent.co.uk/news/world/africa/10000-still-missing-in-gaddafis-killing-fields-7901927.html>. The appalling massacre was a contributing factor to the recent revolution when some of those calling for investigation were arrested. See Human Rights Watch, *Libya: Arrests, Assaults in Advance of Planned Protests*, 17 February 2011 <http://www.hrw.org/news/2011/02/16/libya-arrests-assaults-advance-planned-protests>.

Libya's first free election in decades was scheduled to be held on 7 July 2012: Make Every Woman Count, *Libya: Equal Participation of Women Vital for Building New Libya, Says UN Envoy*, 27 June 2012, <http://www.peacewomen.org/news_article.php?id=5069&type=news>.

8 The grandiloquent *al-Jumhūriyyah al-'Arabiyyah al-Lībiyyah* or the Great Socialist People's Libyan Arab *Jamahiriya* or Libyan Arab has given way to 'Libya' – or, less frequently, to 'Republic of Libya' (Libyan *Jamahiriya*) – since the 2011 Revolution.

9 For more details regarding this and the far less frequently spoken minority languages, see Paul M Lewis (ed), *Ethnologue: Languages of the World* (9 June 2011) SIL International <http://www.ethnologue.com/show_country.asp?name=libya>. It is worth noting that Arabic is also the most commonly spoken language used by young people in their homes in Australia, being spoken by 11.8% of the AEDI 2009 survey sample (of 261,203, which comprises 97.5% of the estimated population of five-year-olds in their first year of full-time schooling): Centre for Community Child Health and Telethon Institute for Child Health Research, 'A Snapshot of Early Childhood Development in Australia: Australian Early Development Index (AEDI) National Report 2009' (Australian Government, 2009) 3, 8 Table 2.6.

10 As was reflected in the wording of the *Great Green Charter of Human Rights in the Jamahiriya Era 1988* (Libya) art 11.

11 *Constitution Declaration of 1969* (Libya) arts 1, 2, 3, 4.

12 The League of Arab States (Arab League) is a 'voluntary association of independent countries whose peoples are mainly Arabic speaking'. Its goals are to 'strengthen ties among the member states, coordinate their policies, and promote their common interests … and [it] is involved in political, economic, cultural; and social programs designed to promote [those] interests … and has helped advance the role of women in Arab

former colonial power, Italy, as well as from France and Britain, in the post-World War II era) was the first issue considered by the League of Arab States at its initial session when its charter was adopted in 1945.

The issue of Libyan independence was also considered by the new post-war international organisation, the United Nations (UN),[13] in the third and fourth sessions of the General Assembly, held in 1948 and 1949 respectively. For this reason, Libya 'is sometimes referred to as the United Nations born daughter'.[14] Libya became independent from Italy on 24 December 1951[15] and a member of the UN on 14 December 1955, the sixth Arab state and the fifth African state to do so.[16]

On 25 May 1963, the Organisation of African Unity (OAU) was established, and Libya was one of the 32 African states to sign the charter of the OAU on that date. On 26 May 2001, the OAU was legally transformed into the African Union (AU), of which Libya continues as a member.[17]

Libya has ratified or acceded to numerous international legal agreements on human rights. Among these are 29 conventions of the ILO,[18] and a further seven human rights conventions created under the auspices of the United Nations.[19] However, a number of reservations have been entered where the government considers that the provisions of a convention or treaty conflict with

---

societies, and promoted child welfare activities': Arabic German Consulting, *The Arab League: The League of Arab States* (18 April 2011) <http://www.arab.de/arabinfo/league.htm>.

13 *Charter of the United Nations*, opened for signature 26 June 1945 (entered into force 26 June 1945).

14 Libyan Mission, *Libya at the UN* (12 November 2008) <http://www.libyanmission-un-org/welcome.htm>.

15 Library of Congress, *Country Profile: Libya*, above n 2, 1.

16 Libyan Mission, above n 14.

17 James Martin Center for Nonproliferation Studies, *Inventory of International Nonproliferation Organizations and Regimes: African Union (AU)* (2011) <http://cns.miis.edu/inventory/pdfs/au.pdf>.

18 International Labour Organization, *List of Ratifications of International Labour Conventions Libyan Arab Jamahiriya* (7 April 2011) <http://webfusion.ilo.org/public/applis/appl-byCtry.cfm?lang=EN&CTYCHOICE=1520>. However, one of the ILO conventions (C59 *Minimum Age (Industry) Convention (Revised) 1937*) was later renounced. Some eight conventions are considered directly related to human rights by the United Nations Development Programme's (UNDP) *Arab Human Rights Index* (AHR Index): *Convention on the Freedom of Association and Protection of the Right to Organise 1948* (2000); *Convention on the Right to Organise and Collective Bargaining 1949* (1962); *Convention on the Abolition of Forced Labour 1957* (1961); *Convention on Forced Labour 1930* (1961); *Convention on Equal Remuneration 1951* (1962); *Convention on Elimination of Discrimination in Respect of Employment and Occupation 1958* (1961); *Convention on Minimum Age 1973* (1975); *Convention on Worst Forms of Child Labour 1999* (2000). Note: the year in brackets is the year the particular convention was ratified by Libya. Strangely, the AHR Index omits reference to the *Convention on Maternity Protection 1919* (ratified 1971) and its 1952 revision (1975) as a human rights-related convention. See UNDP, AHR Index, *Libya: Human Rights Profile. International Conventions* (undated) (17 March 2011) <http://www.arabhumanrights.org/en/countries/country.aspx?cid=10>.

19 It has also signed a further seven relevant treaties under the auspices of the United Nations. See AHR Index, *Libya: Human Rights Profile*, above n 18. These comprise: the *International Covenant on Economic, Social and Cultural Rights 1966* (1970); *International Covenant on Civil and Political Rights 1966* (1970); *International Convention on the Elimination of All Forms of Racial Discrimination 1965* (1968); *Convention on the Elimination of All Forms of Discrimination against Women 1979* (1989); *Convention Against Torture and Other Cruel, Inhuman or Degrading Treatment or Punishment 1984* (1989); *Convention on the Rights of the Child 1989* (1993); and the *International Convention on the Protection of All Migrant Workers and Members of Their Families 1990* (2004). Libya is also a signatory to the first *Optional Protocol to the Covenant on Civil and Political Rights 1966* (1989); *Optional Protocol to the Convention on the Rights of the Child on the Involvement of Children in Armed Conflict 2000* (2004); and *Optional Protocol to the Convention on the Rights of the Child on the Sale of Children, Child Prostitution and Child Pornography 2000* (2004):

the spirit and teachings of the *Holy Qur'ān*. The basis for these reservations is the view that a state governed in accordance with Islam is expected to uphold and maintain the teaching of the *Holy Qur'ān*, which is regarded as of Divine origin, and which, therefore, must take precedence over the writings or philosophies of mere mortals.[20]

Provisions of international treaties to which Libya is a party are enforceable through domestic legislation.[21] Libya ratified CEDAW[22] on 16 May 1989.[23] However, on 5 July 1995 Libya entered reservations in relation to Articles 2 and 16[24] on the basis that they were inconsistent with the principles of equality between men and women in Libya as understood in the light of the *Holy Qur'ān*.[25] Article 16(d), for example, states that men and women have '[t]he same rights and responsibilities as parents'.[26] Under *Shar'iah* (Islamic law), introduced during the early 1970s in Libya,[27] the head of the household and the person who has responsibility for the family is the man, while the woman has no financial obligations to support the family, even if she works.[28] *Shar'iah* also influenced the *Marriage and Divorce Act No 10 of 1984*,[29] which affirms (in Articles 17, 40 and 71) that the man, who is the head of the family, is responsible for the family's welfare. Under Article 396 of the *Libyan Criminal Act*,[30] if a man does not take his family responsibilities

---

AHR Index. See also United Nations, *List of 24 Multilateral Treaties on the Protection of Civilians* (9 June 2011) <http://treaties.un.org/doc/source/events/2004/list.pdf>.

20 UNDP, AHR Index, *Libya: Human Rights Profile* (12 May 2011), above n 18. A similar provision for what must occur when there is a conflict between what is ordered by men and what is perceived to be the will of God appears in the Christian Scriptures where one of the first Apostles (Peter) and others are recorded as saying: 'We must obey God rather than men' (Acts 5:29b), *Holy Bible* (Oxford University Press, 2nd ed, 1971).

21 Aly Dawy, *Alqanwn Aldwly Alaam* (Dar Alkotop Alwatanyah, Bnghazy, 2nd ed, 2005) 62 [Trans: *Public International Law* (National Library, Benghazi)].

22 *Convention on the Elimination of All Forms of Discrimination against Women* (*CEDAW*), opened for signature 1 March 1980, 1249 UNTS 13 (entered into force 3 September 1981).

23 United Nations Division for the Advancement of Women/Department of Economic and Social Affairs (DESA), *Convention on the Elimination of All Forms of Discrimination against Women: States Parties* (10 May 2011) <http://www.un.org/womenwatch/daw/cedaw/states.htm>.

24 United Nations Division for the Advancement of Women/Department of Economic and Social Affairs, *Convention on the Elimination of All Forms of Discrimination against Women: Declarations, Reservations and Objections to CEDAW* (10 May 2011) <http://www.un.org/womenwatch/daw/cedaw/reservations-country.htm>.

25 UNDP, *Human Rights Profiles: Libya* (12 May 2011) above n 18. In regard to the reservation for Article 2: 'on the obligation of states to integrate the principle of gender equality in their national legislation, and guaranteeing actual realization of this principle, Libya said the principle would be applied according to Islamic law (Shari'a). [In regard to] Article (16/1) that commits states to take proper measures to eliminate discrimination against women in marriage and family affairs, Libya abides by women's rights guaranteed by Islamic Shari'a': at 2.

26 *CEDAW* art 16(d).

27 *Shar'iah* was declared the 'principle source of legislation' by the Revolutionary Command Council after the 'First of September Revolution' of 1 September 1969 which ousted the monarchy: Ali Omar Ali Mesrati, *The Best Interests of the Child: International Child Law as Interpreted in the Libyan High Court Jurisdiction* (PhD Thesis, University of Wollongong, 2009) 148–9; see also *Libyan Civil Code* art 1, and *Constitution Proclamation* art 2: Mesrati at 149–50.

28 Al-Sadq Abdul Rhman Al-Ghryani, *Mudunt Al-Fqh Al-Maliky wa Ta'diylatuh* (Mu'sast Al-Ryan, 2002) 105 [Trans: *Code of Maliki Jurisprudence and its Amendments* (Foundation Rayyan)]. This will be elaborated upon further below.

29 *Marriage and Divorce Act No 10 of 1984* (Libya); see also Mesrati, above n 27, 148.

30 *Criminal Act 1953* (Libya).

seriously, he can be adjudged a criminal and either jailed for no less than one year or asked to pay a fine of 50 Libyan dinars (LYD).[31] As elsewhere, men may try to avoid maintenance by claiming they have no employment or by understating income while employed. This highlights the need for women to be able to combine motherhood and paid employment.

Are There Problems for Women in Combining Work and Family? What Are They and to What Extent Do They Affect Women?

According to many of those who write on the subject of working women, '[f]amily responsibilities are the biggest determining factor in female participation in today's workforce'.[32] These findings do not come as a surprise to many women, but rather confirm their own personal experience or observation of their own experience or that of others. Women have the primary responsibility for taking care of other family members. Female participation in the workplace is commonly negatively related to the number and age of children in the household; that is, the more children in a household, the less likely a woman is to be employed or, if employed, the lower her hours of workplace participation are likely to be. Again, the younger the age of the youngest child, the less likely a woman is to participate in the workplace, or the lower her hours are likely to be.[33] Women, however, may have other caring responsibilities that impact on their workplace participation. Women are the most frequent carers, not only for children but also for the sick, the intellectually and/or physically disabled,[34] the elderly[35] and the mentally ill among family members. Therefore it can come as no surprise that, given 'the fact that women still shoulder the majority of unpaid household labor and care-giving responsibilities',[36] it is women who bear the brunt of conflict between family and work responsibilities.

While research over time and in various countries has shown this to be the case, in Libya it is even more pronounced, as women are almost universally expected to take on these responsibilities. It has also been commonly observed that '[w]omen do much more housework including childcare, than their partners, no matter how educated they are, how much they earn or how many hours they

---

31 The international code for the Libyan dinar is LYD: *Exchange Rate: Currency Information Libyan Dinar* (25 October 2011) <http://www.exchangerate.com/currency-information/libyan-dinar.html>.

32 Kandra Drayton, *Motherhood: How it Affects Women Journalists' Experiences* (LLM Thesis, University of Florida, 2004) 1; see also Organisation for Economic Cooperation and Development (OECD), *Babies and Bosses: Reconciling Work and Family Life: A Synthesis of Findings for OECD Countries* (OECD, 2007) 14, 6, where the younger the children, the lower the participation rate in the workforce.

33 See, e.g., Lixin Cai, 'Work Choices of Married Women: Drivers of Change' (Productivity Commission, Canberra, 2010) 3, 5–7, 50–58.

34 Productivity Commission, 'Disability Care and Support' (Draft Inquiry Report, February 2011), Section 2.2 'Disability and Disadvantage', where the report notes that '[f]amilies caring for people with disability are ... more likely to experience relationship breakdown'. Some 30% of female carers 30–50 years of age separate or divorce in the first 10 years of caring. Carers are far less likely than those in other families to participate in the workforce, or have participation limited due to their caring duties; 40% spend more than 40 hours per week caring for a family member.

35 Emily K Abel, 'Adult Daughters and Care for the Elderly' (1986) 12(3) *Feminist Studies* 479, 480; see also Naohiro Ogawa, Robert D Retherford and Yasuhiko Saito, 'Caring for the Elderly and Holding Down a Job: How Are Women in Japan Coping?' (2003) 65 *Asia-Pacific Population and Policy* 1, Figure 3.s.

36 Elizabeth Hirsh and Christopher J Lyons, 'Perceiving Discrimination on the Job: Legal Consciousness, Workplace Context, and the Construction of Race Discrimination' (2010) 44(2) *Law and Society Review* 269, 274.

spend in paid work'.[37] This is clear even in the most developed countries in the world. It is even clearer in developing countries, where 'there is still considerable reliance on the extended family'.[38]

It has been observed internationally that while women's workplace participation has increased substantially in recent decades, they 'continue to bear the primary responsibilities for unpaid work in the households, including both the provision of care to family members and domestic tasks'.[39] The unpaid labour of women is vital to the continued functioning and well-being of the entire society as their 'non-economic activities ... enable the care and maintenance of every member of society, underpinning societal health and survival'.[40] A 1997 study (undertaken using time diaries) found that while women spent less time on average in paid employment (30.8 hours as opposed to the average of 39.7 hours for men), women on average spent 25.6 hours and men 14.3 hours in duties that revolved around 'family care', including shopping, housework and caring for children.[41] The study revealed both a gender-based paid working hours' imbalance and the maintenance of traditional gender roles for the preponderance of care for home and family.

An Australian Institute of Family Studies investigation confirmed that women still 'shoulder the bulk of and the burden of family care'.[42] As Burrow so correctly observes:

> [T]he social and economic revolution which has led to more women being employed has not been matched with a cultural shift at the workplace or in the home which provides for the necessary flexibility to enable women and men to manage work and family.[43]

Across the world, in developing and least developed countries, women also bear the greater part of the responsibility for caring duties and other domestic responsibilities (which may include food-growing as well as preparation).

A UN report on equal sharing of responsibilities (including in an HIV/AIDS context) found that particular challenges have arisen due to the devastating effects of the HIV/AIDS epidemic with the caring role falling as it does largely on women and girls. This has made it difficult for younger women and girls to continue in education and for women particularly to continue in or seek paid employment at a time when there is ever more need for them to supply income as well as care.[44] The 'double burden' can be exacerbated by traditional expectations and a lack of social services and appropriate medications in poorer countries. The growing of food on a domestic plot may also suffer when a woman's time is taken up by her caring role, affecting family nutritional status. If it is the mother who is ill, then the risk of children becoming child labourers increases in poorer families, while adopting a carer role at the expense of education can adversely impact on the future

---

37 Neil Rees, Katherine Lindsay and Simon Rice, *Australian Anti-Discrimination Law: Text, Cases and Materials* (Federation Press, 2008) 333.

38 International Labour Office, 'Women's Employment: Global Trends ILO Responses, 49th sess of the Commission on the Status of Women' (United Nations, New York, 28 February–11 March 2005) 8.

39 Laura Addati and Naomi Cassirer, 'Equal Sharing of Responsibilities Between Women and Men, Including Care-Giving in the Context of HIV/AIDS' (EGM/ESOR/2008/BP.2, Division for the Advancement of Women Department of Economic and Social Affairs United Nations, 19 September 2008) 3.

40 Ibid.

41 Melissa A Milkie and Pia Peltola, 'Playing All the Roles: Gender and the Work-Family Balancing Act' (1999) 61(2) *Journal of Marriage and Family* 476, 478.

42 Sharan Burrow, 'An Unequal World' (2004) 27(3) *UNSW Law Journal* 884, 887.

43 Ibid.

44 Addati and Cassirer, 'Equal Sharing of Responsibilities' UN doc EGM/ESOR/2008/BP.2, above n 39, 6.

prospects of girls. Those without access to resources – the poor, rural dwellers, and racial and ethnic minorities who lack economic and social capital – are 'often hit hardest'.[45]

As mentioned earlier, in Libya, prevailing cultural stereotypes and traditional views of women make it very clear that the best (most acceptable) place for women is the home, and that the most significant role women can play is inside the home rather than outside it. They are not supposed to get help with housework, particularly from their husbands, as it is regarded as shameful for men to do domestic work[46] in Libyan society.[47] All these factors have made it difficult for women to find ways to balance work with motherhood.

Fortunately, this negative view of the role of women as workers in Libyan society is gradually changing for the better. Many laws have been enacted to support women socially and economically. However, there is still a big gap between the policy and the practice of these laws that makes it difficult for working women to enjoy both rights, that of work and that of motherhood. This is evidenced by the number of instances where there exists only short periods of maternity leave, and that leave which does exist has insufficient benefits. This creates conflict for working mothers and pushes them to choose between having children and having a career.

Another factor contributing to the struggle faced by working mothers is the lack of legislation providing suitable childcare facilities for their children in the workplace during working hours. Yet it has been shown that family-friendly workplace polices can help professional women tremendously by enabling them to remain in the workforce after having children and by reducing their work–family conflict.[48] In addition, there are no part-time positions or 'work from home' occupations in Libya. Such arrangements can offer a level of flexibility to mothers during transitional periods in their lives such as pregnancy and post-delivery.

The way in which working mothers are prevented from enjoying both rights – work and motherhood – amounts to discrimination and represents a denial of equal employment opportunity. Article 11 of CEDAW, to which Libya has been a State party since 1998, states that:

> States Parties shall take all appropriate measures to eliminate discrimination against women in the field of employment in order to ensure, on a basis of equality of men and women, the same rights.

Consistent with Libya's obligations under CEDAW, reform of the existing legal and regulatory regimes governing employment and maternity leave is imperative. As this book documents a legal study which is the first of its kind in Libya, some specific recommendations will be provided at the end of the volume to help achieve this objective.

Overview: International Conventions and Libyan Efforts to Prevent Discrimination

Gender discrimination negatively impacts on equal employment opportunities in the workplace for women around the world. Where significant gender stereotyping in the workplace is evident, in both the public and the private sectors, access to equal employment opportunities is more difficult. Even though there are many international human rights conventions and employment laws for the

---

45 Ibid.

46 For instance, cooking, cleaning and taking care of children.

47 Amal Obeidi, *Political Culture in Libya* (Curzon Press, 2001) 171.

48 Marissa Martino Golden, 'Women in the Administrative State: The Impact of Motherhood and Family-Friendly Policies on Women's Career Paths in the Federal Civil Service' (University of California, 2006) 15.

eradication of discrimination, working women still encounter difficulties in relation to family issues such as caring responsibilities (referred to earlier), pregnancy and childcare in Libya and elsewhere. As to pregnancy, there has been much debate about the extent to which women should be protected against pregnancy-related discrimination.[49] There is a negative relationship generally between having family responsibilities and being in paid employment; that is, the more responsibilities a woman has, the less likely she is to be able to enter the workforce, and maintain employment. It is the experience of women across the developed world that the more children a working mother has, the less likely she may be to re-enter the workforce after leaving for pregnancy, childbirth and early childcare duties.[50] The age of her youngest child is also an important determinant of the date at which a woman may return to work.[51]

To what extent, however, do these patterns reflect free and genuine choice; and to what extent are they the result of blatant discrimination against mothers wishing to continue working (as embodied in a lack of provision of opportunities for such employment or the failure to create an environment that makes employment possible)? Across the world the attempt to combine work and motherhood is not without its difficulties.

As the combination of employment and motherhood is an area of concern for all people, the relevant international norms and instruments will be examined. The particular focus of this study is the Libyan legal system and the rights of working women, together with their rights to motherhood in Libyan society. This overview is therefore divided into two sections. The first section reviews the body of international human rights conventions that deal with discrimination against working mothers. The second section reviews the steps that have been taken within the Libyan legal system to prevent discrimination and encourage participation, and identifies ways in which participation continues to be limited.

International Human Rights Conventions Relevant to the Rights of Working Women and their Children

This section will outline the conventions concerned with the prevention of discrimination against women. This includes human rights conventions of general application which prohibit discrimination against all – regardless of race, gender, religion, colour, language, political or other opinion, national or social origin, property, birth or other status[52] – as well as conventions concerned specifically with women's rights.

49 Karon Monaghan, *Equality Law* (Oxford University Press, 2007) 205.

50 OECD, *Babies and Bosses*, above n 32, 16–17.

51 Ibid. 46.

52 For instance, *Universal Declaration of Human Rights* (*UDHR*), GA Res 217A (III), UN GAOR, 3rd sess, 183rd plen mtg, UN Doc A/810 (10 December 1948); *Discrimination (Employment and Occupation) Convention* (C111), opened for signature 25 June 1958, ILO (entered into force 15 June 1960), *International Convention on the Elimination of All Forms of Racial Discrimination (ICERD)*, opened for signature 21 December 1965, 660 UNTS 195 (entered into force 4 January 1969); *International Covenant on Civil and Political Rights (ICCPR)*, opened for signature 16 December 1966, 999 UNTS 171 (entered into force 23 March 1976); *CEDAW*; *Maternity Protection Convention* (C183), opened for signature 15 June 2000, ILO, (entered into force 7 February 2002); *International Convention on the Protection of the Rights of All Migrant Workers and Members of Their Families (ICRMW)*, opened for signature 18 December 1990, 2220 UNTS 3 (entered into force 1 July 2003).

This section will outline four conventions: two from the United Nations and a further two from the International Labour Organization. The primary UN convention concerning women is the *Convention on the Elimination of All Forms of Discrimination against Women* (CEDAW). Also of specific importance in relation to the issue of working mothers and the needs of their children is the *Convention on the Rights of the Child* (CRC),[53] as the rights of women and those of their children are inextricably linked in the matters here examined. These UN conventions are discussed in depth in Chapter 2.

The two ILO conventions of particular relevance to working mothers are the *Maternity Protection Convention* and the *Discrimination (Employment and Occupation) Convention* (C111). These have been ratified by the Libyan government and will be discussed briefly below and in depth in Chapter 3.

UN Convention on the Elimination of All Forms of Discrimination against Women (CEDAW)

Similar to other international conventions, CEDAW elaborates on the norms and ideals put forward by the *Universal Declaration of Human Rights* (UDHR) and the *International Covenant on Civil and Political Rights* (ICCPR).[54] The Preamble of CEDAW recognises the great contribution of women to the welfare of the family and to the development of society, and it further mentions that the role of women in procreation should not be a basis for discrimination.[55] This convention also recognises that in order to change the traditional role of men and women in the family, as well as in society, it is crucial to achieve equality between men and women in all spheres of life.[56] Often referred to as a 'Bill of Rights' for women,[57] CEDAW is a comprehensive international agreement that aims to improve the status of women.

Libya is one of its many signatories, and while it has entered a number of reservations to this convention, they are not relevant to the topic of this volume. The problem is not so much the reservations but the *lack of compliance with Articles to which no reservation has been entered.* Under its obligations to this convention, Libya is required to submit a national report every four years. The difficulty Libya has experienced in complying with CEDAW is, however, reflected in the tardy submission of reports.[58] This convention is explored in detail in Chapter 2 and its relationship to the subject of women's rights in motherhood and employment is explored in depth in Chapter 4.

---

53 *Convention on the Rights of the Child* (*CRC*), opened for signature 20 November 1989, 1577 UNTS 3 (entered into force 2 September 1990).

54 *International Covenant on Civil and Political Rights (ICCPR),* opened for signature 16 December 1966, 999 UNTS 171 (entered into force 23 March 1976).

55 *CEDAW* Preamble.

56 Henry J Steiner, Philip Alston and Ryan Goodman, *International Human Rights in Context: Law, Politics, Morals: Text and Materials* (Oxford University Press, 3rd ed, 2008) 183.

57 Australian Government: Department of Families, Housing, Community Services and Indigenous Affairs, and Australian Human Rights Commission, *Women's Human Rights: United Nations Convention on the Elimination of All Forms of Discrimination against Women: CEDAW (What is CEDAW?)* (Commonwealth of Australian and the Human Rights and Equal Opportunity Commission, 2008) fact sheet 5.

58 Just three reports have been submitted since 1989, namely in 1991, 1999 and 2009: United Nations Committee on the Elimination of Discrimination Against Women (CEDAW Committee), *Consideration of Reports Submitted by States Parties Under Article 18 of the Convention on the Elimination of All Forms of Discrimination Against Women Initial Reports of States Parties – Libya*, UN Doc CEDAW/C/LIB/1 (18 February 1991), *Second Periodic Report – Libya*; United Nations Committee on the Elimination of Discrimination Against Women, *Consideration of Reports Submitted by States Parties Under Article 18 of the Convention on the Elimination of All Forms of Discrimination Against Women, Second Periodic Reports by States Parties –*

UN Convention on the Rights of the Child (CRC)

The *Convention on the Rights of the Child* (CRC)[59] was adopted by the United Nations General Assembly on 20 November 1989 and entered into force on 2 September 1990.[60] This convention has been ratified by more nations than any other convention, highlighting its significance.[61] There are 140 signatories to this convention and 194 States parties have ratified it.[62] The CRC contains material relevant to the right of children not to suffer from discrimination.[63] This convention is essential to this study, as the need to support working mothers is mentioned in many of its Articles. For instance, Article 18(3) states that all States parties have to provide childcare services for working parents, while Article 3(3) requires standards to be established for childcare facilities and their staff. Also, Article 24(2)(d) affirms that actions should be taken 'to ensure appropriate pre-natal and post-natal health care for mothers'. Libya ratified the *Convention on the Rights of the Child* on 15 May 1993,[64] and did not enter any reservations for this convention.[65] More information about this convention is found in Chapter 2, while the discrepancy between this convention and Libyan domestic law will be further discussed in Chapter 4.

ILO Maternity Protection Convention

In 1919, the League of Nations (the predecessor of the United Nations) established the International Labour Organization, which continues to the present day. It administers a number of conventions which militate against discrimination in the workplace. They include the *Maternity Protection Convention 1919*,[66] the third of the conventions formulated by the ILO (C3). Its language reflects the original concern of the organisation to protect women from danger in the workplace or conditions such as working at night rather than the more contemporary concerns for equality of access to employment and the provision of maternity leave. These were not to be major concerns until the mid-twentieth century when a major revision was undertaken. Further revision occurred in 2000.

Libyan Arab Jamahiriya, UN Doc CEDAW/C/LBY/2 (15 March 1999); and United Nations Committee on the Elimination of Discrimination Against Women, *Consideration of Reports Submitted by States Parties under Article 18 of the Convention on the Elimination of All Forms of Discrimination against Women, Combined 2nd, 3rd, 4th and 5th Periodic Reports of States Parties – Libyan Arab Jamahiriya*, UN Doc CEDAW/C/LBY/5 (4 December 2008): United Nations Committee on the Elimination of Discrimination against Women, *Concluding Observations of the Committee on the Elimination of Discrimination against Women – Libyan Arab Jamahiriya*, 43rd sess (19 January–6 February 2009) UN Doc CEDAW C/LBY/CO/5 (6 February 2009).

59 *Convention on the Rights of the Child* (CRC), opened for signature 20 November 1989, 1577 UNTS 3 (entered into force 2 September 1990).

60 Ibid.

61 Adrien Katherine Wing, 'International Conventions' in Joseph Suad (ed), *Encyclopedia of Women and Islamic Cultures: Family, Law and Politics* (Brill, 2005) vol 2, 306, 307.

62 At 10 December 2011: United Nations, *Treaty Collection: Convention on the Rights of the Child* <http://treaties.un.org/Pages/ViewDetails.aspx?src=TREATY&mtdsg_no=IV-11&chapter=4&lang=en>.

63 See *Convention on the Rights of the Child* art 2.

64 Office of the United Nations High Commissioner for Human Rights, *Status of Ratifications of the Principal International Human Rights Treaties 2006* (OHCHR) 7.

65 United Nations, UN GAOR, 27th special sess, 5th mtg, UN Doc A/S-27/PV.5 (10 May 2002) 9.

66 *Maternity Protection Convention* (C3), opened for signature 28 November 1919, ILO (entered into force 13 June 1921).

This legislation is of great relevance. However, it should be noted that while the Libyan Government ratified both the first and the second conventions – in 1971[67] and 1975[68] respectively – it has yet to ratify the third. This may reveal a certain degree of discomfort with its contents. A more detailed examination of the changing nature of the *Maternity Protection Convention* will be provided in Chapter 3.

ILO Discrimination (Employment and Occupation) Convention (C111)

The fundamental ILO instrument on discrimination is the *Discrimination (Employment and Occupation) Convention 1958* (C111),[69] which was adopted in 1958 upon request by the UN, and ratified by Libya on 13 June 1961.[70] The large number of countries that have ratified the convention (some 169 countries in addition to Libya)[71] indicates the broad acceptance of its provisions and its importance globally. This convention calls for the elimination of discrimination in the area of employment and occupation. Discrimination includes: any act of denying, excluding or preferring another human based on their race, colour, gender and so on, which will have the effect of nullifying or impairing equality of any opportunities or treatment in the workplace (Article 1(1)(a)).

This convention is relevant to this study for many reasons. Of particular significance are the sections concerning discrimination in respect of employment and occupation in both public and private sectors. C111 was the first treaty concerning non-discrimination in the workforce. However, while C111 is closely related to the requirements of other human rights treaties concerning equality and work,[72] its failure to make compulsory the provision of special measures for those with family responsibilities may be viewed as a shortcoming. However, its provision that any such measures (as supplied by member states in consultation with employers and employees) for those with these and other needs are not in themselves to be viewed as discriminatory is heartening. This convention will be addressed further in Chapter 3.

The Role of the Libyan Legal System in Preventing Discrimination against Libyan Working Women

This section will identify the Libyan employment legislation that has been put in place to prevent discrimination. It will focus on the primary sources for Libyan employment law for working mothers, as there is a lack of secondary literature on this topic.

67 International Labour Organization, *C3 Maternity Protection Convention, 1919: Ratified by Libyan Arab Jamahiriya on 27:05:1971* (24 September 2011) <http://www.ilo.org/ilolex>.

68 International Labour Organization, *C103 Maternity Protection Convention (Revised), 1952: Ratified by Libyan Arab Jamahiriya on 19:06:1975* (24 September 2011) <http://www.ilo.org/ilolex>.

69 *Discrimination (Employment and Occupation) Convention* (C111), opened for signature 25 June 1958, ILO (entered into force 15 June 1960).

70 *Discrimination (Employment and Occupation) Convention* (C111) *1958: Ratified by Libyan Arab Jamahiriya on 13 June1961*, ILOLEX Doc No 191961 LBY111.

71 ILOLEX, *Database of International Standards: Ratifications: Convention C111* (11 May 2011) <http://www.ilo.org/ilolex/english/newratframeE.htm>.

72 *Eliminating Discrimination against Indigenous and Tribal Peoples in Employment and Occupation*, opened for signature 29 February 2008 (entered into force 29 February 2008).

The Libyan legal system is derived from Italian and French civil law on the one hand, and *Shar'iah* on the other.[73] This overview will, therefore, consider aspects of both French-derived Libyan civil law and *Shar'iah* in relation to their impact on Libyan women's entitlements to work. The tensions that arise between the two legal systems have a direct impact on limiting women's ability to work, and also the type of work women can do. This is covered in detail in Chapter 4.

History of Legislation Preventing Discrimination

The Libyan Government has tried to encourage women to participate more actively in the economy. The position and role of women in the economy has become one of the focal issues of the past three decades.[74]

A number of pieces of Libyan legislation support non-discrimination on the basis of gender. Under Article 5 of the *Constitutional Declaration of 1969*,[75] all citizens are equal before the law, while the *Labour Code Act No 58 of 1970*[76] and the *Civil Service Act No 55 of 1976*[77] also contain a number of important provisions related to the rights of working mothers (though the applicable Act depends on the categorisation of the employer). Article 31 of the *Labour Code Act No 58 of 1970* (as does the *Civil Service Act*) states, for example, that there is to be no differentiation between genders in terms of salary.

Article 43 of the *Labour Code* provides women with paid maternity leave (subject to a number of conditions) in addition to a compulsory confinement leave period, and grants a number of entitlements related to continuation of employment or its cessation due to pregnancy or childbirth (again subject to certain conditions). Article 97 of the *Labour Code* also guarantees working women the right to nursing breaks for their infants. Larger employers must also make provision for childcare for female employees' children under Article 98. The *Child Protection Act No 5 of 1997*[78] has similar provisions. The provisions of both the above Acts and of the *Social Security Act No 13 of 1980*,[79] which also provides a period of paid maternity leave for Libyan working mothers, are discussed in Chapter 4.

Since the beginning of the 1980s, more radical changes have been observed. A number of cultural assumptions have been challenged by the state[80] as it seeks to balance its obligations as a state that recognises and upholds Islam as the faith of its citizens, and those aspirations that as a socialist state it holds dear, though the two are not necessarily in conflict.

---

73 Abdullahi A An-Na'im, *Islamic Family Law in a Changing World: A Global Resource Book* (Zed Books, 2002) 174.

74 Obeidi, *Political Culture in Libya*, above n 47, 169.

75 *Constitution Declaration of 1969* (Libya).

76 *Labour Code Act No 58 of 1970* (Libya) Article 1 states: 'The provisions of this Code shall apply to all persons working under a contract of employment. Also, this Code shall apply to manual workers employed by Government and public bodies unless their status has been defined by special regulation made by the Council of Ministers'.

77 *Civil Service Act No 55 of 1976* (Libya).

78 *Child Protection Act No 5 of 1997* (Libya).

79 *Social Security Act No 13 of 1980* (Libya) This Act is comprehensive in the area of social security, providing protection in the event of old age, disability, sickness, work injury or occupational disease, loss of breadwinner, and general welfare assistance or assistance in the event of calamities, disasters and death.

80 Obeidi, *Political Culture in Libya*, above n 47, 174.

Article 21 of the *Great Green Charter of Human Rights* (GGCHR), adopted by the Basic People's Congress on 12 June 1988,[81] further emphasised the principle of equality and stated that:

> The members of Jamahiriyan society, men or women, are equal in everything which is human. The distinction of rights between men and women, is a flagrant injustice which nothing justifies.

New laws were incorporated into the legislation to encourage women to participate more actively in the workplace, including the military[82] and the judiciary.[83] The *Order of the General People's Committee No 164 of 1988 on Employment of Arab and Libyan Women*[84] aims to support any employed woman who is able to work in any situation other than the police force or customs (which are covered under separate legislation). Article 2 indicates that women are able to undertake professional training and work in various occupations, and both part-time and full-time work is to be made available for women in the administrative services and the production sectors. Women working part time are also accorded rights to maternity leave under the *Social Security Act No 13 of 1980*.[85]

Two additional Acts also provide protection for equal rights of all citizens regardless of gender. Article 1 of the *Promotion of Freedom Act No 20 of 1991*[86] stipulates that '[c]itizens of the Great Jamahiriya, male and female, are free and enjoy equal rights', while the *Charter of Women Rights and Obligations in Republic Society 1997*[87] states that women and men should have equal rights in the workplace to position and treatment based on their knowledge and experience as well as their abilities.[88]

Although the legislation indicates that there should be no discrimination against working women in Libyan society, in practice the participation of working mothers in the workplace is still limited in almost every area of work, especially in the political system and public affairs.[89] The difficulty of managing family and work responsibilities remains the main barrier. Legislative advances, though praiseworthy, have been limited, often due to poor implementation of the law. Problems include inadequate duration and inconsistency of maternity protection periods; paucity of part-time occupations; generally inflexible working hours; and an absence of workplace-based childcare facilities. Chapter 4 examines this legislation in greater detail.

---

81 *Great Green Charter of Human Rights in the Jamahiriya Era 1988* (Libya). Early indications from the post-2011 regime are similarly committed to the principle of equality – at least in its Constitution – and are guaranteed a vote in elections; but the situation remains somewhat fragile: See, e.g., material by Libyan resident, trainer, researcher and translator Rhiannon Smith, 'Are Libyans For or Against Women's Rights?' *Libya Herald: The New Independent Libya Daily*, 30 June 2012. <http://www.libyaherald.com/are-libyans-for-or-against-womens-rights/>. For evidence of women's activism, see The Voice of Libyan Women website (30 June 2012) < http://www.vlwlibya.org/>.

82 *Army Act No 3 of 1984* (Libya).

83 *Right of Women to Assume Posts in the Judiciary Act No 8 of 1989* (Libya).

84 *Order of the General People's Committee No 164 of 1988 on Employment of Arab Libyan Women* (Libya).

85 Ibid. arts 2, 3, 4, 9 and 11.

86 *Promotion of Freedoms Act No 20 of 1991* (Libya).

87 *Charter of Women Rights and Obligations in Republic Society 1997* (Libya).

88 Ibid. art 12.

89 Obeidi, *Political Culture in Libya*, above n 47, 175.

Discrepancies between Libyan Domestic Law and International Human Rights Law

Not only are gaps observed between national law and implementation but also between national obligations under human rights instruments which Libya has ratified and national legislation (both in theory and practice). For example, Libyan domestic law has separate prescriptions for maternity leave that depend on the nature of employment. This is clearly discriminatory between working mothers who live in the same society and who should be granted equal maternity rights in their places of work. Although women theoretically have equal access to employment and political participation,[90] women do not fully participate in the political system or across the workforce, and it is quite rare for women in Libya to hold senior positions.[91]

Although Libya has ratified a number of important international conventions protecting the rights of working women,[92] it has not fully implemented these conventions. Libya has failed to comply with the provisions and responsibilities provided by these conventions for the protection of women's maternity rights and the prevention of all forms of discrimination against them. Of particular concern are the inadequate provisions related to maternity leave (as provided under the *Maternity Protection Convention*), the provision of childcare (as provided under Article 11(2)(c) of CEDAW and Article 18(3) of the *Convention on the Rights of the Child*) and in many instances the inadequate enforcement of the provisions that do exist.

Background to the Research Project on which this Publication is Based: Its Aims, Objectives and Limitations

As noted earlier, the original research project aimed to examine the theoretical and practical operation of relevant Libyan laws in the context of the standards set by international human rights law, including the UN conventions (CEDAW and CRC), the ILO conventions (the *Discrimination (Employment and Occupation) Convention* (C111) and the *Maternity Protection Conventions*) and other UN and ILO instruments dealing with discrimination against working mothers and their children (which documents also formed its normative framework).

The project was an attempt to shed light on the problem posed by the perception that there is an unsolvable conflict between the right of women to work and their right to motherhood, and to resolve the practical obstacles that lie between the enjoyment by working women of their rights as independent workers and as mothers, without requiring a choice of one over the other. Libyan employment legislation was also examined with regard to the issues of working mothers; the steps that had been taken within the Libyan legal system to prevent discrimination and encourage participation were examined; and the ways in which participation continues to be limited were identified. The adequacy of existing Libyan laws was evaluated and, where warranted, recommendations made as to amendments and reforms to ensure the protection of both work and motherhood rights.

---

90 CEDAW Committee, *Consideration of Libya's Second Periodic Report* (15 March 1999), above n 58.

91 As is later discussed and proven in Chapter 4.

92 For example, Libya ratified the *Maternity Protection Convention (Revised) 1952* on 19 June 1975; the *Convention on the Political Rights of Women* on 16 May 1989; the *Discrimination (Employment and Occupation) Convention 1958* (C111) on 13 June 1961; the *Equality of Treatment (Social Security) Convention 1962* on 19 June 1975; and CEDAW on 16 May 1989. Libya has also ratified the Optional Protocol of CEDAW on 18 June 2004, which allows the CEDAW Committee to receive and consider complaints from individuals or groups.

Issues Involved

The primary issue explored in this volume is how the rights of women to work and to motherhood, as articulated in international human rights instruments, can be best promoted within the context of the Libyan legal system.

A number of secondary issues flowed from and are involved in such an evaluation. These included the conceptual compatibility of a mother's rights at work (and to work) and as a mother; whether international human rights law has resolved the perceived tension/conflict between these 'sets' of rights; and the nature of the obligations (if any) imposed on States parties to the treaties and conventions that are related to the rights of working women/mothers, such as CEDAW and the ILO *Maternity Protection Convention*, among others. In this regard, the role of Libya's reservations in relation to such conventions (particularly those to parts of Articles 2 and 16 of CEDAW) is examined. And again, the issue of whether Libyan law meets international expectations is one thing; it is yet another for Libyan practice to do so. The extent to which Libyan law and practice adequately protect both a woman's rights at work and her rights of motherhood is examined, including whether existing Libyan maternity leave legislation and other provisions provide a solution, and how such provisions compare internationally.

Libyan law and practice are weighed and found wanting. The author proposes a number of steps to be taken by Libyan law-makers to ensure that working women are in a position to enjoy both paid employment and their role as mothers, and includes consideration of the possibility of state provision of welfare benefits to parents as appropriate additional/alternative policy measures to those already in existence.

Contribution of the Study: The First in its Field

This study sheds light on the past and present situation of Libyan employment laws regarding working women, especially working mothers. It does so by analysing and comparing the situation with the broader context of international human rights law. The study's thorough appraisal of the existing situation as well as of Libya's obligations under international law will enable a practical – and perhaps at times radical – contribution to be made in relation to the Libyan legal regime. The adoption of recommendations made subsequent to its findings could lead to an improvement of employment laws regarding maternity leave and other provisions to benefit working mothers in Libya.

As the first study in this field in Libya, it will make a contribution to the scholarly literature in this area of human rights norms, as well as offering some practical steps to strengthen Libyan legislation and regulations in this area. These changes would be beneficial to Libyan women and provide them with ways to possess and enjoy their rights both as mothers and as independent working women who can play an effective role in Libyan society. It is particularly relevant given the current state of flux and the evolution of a new Libya in the post-2011 revolutionary period.

If implemented, the changes suggested would have a positive effect on the Libyan economy by increasing women's workforce participation rates and allowing them to make a greater overall contribution. The country would also enjoy the benefits offered by greater workplace participation by the nation's increasingly educated women.

This study ultimately aims to help bring about change and development in the economy on the national level by encouraging any legislative amendments that are revealed by the research to be necessary for women to enjoy their rights as mothers and as workers to be put in place in Libyan law – both in form and practice.

Methodology Adopted

As briefly indicated earlier, the methodology adopted to explore these issues involved:

1. A review of primary and secondary materials on relevant international human rights law in order to determine what is expected of States parties in relation to respecting both rights at work and motherhood rights, including maternity leave, childcare availability and hours of work.
2. A review of primary and secondary materials on relevant Libyan law to assess the extent to which Libya fulfils its obligations under or otherwise meets the standards set by international human rights law (with any translation of materials from Arabic to English undertaken by the author).
3. The collection of original qualitative data by conducting semi-structured interviews with Libyan women on their experiences as working mothers in Libya. Using this highly flexible type of interview involving 'a few defined' but open-ended questions, the researcher remains ready and able 'to pursue any interesting tangents that may develop'.[93] (Again, since these interviews were conducted in the interviewees' mother tongue (Arabic) for their convenience, translation into English was required and, in this instance, was undertaken by Maha Elhage.) The purpose of collecting empirical data (via interviews) with working women was to inform a more complete assessment of the adequacy, in practice, of Libyan law and policy. The interviewees were working women from the most common work fields in Libya in both the public and private sectors.
4. A review was necessarily conducted of relevant literature (including case studies from other countries) on best practice regarding conditions for working women in order to develop comprehensive recommendations for reform within the Libyan legal system.

Chapter Outline

Following this introductory chapter are five further chapters. Chapter 2 focuses on the UN human rights conventions relevant to the rights of working women and their children, and examines the history of such conventions, particularly those concerned with the elimination of discrimination against women. Thus it includes human rights conventions concerned specifically with women's rights, with two conventions covered in detail, namely CEDAW and the CRC.

Chapter 3 focuses on other international human rights conventions that address the issues raised. In this instance they are conventions created by the International Labour Organization (ILO), namely the *Discrimination (Employment and Occupation) Convention* (C111) and the three successive *Maternity Protection Conventions*. All of these conventions (with the exception of the most recent *Maternity Protection Convention*) have been ratified by the Libyan Government. In regard to the *Maternity Protection Convention*, the second still applies to Libya until it ratifies the third.

93 Zina O'Leary, *The Essential Guide to Doing Research* (Sage, 2004) 164.

Chapter 4 is divided into two sections. First, it explores Libyan employment law in relation to working women. It considers equal rights in the workplace for women as guaranteed by Libyan employment legislation. Following a short account of the history of legislation that aims to prevent discrimination, the principle of equality in Libyan law in general is clarified. The growth of equal rights for working women is documented, as is all legislation linked to working women in Libya.

The first section of the chapter details the legislative changes that encourage increased workplace participation by women in general, such as equal pay provisions. It also details the specific legislation that provides for broader workplace participation by women in what were previously restricted areas (including military service and the judicial system). More particularly, the chapter deals in detail with legislation facilitating greater participation in the workplace by women *with children*, such as that related to paid maternity leave, the right to return to work after childbirth, rights for nursing mothers, and the provision of childcare, healthcare and support.

The second section of this chapter analyses all aspects of Libyan employment law with regard to working mothers and international human rights law, and examines the discrepancies between Libyan domestic law and international human rights law.

Chapter 5 provides concrete evidence of the situation of working mothers in Libya. It examines the extent to which the rights that exist in Libyan law and policy to protect the rights of working mothers to work and to motherhood are actually enjoyed in practice. Observations are based upon interviews conducted with working mothers from the most common fields of work in Libya, in both the public and the private sectors. This chapter contains a brief outline of the methodology adopted as well as the results obtained, and exposes the gap between theory and practice. Reasons for this huge gap are also suggested.

Chapter 6 presents the major findings of the author's study on the essential question of how the rights of women to work and to motherhood (as articulated in international human rights instruments) can best be promoted within the context of the Libyan legal system. This chapter also provides recommendations and solutions for the problems that Libyan women face.

Chapter 2
International Human Rights Standards: United Nations

There are today a number of key presuppositions about 'law' and 'society' and about 'human rights', many of which are embodied in international instruments. Primary among these are the following: all human beings are equal before the law; access to the law is crucial; law is just and impartial, and not influenced by wealth, race, religion, gender or status. Absence of law within a society would render that society anarchic. Indeed, the presence of law (or 'lore') as an organising principle for behaviour is characteristic of human society. Moreover, all human beings deserve, or rather have the right to be (live, work and so on) in a society where human rights (to shelter, adequate nutrition, equality before the law and so on) are understood to be inherent.[1] If this is not the case and human rights are abused, corrupt or simply non-existent, society is then basically denying its civilians dignity, equality and justice.

> Human rights constitute the moral discourse of our time. Their claim to universality offers a bridge between diverse, cultural, religious and philosophical worldviews. Human rights exist in law, but precede law, demanding legal recognition.[2]

Today there is a lot of pressure, both on an international and a national scale, to ensure that all human beings are recipients of equal opportunities and treatment, whether in the workplace, home or community.

As Melton writes, 'The power of international human rights law lies in large part in its universality'.[3] Human rights apply to both males and females – to all human beings. Yet women are deprived of enjoying some rights solely on the basis of their sexual identity. This is inhumane. Indeed, '[g]ender equality and non-discrimination on the basis of sex is one of the most frequently recognised norms of international human rights law'[4] and is considered the 'cornerstone of every democratic society [that] aspires to social justice and human rights'.[5]

The *Universal Declaration of Human Rights* (UDHR) expresses this belief,[6] and clearly states on countless occasions (especially in many of its Articles) that women should not be

1 'Human rights are increasingly portrayed as critical standards for evaluating the merits of state actions': Luke McNamara, *Human Rights Controversies: The Impact of Legal Form* (Routledge-Cavendish, 2007) 1.

2 Olivia Ball, 'Breastmilk is a Human Right' (2010) 18(3) *Breastfeeding Review* 9, 9.

3 Gary B Melton, 'Building Humane Communities Respectful of Children: The Significance of the Convention on the Rights of the Child' (2005) 60(8) *American Psychologist* 918, 919.

4 Niaz A Shah, *Women, the Koran and International Human Rights Law: The Experience of Pakistan* (Martinus Nijhoff, 2006) 167.

5 Office of the United Nations High Commissioner for Human Rights, *Fact Sheet No 22, Discrimination against Women: The Convention and the Committee* (9 July 2011) <http://www.unhcr.org/refworld/docid/47947740d.html>.

6 *Universal Declaration of Human Rights* art 2.

ignored or deprived of their rights on the basis of gender. One such 'occasion' where the UDHR clearly indicates its zero tolerance of discrimination is Article 2, which states:

> Everyone is entitled to all the rights and freedoms set forth in this Declaration, political or other opinion, national or social origin, property, birth or other status. Furthermore, no distinction shall be made on the basis of the political, jurisdictional or international status of the country or territory to which a person belongs, whether it be independent, trust, non-self-governing or under any other limitation of sovereignty.[7]

The United Nations (UN) has created many international conventions that concern women and children, reflecting the many issues raised in regard to them.[8]

This chapter and the following one aim to focus on the several international human rights conventions and other instruments created to protect and conserve the human rights of individuals around the globe. However, only those dealing with discrimination against working mothers will be examined in detail. These two chapters will consider conventions concerned with the prevention of discrimination against women. This includes human rights conventions of general application which prohibit discrimination against all, regardless of race, gender, religion, colour, language, political or other opinion, national or social origin, property, birth or other status[9] – as well as conventions concerned specifically with women's rights.

The primary focus in this chapter will be on the UN *Convention on the Elimination of All Forms of Discrimination against Women* (CEDAW)[10] and the *Convention on the Rights of the Child* (CRC),[11] while Chapter 3 will consider other treaties relevant to the present study, namely the International Labour Organization (ILO) *Discrimination (Employment and Occupation) Convention* (C111)[12] and the *Maternity Protection Convention.*[13]

The conventions will be discussed in chronological order in their respective chapters. This chapter will commence with a brief history of the United Nations, the 'how and why' it came into existence.

---

7 Ibid.

8 Doris Weichselbaumer and Rudolf Winter-Ebmer, 'The Effects of Competition and Equal Treatment Laws on Gender Wage Differentials' (2007) 22 *Economic Policy* 235, 245.

9 For instance, *Universal Declaration of Human Rights*, *Discrimination (Employment and Occupation) Convention* (C111), ICCPR, CEDAW, ICRMW, *Maternity Protection Convention* (C183).

10 *Convention on the Elimination of All Forms of Discrimination against Women* (CEDAW), opened for signature 1 March 1980, 1249 UNTS 13 (entered into force 3 September 1981).

11 *Convention on the Rights of the Child* (CRC), opened for signature 20 November 1989, 1577 UNTS 3 (entered into force 2 September 1990).

12 *Discrimination (Employment and Occupation) Convention* (C111), opened for signature 25 June 1958, ILO (entered into force 15 June 1960).

13 For instance, *Maternity Protection Convention* (C3), opened for signature 28 November 1919, ILO (entered into force 13 June 1921); *Maternity Protection Convention(Revised)* (C103), opened for signature 28 June 1952, ILO (entered into force 7 September 1955); and the *Maternity Protection Convention* (C183), opened for signature 15 June 2000, ILO (entered into force 7 February 2002).

History and Background of the United Nations

Established in 1945 in the aftermath of World War II, the United Nations (UN) is an intermediary between states and a global respondent to threats to security, which has made it a symbol of hope for peace and security for most of the international community.[14] It embodies aspirations that had been dashed when the existence of its predecessor, the League of Nations, had failed to avert a second 'global' war. Although the *Atlantic Charter* of 14 August 1941 may have contained the roots of the idea of a new international organisation,[15] the main impetus for the creation of the UN was the tragedy of World War II.[16] It is this experience that has made it far more than a broker for international relations.

There was not only a desire to avoid the reoccurrence of global conflict or of any conflict that is devastating in terms of the sheer numbers of injured and dead combatants and property loss, but also of any conflict (actual or potential) that might result in the destruction of, and enduring damage to, the lives of non-combatants and future generations. Images of the damage wrought by the 'modern approach to war' were uppermost in people's minds: the use of the atomic bomb, the blanket bombing of cities (regardless of the limited area involved in a military role) to intimidate entire populations and so forth. Also of particular concern were the problems posed by horrific policies of persecution adopted by governments towards their own citizens: for example, genocide of particular populations, including vulnerable persons (such as the mentally ill, the infirm, aged and those with physical and intellectual disabilities), and also of those of a particular religious faith or ethnicity. The images that flooded the world after the fall of Nazi Germany, as well as the subsequent Nuremberg trials, brought the concept of 'human rights' to the fore.

Hence, while intergovernmental conferences have been held for many centuries, especially following wars, essentially in order to determine the post-war political scene[17] (involving 'adjusting' borders if not 'carving up' the defeated nations among the victors), the establishment of the United Nations was also intrinsically concerned with the rights of persons (and not just on an international basis in times of war but, more problematically, within their own countries). The UN's aim to protect 'succeeding generations from the scourge of war' would more generally mean the prevention of the 'broad assaults on human dignity'.[18]

The primary purpose of the UN to achieve international peace thus extends far beyond the mere prevention of war to the betterment of the economic, social and humanitarian conditions of all people and the improvement of international law and its application, as well as a broad concern for advancing development.[19] So it is that today almost every organ and agency of the UN is concerned with the protection of human rights to a greater or lesser extent.[20]

Initially, 50 nations signed the *Charter of the United Nations*, which established the organisation at a meeting in San Francisco on 26 June 1945. This number rose to 51 when Poland was allowed to sign the Charter as an original member in the following months, even though it was not at the

---

14 Jean E Krasno, 'Founding the United Nations: An Evolutionary Process' in Jean E Krasno (ed), *The United Nations: Confronting the Challenges of a Global Society* (Lynne Rienner, 2004) 19, 19.

15 Lawrence Ziring, Robert E Riggs and Jack C Plano, *The United Nations: International Organization and World Politics* (Thomson Learning, 3rd ed, 2000) 19.

16 Joe Sills, 'The United Nations and the Formation of Global Norms' in Jean E Krasno (ed), *The United Nations: Confronting the Challenges of a Global Society* (Lynne Rienner, 2004) 47, 61.

17 Ibid. 63.

18 Ibid. 61.

19 Sven Bernhard Gareis and Johannes Varwick, *The United Nations: An Introduction* (Lindsay P Cohn trans, Palgrave Macmillan, 2005) 2–3.

20 Sills, above n 16, 61.

meeting.[21] With its 19 Chapters and 111 Articles containing extensive provisions, the Charter came into force following ratification by the then USSR on 24 October 1945.[22]

Since then, membership has increased significantly, primarily as a result of the rise in the number of independent nations in the world following decolonisation.[23] Today, the UN is an international organisation made up of 191 member states (having reached that level with the accession of Switzerland and East Timor in 2002). All have voluntarily accepted a common duty of ensuring and maintaining world peace and 'humane living conditions' for the world's citizens.[24]

The UN can rightfully justify its claims regarding the universality of the objects, norms and principles that it adopts (see further below), as its level of membership is exceptionally high compared to that of other international organisations. Even the outstanding non-member, the Vatican state, is actively involved with the organisation.[25]

The significant increase in membership of the UN had a great impact on the extent and nature of its work. It has given rise to new agendas (such as development) as well as to the establishment of new bodies, organisations and programmes. Developing countries now form a two-thirds majority in the General Assembly.[26]

The UN, in a general sense, regards itself as a platform for international collaboration whose specific obligations are difficult to determine. The UN was promised extensive competence when it was established as a comprehensive organisation. It took responsibility for 'the whole world' and as such was concerned with all issues (including environmental, security, humanitarian) in need of international focus. In practice, this means that every party will try to bring forward its own area of interest within the UN: those who are concerned with development policies highlighting development; those concerned with security highlighting security and so on.[27]

The high membership brings with it other implications. The broader the inclusion internationally of country and cultures, the broader can be expected to be the range of issues and the various approaches to those issues. This is particularly the case with regard to human rights, where individual, national, cultural and faith rights interact on domestic and international levels, and where a degree of consensus is sought.

Yet the United Nations remains the only international organisation in the world today that can formulate internationally accepted principles and norms of behaviour. This normative power extends to all of its agencies, programmes and funds as well as to the international agreements that fall under its auspices.[28]

The United Nations Charter

Like any constitutive document, the UN Charter itself is 'organic';[29] its constituent parts are interrelated and it has the potential to change and grow. The creation of the UN Charter was a true turning point in international law. It is much broader in application compared to the League

21 Krasno, above n 21, 40.

22 Gareis and Varwick, above n 19, 7.

23 Ibid. 1.

24 Ibid. 1, 55.

25 Ibid. 1.

26 Ibid.

27 Ibid. 55.

28 Sills, above n 16, 47.

29 Charles Norchi, 'Human Rights: A Global Common Interest' in Jean E Krasno (ed), *The United Nations: Confronting the Challenges of a Global Society* (Lynne Rienner, 2004) 79, 81.

Covenant as it extends beyond determining terms for mandated territories to address the needs of all dependent world citizens.[30] Where earlier there were very few measures available to citizens against infringement of rights by their states, the Charter established a number of protections for individuals against their state, acknowledging the increasing demand for such protection.[31]

It is characterised by a number of firm commitments in relation to human rights, dignity of the human person and equality between genders and nation states. There is an emphasis on social tolerance and peaceful coexistence on an individual and state level, as well as on the determination to achieve international cooperation on the improvement of economic and social standards for all the world's citizens.[32]

However, all discussions concerning international human rights and their realisation must give consideration to the overall global system in which the UN functions. The states as sovereign powers continue to be at the centre stage of this structure, even though international organisations play an important role in forming the connections between them. The maintenance or infringement of individual human rights is a matter mainly in the hands of each nation state. In certain cases, a state may be able to successfully argue that its citizens are being mistreated by foreign nations and obtain remedies. However, generally in international law, states have the freedom to treat their nationals according to their own standards, and this is the cause of the most common and important breaches of human rights.[33]

Although the UN is able to formulate internationally accepted principles and norms of behaviour, and this normative power extends to the agencies and international agreements under its control,[34] it should be noted that norms are commonly accepted behaviours or behaviour sets which can differ significantly in various regions of the world. There is a clear distinction between 'global' and 'local' norms, and the difficulty lies in establishing global norms that can transcend the many subtle variations between and within societies. The significance of global norms rests in their potential to bring order where there might otherwise be chaos due to a lack of standards.[35] One of the most noteworthy achievements of the UN has been its ability to establish commonly accepted principles in the field of human rights.[36]

As former UN High Commissioner for Human Rights Mary Robinson states, the individual person lies at the core of all the UN's work. She suggests that every person has a role to play in the promotion of the implementation of international standards, and that each person needs to be aware of the implication of those standards for their everyday lives and that of others.[37] That progress, however substantial, still has a way to go, is reflected in her observation that although '[h]uman rights have universal ownership' and are a much celebrated idea, they remain to be turned into 'a reality'.[38]

30 Ziring, Riggs and Plano, above n 15, 310.
31 Norchi, above n 29, 80.
32 Ibid.
33 Ziring, Riggs and Plano, above n 15, 334–5.
34 Sills, above n 16, 47.
35 Ibid.
36 Ibid. 49.
37 Norchi, above n 29, 79.
38 Ibid. 80.

Universal Declaration of Human Rights (UDHR)

The United Nations *Universal Declaration of Human Rights* lies at the core of the International Bill of Human Rights and 'reflects the claims of humanity in a community of states'.[39] Its first Article clearly states that:

> All humans are born free and equal in rights. They are endowed with reason and conscience and should act towards one another in a spirit of brotherhood.[40]

Formerly, states were able to hide behind the 'veil of sovereignty',[41] but now a new era was heralded as the rights of the individual state and the international community's representative body became increasingly a contested area, particularly when countries agreed to participate in various treaties and conventions to which they then became bound and which involved them in an inspectorial or reporting process (for example, CRC, CEDAW and so on). The crucial shift was from 'the protection of the sovereigns to the protection of the people'.[42]

Article 21(3) raises a quite obvious challenge to the notion of state sovereignty by stating that government power and authority has to be based 'on the will of the people'.[43] This must pose a particular challenge for both true monarchies and autocratic dictatorships, neither of which satisfy the apparent demand for elected forms of government. There is an issue, too, in regard to the acceptability of socialist dictatorships, where such states argue forcefully that a single-party state with multi-level and multi-area representative structures satisfies such a requirement, an argument often not accepted by western-style democracies.

The Convention on the Elimination of All Forms Discrimination against Women (CEDAW)

In this section, a number of issues related to the *Convention on the Elimination of All Forms Discrimination against Women* (CEDAW) will be discussed.[44] Following an initial overview and history of the Convention, its importance and the obstacles it faces, this section will turn more specifically to Libya and CEDAW. The nature of the reservations that Libya entered to this Convention and the reasons for this action will be provided, as will information regarding Libya's ongoing relationship with the Convention's administering body, the CEDAW Committee.

CEDAW: An Overview and Account of Its Origins

Similarly to other international conventions, CEDAW elaborates the norms and ideals of the *Universal Declaration of Human Rights* (UDHR),[45] the *International Covenant on Civil and*

---

39 Ibid. 81.

40 *Universal Declaration of Human Rights*, art 1.

41 Norchi, above n 29, 85–6.

42 Ibid. 86, where the author quotes W Michael Reisman, 'Sovereignty and Human Rights in Contemporary International Law' (1990) 84(4) *American Journal of International Law* 866, 869.

43 Norchi, above n 29, 85.

44 *Convention on the Elimination of All Forms of Discrimination against Women* (*CEDAW*), opened for signature 1 March 1980, 1249 UNTS 13 (entered into force 3 September 1981).

45 *Universal Declaration of Human Rights*.

Political Rights (ICCPR)[46] and the *International Covenant on Economic, Social and Cultural Rights* (ICESCR).[47] The Preamble of CEDAW recognises the great contribution of women to the welfare of the family and to the development of society. It further states that the role of women in procreation should not be a basis for discrimination.[48] This convention also recognises that change in the traditional role of men and women in the family as well as in society is crucial in order to achieve equality between men and women in all spheres of life.[49]

After World War II, which marked the League of Nations' failure, the Allied powers took the first steps to build a new international organisation for cooperation, development and the preservation of peace and security among the members of the world community. At the founding conference of the United Nations in San Francisco in 1945, some women participants insisted that the principle of equal rights for men and women be included in the Charter of the United Nations.[50] Therefore, 'the fundamental rights of individuals, the dignity and value of human beings, equal rights of men and women' are specified in the Preamble of the UN Charter.[51] However, while the UDHR was proclaimed just three years later (and the ICCPR and ICESCR opened for signature in the mid-1960s and entered into force almost 10 years later in 1976) and the *International Convention on the Elimination of All Forms of Racial Discrimination* (ICERD) was adopted in 1965,[52] consultations and negotiations for a convention that was specifically focused on women's rights were ongoing.

This began with the formation of a subcommittee to the Human Rights Commission (HRC) in 1946. Within a year it became the Commission on the Status of Woman, reporting directly to the Economic and Social Council of the UN.[53] The Commission worked tirelessly to secure a number of individual conventions that addressed various issues that particularly affected women or where women were 'particularly vulnerable'. These included the *Convention on the Political Rights of Women* (1952)[54] and the *Convention on Consent to Marriage, Minimum Age for Marriage and Registration of Marriages* (1962).[55] The Commission was convinced that a universal document rather than a 'piecemeal' approach was required. The existing international

46 *International Covenant on Civil and Political Rights* (ICCPR), opened for signature 16 December 1966, 999 UNTS 171 (entered into force 23 March 1976).

47 *International Covenant on Economic, Social and Cultural Rights* (ICESCR), opened for signature 16 December 1966, 999 UNTS 3 (entered into force 3 January 1976).

48 *CEDAW* Preamble.

49 Henry J Steiner, Philip Alston and Ryan Goodman, *International Human Rights in Context: Law, Politics, Morals: Text and Materials* (Oxford University Press, 3rd ed, 2008), 183.

50 *Charter of the United Nations*, opened for signature 26 June 1945 (entered into force 26 June 1945).

51 Dorothea Gaudart, 'What Are the Origins of CEDAW? The History of the UN Convention on the Elimination of All Forms of Discrimination against Women' in Sylvia Kölbl (ed), *What is CEDAW? The UN Convention on the Elimination of All Forms of Discrimination against Women: The Human Rights of Women and What They Mean* (Federal Chancellery, Federal Minister for Women, Media and Civil Service, 2007) 12, 12.

52 *International Convention on the Elimination of All Forms of Racial Discrimination (ICERD)*, opened for signature 21 December 1965, 660 UNTS 195 (entered into force 4 January 1969).

53 United Nations, *Convention on the Discrimination against Women and Its Optional Protocol: Handbook for Parliamentarians* (UN and Inter-Parliamentary Union, 2003) 11–12.

54 *Convention on the Political Rights of Women*, opened for signature 31 December 1953, 193 UNTS 135 (entered into force 7 July 1954), GA Res 640 (VII) UN GAOR 7th sess, 409th plen mtg (20 December 1952) UN Doc A/RES/640Annex.

55 *Convention on Consent to Marriage, Minimum Age for Marriage and Registration of Marriages*, opened for signature 7 November 1962, 521 UNTS 231 (entered into force 9 December 1964).

human rights instruments (for example, UDHR) were viewed as inadequate. As Hoq observes, 'The Convention is based on the understanding that existing international human rights laws were not effectively addressing the specific disadvantages and injustices faced by women'.[56] Work started first on the non-binding *Declaration on the Elimination of Discrimination against Women* (DEDAW),[57] and then, once that was secured, on an overarching binding convention.[58] The extent of the negotiations already undertaken for DEDAW and then CEDAW may go some way to explain why, once CEDAW was adopted, entry into force followed so rapidly.

After prolonged consultation and negotiation, CEDAW was adopted by the United Nations General Assembly on 18 December 1979.[59] It was signed by 64 States at the Copenhagen Conference on 17 July 1980, and two other states also submitted their instruments of ratification.[60] CEDAW entered into force on 3 September 1981,[61] reflecting a faster rate of adoption by the world community than any other previous human rights convention.[62] Another contributory factor may be the ability of member states to lodge reservations, subject to the proviso that such reservations 'are not incompatible with the object and purpose of the Convention'.[63] In the eyes of some member states, other signatories appear, at the very least, to sail 'very close' to doing so or contravene that provision (see further below).[64] Its implementation continues to be an ongoing dialogue between signatories and the CEDAW Committee.

Nevertheless, CEDAW was a milestone in the history of the United Nation's efforts to codify exhaustively international legal standards for women.[65] At present, 187 countries – representing

56 Laboni Amena Hoq, 'The Women's Convention and Its Optional Protocol: Empowering Women to Claim their Internationally Protected Rights' (2001) 32 *Columbia Human Rights Law Review* 677, 680.

57 *Declaration on the Elimination of Discrimination against Women*, GA Res 2263 (XXII) UN GAOR 22nd sess, UN Doc A/RES/2263 (7 November 1967).

58 For an account of the history of CEDAW, see Committee on the Elimination of Discrimination against Women, 'Progress Achieved in the Implementation of the Convention on the Elimination of All Forms of Discrimination against Women' (Paper presented at the Fourth World Conference on Women, Beijing, 4–15 September 1995), UN Doc A/CONF.177/7, 4 [6]–[14].

59 UN, *CEDAW and Its Optional Protocol*, above n 53, 9.

60 Ibid.

61 *Convention on the Elimination of All Forms of Discrimination against Women* (CEDAW), opened for signature 1 March 1980, 1249 UNTS 13 (entered into force 3 September 1981).

62 Vedna Jivan and Christine Forster, 'Challenging Conventions: in Pursuit of Greater Legislative Compliance with CEDAW in the Pacific' (2009) 10 *Melbourne Journal of International Law* 655, 657.

63 *CEDAW* art 28(2).

64 See, e.g., Austria on Saudi Arabia's reservation to Articles 2(f), 9, 15(2), 16, 29(1): United Nations, *Declarations, Reservations, Objections and Notifications of Withdrawal of Reservations Relating to the Convention on the Elimination of All Forms of Discrimination against Women*, Meeting of the States Parties to the Convention CEDAW 14th mtg, 23 June 2006, Item 6 of the Provisional Agenda, UN Doc CEDAW/SP/2006/2 (10 April 2006). See 'D. Objections to certain declarations and reservations', 36. For reservations by country, see UN Women, *Convention on the Elimination of All Forms of Discrimination against Women: Declarations, Reservations and Objections to CEDAW* (22 October 2011) <http://www.un.org/womenwatch/daw/cedaw/reservations-country.htm>.

65 United Nations Secretary General (Kofi Annan), *Secretary General Says It is Duty of All to be 'Vigilant and Articulate Custodians' of Women's Anti-Discrimination Convention*, UN Doc SG/SM/7258, WOM/1152 (Press Release, 10 December 1999). See also UN, *CEDAW and Its Optional Protocol*, above n 53, 10.

more than 90 per cent of the members of the United Nations – are parties to CEDAW. Libya is among them.[66]

CEDAW is a comprehensive international agreement that aims to improve the status of women. Often referred to as a 'Bill of Rights' for women,[67] CEDAW established a platform for women to raise their voices to the world and be noticed as equal to men. It also created many opportunities for women to be equal to men through the obligations incurred by signatories. The reporting mechanism of this Convention also ensured that this was not a document to be regarded as 'mere words'.[68] It is one of nine core international human rights treaties.[69] It was the first international treaty to address fundamental rights for women as women,[70] and not simply as included as part of humanity, an approach that the Commission had found wanting.[71] CEDAW is 'first and foremost a treaty, an international legal instrument'.[72] It is legally binding on those States parties that have ratified it.[73] This is confirmed in Article 26 of the *Vienna Convention on the Law of Treaties* (VCLT, 1969), which states that: 'Every treaty in force is binding upon the parties to it and must be performed by them in good faith'.[74]

CEDAW's Importance

CEDAW has been referred to as the 'definitive international legal instrument requiring respect for and observance of the human rights of women'.[75] It is clear from its Preamble and definition of discrimination in Article 1 (and the terms of Articles 2, 3 and 24 and elsewhere in the practice of the CEDAW Committee) that CEDAW:

---

66 As at 15 October 2011: United Nations, *Treaty Collection: Status of Treaties: Convention on the Elimination of All Forms of Discrimination against Women* (5 September 2011) <http://treaties.un.org/Pages/ViewDetails.aspx?src=TREATY&mtdsg_no=IV-8&chapter=4&lang=en>.

67 UN, *CEDAW and its Optional Protocol*, above n 53, 3.

68 Gaudart, above n 51, 12.

69 There are nine core international human rights treaties: *International Convention on the Elimination of All Forms of Racial Discrimination* (ICERD); *International Covenant on Civil and Political Rights* (ICCPR); *International Covenant on Economic, Social and Cultural Rights* (ICESCR); *Convention on the Elimination of All Forms of Discrimination against Women* (CEDAW); *Convention against Torture and Other Cruel, Inhuman or Degrading Treatment or Punishment* (CAT); *Convention on the Rights of the Child* (CRC); *International Convention on the Protection of the Rights of All Migrant Workers and Members of Their Families* (ICRMW); *International Convention for the Protection of All Persons from Enforced Disappearance, Convention on the Rights of Persons with Disabilities* (CRPD).

70 For example, in politics, healthcare, education, economics, employment, law, property and marriage and family relations. See Karin Tertinegg, 'Women's Human Rights and Obligations for Austria' in Sylvia Kölbl (ed), *What is CEDAW? The UN Convention on the Elimination of All Forms of Discrimination against Women the Human Rights of Women and What They Mean* (Federal Chancellery, Federal Minister for Women, Media and Civil Service, 2007) 19, 19.

71 Gaudart, above n 51, 14.

72 Andrew Byrnes, Maria Herminia Graterol and Renee Chartres, 'State Obligation and the Convention on the Elimination of All Forms of Discrimination against Women' (University of New South Wales, 2007) 8.

73 Rebecca J Cook, 'Reservations to the Convention on the Elimination of All Forms of Discrimination Against Women' (1989–1990) 30 *Virginia Journal of International Law* 643, 649.

74 *Vienna Convention on the Law of Treaties*, opened for signature 23 May 1969, 1155 UNTS 331 (entered into force 27 January 1980) art 26.

75 Cook, above n 73, 643.

> guarantees women's equal enjoyment not only of the rights explicitly dealt [within] ... the fields covered in Articles 6–16 of the Convention, but also extends to the equal enjoyment of all internationally recognised human rights and fundamental freedoms.[76]

Therefore, this Convention is crucial to this study, as it is specifically for 'women' – all women young and old, married or unmarried, mothers or childless. For this volume, however, the position of working mothers is the focus. Mention is made in many of CEDAW's Articles in regard to women generally, but also in particular in regard to the need to support working mothers, regardless of whether they working in the public or private sector.

CEDAW has 30 Articles, and all of them are significant. The initial Articles oblige States parties to refrain from discrimination on the basis of gender and also to take measures towards achieving equality in all spheres of life, including by breaking down discriminatory attitudes, customs and practices in society.[77] The Convention begins by defining discrimination on the basis of sex. Article 1 defines 'discrimination against women' as:

> [a]ny distinction, exclusion or restriction made on the basis of sex which has the effect or purpose of impairing or nullifying the recognition, enjoyment or exercise by women, irrespective of their marital status, on a basis of equality of men and women, of human rights and fundamental freedoms in the political, economic, social, cultural, civil or any other field.[78]

Article 4(2) permits States parties to adopt 'special measures' aimed at 'protecting maternity', with such measures not being considered 'discriminatory', including 'those measures contained in the present Convention'. This provision recognises that 'equality' of treatment is insufficient to guarantee equality of outcomes or to take account of conditions inherent in pregnancy and maternity that must be addressed to ensure workforce participation. For example, given that the internationally recognised desirability of breastfeeding[79] is a particular focus of this publication in relation to workplace practices, it can be seen that this Article allows for 'special measures' to be put in place by the government without these being considered 'discriminatory'.

Article 11 provides that States parties are obliged to take all appropriate measures to eliminate discrimination against women in employment. Article 11(1) states general rights applicable to all women. States parties are:

> to take all appropriate measures to eliminate discrimination against women in the field of employment in order to ensure, on the basis of equality of men and women, the same rights, in particular ... .
>
> (b) The right to the same employment opportunities ...

---

76 Byrnes, Graterol and Chartres, above n 72, 117. The authors recommend that this be explicitly included in a 'clear statement' within the Convention. They do not here appear to differentiate between binding and non-binding instruments and include those rights recognised by the UDHR as well as international covenants on human rights and other 'UN and regional human rights treaties and other human rights instruments': ibid.

77 UN, *CEDAW and its Optional Protocol*, above n 53, 12.

78 *CEDAW* art 1.

79 See generally, Ball, above n 2, 9.

(c) … to free choice of profession and employment, … promotion, … job security and all benefits and conditions of service, … vocational training and retraining, … apprenticeships …

(d) … equal remuneration, including benefits, and to equal treatment …

(e) social security, … in … retirement, unemployment, sickness … old age …

(f) … protection of health and to safety in working conditions, including the safeguarding of the function of reproduction.[80]

Article 11(2) addresses more specifically the needs of women who are pregnant or who have given birth. It requires that specific measures need to be taken to prevent discrimination against women in employment on the basis of marriage or maternity. Dismissal on the grounds of pregnancy, maternity leave or marital status is prohibited, with breaches to be subject to sanctions.[81] In addition, States parties are requested to introduce paid maternity leave (or maternity with comparable social benefits) without the loss of 'employment, seniority or social allowances'.[82] States are also required to 'encourage the provision of the necessary supporting social services to enable parents to combine work and family responsibilities and participation in public life', especially by 'promoting the establishment … of a network of childcare facilities'.[83] In addition, during pregnancy special protection must be provided to women 'in types of work proved to be harmful to them'.[84] Again, the safety and needs of pregnant women (and their foetuses) are to be given the consideration that the state of pregnancy requires.

In order to ensure that women have access to healthcare equal to men, including that relating to family planning, Article 12(1) requires States parties to take measures to eliminate discrimination against women regarding access to healthcare services (including family planning). Particularly relevant to this volume are the provisions under paragraph 2 of the same Article, which decrees that States parties are also required to ensure that women have appropriate services (free of charge where necessary) with regard to pregnancy, confinement and the postnatal period. During pregnancy and lactation women are also required to be provided with adequate nutrition.

Fully implemented, CEDAW offers great advances for women in general, and working mothers in particular. CEDAW can be an effective weapon against different forms of discrimination. It can be used by women in their battle against poverty and violence. It also provides them with their rights in employment, legal protection, inheritance, property and access to credit. This has been witnessed in countries where CEDAW was ratified (and no reservation entered in regard to such

80 *CEDAW* art 11(1).

81 Ibid. art 11(2)(a). See also Linda M Keller, 'The Convention on the Elimination of Discrimination against Women: Evolution and (Non)Implementation Worldwide' (2004–05) 27 *Thomas Jefferson Law Review* 35, 36.

82 *CEDAW* art 11(2)(b).

83 Ibid. art 11(2)(c).

84 Ibid. art 11(2)(d).

areas).[85] For instance, women in Libya have been given extensive rights in terms of employment in the judicial system[86] since the ratification of CEDAW by Libya in 1989.[87]

However, while CEDAW is a 'powerful tool to promote gender equality', as Keller observed, its actualisation depends on the willingness of the States parties to implement CEDAW's provisions. Now, as then, this is yet to be the case for many States parties.[88]

Obstacles to CEDAW

Despite its advantages and potential benefits, CEDAW has some serious obstacles that affect its usefulness. These stem from two major sources: reservations entered by States parties; and poor reporting practice, including late submission of progress reports required under the Convention as well as failure to include material requested, and even failure to report.

Reservations

Reservations entered by States parties to core Articles of the Convention[89] are often directly linked to strong cultural understandings within particular countries. CEDAW Committee members may view these understandings as 'discriminatory traditional culture ... often manifested in ... gender role stereotyping' and believe that it is 'the most difficult issue to tackle',[90] probably because it is so deeply embedded in the existing culture. Keller observes that '[r]eservations to CEDAW are often based on assertions of cultural or religious belief'.[91]

It should, however, be recalled that a number of countries source their law, legislation, judicial system and cultural practices in a context that privileges particular interpretations of writings considered sacred by the vast majority of their populations. In most instances, the prime text is the *Holy Qur'ān*, believed to be of Divine origin, and the *Sunnah* and (according to the area in question) various interpretations of major schools of Islamic thought. One could argue that in many cases a state's position merely reflects the strongly held beliefs of its people. In Libya, for instance – as in a number of states with an overwhelmingly Muslim population – Islam is recognised as the 'official state religion' and the *Qur'ān* has been long considered the country's very constitution,[92] and thus *Shar'iah* a continuing principal source of law and jurisprudence. Recent events are not expected to change this substantially.[93]

85 Amnesty International, *A Fact Sheet on CEDAW: Treaty for the Rights of Women* (25 August 2005) <http://www.amnestyusa.org/women/pdf/cedaw.pdf>.

86 *Right of Women to Assume Posts in the Judiciary Act No 8 of 1989* (Libya).

87 UN Division for the Advancement of Women/Department of Economic and Social Affairs, *CEDAW States Parties* (2007) <http://www.un.org/womenwatch/daw/cedaw/states.htm>.

88 Keller, above n 81, 35.

89 Those to which Libya entered reservations are Articles 2 and 16.

90 Heisoo Shin, 'CEDAW and Women's Human Rights: Achievements and Obstacles' (Paper presented at Human Rights 2004: The Year in Review, Castan Centre for Human Rights Law Annual Conference, 3 December 2004) (unpaginated).

91 Keller, above n 81, 39.

92 Bureau of Near Eastern Affairs, *Background Note: Libya* (US Department of State, 7 July 2011) <http://www.state.gov/r/pa/ei/bgn/5425.htm>. It is also the source of law for the legislature: *Al-Mahkama Al-'Ulya*, GM, decision 197/39, 3 November 1997: see Ali Omar Ali Mesrati, *The Best Interests of the Child: International Child Law as Interpreted in the Libyan High Court Jurisdiction* (PhD Thesis, University of Wollongong, 2009) 151 n 374.

93 This is expected to remain essentially the case after the 2011 Revolution. See, e.g., *Draft Constitutional Charter for the Transitional Stage* (23 October 2011) <http://www.al-bab.com/arab/

This is in contrast to the now generally secular 'west', whose values manifested in law still contain some remnants of Judaeo-Christian beliefs and practices[94] as well as practices that reflect a far more recent (and CEDAW-compliant) understanding of equality (for example, in regard to inheritance). Many countries around the world have registered a reservation in regard to one Article or more, though for different reasons.[95] CEDAW may have the highest number of signatories of any convention, but 'it also has the highest number of reservations imposed'.[96] Indeed, the openness of CEDAW to the entry of reservations has made it a document able to be signed by many countries, but it has also contributed to the ongoing debate between the CEDAW Committee and a number of States parties over matters where faith and cultural practices and CEDAW's directives represent 'competing values of universality and integrity'[97] (for example, in regard to inheritance and custody).

Islamic understandings and practices also vary significantly for, as Heisoo Shin (CEDAW vice chair) observed, some Islamic countries ratified CEDAW without entering a single reservation.[98] The level of compliance or implementation may be a separate issue, however. As McNamara observes:

> notwithstanding the claimed universality of the value embodied in human rights instruments, there is significant variation in the legal 'shape' of ... [such] values in different countries, and ... there is a qualitative difference in the extent to which in practice individuals and groups in different states enjoy [them] ... and are able to use human rights law as a vehicle for achieving particular social justice goals.[99]

In reality, a number of substantial reservations exist that are often to the core Articles (such as Articles 2 or 16) and which are considered 'incompatible with the purpose and objectives of the Convention'.[100] Indeed, '[t]hese reservations are one of the reasons that the right to non-discrimination on the ground of sex still has not reached the status of customary international law, in contrast with the right to non-discrimination on the ground of race'.[101]

Poor reporting practices

Non-reporting or overdue reports also severely weaken the process. This problem can be at least partly attributed to a country being committed to produce reports to various international bodies under their respective human rights and other legislation. Also a problem can be the level of information required and its degree of sophistication. This might pose a particular problem for countries just beginning to develop such records. The absence of reports has in a number of cases

---

docs/libya/Libya-Draft-Constitutional-Charter-for-the-Transitional-Stage.pdf>. Note: in Arabic this is a 'Constitutional Declaration'.

94 For example, monogamy rather than polygamy.

95 Including Switzerland and the United Kingdom, where countries claim more protection is granted under national legislation than under CEDAW. Australia has a (now outdated) reservation to Article 3 regarding the provision of paid maternity leave. For details regarding this and other countries (including the US), see UN, *Treaty Collection: Status of Treaties: CEDAW*, above n 66. The United States, on the other hand, has signed but not ratified the Convention.

96 Cheshmak Farhoumand-Sims, 'CEDAW and Afghanistan' (2009) 11(1) *Journal of International Women's Studies* 136, 138.

97 Ibid. 139 (citation omitted).

98 Shin, above n 90.

99 McNamara, above n 1, 4.

100 Shin, above n 90.

101 Farhoumand-Sims, above n 96, 138 (citation omitted).

been so prolonged that the CEDAW Committee has considered issuing a 'report on progress' in the absence of a report submitted by the country involved. Shin noted that the 2004 announcement of this alternative 'as a last resort' may spur countries to produce reports.[102] The Committee is also considering more streamlined reports following meetings with States parties experiencing difficulties.[103] However, it can already be called upon for assistance in such matters.

The process itself also has the potential to delay further submissions, as is shown in the result of the CEDAW Committee's early inability to deal with submissions in a timely manner (a problem now afflicting the CRC Committee). There had been recurring backlogs of reports, with these having accumulated despite delays in submissions and, on at least one occasion, the timetabling of an additional exceptional session.[104] Since January 2005, the CEDAW Committee has met three times a year in working sessions in order to keep abreast of material submitted.[105] This, and the adoption of a constructive dialogue approach and pre-sessional consultations,[106] appears to have largely eliminated any delay on the Committee side of the equation, but not on the part of the States parties.

States parties are still submitting reports late (or failing to submit). Due to the system of conventions working within a framework of national sovereignty, there is no consequence in terms of formal sanctions able to be applied to a State party involved.[107] What remains is a 'shaming' among peers or the application of external or internal political pressure.[108] This is, perhaps, one reason that can be given for the continuing problem for the CEDAW Committee and other human rights bodies to which reports are due. However, the existence of the Convention is in itself a powerful articulation of the rights of women and a standard against which legislation and practice are compared.[109]

In spite of all the advances achieved by CEDAW and the ongoing dialogue between parties and the CEDAW Committee, women still have not achieved full equality with men legally and economically. This is still a problem which is faced by women in developing and developed countries alike.[110]

Libya and CEDAW

In this part of the chapter, the action of the Libyan Government in relation to CEDAW will be addressed. The reservations entered and Libya's working relationship with the CEDAW Committee will be discussed.

---

102 Shin, above n 90.

103 For example, in 2003: Shin, above n 90.

104 In 2002: Shin, above n 90.

105 *CEDAW, Convention on the Elimination of All Forms of Discrimination against Women, 14th mtg, 23 June 2005* (20 October 2011) <http://www.un.org/womenwatch/daw/cedaw/statesmeeting/fourteenth.htm>.

106 Shin, above n 90.

107 Sally Engle Merry, 'Constructing a Global Law: Violence against Women and the Human Rights System' (2003) 28 *Law and Social Inquiry* 941, 942–3.

108 Ibid. 942.

109 Ibid. 941–2.

110 Cynthia G Wagner, 'Progress Report on Discrimination against Women' (2008) 42(3) *Futurist* 9, 9.

Libya ratified CEDAW on 16 May 1989[111] and the Optional Protocol[112] to CEDAW on 18 June 2004.[113] However, on 5 July 1995 Libya entered reservations in relation to Articles 2 and 16 of CEDAW.[114] It should be noted that ratification 'obliges states parties to enact or modify domestic legislation and constitutions to accord with the substantive articles of the convention'.[115]

Libya's reservations to CEDAW

In total, Libya has ratified some 39 international legal agreements on human rights, comprising 28 conventions of the International Labour Organization[116] and a further 11 human rights conventions created under the auspices of the United Nations.[117] In terms of international law and women's rights in Libya, the problem remains that although Libya has ratified such a large number of conventions[118] and has not entered any reservations (with the sole exception of the reservations to Articles 2 and 16 of CEDAW),[119] it has failed to fully comply with the provisions and responsibilities imposed by these conventions in regard to the protection of women's maternity rights and the prevention of all forms of discrimination against them.

The reservations that Libya did enter on 5 July 1995[120] in relation to Articles 2 and 16 of CEDAW were entered on the basis that the Articles are inconsistent with the principles of equality that apply between men and women in Libya. In particular, Libya regards these Articles as being against the principles and spirit of the *Holy Qur'ān*, which is an integral part of the formulation of its domestic law.[121]

---

111 UN, *Treaty Collection: Status of Treaties: CEDAW*, above n 66.

112 *Optional Protocol to the Convention on the Elimination of All Forms of Discrimination against Women*, opened for signature 6 October 1999, 2131 UNTS 83 (entered into force 22 December 2000) (*CEDAW Optional Protocol*).

113 United Nations, *Treaty Collection: Status of Treaties: Optional Protocol to the Convention on the Elimination of All Forms of Discrimination against Women* (6 September 2011) <http://treaties.un.org/Pages/ViewDetails.aspx?src=TREATY&mtdsg_no=IV-8-b&chapter=4&lang=en>.

114 UN Division for the Advancement of Women/Department of Economic and Social Affairs (DESA), *CEDAW: Declarations, Reservations and Objections to CEDAW* (10 May 2011) <http://www.un.org/womenwatch/daw/cedaw/reservations-country.htm>.

115 Jivan and Forster, above n 62, 656.

116 For instance: *Discrimination (Employment and Occupation) Convention* (C111); *Maternity Protection Convention* (C3); *Maternity Protection Convention* (C103); *Minimum Age (Industry) Convention* (C5) 1919, opened for signature 28 November 1919, ILO (entered into force 13 June 1921); *Discrimination (Employment and Occupation) Convention* (C111); and the *Employment Policy Convention* (C122), opened for signature 9 July 1964, ILO (entered into force 15 July 1966).

117 For example: *Universal Declaration of Human Rights*, *Convention on the Political Rights of Women*, *ICERD*, *ICCPR*, *Convention on the Rights of the Child* (CRC), *ICRMW*.

118 For example: *Declaration of the Rights of the Child*, LON (26 September 1924); *Charter of the United Nations*, opened for signature 26 June 1945 (entered into force 26 June 1945); *Universal Declaration of Human Rights*; *Convention on the Political Rights of Women*; *Declaration of the Rights of the Child*, GA Res 1386 (XIV), UN GAOR, Sup No 16, UN Doc A/4354 (20 November 1959); *ICERD*; *ICCPR*; *Convention on the Rights of the Child* (CRC); *ICRMW*; *Discrimination (Employment and Occupation) Convention* (C111); *CEDAW*.

119 UN Division for the Advancement of Women/DESA, *CEDAW: Declarations, Reservations and Objections*, above n 114.

120 Ibid.

121 UNDP, AHR Index, *Human Rights Profiles: Libya. International Conventions* (undated) (12 May 2011) <http://www.arabhumanrights.org/en/countries/country.aspx?cid=10>

It should be noted that the ability of nations to enter reservations to a convention allows countries that otherwise would be reluctant to sign and ratify a convention to do so. The relevant committee for the convention then attempts to persuade such countries to withdraw their reservations and more fully implement the convention. Such conventions are informed by certain cultural norms and expectations, and often embody norms that may not fully align with the social, cultural and religious norms of the signatory, norms that the country wishes to preserve.[122]

In Article 2, signatories agree to 'pursue by all appropriate means and without delay a policy of eliminating discrimination against women'. This is to include the government undertaking:

> (a) To embody the principle of the equality of men and women in their national constitutions or other legislation ... and to ensure, through law and other appropriate means, the practical actual realization of this principle;
>
> (b) To adopt appropriate legislative and other measures ... to prohibit discrimination;
>
> (c) To establish legal protection of the rights of women on an equal basis with men ... and ensure through competent national tribunals and other public institutions the effective protection of women against any act of discrimination;
>
> (d) To refrain from ... any act or practice of discrimination against women and ensure that public authorities and institutions [do likewise];
>
> (e) To take all appropriate measures to [ensure] eliminate discrimination against women by any person, organization or enterprise;
>
> (f) To take all appropriate measures, including legislation, to *modify or abolish existing laws, regulations, customs and practices* which constitute discrimination against women[123]

Libya undertook to implement Article 2 but 'with due regard for the peremptory norms of the Islamic *Shar'iah* relating to determination of the inheritance portions of the estate of a deceased person'.[124] Such norms entitle male children to a double portion of an estate.[125] This is due to family responsibilities that are imposed on them under the norms created by the same *Shar'iah*. In the

---

122 Afroza Begum, *Protection of Women's Rights in Bangladesh: A Legal Study in an International and Comparative Perspective* (PhD Thesis, University of Wollongong, 2004) 16–17, 59, 62.

123 *CEDAW* art 2 (emphasis added).

124 *Declarations, Reservations, Objections and Notifications of Withdrawal of Reservations Relating to the Convention on the Elimination of All Forms of Discrimination against Women*, UN Doc No CEDAW/SP/2006/2 (Libyan Arab Jamahiriya, Reservations, 5 July 1995) 17–18.

125 *Qur'ān* 4:11–12, 4:176. These sections detail inheritance portions due in various circumstances, including a person dying without offspring, or with female children or a mixture of male and female children, with or without siblings etc. Such sections have the force of law (guaranteed under Libyan law). Thus Libya entered reservations concerning Article 2 in regard to inheritance, where Libya maintained the right to implement it in accord with Islamic law (*Shar'iah*). Libya also entered a reservation concerning Article 16(1) that 'commits states to take proper measures to eliminate discrimination against women in marriage and family affairs'. Here again, 'Libya abides by women's rights guaranteed by Islamic Shari'a'). For more information, see Mesrati, above n 92, 96.

case of women, however, any inheritance is under her personal control and there is no obligation to distribute it or use it to care for other family members, although (in practice) many naturally do so.[126]

CEDAW does not recognise the differences in levels of responsibility accorded to men and women by the *Qur'ān* and thus reflected in the legislation of Muslim countries.[127] Inheritance under *Shar'iah* stems from that distribution of responsibility. In Libya, the *Protection of Women's Right to Inheritance Act of 1959*[128] guarantees that a woman receives the inheritance to which she is entitled under *Shar'iah.*

Libya, together with a number of other nations, not all of them Muslim,[129] has lodged a reservation regarding Article 16(1)(c) and (d) of the Convention, which refer to the issue of equal rights and responsibilities. Generally, rights and responsibilities are seen not as identical but as complementary.

Key areas of difference between CEDAW and Libyan law remain the provisions related to 'the dissolution of marriage, the custody and guardianship of children upon dissolution of a marriage, and polygamy' that are covered by Article 16.[130] Article 16(1)(c) states that men and women 'have the *same* rights and responsibilities during marriage and its dissolution' (emphasis added) and Article 16(1)(d) states that men and women have 'the same rights and responsibilities as parents irrespective of their marital status, in matters relating to their children – in all cases the interests of the children are paramount'.

Under *Shar'iah*, which is acknowledged as a source of law for Libya, the head of the household and the person who holds the responsibility for the family is the man, while the woman has no financial obligations to support the family even if she works.[131] In practice however most women – particularly wives and mothers – use their income either directly or indirectly (by surrendering it to their husband) to assist in supporting the family. Very few use it exclusively for themselves.

The reservation entered is that the 'implementation of Article 16, paragraph 1(c) and (d) of the Convention shall be without prejudice to any of the rights guaranteed to women by the Islamic [*Shar'iah*]'.[132] To guarantee the rights of women (and the interests of their children) in accord with *Shar'iah*, Libya enacted the following legislation.

The *Marriage and Divorce Act No 10 of 1984*[133] affirms (in Articles 17, 40 and 71) that the man, who is the head of the family, is responsible for the family's welfare. Libya has enacted legislation

126 Sherif Abdel Azeem, *Women in Islam Versus Women in the Judaeo-Christian Tradition: The Myth and the Reality* (World Assembly of Muslim Youth, 1995) 13.

127 Begum, above n 122, 63.

128 *Protection of Women's Right to Inheritance Act 1959* (Libya).

129 These include Lebanon, Bahrain, India, Israel and Egypt. India referred to the rights of the communities not to have such restrictions imposed without their consent (India, Declaration: 14); and Israel lodged its reservation 'to the extent that the laws on personal status which are binding on the various religious communities in Israel do not conform with the provisions of that article' (Israel, Reservation: 15). See CEDAW, *Declarations, Reservations, Objections and Notifications of Withdrawal of Reservations Relating to the Convention on the Elimination of All Forms of Discrimination against Women*, UN Doc No CEDAW/SP/2006/2, 9 (Bahrain), 17 (Lebanon), 14 (India), 15 (Israel), 11 (Egypt).

130 Ekaterina Yahyaoui Krivenko, *Women, Islam and International Law: Within the Context of the Convention on the Elimination of All Forms of Discrimination Against Women* (Martinus Nijhoff, 2008) 152.

131 Al-Sadq Abdul Rhman Al-Ghryani, *Mudunt Al-Fqh Al-Maliky wa Ta'diylatuh* (Mu'sast Al-Ryan, 2002) 105 [Trans: *Code of Maliki Jurisprudence and its Amendments* (Foundation Rayyan)].

132 CEDAW, *CEDAW Reservations – Libya*, UN Doc CEDAW/SP/2006/2 (5 July 1995), above n 124, 17–18.

133 *Marriage and Divorce Act No 10 of 1984* (Libya).

to protect women and their children. Under Article 396 of the *Libyan Criminal Act*,[134] if a man does not take his family responsibilities seriously, he can be judged as a criminal and either jailed for no less than one year[135] or asked to pay a fine of LYD 50.[136]

Men, therefore, have a legal responsibility to support their families. Women too, however, while they do not have the same obligation to do so, are able to assist and are in no way prohibited from assisting in the support of their families.

To ensure the healthy development of children in a family (and in particular in regard to the nurture of young infants), the *Qur'ān* – and the legislative framework derived from it – places a responsibility on mothers in relation to the care of those children.[137] The responsibility of the law, in this context, is to facilitate workplace participation in a manner that does not negatively impact on children and families. The primacy of parenting responsibilities, particularly in regard to the care of young children, is clearly maintained as being the role of the mother; meanwhile CEDAW's emphasis is rather on equality of outcomes in terms of workplace participation by women and in terms too of fostering a greater direct parenting role by men in a role distribution that is increasingly gender free or non gender specific.

The Libyan Government and the CEDAW Committee

The ratification of CEDAW requires States parties to implement various measures in order to overcome discrimination domestically. These may include the adoption of the principle of gender equality within the legal system and the foundation of organisations to deal with individual and institutional discrimination against women.[138] Once a state ratifies CEDAW, it must submit reports to the CEDAW Committee, the first to be submitted a year after ratification and then one every four years thereafter. Each report is to outline measures taken by the country to comply with their treaty obligations. Libya as a State party must adhere to these requirements.

The CEDAW Committee generally meets three times a year to discuss, examine and evaluate state reports.[139] It makes recommendations where necessary, and monitors the progress and achievements of each state through the submitted reports and interviews with the reporting countries' delegations, as well as through the input from relevant non-governmental organisations (NGOs).[140]

Since Libya ratified CEDAW, it has submitted official periodic reports on three occasions to the CEDAW Committee. The Committee received the first report (due on 15 June 1990) on

---

134 *Criminal Act 1953* (Libya).

135 Families so affected must then rely on government support.

136 Approximately AUD 40. See *Exchange-Rates* (15 October 2011) <http://www.exchange-rates.org>.

137 For more details see, Maryam Bent Hasan Al-Khlyfah and Abdulkareem Alwan, *Moltqa Albhryn fy Hoquq Alnsln wa Huryath Alasasyah* (Jameat Al-Bahryn, 2007) 117–25 [Trans: *Forum in Bahrain Human Rights and Fundamental Freedoms* (University of Bahrain)].

138 Weichselbaumer and Winter-Ebmer, above n 8, 246.

139 Office of the United Nations High Commissioner for Human Rights, *Committee on the Elimination of Discrimination against Women: Sessions* (15 October 2011) <http://www2.ohchr.org/english/bodies/cedaw/sessions.htm>. Note the OHCHR has had responsibility for the CEDAW Committee since 1 January 2008. Before 2005, it met twice a year only.

140 Weichselbaumer and Winter-Ebmer, above n 8, 246.

18 February 1991;[141] the second report (due on 15 June 1994) on 18 February 1999;[142] and the combined third, fourth and fifth periodic reports (due on 15 June 1998, 2002 and 2006 respectively) on 4 December 2008.[143]

Introducing the initial report, the Libyan representative maintained that there were 'no laws that were in any way discriminatory against women' and pointed to the fact that Libyan legislation contained the principle of gender equality, adding that '[*Shar'iah*] equally emphasised the importance of women in society'.[144] Indeed, he said that gender stereotypes were being eliminated through education,[145] that women were 'considered as the cornerstone of the society ... equal to men before the law ... had equal rights with regard to custody of their children ... able to write wills, independent of men, and [had] the right to choose their husbands'.[146]

The CEDAW Committee examined the initial report on 19 and 21 January 1994.[147] Having considered the initial report (and its addendum), the Committee noted a number of areas where progress had been made. These included greater participation in education and in the workforce.[148] The Committee also noted a number of principal concerns; among them was the 'State party's general reservation on ratifying the Convention', which the Committee considered to be 'incompatible with the Convention's purpose and objective'.[149] The Committee also argued that, as *Shar'iah* 'had given equality to women', it was unclear why Libya persisted with the general reservation.[150] The Committee also 'noted with concern' that:

> While the State party was on the one hand introducing revolutionary measures for the emancipation of women, it was on the other hand emphasizing their role as mothers and housewives, thus reinforcing what was already stiff cultural resistance to substantial change.[151]

The Committee regretted the lack of any specific information in the State party's report on the implementation of Articles 2 and 5 of the Convention. It also noted a lack of statistical data (particularly gender-disaggregated data)[152] and a scarcity of information on the particular problems of women in rural areas and the important role they played in the family economy.[153] Other areas

141 CEDAW Committee, *Consideration of Libya's Initial Report*, UN Doc CEDAW/C/LIB/1 (18 February 1991), above ch 1 n 58, 1.

142 United Nations Committee on the Elimination of Discrimination against Women, *Ways and Means of Expediting the Work of the Committee Report of the Secretariat*, 29th sess (30 June–18 July 2003), *Provisional Agenda*, UN Doc CEDAW/C/2003/II/4 (14 May 2003) Annex II, Item 6b, 17 where it is reported as yet to be considered. For access to relevant documents, see UNDP Arab Human Rights website.

143 CEDAW Committee, *Consideration of Libya's Combined 2nd–5th Reports*, UN Doc CEDAW/C/LBY/5 (4 December 2008), above ch 1 n 58.

144 United Nations, GAOR 49th sess, Supp No 38 (CEDAW Committee, *Report*, 13th sess (17 January–4 February 1994) UN Doc A/49/38 (1994) (*Concluding Observations – Initial Report – Libya)* [127].

145 Ibid. [128].

146 Ibid. [129].

147 United Nations, GAOR 49th sess, Supp No 38 (CEDAW Committee, *Report*, 13th sess (17 January–4 February 1994) UN Doc A/49/38, (1994) (*Concluding Observations – Initial Report – Libya)* [126]–[185].

148 Ibid. [137], [177].

149 Ibid. [179].

150 Ibid. [130]–[132].

151 Ibid. [180].

152 Ibid. [133], [145], [155], [156], [163], [184].

153 Ibid. [182].

of concern included inheritance[154] and contradictory reports regarding custody of children after divorce.[155] In regard to childcare, Committee members noted that the '50 employee rule' for childcare provision worked against the provision of childcare, as few enterprises employed that many women.[156]

Libya's second periodic report[157] was received on 18 February 1999.[158] However, it was almost a decade later before a pre-session working group considered, it in January 2009, after responses were received to questions issued in August 2008.[159] It was then considered in conjunction with a number of later reports.

In January and February 2009, the CEDAW Committee considered Libya's second periodic report and the combined third, fourth and fifth periodic reports.[160] Following these sessions, the Committee released comments regarding Libya's progress in implementing CEDAW, as well as areas of concern.[161] A number of positives were highlighted, including the *Charter on the Rights and Duties of Women in the Libyan Arab Society* – approved by the General People's Committee (GP Cttee) in March 1997 – and the nation's accession to the Optional Protocol to CEDAW in 2004.[162]

The CEDAW Committee also expressed its appreciation to the State party for its written replies to the list of issues and questions that had been raised by the pre-session working group, but regretted that they had not provided specific information in response to the questions posed. The Committee commended the State party for its high-level delegation. It also expressed its appreciation for the second periodic report and the combined third to fifth periodic reports; but in regard to the latter combined report the Committee reminded Libya 'of the need to comply with its reporting obligations in a timely manner, as delays in reporting may have a negative impact on the implementation of the Convention'.[163] It also regretted that the State party did not follow its guidelines for the preparation of periodic reports. The Committee again expressed regret at the Libyan government's failure to provide gender-disaggregated data or sufficient information on all areas covered by the Convention. The Committee cited the areas of health and education

---

154 Ibid. [174] where the Committee members 'felt that there was no need to enter a reservation, because, with that interpretation [i.e. responsibility for males means a double share of inheritance], women were treated equally to men'.

155 Ibid. [169].

156 Ibid. [164].

157 CEDAW Committee, *Consideration of Libya's Second Periodic Report* (15 March 1999), above ch 1 n 58.

158 See, UNDP, AHR Index, *Libya: Country Reports: Convention on the Elimination of All Forms of Discrimination against Women* (15 October 2011) <http://www.arabhumanrights.org/en/countries/convreports.aspx?cid=10&cnv=6>.

159 United Nations Committee on the Elimination of Discrimination against Women, *List of Issues and Questions with Regard to the Consideration of Periodic Reports: The Pre-Session Working Group Considered the Second Periodic Report of the Libyan Arab Jamahiriya*, 43rd sess (19 January–6 February 2009), UN Doc CEDAW/C/LBY/Q/2 (12 August 2008). For responses, see United Nations Committee on the Elimination of Discrimination against Women, *Responses to the List of Issues and Questions with Regard to the Consideration of the Second Report Libyan Arab Jamahiriya: Pre-session Working Group*, Addendum, 43rd sess (19 January–6 February 2009) UN Doc CEDAW/C/LBY/Q/2/Add.1 (9 January 2009).

160 CEDAW Committee, *Concluding Observations – Libya* (6 February 2009) above ch 1 n 58.

161 Ibid.

162 Ibid. [4]–[5].

163 Ibid. [2].

in particular, as well as employment (including the issue of maternity leave).[164] It encouraged the government to utilise the technical assistance available from the UN Office of the High Commissioner for Human Rights (OHCHR).[165] The Committee also regretted that the government had failed to provide 'information on the impact and results of measures taken to achieve equality between women and men'.[166] This made it difficult for the Committee 'to assess progress in the implementation of the Convention in the State party'.[167]

The 'persistence of entrenched, traditional stereotypes regarding the roles and responsibilities of women and men in the family and society at large'[168] remained a source of concern. The Committee noted that these were 'reflected ... in women's educational choices, their situation in the labour market and their low participation rate in political and public life'.[169] The Committee urged Libya to adopt a national strategic plan to promote the human rights of Libyan women and eliminate gender stereotypes, and thus promote 'equal sharing of family responsibilities ... and equal status and responsibilities in the private and public spheres'.[170]

Legal Status of CEDAW and the Definition of Discrimination

In terms of the legal status of the Convention, the Committee noted that while Libya had affirmed that all laws in force there embodied the principle of gender equality, it remained 'concerned at the lack of clarity with respect to the status of the Convention in the domestic legal order'.[171] It reaffirmed its concern in regard to the absence of a prohibition of discrimination against women in domestic legislation in line with Articles 1 and 2(b) of the Convention:

> It recalls that the absence of such a specific provision on prohibition ..., which encompasses both direct and indirect discrimination in both the public and private spheres, constitutes an impediment to the full application of the Convention in the State party.[172]

The Committee also expressed concern 'that the provisions of the Convention have not been invoked in national courts'.[173]

The Committee urged greater dissemination of the concluding comments and other relevant material to government officials, parliamentary members and women's and human rights organisations so that these would be 'aware of the measures that have been taken to ensure the de jure and de facto equality of women, as well as the further steps ... required in this regard'.[174]

The Committee requested that a combined sixth and seventh periodic report (in which the government could respond to the Committee's observations and report on further progress) be submitted in 2014, but asked that information on steps taken to implement certain recommendations

---

164 Ibid. [2]–[43]. See for education [31]–[32]; employment [33]–[34] (maternity leave [34]); health [35]–[36].

165 Ibid. [2].

166 Ibid. [43].

167 Ibid. [43].

168 Ibid. [21].

169 Ibid. [21].

170 Ibid. [21]–[22].

171 Ibid. [9].

172 Ibid.

173 Ibid. [11].

174 Ibid. [48].

be submitted in 2011.[175] Again the Committee recommended that the available technical assistance be sought. (The events of February 2011, however, are likely to have prevented the submission of such an interim report; but nor can any notice be found of a request being submitted to the OHCHR for assistance.)

This continued reluctance to implement changes identified by the Committee as ones that would contribute to women's equal participation in the workforce reflects an overall attitude that manifests itself in the government's apparent inability to properly monitor regulations and legislation that are in place. Superficial gestures (up to and including those of legislation) carry little weight without concrete measures such as an active inspectorate and adequate sanctions where breaches occur. The attitudinal change supportive of the rights of women to participate more fully in the workforce and yet be able to maintain their roles as wives and mothers is still notable by its absence. Despite a generation of well-educated women becoming available to enter the workforce, their skills remain underutilised due to the persistent attitude that is also manifested in the communications between the government and the Committee.

Convention on the Rights of the Child (CRC)

In this section many issues related to the *Convention on the Rights of the Child* (CRC) will be discussed. These include the importance of children to society; the history of and background to the Convention; the CRC in comparison to the UN Charter and other documents concerning children; the importance of the CRC; Libya and the CRC, and its relations with the CRC Committee.

The Significance of Children to Society and the Major Role They Play

As Diane Whitehead wrote, 'Because children are both the present and the future of every nation, they have needs, rights, and intrinsic worth that must be recognised and supported'.[176] Today's children are not only the children of today, but also represent the future of every nation. As such, their rights and needs must be supported; but, most importantly, their 'intrinsic worth' as human beings in their own right must be recognised. Their small stature, their dependent status, their vulnerability does not mean that they should be any less well treated than other humans who happen to be adults. Indeed, their very vulnerability gives them a special status, and demands, for example, that they be given special care with regard to their health and welfare. As Whitehead noted, 'Children occupy a unique status in society ... [and] ... [t]his status should be both recognised and respected'.[177]

The children of today are 'the next generation's decision-makers and leaders ... [and] will shape the future of our society and culture'.[178] It is, therefore, crucial that their basic rights be protected and safeguarded so that they are able to 'grow and develop to meet their full potential'.[179]

---

175 Ibid. [50].

176 Whitehead in Association for Childhood Education International (ACEI) and US National Committee of the World Organization for Early Childhood, 'Global Guidelines for Early Childhood Education and Care in the 21st Century' (ACEI-OMEP, 2000) 1 <http://acei.org/acei/omep-joint-statement-in-support-of-ratification-of-the-crc>.

177 Diane Whitehead, 'Convention on the Rights of the Child' (2009) 85(3) *Childhood Education* 178, 178.

178 Ibid.

179 Ibid.

Only in this way can both the society and its individual members reach their individual and collective potential. Thus, correctly understood, guaranteeing children's rights so as to ensure their healthy development as human beings is a valuable societal goal rather than an individualistic indulgence or even as something destructive of families and of parental rights (which is how it is sometimes portrayed by the most conservative factions, particularly those with reservations relating to religious instruction and practice, in almost every nation).[180]

The History of the Convention on the Rights of the Child

There was a growing recognition in Europe in the late nineteenth century of childhood as a time before adult responsibilities were taken on, and of children as other than potential or actual workers for their parents in fields, or later for others in factories. This has been termed by some as a sentimentalisation of childhood[181] made possible by medical advancement and increased survival rates;[182] but for others it represented a long overdue recognition of the intrinsic worth of children, their value as human beings. It was a period of great change – which began with the Enclosure Acts and the beginning of what we now term 'urbanisation' and burgeoning industrialisation, with all its attendant abuses and suffering – that ushered in a period of great reform.[183] In many countries, and internationally, this was reflected in legislation designed to exclude children from dangerous workplaces;[184] to impose a minimum age for employment;[185] to ensure a minimum level of schooling provided by the state;[186] and even to guarantee support for families in the worst circumstances so that their children might survive.[187] Famine in Europe, such as the Potato Famine in Ireland, now unthinkable, saw innocent children perish in their thousands in the mid-nineteenth century. There was also a growing awareness of the conditions in which the middle class saw others live, which generated revulsion and social activism rather than acceptance. It was this as much perhaps as fear of revolution that prompted social change on a broad scale.

There was an almost universal passion evident for improving 'child care and children's lives'.[188] This is exemplified by the proclamation by the Swedish progressive writer Ellen Key[189] of the

180 Robert Karolis, *The Convention on the Rights of the Child: The Making of a Deception* (Constitutional Heritage Protection Society, 1990). See also M Siraj Sait, 'Islamic Perspectives on the Rights of the Child' in Deirdre Fottrell (ed), *Revisiting Children's Rights: 10 Years of the UN Convention on the Rights of the Child* (Kluwer Law International, 2000) 31, 31.

181 Paula S Fass, 'A Historical Context for the United Nations Convention on the Rights of the Child' (2011) 633(1) *Annals of the American Academy of Political and Social Science* 17, 22.

182 Ibid. 19.

183 Ibid.

184 Ibid. 19–20.

185 See, among others, *Minimum Age (Industry) Convention* (C5) 1919, opened for signature 28 November 1919, ILO (entered into force 13 June 1921); *Minimum Age (Sea) Convention* (C7), opened for signature 9 July 1920, ILO (entered into force 27 September 1921); *Minimum Age (Agriculture) Convention* (C10), opened for signature 16 November 1921, ILO (entered into force 31 August 1923). See also OHCHR, *Legislative History of the Convention on the Rights of the Child* (United Nations, 2007) 3.

186 Fass, above n 181, 19–20.

187 Ibid. 19.

188 Ibid. 21.

189 Prominent Swedish writer, feminist, educationalist, and liberal yet socialist thinker of the late nineteenth and early twentieth century.

twentieth century as the 'Century of the Child' in her two-volume work so titled.[190] She had then 'every reason to expect that continuing improvement would proceed with the unfolding century and that progressive nations and progressive mothers, especially, would protect their children and enhance their lives',[191] but this was not to be. As Paula Fass observes, these positivist views collided with the events of World War I (and, later, World War II). Children were among the most vulnerable, and therefore suffered disproportionately both in the war and its aftermath. Blockades were consciously used not simply to target the military but also entire civilian populations, resulting in malnutrition and starvation of millions in World War I[192] (and again in later conflicts).

Aware of the particular vulnerability of children and their need for protection, the newly formed League of Nations established the Committee for the Protection of Children in 1919. In its 5th Assembly, the League of Nations adopted the *Geneva Declaration of the Rights of the Child* on 26 September 1924.[193] This Declaration was reaffirmed in 1934. However, this was insufficient to ensure children's access to the means (both material and spiritual) to develop normally (Article 1) or guarantee their right to food, care if sick or delinquent, shelter if orphaned or abandoned (Article 2), or to 'relief in times of distress' (Article 3)[194] as well as safeguarding them from exploitation in time of war or peace (Article 4). This was clearly demonstrated by the events of the Great Depression of the 1930s and World War II.

World War II, with the direct targeting by all parties of civilian populations for obliteration, as well as the Nazi regime's programme of 'scientific' experimentation on the most vulnerable (including children) and the acceptance by all parties of 'collateral damage', called into question the very nature of 'civilised' society. These events demanded a response.

Both wars and the sense of horror they generated resulted in an upsurge of support for children's rights. As Paula Fass observes, 'the need for a children's charter of some kind became obvious'.[195] While the Depression between the two major conflicts again showed the impact on the young of economic events beyond their control, it was war that most chillingly revealed that simply having the 'right to childhood' was unfortunately not enough – children could not rely on this right to protect them during these times of hardship and horror.[196] The sufferings of children in World War II and its aftermath demonstrated not only the shortcomings of earlier moves to protect children, but also emphasised the need for greater participation in and recognition of the 'full humanity' of children. For Fuss, it was 'their full humanity … not their childhood, to which they had a right and to which new international commitments should … be directed'.[197] The collision of optimism for children's rights and the 'overwhelming facts on the ground [and] the way these facts were engaged … had important influences on the particular history of the CRC'.[198]

190 Key's two-volume book was entitled *Barnets Århundrade* (Swedish edition, 1900) [*The Century of the Child*, 1909]. For the Swedish text, see <http://runeberg.org/barnets/>: Ellen Key, *Barnets Århundrade* (Bonniers, 1900). It begins with a quotation from Friedrich Nietzsche (in *Also sprach Zarathustra/Thus Spoke Zarathustra* (1891) about childhood as the 'undiscovered land' and the one that people must love and where they must live, emphasising that one should live to create the future not simply reproduce the past: Part III, ch 56.

191 Fass, above n 181, 21.

192 Ibid. 22.

193 OHCHR, *Legislative History of the CRC*, above n 185, 3.

194 Ibid.

195 Fass, above n 181, 23.

196 Ibid.

197 Ibid.

198 Ibid.

These are among the many significant factors that 'contributed historically to the creation of the CRC'[199] and to the documents that preceded it, including the pre-World War I ILO materials, but more particularly the *Geneva Convention of the Rights of the Child* adopted by the League of Nations on 26 September 1924 (reaffirmed in 1934) and the creation of an international organisation specifically directed at children – the Save the Children Union.[200]

It should be noted that work once again began in the immediate aftermath of World War II, not only via the formation of international organisations specifically for children – for example, the Save the Children Fund and the United Nations International Children's Education Fund (1946)[201] – but also via the construction of a new children's rights document, with preparation beginning as early as 1946.[202] It was anticipated that this would be an improvement on the earlier League of Nations Geneva Declaration. The drafting of the CRC took place during the Cold War.[203] While the Cold War deepened and reflected a world increasingly divided into two blocs – one communist, the other the 'free world' – socialist Poland was among those countries that made a significant contribution to the formulation of the new document.[204] This was a truly international concern. The Social Commission, which had been charged with the formulation of a new Charter for Children's Rights almost immediately after the war, recommended that:

> [E]ven though great weight should be given to the Geneva Declaration, the proposed Charter should nevertheless include additional principles which would transform the document into a United Nations Charter of the Rights of the Child, embodying the main features of the newer conception of child welfare.[205]

The Social Commission also stated that both member states and NGOs should be consulted, and this was agreed. It was decided that a new instrument would be drafted, but it would be a 'non-binding declaration rather than a charter'.[206] The draft, amended by the Commission, was adopted in 1950[207] and then referred to the Commission on Human Rights.[208]

In 1948, meanwhile, the United Nations General Assembly had adopted the *Universal Declaration of Human Rights*, which implicitly grants rights to children as well as to adults.[209] The specific needs of children in regard to rights over and above those accorded adults or human beings generally continued to be recognised. Their vulnerability and dependency were prominent. However, the referral of the document on the 'rights of the child' to the Commission on Human Rights was only natural and logical.

By 1950, the first draft of the UN *Declaration of the Rights of the Child* (UNDRC) was released by the Social Commission which had been charged with its formulation.[210] The body charged with the responsibility for the document became the Commission on Human Rights, and this body

199 Ibid. 25.
200 OHCHR, *Legislative History of the CRC*, above n 185, iv.
201 Ibid. vii.
202 Ibid. 4.
203 Melton, above n 3, 920.
204 OHCHR, *Legislative History of the CRC*, above n 185, xxvii–xxxviii.
205 Ibid. 4.
206 Ibid.
207 Ibid. 5–6 [59].
208 Ibid. 5–7.
209 *Universal Declaration of Human Rights*.
210 OHCHR, *Legislative History of the CRC*, above n 185, 4–6.

issued the *Draft Declaration of the Rights of the Child* in 1959. The resulting *Economic and Social Council Resolution No 728* was adopted on 30 July and, following discussion the *Declaration of the Rights of the Child*, was proclaimed by the General Assembly of the *United Nations Resolution No 1386* of 20 November 1959.[211]

Following the adoption of a resolution in late 1976 on the International Year of the Child,[212] further discussions began in relation to the possibility of a more stringent and binding document. By 1978, draft resolutions were being created regarding the question of a convention on the rights of the child, and a second United Nations Economic and Social Council resolution on an international Year of the Child adopted.[213] In 1979, the United Nations 'began developing an international treaty that would protect the rights of children everywhere'.[214] However, in contrast to previous efforts, this treaty was to be 'an inclusive, *legally binding* human rights treaty for all the world's children'.[215] The negotiations were ongoing from 1978 to 1979, with various drafts, discussions in the Commission on Human Rights, contributions by NGOs, United Nations Economic and Social Council resolutions, working groups, reports, technical reviews and resolutions at the General Assembly of the United Nations.[216] Various Articles were adopted each year from 1979 onwards[217] in the lead-up to the adoption of a new convention some ten years later.[218]

The CRC in Comparison with the UNDRC

Many saw a stark contrast between the 1959 Declaration and the 1989 Convention. Melton, for example, commented on the distinctions between the two:

> Historically, child advocacy has been divided between people who primarily favour recognition of children's autonomy and privacy and those who primarily favour support for their care and protection. ... Documents expressing children's rights typically took one position but not the other (see, e.g., Declaration on the Rights of the Child, 1959, expressing children's rights to care and protection).[219]

The CRC recognised the many limitations that had marred earlier attempts at guaranteeing child rights, namely the limitations created by their dependency.[220] There was a renewed emphasis on the inherent or intrinsic value of the child and an added emphasis on the child's dignity. Indeed, as Melton observes: 'The integrating construct, remarkably sustained during the lengthy drafting process,

211 Ibid. 4–26.

212 Ibid. 29.

213 For details, see ibid. 31–48.

214 Whitehead, above n 177, 178.

215 Ibid. (emphasis added).

216 OHCHR, *Legislative History of the CRC*, above n 185, 31–47 (1978), 48–78 (1979), 79–81 (1980), 82–93 (1981), 94–101 (1982), 102–6 (1982–83), 107–14 (1983), 115–23 (1984), 124–38 (1985), 139–52 (1986), 153–64 (1987), 165–92 (1988).

217 Ibid. 69 (1979), 79 (1980), 83 (1981), 95–6 (1982), 108 (1983), 117 (1984), 125–6 (1985), 141–2 (1986), 154 (1987), 169–72 (1988).

218 For full details and copies of the various texts as well as commentary on the various articles, see ibid. Part III, 275–907.

219 Melton, above n 3, 920.

220 Fass, above n 181, 26.

was protection of the *dignity* of the child, a term appearing eight times in the CRC'.[221] Prior to the enactment of the CRC in 1989, the focus in human rights documents was divided between those who emphasised the 'civil and political rights of a child, and those [who emphasised] ... social, economic, and cultural rights'.[222] With the enactment of the CRC, the rights of the child expanded to embrace far broader dimensions than those envisaged by either of these two perspectives. The child now had cultural, social, economic, civil and political rights,[223] indeed human rights that were to be observed.

Adopted in 1989, the CRC was recognised by the international community as a supersession of the two earlier declarations concerning the rights of the child, that is, the League of Nations *Declaration of the Rights of the Child* in 1924[224] and the United Nations *Declaration of the Rights of the Child* in 1959.[225] The CRC differs in many aspects from its predecessors (see further below),[226] but:

> [P]erhaps more than any other instrument, the CRC (1989) is illustrative of the potential of international human rights law to guide policy in a manner that transforms life at the neighbourhood level. That potential rests in several characteristics of the CRC itself and of the response that it has engendered in the global community.[227]

The CRC is broad-ranging in its impact on children's lives, and the degree of its acceptance by the international community further multiplies that impact across the globe.

The CRC was adopted unanimously by the United Nations General Assembly on 20 November 1989 and entered into force on 2 September 1990.[228] An important convention, it has 'both policy and practice implications'.[229] The CRC is the main international treaty that 'addresses the rights of the world's children'.[230] It provides the 'most comprehensive legal framework for basic human rights for children everywhere'.[231] The CRC is a renowned and well-respected convention worldwide. Scholars and children's rights advocates alike celebrate and applaud its 'innovative approach to children's rights'.[232] It is genuinely believed that the CRC has not only far surpassed the two earlier declarations by providing the world with a 'child-centred' convention, but that it has also initiated a 'sudden and dramatic change' in our thinking, expectations and stereotypes of children's rights.[233]

---

221 Melton, above n 3, 920.

222 Ibid.

223 Deirdre Fottrell, 'One Step Forward or Two Steps Sideways? Assessing the First Decade of the Children's Convention on the Rights of the Child' in Deirdre Fottrell (ed), *Revisiting Children's Rights: 10 Years of the UN Convention on the Rights of the Child* (Kluwer Law International, 2000) 1, 4.

224 *Declaration of the Rights of the Child*, LON (26 September 1924).

225 *Declaration of the Rights of the Child*, GA Res 1386 (XIV), UN GAOR, Sup No 16, UN Doc A/4354 (20 November 1959).

226 Doris E Buss, '"How the UN Stole Childhood": The Christian Right and the International Rights of the Child' in Jo Bridgeman and Daniel Monk (eds), *Feminist Perspectives on Child Law* (Cavendish, 2000) 271, 281–2.

227 Melton, above n 3, 919.

228 *Convention on the Rights of the Child* (CRC). See also Whitehead, above n 177, 178.

229 Robin S Mama, 'Needs, Rights, and the Human Family: The Practicality of the Convention on the Rights of the Child' (2010) 89(5) *Child Welfare* 177, 177.

230 Ibid. 178.

231 Whitehead, above n 177, 178.

232 Buss, above n 226, 282.

233 Ibid.

There are three main aspects that make the CRC a unique, practical and almost universally accepted convention.[234] Firstly, according to Article 3 of the Convention, the child's best interests shall be a 'primary consideration'. Secondly, Articles 12–15 recognise a child's right to 'self-expression and freedom of thought'. Thirdly, Articles 5 and 14 note that the exercise of the 'responsibilities, rights and duties of parents' are to be consistent with the 'evolving capacities of the child'.[235] As Melton observes, '[i]n principle, the CRC is developmentally elastic',[236] and thus it is uniquely suited to the developing child and their changing capacities and abilities.

The CRC's breadth in terms of the 'diversity of domains it addresses' and its extraordinary attention to detail makes it a convention full of diversity.[237] It addresses all issues concerning children at different stages of development, and demonstrates a belief that children should be treated and dealt with in a way that is consistent with their evolving capacities:[238]

> The CRC … goes beyond kiddie-lib and child-saving orientations to ensure that the entitlements necessary for children's development as members of the community are provided in a manner consistent with their status as persons.[239]

The CRC is successful and universally accepted, as it employs unique theories and analogies. It 'promotes a climate in which children are given a chance to have a say and be treated with respect'.[240] It also outlines and defines children's rights 'in terms of children's own understanding and experience'.[241] This flexibility, practicality and ingenious design are what make the CRC a successful, celebrated convention at governmental level, while its inclusion of the child's own understanding and perspective renders it acceptable to those whose rights it seeks to recognise.[242] The respectful attitude towards children themselves is embodied in the document. Its general approach to children is that they are 'human beings who deserve dignity and human rights'. It should be noted that the Convention defines children as 'people under the age of 18'.[243]

The CRC's Importance as a Treaty

The CRC is particularly significant because it is the 'first *binding* universal treaty dedicated solely to the protection and promotion of children's rights'.[244] It aims to safeguard and advance the rights of all children,[245] and 'supports children and families and provides measures that will enable the child to eventually be prepared to lead a full life'.[246]

---

234 Just two member countries have not ratified the CRC: the United States and Somalia (which has no extant government at the time of writing). Adrien Katherine Wing, 'International Conventions' in Joseph Suad (ed), *Encyclopedia of Women and Islamic Cultures: Family, Law and Politics* (Brill, 2005) vol 2, 306, 307.

235 Buss, above n 226, 282.

236 Melton, above n 3, 920.

237 Ibid. 919–20.

238 Ibid. 920.

239 Ibid.

240 Ibid.

241 Ibid.

242 Ibid.

243 Mama, above n 229, 178.

244 Fottrell, above n 223, 11 (emphasis added).

245 Whitehead, above n 177, 179.

246 Mama, above n 229, 179.

It is the world's most recognised, ratified and respected human rights treaty. The nations that have ratified this essential convention use it to guide them in developing legal systems and programmes and policies that fully address children's needs and rights.[247] Indeed, it is the single most approved treaty in the world,[248] with 140 signatories and 193 States parties that have ratified it.[249] The legitimacy of its adoption was enhanced by a process which involved consensus-based drafting that took place over a decade 'with an unprecedented level of input' and involved both governmental and non-governmental organisations as well as technical and expert working parties.[250] The widespread respect for the adoption process and outcome resulted in something of a human rights 'success story' according to Buss,[251] and is signalled by its rapid entry into force and expansion of the number of signatories. Within a single year the Convention was ratified by the required minimum of 20 countries and entered into force in 1990,[252] and the number of countries that have ratified it has grown rapidly to the current 193.[253] Each country is involved in a process of ongoing reporting to the relevant body in regard to their implementation of the Convention.

Many have said that the CRC 'should be read as a whole'. For example, those interested in knowing what the CRC states in regard to childcare should not limit themselves to the Articles dedicated to it (such as Article 18); rather, the CRC should all be read from Article 1 to Article 54 to gain the full import of the document.[254] The implementation by governments of the CRC is based on a broad principle of non-discrimination.[255] It is emphasised that States parties are not to employ it selectively.

Just as CEDAW recognises the rights of women, so too, the CRC recognises the rights of the child. It is these two sets of rights that are to be so carefully balanced when women with children seek to enter or remain in the workforce. Children should not suffer by their mother entering the workforce, but should benefit, as should the entire society. Therefore the role of children and their rights and how these rights should also be enjoyed and their needs met is an important part of the consideration of a mother's right to enjoy both the right to motherhood and a right to participate in the workforce on an equal basis with men wherever possible. Mothers are one half of the motherhood equation – children form the other half of that same equation. Their right to nourishment from breastfeeding is probably the prime example of where the two needs and rights intersect in a way that can only be met with the aid of adjustments on the part of the employer and the State. The CRC is essential to this study because mention is made in many of its Articles of the need to maintain working mothers, illustrating the important intersection of the rights and responsibilities of mothers and the rights and needs of children.

The most important relevant Articles will be highlighted. It is imperative, therefore, that the following Articles be specifically mentioned: namely, Articles 2(2), 18(2) and (3), 24(2)(d), 26 and 27.

---

247 Whitehead, above n 177, 178.

248 Wing, above n 234, 307.

249 UN, *Treaty Collection, Status of Treaties: CRC*, above ch 1 n 62. As already mentioned, the sole exceptions in terms of member country ratifications are the United States and Somalia: Wing, above n 234, 307.

250 Melton, above n 3, 919. For a full and comprehensive account, see OHCHR, *Legislative History of the CRC*, above n 185.

251 Buss, above n 226, 271.

252 Ibid.

253 UN, *Treaty Collection*: *Status of Treaties: CRC*, above ch 1 n 62.

254 Melton, above n 3, 921.

255 See *Convention on the Rights of the Child* (CRC) art 2.

Article 2(2) involves the principle of non-discrimination against the child which, in terms of this study, could be taken to include equal access to adequate childcare services and care for children of those mothers who are in the workforce.

Also, paragraphs 2 and 3 of Article 18 encompass the State's duty to provide 'appropriate assistance to parents and legal guardians in the performance of their child-rearing responsibilities' and 'ensure the development of institutions, facilities and services for the care of children'. Paragraph 3 of Article 18 proclaims that, 'States parties shall take all appropriate measures to ensure that children of working parents have the right to benefit from child-care services and facilities'.[256] Many other Articles are also important. For instance, Article 24 concerning health affirms in paragraph 2(d) that the State is '[t]o ensure appropriate pre-natal and post-natal health care for mothers', while Article 26 states that every child should be able to benefit from adequate levels of social security provision. Such benefits may be determined taking into account the 'resources and circumstances' of the child and of those responsible for his or her welfare. Paragraph 1 of Article 27 refers to the right of a child to a 'standard of living adequate for the child's physical, mental, spiritual, moral and social development', while paragraph 3 provides that States parties shall:

> [I]n accordance with national circumstances ... take appropriate measures to assist parents and others responsible for the child to implement this right and shall in case of need provide material assistance and support programmes, particularly with regard to nutrition, clothing and housing.[257]

These Articles are relevant because they involve all those responsible for the care of children, including those providing care and services for the children of working mothers. The breadth and degree of detail in the CRC make it an ideal 'analytic tool useful in developing, monitoring and evaluating child policy, regardless of the specific issue under consideration'.[258]

Libya and the CRC

The relationship between Libya and the Committee on the Rights of the Child (CRC Committee) regarding the *Convention on the Rights of the Child* will be explored in this section.

Libya acceded to the *Convention on the Rights of the Child* on 15 May 1993.[259] It is significant that, unlike many other nations, Libya did not enter any reservations for this convention.[260] It is imperative, however, that Libya fully cooperate and fulfil the responsibilities required of it as a member state. As Melton states, 'ratification of the CRC or an announcement of a moral commitment to apply its provisions is just the beginning'.[261] This is perhaps a responsibility of which the Libyan government should be reminded, given its subsequent, quite tardy submission of the required reports, the rather dubious nature of some of the claims made in those reports and its subsequent statements made to the relevant committee, in this instance the CRC Committee[262] (see further below).

---

256 Ibid. art 18(2) and (3).

257 Ibid. art 27(3).

258 Melton, above n 3, 920.

259 OHCHR, *Status of Ratifications of the Principal International Human Rights Treaties 2006*, above ch 1 n 64, 7.

260 United Nations, UN GAOR, 27th special sess, 5th mtg, UN Doc A/S-27/PV.5 (10 May 2002) 9.

261 Melton, above n 3, 921.

262 Mama, above n 229, 178.

The CRC, like any other convention, should be 'realistically interpreted'. It also needs to be 'actively promoted'[263] to achieve the impact envisaged by those who framed it. The CRC has remarkable potential to truly assist a country in maintaining and safeguarding a childhood for its children, one full of respect, honour and justice; however, the CRC's practicality 'hinges in its implementation' (including its enforcement).[264] A key to successful implementation at the international level was the establishment of the CRC Committee, an 'independent group of experts'[265] that tracks the implementation of the convention (or lack thereof) by States parties by monitoring and receiving the obligatory periodic country reports,[266] and responding to those reports.

While countries are obligated to submit periodic reports, the Committee in turn is required to examine the reports. It responds to each report, issuing a response which includes 'Concluding Observations'. These may include recommendations, comments and requests (sometimes for further clarification regarding material submitted). Prior face-to-face consultative meetings are also held, which enables spokespersons for a particular government to present their arguments directly to the Committee and for Committee members to directly interrogate national representatives regarding the nature and content of their report. In regard to individual complaints, the Committee is unable to consider them; however, child rights may be raised before other committees with competence to consider 'individual complaints'.[267]

The Libyan Government and the CRC Committee

In accordance with Article 44, each State party is required to submit regular reports to the Committee (initially two years after ratification and every five years thereafter), with such reports to the Committee required to outline the steps and procedures taken to ensure the Convention's implementation.[268]

The CRC Committee attempts to independently verify the content of the State party's report by obtaining information from a number of sources. This includes organisations such as the United Nations International Children's Emergency Fund (UNICEF), the ILO and the United Nations High Commissioner for Refugees (UNHCR), as well as international and national NGOs. 'Significantly', notes Cohen, 'it is this latter group that frequently supplies the most important information'.[269] This information is considered by the Committee in a closed pre-sessional meeting where the Committee 'reviews States Parties' reports that will be examined at the next session'.[270]

---

263 Ibid. 177.

264 Ibid.

265 Cynthia Price Cohen, 'Implementing the U.N. Convention on the Rights of the Child' (1999–2000) 21 *Whittier Law Review* 95, 95–6. Details of its current 15 members can be obtained at Office of the United Nations High Commissioner for Human Rights (OHCHR), *Committee on the Rights of the Child* (15 August 2011) <http://www2.ohchr.org/english/bodies/crc/members.htm>.

266 Mama, above n 229, 178.

267 OHCHR, *Committee on the Rights of the Child* (15 August 2011) <http://www2.ohchr.org/english/bodies/crc/>.

268 United Nations Committee on the Rights of the Child (UN CRC Committee), *Treaty-Specific Guidelines Regarding the Form and Content of Periodic Reports to be Submitted by States Parties under Article 44, Paragraph 1(b), of the Convention on the Rights of the Child*, 55th sess, UN Doc CRC/C/58/Rev.2 (23 November 2010) 1.

269 Cohen, above n 265, 101.

270 Ibid. 100.

The Committee formulates 'a list of issues' which is then forwarded to the State party so that a written response can be submitted prior to the oral hearing.[271]

The oral examination comprises three half-day sessions that follow the pattern of the report. This concludes with the Committee making comments to which the head of the government delegation responds. Finally, the Committee issues its *Concluding Observations*. This document reports on both positive developments and 'areas of concern', and may make a number of recommendations. This is then submitted to the United Nations General Assembly.[272]

The Libyan Government submitted its initial report (due on 14 May 1995) a year late (on 23 May 1996).[273] The second periodic report was submitted on 8 August 2000.[274] The third periodic report, due in 2005, was not submitted as an individual document or on time; rather, Libya combined the third and fourth periodic reports. The CRC Committee received this combined report on 1 September 2009.[275] However, it has not yet been considered by the Committee.[276] The author has been unable to source any further reports to indicate whether an oral examination and/or a pre-sessional meeting occurred, and the recent unrest in Libya (February–October 2011) may contribute to further delays in these matters.

In regard to Libya's initial periodic report, the Committee expressed 'its appreciation to the State party for its report, which has been prepared in conformity with the Committee's guidelines, and for the submission of written replies to its list of issues'.[277] However, the Committee had a number of principal subjects of concern remaining.[278] These included that:

> [T]he State party does not appear to have fully taken into account the provisions of the Convention, especially its general principles, as reflected in its articles 2 (non-discrimination), 3 (best interests of the child), 6 (right to life, survival and development) and 12 (respect for the views of the child), in its legislation, its administrative and judicial decisions, as well as in its policies and programmes relevant to children. While noting the existence of mechanisms to register and address complaints,

---

271 Ibid. 102.

272 Ibid.

273 UN CRC Committee, *Consideration of Reports Submitted by States Parties under Article 44 of the Convention: Initial Reports of States Parties Due in 1995 Addendum – Libyan Arab Jamahiriya (23 May 1996)*, UN Doc CRC/C/28/Add.6 (26 September 1996).

274 UN CRC Committee, *Consideration of Reports Submitted by States Parties under Article 44 of the Convention: Second Periodic Reports of States Parties Due in 2000 – Libyan Arab Jamahiriya (8 August 2000)*, UN Doc CRC/C/93/Add.1 (19 September 2002).

275 UN CRC Committee, *Consideration of Reports Submitted by States Parties under Article 44 of the Convention: Third and Fourth Periodic Reports of States Parties Due in 2005 – Libyan Arab Jamahiriya (1 September 2009)*, UN Doc CRC/C/LBY/3–4 (2 June 2010).

276 Nor does it appear likely before late 2012: See OHCHR, *Committee on the Rights of the Child: Sessions* <http://www2.ohchr.org/english/bodies/crc/sessions.htm>. Sessions to 3 February 2012 as at 15 October 2011 (though 'schedules are subject to change without notice') do not include a scheduled consideration of the report by Libya. (Note: the CRC Committee meets three times a year (usually January, May and September) for three weeks per session.)

277 UN CRC Committee, *Consideration of Reports Submitted by States Parties under Article 44 of the Convention: Concluding Observations of the Committee on the Rights of the Child: Libyan Arab Jamahiriya Initial Report*, 17th Session UN Doc CRC/C/15/Add.84 (4 February 1998) 1 [2] (where reference is made to CRC/C/Q/LIBYA.1).

278 Ibid. *Concluding Observations – Libyan Arab Jamahiriya Initial Report*, CRC/C/15/Add.84, 2 [6]–[17].

> the Committee is concerned at the absence of an independent mechanism to register and address complaints from children concerning violations of their rights under the law.[279]

A lack of coordination among bodies concerned for child welfare in Libya and a shortfall of training in this matter among professionals working in this area were issues particularly highlighted by the Committee, as was the lack of promotion of the principles applying under the Convention and the omission of appropriately disaggregated statistical data.[280] Despite progress in the area of child nutrition, the extent of chronic under-nutrition and child health also remained a concern.[281] The status accorded the children of migrant workers and non-citizens was a particular source of concern, as they were discriminated against in terms of their treatment and access to services on that basis.[282] Also of concern were: the continued use of the term 'illegitimate'; the determination of citizenship rights; the inheritance regime;[283] the use of corporal punishment in the home; child abuse;[284] and the retention of certain penal provisions,[285] as well as the administration of justice for juveniles.[286] The Committee made some 17 recommendations and suggestions in regard to the above matters.[287]

The 'timely submission' by Libya of its second periodic report was welcomed by the Committee;[288] however, it regretted a continuing lack of suitable data which, 'together with scarce information on practical implementation hindered a full assessment'.[289]

However, for all its many faults, Libya seems to have pleased the Committee in some regard. First, the Committee commends the founding of the Higher Committee for Children (1997). Secondly, it supports and congratulates the State party's 'generous assistance in humanitarian matters, including in collaboration with United Nations agencies'. Lastly, the Committee also expresses appreciation for 'the State party's achievements in the areas of education, particularly in raising enrolment and literacy rates, and health, including the coverage of its immunization programmes and access to basic services'.[290] However, the Committee in its *Concluding Observations* states that, unfortunately, many of the same issues of concern raised in the last report are still of relevance and concern in the current report. These include the following areas.

Legislation

The Committee notes that while the country had adopted numerous pieces of legislation to improve child welfare, 'many' of those measures 'reflect a predominantly welfare rather than rights based approach' – for example, the *Child Protection Act No 5 of 1997*.[291] Again, the principles of non-

279 Ibid. 2 [10].

280 Ibid. 2 [6]–[8].

281 Ibid. 2 [16].

282 Ibid. 2–3 [11].

283 Ibid. 2–3 [11]–[12].

284 Ibid. 3 [14]–[15].

285 Ibid. 3 [13]: namely that a perpetrator of rape of a minor could be immune from prosecution if he married the victim.

286 Ibid. 3 [17].

287 Ibid. 3–6 [13]–[34].

288 UN CRC Committee, *Thirty-Third Session Consideration of Reports Submitted by States Parties under Article 44 of the Convention: Concluding Observations – Libyan Arab Jamahiriya Second Report*, UN Doc CRC/C/15/Add.209 (4 July 2003) 1 [2].

289 Ibid.

290 Ibid. 1 [3].

291 Ibid. 2 [7].

discrimination and best interests of the child were evoked in regard to personal status laws and juvenile justice legislation. More generally, the International Bureau for Children's Rights has observed: 'Libyan legislation does not appear to prioritise the best interests of the child and the right of children to participate in all decisions affecting them'.[292]

Coordination

The Committee notes that the Libyan system for child welfare 'lacks necessary and effective coordination'.[293] The Higher Committee for Children is responsible for formulating 'child welfare plans and programmes and coordinating their implementation through 26 categories of public authority for example, day nurseries, schools, health centres, social welfare homes',[294] yet there also exists local authorities that provide child services without any apparent centralised oversight. Also, as the Higher Committee is 'composed of volunteers and officials seconded from government ministries, there may be some doubt as to whether its structures are sufficiently robust to perform its functions'.[295] Additional powers are recommended for the Higher Committee, as is a strengthened level of 'intersectoral coordination and cooperation at and between national and local levels of government'.[296]

Data

The National Organisation for Information and Documentation and other information and database sectors are responsible for providing data in regard to children to the Committee and other institutions. The Committee urges Libya to continue to progress in this area. It also advises Libya to 'seek technical assistance from, among others, UNICEF', as this will help Libya improve the quality of its data, which in turn will help the country to 'assess progress and design policies and programmes to implement the Convention'.[297]

Monitoring structures

While the Committee welcomed advances made, it noted two particular problems that it perceived as hampering further progress. The first is a lack of 'a fully independent mechanism with a mandate regularly to monitor and evaluate progress in the implementation of the Convention, and which is mandated to receive and address complaints by children of violations of their rights'.[298] The second obstacle is the existence of two entities, the Higher Committee for Children and the Secretariat for Legal Affairs and Human Rights, with essentially the same functions: the former in regard to monitoring children's rights; the latter having responsibility regarding human rights, necessarily including those of children. The Committee feared that this situation 'may result in overlap and problems of coordination which may have a negative impact on the effectiveness of these governmental (self-)monitoring bodies'.[299] It was recommended that this situation be amended.[300]

---

292 International Bureau for Children's Rights (IBCR), 'Making Children's Rights Work in North Africa: Country Profiles on Algeria, Egypt, Libya, Morocco and Tunisia' (IBCR, 2007) 104.

293 UN CRC Committee, *Concluding Observations – Libyan Arab Jamahiriya Second Report*, UN Doc CRC/C/15/Add.209, above n 288, 2–3 [9].

294 Ibid.

295 Ibid. 3 [9].

296 Ibid. 3 [10(a)].

297 Ibid. 3 [12].

298 Ibid. 3 [13].

299 Ibid.

300 Ibid. 3 [14].

Training
The need to better and more widely disseminate information and improve training regarding the Convention was again noted.[301] Training was to include those in the legal area (judges, magistrates and legal practitioners) who were singled out as requiring additional training in this area, in addition to teachers and others working with children (health workers, social workers and so on). Special programmes to reach the illiterate were also recommended.[302]

Migrant and non-citizen children
Special mention was again made of the position of children of migrant workers and non-citizens,[303] and of those born out of wedlock.[304] The CRC Committee also remained 'unconvinced' that custody (as effected under Libyan law) takes adequate cognisance of the 'best interests of the child'.[305]

Other concerns
The Committee also made recommendations in regard to the adoption of nationality.[306] While the Committee welcomed the prohibition of corporal punishment in schools and the introduction of 'measures to report and investigate maltreatment of children', it again regretted the lack of available data on implementation, and also recommended further efforts by the State party in regard to familial violence, abuse, neglect or maltreatment.[307] In addition to progress made, greater efforts were also recommended in regard to children with disabilities, particularly in regard to non-discrimination and education.[308] The lack of preschool education was also a subject of concern.[309] Penal provisions and the lack of conformity with the definition of the child once again came in for criticism, as did the continued practice of corporal punishment. A call was made for training for the provision of rehabilitation services for juveniles, as well as for a raising of the age of criminal responsibility and an end to criminalisation of status offences (for example, homelessness) and of 'collective punishment'.[310]

Overall, the Committee noted that Libya in its second report did not provide it with complete data in regard to 'demographic and budgetary matters' necessary for a full evaluation of implementation of the Convention. Libya also failed to fully explain and outline the methods taken to ensure its implementation.[311]

As for Libya's third and fourth periodic reports, which were combined and submitted as a document on 1 September 2009, the author has been unable to discover much progress. A meeting by the Committee is due to be held after each submission; however, as of October 2011 this meeting had still not been scheduled at least until February 2012. No trace has been found of references to any pre-sessional meeting, or of an oral hearing, as a prelude to the issuing of its *Concluding*

301 Ibid. 5 [19]–[20].
302 Ibid. 5 [20].
303 Ibid. 6 [23]–[24].
304 Ibid.
305 Ibid. 7 [27]–[28]. Custody/guardianship is determined in accordance with *Shar'iah* principles. For a comprehensive discussion on this issue, see generally Mesrati, above n 92.
306 UN CRC Committee, *Concluding Observations – Libyan Arab Jamahiriya Second Report*, UN Doc CRC/C/15/Add.209, above n 288, 7 [31]–[32].
307 Ibid. 8 [33]–[34].
308 Ibid. 8–9 [35]–[36].
309 Ibid. 10 [39]–[40].
310 Ibid. 8–9 [45]–[46]. See also 5–6 [21]–[22] (re age of criminal responsibility).
311 Ibid. 1 [2].

Observations. As of October 2011, the Committee had not yet released/published its observations, recommendations and further comments in regard to this report.[312] Further delays may be expected in the process due to the reconstruction of the Libyan administration after the events of 2011.

Concluding Comments Regarding the CRC

The area of child welfare particularly intersects with the rights of working women. It is a mother's primary concern at home and at work. Women are generally considered 'by their nature' to be particularly suited to roles allied with caring for children (particularly their health and education), and it is therefore unsurprising that these areas are the main fields of women's education in Libya. However, this makes their continued presence in such roles following maternity particularly important. In this regard 'out of home' care for the children of working mothers is important, and the international requirements in this matter should be considered by the government when formulating legislation and regulations.

In terms of cooperation from the Libyan Government in regard to the CRC Committee, the level of cooperation is similar to that of the government in regard to the reporting mechanism of CEDAW and its interaction with the CEDAW Committee. The CRC Committee repeatedly notes a lack of progress or reluctance to change in regard to numerous matters involving the rights of the child, a number of which also intersect with the rights of mothers to enjoy their rights to motherhood and work. From their correspondence, the necessary widespread attitudinal change (so necessary for genuine change to occur in terms of legislation, regulation and real implementation 'on the ground') appears to be slow in coming.

Conclusion in Regard to the Relevant UN Conventions

In conclusion, the UN human rights conventions are of great importance and relevance to the issues in hand. These treaties have the potential to make a huge difference to the level of discrimination faced by working mothers in Libya, and particularly to the discrepancies in regard to legislation and its implementation in practice. Their respective committees continue to challenge governments to fulfil obligations that were made incumbent upon them by ratification. It is not ratification alone, however, that makes this change possible. It is through the enforcement of these treaties that it will become possible for the Libyan working mother to experience real change.

There are many issues associated with this, particularly the slow pace of change even after ratification. Firstly, the UN's system of inspection and monitoring is a purely supervisory one, and does not involve actual enforcement of the treaty in terms of imposition of sanctions in the event of non-compliance. Implementation is left to the member state. Libya, however, appears to find the task a difficult one; the proper implementation of UN treaties in domestic legislation and regulations (and *their* enforcement) is not occurring. Indeed, as Li Weiwei so accurately observes: 'a big step forward in eliminating discrimination can only be achieved if a collective effort is made both at the international level and by governments'.[313] The latter is only possible when the necessary attitudinal change regarding women (particularly mothers) in the workplace is shared by political representatives and legislators. When it is shared by the majority of the population, change

312 OHCHR, *Committee on the Rights of the Child: Sessions*, above n 276.

313 Li Weiwei, 'Equality and Non-Discrimination under International Human Rights Law' (Norwegian Centre for Human Rights, 2004) 26.

will become, if not inevitable, at least probable. Attitudinal change (arguably as yet limited) as well as the specifics of each convention is monitored in and through the correspondence and discussions between government and committees, in the reports from NGOs and in the statistics provided in relation to the treaty obligations. This is another reason for the value of such material to researchers and chroniclers of progress in the changing role of women.

The following chapter discusses another two international human rights treaties, those of the ILO that concern working women. The chapter will aim to discuss these treaties and evaluate their importance.

Chapter 3

International Human Rights Standards: International Labour Organization

The International Labour Organization (ILO) is an organisation that creates international conventions aiming to eliminate all forms of discrimination against individuals or parties that are seen to be 'weak' or lacking 'voice'. Women are the largest demographic group subject to discrimination.[1] Therefore, many conventions have been created to protect and conserve the rights of women, whether in regard to employment, health or welfare.

Regarding the relevance of ILO conventions to the present study, it should be noted that Libya became a member state of the ILO in 1952, after freedom from colonial rule was attained in 1951.[2] Of particular relevance are the *Discrimination (Employment and Occupation) Convention* (C111)[3] and the *Maternity Protection Convention* in its three forms (C3, C103 and C183),[4] which will be discussed in depth below. These ILO conventions have been ratified by Libya, the country whose provision for the rights of working mothers is the main focus of this study. This section, however, begins with a brief history of the ILO.

The History and Background of the International Labour Organization

The International Labour Organization (ILO) was founded in the year 1919 in Geneva (Switzerland) as a peacemaking institution that promoted social justice.[5] The ILO began as 'an autonomous body' of the League of Nations, created by the Treaty of Versailles in the aftermath of World War I. While the League of Nations failed to prevent the outbreak of World War II and was replaced by the United Nations when peace was concluded, its many good works and those of its associated bodies (such as the ILO, the Refugee Commission, the Health Organisation and so forth) were not to be allowed to fall apart. The United Nations essentially 'inherited' a number of organisations, conventions and treaties. Significant among them for women were a number of ILO conventions.

---

1 Doris Weichselbaumer and Rudolf Winter-Ebmer, 'The Effects of Competition and Equal Treatment Laws on Gender Wage Differentials' (2007) 22 *Economic Policy* 235, 237.

2 Adnan Kalyl Al-Talawy, *Al-Qanwn Al-Dawly Llaml: Shurwhat Limunzmt Al-Aml Al-Dwlyyh wa Al-Tshriy'a Al-Dwly Llaml 1919–2010* (Almrkz Al-Arabi Al-Swysry Libuhwth Al-Tshghiyl wa Huqwq Al-Ensan Fi Alaml – Geneva, 2011) 478 [Trans: *International Labour Law: Explanations of the International Labour Organization and International Regulation 1919–2010* (Arabic Swiss Centre for Labouring Research and Human Rights in Employment)].

3 *Discrimination (Employment and Occupation) Convention* (C111), opened for signature 25 June 1958, ILO (entered into force 15 June 1960).

4 *Maternity Protection Convention* (C183), opened for signature 15 June 2000, ILO (entered into force 7 February 2002).

5 Weichselbaumer and Winter-Ebmer, above n 1, 245.

The International Labour Organization became an independent body (agency) of the United Nations in 1946, and is widely respected and recognised by a wide range of governments.[6] Today, the ILO has 183 member states,[7] 'many of which are poor, developing countries'.[8]

ILO member states are required, or rather expected, to implement the international standards promulgated by the ILO. This is achieved mainly through the adoption of various ILO conventions and recommendations.[9] The ratification of any ILO convention by a member state amounts to an agreement on the regulations or 'criteria' of the convention. It instigates the responsibility to undertake the measures necessary in order to implement the convention, whether the country is reviewing current legislation, eradicating traditional models of practice or establishing new institutions. It also attaches the obligation to report to the supervisory committee in designated time periods regarding the progress and success of implementation.[10]

In 1999, the ILO pronounced that its main goal was to ensure, enforce and safeguard 'decent work'.[11] Since then it has been functioning and doing everything possible to achieve this grand yet simple goal. However, such a goal is unachievable if it is not universal. Hence, the ILO plays a major role in both promoting and setting international labour standards.[12]

The ILO's Role in Setting International Labour Standards

The ILO sets International Labour Standards mainly by adopting conventions and recommendations.[13] ILO conventions and recommendations (particularly the former) cannot be conveniently categorised into the conventional categories of 'soft' or 'hard' law.[14]

An ILO convention is a multilateral treaty with international obligations and is 'binding upon the Members which ratify it'.[15] An ILO convention is in the same rank as a treaty and becomes automatically legally binding on all member states that have ratified it.[16] There is a clear distinction between provisions that entail legally binding obligations and non-binding recommendations. The former are usually characterised by the use of particular terms: '[F]ormulations such as "each member *shall* … " or "each worker *shall* receive … " creates a legal obligation and/or a legal right'

6 Roger Blanpain et al, *The Global Workplace: International and Comparative Employment Law – Cases and Materials* (Cambridge University Press, 2007) 53.

7 International Labour Organization, *Alphabetical List of ILO Member Countries* (14 July 2011) <http://www.ilo.org/public/english/standards/relm/country.htm>.

8 Blanpain et al, above n 6, 56.

9 Ibid. 53.

10 Maternity Protection Coalition (MPC), 'ILO and the Ratification Process' in Lakshmi Menon (ed), *Maternity Protection Campaign Kit: A Breastfeeding Perspective* (World Alliance for Breastfeeding Action, 2003) 12.

11 Blanpain et al, above n 6, 57.

12 Ibid. 19.

13 Ibid. 58.

14 Leah F Vosko, 'Gender, Precarious Work, and the International Labour Code: The Ghost in the ILO Closet' in Judy Fudge and Rosemary Owens (eds), *Precarious Work, Women, and the New Economy: The Challenge to Legal Norms* (Hart, 2006) 53, 55.

15 *International Labour Organization Constitution*, art 20.

16 Mark Anner and Teri Caraway, 'International Institutions and Workers' Rights: Between Labor Standards and Market Flexibility' (2010) 45 *Studies in Comparative International Development* 151, 152.

respectively.[17] However, when it comes to 'punishment', that is, the sanctions that are in place in case of violation of the provisions of ILO conventions, such sanctions as are available are weak.[18]

On the other hand, ILO recommendations are 'non-binding guidelines to orient national policy and practice ... and may supplement the provisions ... [of] a parallel Convention'.[19] They are 'designed to provide guidance only, need not be ratified by ILO member governments, and do not constrain their actions'.[20] The recommendations of the ILO are not legally binding on states, and there is an increasing reliance on protocols and codes of conduct by the ILO for setting labour standards.[21]

There are three main ILO bodies: the International Labour Conference (ILC), the Governing Body (GB) and the International Labour Office (the 'Office'). These three bodies 'play a [major] role in setting International Labour Standards'.[22] The ILC specifically 'has influence through its construction of normative principles and frameworks that can be used by individual nations to translate principles into substantive labour standards'.[23]

The ILO enforces International Labour Standards by (a) examining reports submitted from the member states and (b) dealing with, and solving, any complaints, disputes or issues that may arise in the process.[24]

The ILO has created many conventions; however, only those relevant to this study (that is, those specifically related to working mothers) will be considered here. Therefore, the *Discrimination (Employment and Occupation) Convention* (C111) and the *Maternity Protection Convention* will be examined in detail. It is important to recall that earlier conventions – for example, the *Maternity Protection Convention 1952* (C103) – remain binding upon those countries that have ratified them (as is the case with Libya), even when those conventions have themselves been superseded by more recent versions,[25] which a party may be reluctant to ratify.

ILO Conventions Relevant to Working Women, Particularly Mothers

There are many conventions put in place that are highly relevant and have great significance in regard to employment in general and for working women especially, in particular working mothers. A few conventions are worth highlighting, including: the *Social Policy (Basic Aims and Standards) Convention*,[26] the *Employment Policy Convention*[27] and the *Paid Educational Leave Convention*,[28] specifically Article 8, which states:

---

17 International Labour Office, *ABC of Women Workers' Rights and Gender Equality* (International Labour Organization, 2nd ed, 2007) 2–3 (emphasis added).

18 Vosko, above n 14, 55.

19 ILO, *ABC of Women Workers' Rights and Gender Equality*, above n 17, 5.

20 Blanpain et al, above n 6, 58.

21 Vosko, above n 14, 55.

22 Blanpain et al, above n 6, 59.

23 Vosko, above n 14, 55.

24 Blanpain et al, above n 6, 60.

25 ILO, *ABC of Women Workers' Rights and Gender Equality*, above n 17, 2.

26 *Social Policy (Basic Aims and Standards) Convention* (C117), opened for signature 22 June 1962, ILO (entered into force 23 April 1964).

27 *Employment Policy Convention* (C122), opened for signature 9 July 1964, ILO, (entered into force 15 July 1966).

28 *Paid Educational Leave Convention* (C140), opened for signature 24 June 1974, ILO (entered into force 23 September 1976) art 8.

> Paid educational leave shall not be denied to workers on the ground of race, colour, *sex*, religion, political opinion, national extraction or social origin.

Others include: the *Workers with Family Responsibilities Convention*[29] and its associated Recommendation; and the *Termination of Employment Convention*,[30] specifically Article 5(d) and (e), which states (emphasis added):

> The following, inter alia, shall not constitute valid reasons for termination:
>
> (d) race, colour, *sex,* marital status, family responsibilities, *pregnancy*, religion, political opinion, national extraction or social origin;
>
> (e) absence from work during *maternity leave.*

Article 5 (above) is highly relevant, as it reflects concern in regard to the working mother when it specifically mentions the terms 'pregnancy' and 'maternity leave'. However, the most relevant ILO convention for this study is the *Discrimination (Employment and Occupation) Convention 1958* (C111).[31]

The Discrimination (Employment and Occupation) Convention (C111)

In this section, the ILO Convention C111 will be discussed in great depth. The background and significance of the Convention will be explored below.

The Background and Significance of Convention (C111)

The *Discrimination (Employment and Occupation) Convention* (C111) was adopted on 25 June 1958 and came into force on 15 June 1960.[32] It was one of the first international non-discrimination treaties to be adopted by the ILO – another being the *Equal Remuneration Convention* (C100) – and is closely related to the requirements of other human rights treaties concerning equality and work.[33] C111 is one of the most fundamental conventions of the ILO. Unsurprisingly then, it is one of the most ratified international labour conventions,[34] and has been ratified by 169 countries.[35]

C111 deals with discrimination in regard to employment and occupation which, according to Article 1(1), includes: any act of denying, excluding, preferring another human based on their race,

---

29 *Workers with Family Responsibilities Convention* (C156), opened for signature 23 June 1981, ILO (entered into force 11 August 1983).

30 *Termination of Employment Convention* (C158), opened for signature 22 June1982, ILO (entered into force 23 November 1985) art 5(d) and (e).

31 *Discrimination (Employment and Occupation) Convention* (C111), opened for signature 25 June 1958, ILO (entered into force 15 June 1960).

32 Ibid.

33 Weichselbaumer and Winter-Ebmer, above n 1, 245.

34 International Labour Office, *Fundamental Rights at Work and International Labour Standards* (ILO, 2003) 59–60.

35 International Labour Organization, *Convention No C111* (2 July 2011) <http://www.ilo.org/ilolex/cgi-lex/ratifce.pl?C111>.

colour, gender so on that would have the effect of 'nullifying or impairing equality' in terms of opportunities or treatment in employment. Thus it is relevant to this study, as it is concerned with discrimination in respect of employment and occupation in both the public and private sectors,[36] which necessarily includes in relation to working mothers (and pregnant women), who are the primary focus of this study.

C111 aims to contribute to the elimination of discrimination in the field of employment and occupation so that 'all human beings, irrespective of race, creed, or sex, have the right to pursue both their material well-being and their spiritual development in conditions of freedom and dignity, of economic security and equal opportunity'.[37] Therefore, C111 simply aims to promote equality and prevent and eliminate any and all forms of discrimination within the workplace.[38] It pays specific attention to, and places great emphasis on, discrimination. It explores and discusses its 'meaning' in paragraph 1(a) and (b) and paragraph 2 of Article 1, which state:

> 1. For the purpose of this Convention the term *discrimination* includes –
>
> (a) any distinction, exclusion or preference made on the basis of race, colour, sex, religion, political opinion, national extraction or social origin, which has the effect of nullifying or impairing equality of opportunity or treatment in employment or occupation;
>
> (b) such other distinction, exclusion or preference which has the effect of nullifying or impairing equality of opportunity or treatment in employment or occupation as may be determined by the Member concerned after consultation with representative employers' and workers' organisations, where such exist, and with other appropriate bodies.
>
> 2. Any distinction, exclusion or preference in respect of a particular job based on the inherent requirements thereof shall not be deemed to be discrimination.

Discrimination is a significant restrictive factor for career initiation and development. It impedes a person from attaining their desired job and prevents men and women from improving their skills and abilities. Discrimination is ignorance of the merits of the subject, and results in disadvantage to certain groups within the community and to the creation of inequalities in labour market outcomes.[39]

According to C111's Committee of Experts on the Application of Conventions and Recommendations (CEACR), discrimination, specifically discrimination against working women, is discreet and can take many forms. The Committee notes that:

> [D]iscrimination against women may take many forms which at first appear to be sex neutral but which actually constitute discrimination because they have a detrimental impact on women. For example, in matters of access to and retention of employment, criteria related to marital

36 International Labour Office, PRO 169 and the Equality Team, *Eliminating Discrimination Against Indigenous and Tribal Peoples in Employment and Occupation: A Guide to ILO Convention No 111* (International Labour Office, 2007) 9.

37 Vosko, above n 14, 56–7.

38 Director-General, 'Time for Equality at Work: Global Report under the Follow-up to the ILO Declaration on Fundamental Principles and Rights at Work, 91st sess 1 (B)' (International Labour Office, 2003) 81.

39 Ibid. 15.

> status, family situation and family responsibilities typically affect only women to their detriment in employment.[40]

As C111 is considered a fundamental convention, the ILO requires a biennial report from states that have ratified it. The reporting procedure includes communication with member states and recommendations by the CEACR, which 'examines the application of international labour standards in member states and points out areas where they could still be better applied'.[41]

Libya, Convention C111 and the Committee of Experts (CEACR)

Libya ratified the *Discrimination (Employment and Occupation) Convention* (C111) on 13 June 1961,[42] and is one of 169 countries to have ratified the Convention.[43] The popularity of C111 clearly reflects its importance, relevance and practicality. Since then Libya has been required to submit a biennial report on its progress and success in applying this convention (in general). However, many issues and complaints have been raised by the Committee of Experts on the application of conventions and recommendations in regard to Libya's conduct and 'progress'.

Prior to the ratification of C111, the Libyan Government should have studied and fully understood all the requirements that were obligatory and the responsibilities that came with ratification. All Articles of the Convention should have been closely analysed, especially Article 3(f) which requests the submission to the CEACR of biennial reports from all member states that have ratified C111. However, on a number of occasions the Libyan Government has not fulfilled its duty to provide a timely report to be examined by the CEACR. This conflicts with Article 3(f) of the Convention, which clearly states that:

> Each Member for which this Convention is in force undertakes, by methods appropriate to national conditions and practice:
>
> (f) to indicate in its annual reports on the application of the Convention the action taken in pursuance of the policy and the results secured by such action.

Libya, for example, failed to submit a report in 1995 as required. The CEACR, in turn, submitted two direct requests, the first in February 1995:

> The Committee notes that the Government's report has not been received. It hopes that a report will be supplied for examination by the Committee at its next session and that it will contain full information on the matters raised in its previous direct request [1993].[44]

40 International Labour Office, *Fundamental Rights at Work and International Labour Standards*, above n 34, 73.

41 Weichselbaumer and Winter-Ebmer, above n 1, 246.

42 *Discrimination (Employment and Occupation) Convention* (C111), ratified by Libyan Arab Jamahiriya on 13 June 1961, ILOLEX Doc No 191961 LBY111.

43 ILO, *Convention No C111* (2 July 2011) <http://www.ilo.org/ilolex/cgi-lex/ratifce.pl?C111>.

44 Committee of Experts on the Application of Conventions and Recommendations (CEACR), *Individual Direct Request Concerning Convention No 111, Discrimination (Employment and Occupation), 1958 Libyan Arab Jamahiriya (ratification: 1961) Submitted: 1995, February*, 65th sess, ILOLEX Doc No 091995 LBY111 (ILO, 1995) 1 [1].

Later that year, the CEACR replied to the Libyan Government's response to its February 1995 request:

> The Committee notes that, in reply to its request for information on the practical application of the principle of the Convention, the Government states that there have been no complaints or legal proceedings concerning discrimination in employment because there is no discrimination in employment and occupation in the country. The Committee draws the Government's attention to paragraph 240 of its 1988 General Survey on equality in employment and occupation where it states that it is difficult to accept statements to the effect that the application of the Convention gives rise to no difficulties or that the instrument is fully applied, especially when no other details are given on the contents and methods of implementing the national policy against discrimination. The Committee therefore repeats its previous request for information on how Act No. 20 of 1991 on the promotion of freedom, which according to the Government is the basis of the country's equality policy, is being applied in practice.[45]

Libya again did not submit the report by 1996, and the CEACR again delivered a similarly direct request.[46] By 1997, however, Libya had submitted, according to the Committee, a 'brief report'.[47]

The CEACR continues to simplify and as far as possible re-word its 'previous direct request'; however, the Libyan Government continues to provide it with repetitive brief reports, each almost identical to its predecessor in content.[48] In response, the CEACR, since Libya's ratification of C111, has continued to reiterate the same requests, recommendations and comments.

In its latest report (2009), Libya has continued to provide the CEACR with general replies to its requests. The CEACR, as it has expressed on countless previous occasions, is concerned with the government's 'lack of consideration'.[49] It also expresses its regret that on the subject of gender equality:

> The [Libyan] Government continues to maintain that the principle of equality and prohibition of discrimination is reflected in the national legislation but fails to provide any information about the concrete measures taken to declare and pursue a national policy on equality in employment and occupation with respect to all grounds covered by the Convention.[50]

45 CEACR, *Individual Direct Request Concerning Convention No 111, Discrimination (Employment and Occupation), 1958 Libyan Arab Jamahiriya (ratification: 1961) Submitted: 1996*, 66th sess, ILOLEX Doc No 091996LBY111 (ILO, 1996) 1 [1].

46 CEACR, *Individual Direct Request Concerning Convention No 111, Discrimination (Employment and Occupation), 1958 Libyan Arab Jamahiriya (ratification: 1961) Submitted: 1997*, 67th sess, ILOLEX Doc No 091997LBY111 (ILO, 1997) 1.

47 CEACR, *Individual Observation Concerning Convention No 103, Maternity Protection (Revised), 1952 Libyan Arab Jamahiriya (ratification: 1975) 1997*, CEACR 1997, 68th sess, ILOLEX Doc No 061998LBY103 (ILO, 1998) 1 [1].

48 CEACR, *Comments Made by the Committee of Experts on the Application of Conventions and Recommendations (from 1990 to 2007) Discrimination (Employment and Occupation) Convention, 1958 (No 111): Libyan Arab Jamahiriya (ratification: 1961)* CEACR, 2009 80th sess 15 [1].

49 CEACR, *Individual Observation Concerning Discrimination (Employment and Occupation) Convention, 1958 (No 111) Libyan Arab Jamahiriya (ratification: 1961)* CEACR 2009, 80th sess ILOLEX No 062010LBY111 (ILO, 2010) 1 [1].

50 Ibid. 1 [2].

According to the CEACR, women's participation in economic activity remained low, at 29.59 per cent.[51] The Committee also mentions that the government's report is a mere repetition of past reports, and notes that it considers the information given by the government insufficient to truly assess the true situation and in regard to progress in Libya.[52] In regard to women, for example, the government has only provided the Committee with statistics that are too general and inadequate to fully assess 'the real progress [that] has been made with respect to the promotion of women's participation in all fields of study and in a wide range of job opportunities at all levels'.[53]

The CEACR has urged the government to fully explain the meaning of various phrases used in *Order No 258 of 1989 of the General People's Committee on the Rehabilitation and Training of Libyan Women.*[54] It has also re-emphasised the importance of statistical data, specifically data that is separated or categorised by gender.[55]

All of the above comments and recommendations by, and requests from, the CEACR are not new. In fact, the CEACR has been repeating itself in many of its reports. This is due to the fact that the Libyan Government merely 'copies and pastes' past reports.

Issues That Have Repeatedly Arisen Since 1961

The CEACR has requested and noted countless issues in regard to the implementation, enforcement and progress of C111 within Libya. Some of these will be considered below.

No complaints does not mean no discrimination

Act No 20 of 1991[56] is the basis of Libya's national policy set to combat discrimination which according to the government does not exist. This can mean that either (a) there is a lack of awareness or (b) there are no effective mechanisms in place to investigate, supervise and monitor the progress, implementation and enforcement of the various Acts (specifically in this case *Act No 20 of 1991* on national policy).

The Libyan Government also repeatedly emphasises that 'there is no discrimination in employment and occupation and gives as evidence of this the lack of complaints concerning this matter'.[57] This was proving hard for the CEACR to accept, because in its experience 'the absence of complaints concerning discrimination, usually means a lack of awareness and/or the insufficient complaint or inspection mechanisms'.[58]

---

51 Ibid. 2 [1].

52 Ibid. 1 [1].

53 Ibid. 2 [2].

54 *Order of the General People's Committee No 258 of 1989 on the Rehabilitation and Training of Libyan Women* (Libya).

55 CEACR, *Individual Observation – Libya* (2010) ILOLEX Doc No 062010LBY111), above n 49, 2 [5].

56 *Promotion of Freedoms Act No 20 of 1991* (Libya).

57 CEACR, *Individual Observation Concerning Convention No 111, Discrimination (Employment and Occupation), 1958 Libyan Arab Jamahiriya (ratification: 1961) 2000*, 71st sess, ILOLEX Doc No 062001LBY111 (ILO, 2001) 1 [2].

58 CEACR, *Individual Observation Concerning Convention No 111, Discrimination (Employment and Occupation), 1958 Libyan Arab Jamahiriya (ratification: 1961) 2002* 73rd sess, ILOLEX Doc No 062003LBY111 (ILO, 2003) 1–2 [3].

It is difficult for the CEACR to accept that 'the application of the Convention gives rise to no difficulties, when no other details are given on the contents and methods implementing the national policy on the promotion of equal opportunity and treatment'.[59]

The Libyan Government continues to use the excuse that there is no discrimination in Libya, and, therefore, there is no need for legal proceedings or reporting on such matters. The CEACR has continually responded that a lack of discrimination can indicate a lack of awareness. It is very clear that employees are unaware of their rights.[60] This again conflicts with yet another Article of the Convention, Article 3(b), which clearly states that:

> Each Member for which this Convention is in force undertakes, by methods appropriate to national conditions and practice:
>
> (b) to enact such legislation and to promote such educational programmes as may be calculated to secure the acceptance and observance of the policy[61]

That women are unaware of their rights is only one of many conflicts with the Convention. Those who are aware of their rights, or those who may have a little knowledge of such conventions as this, may not be aware of the institutions and organisations (such as the employers' and workers' organisations mentioned in Article 3(a) of C111) that are available to them. No knowledge of such institutions does not necessarily mean a level of general ignorance; rather, it means that there has been no concerted campaign to alert people to their rights and to the institutions and organisations that could help them assert those rights.

The existence of law does not equal enforcement: issues of national policy

The Libyan Government must realise that law has no benefit if it is not enforced. The Libyan Government has provided the Committee of Experts with numerous and various legislative *texts* such as Acts of Parliament and *The Green Book*; however, it has not specified or given any indication of the measures taken to ensure that the Convention is *applied* effectively in the community. According to the government's reports and from the results of further research which this study has conducted, the Libyan Government has not put in place any 'complaint or inspection mechanisms'. This course of action again conflicts with Article 3(a) of the Convention, which clearly states its aims at being:

> (a) to seek the co-operation of employers' and workers' organisations and other appropriate bodies in promoting the acceptance and observance of this policy[62]
>
> The Committee *regrets* that the Government continues to maintain that the principle of equality and prohibition of discrimination is reflected in the national legislation but fails to provide any information about the concrete measures taken to declare and pursue a national policy on equality in employment and occupation with respect to all grounds covered by the Convention.[63]

---

59 CEACR, *Comments Made by the Committee of Experts – Libya*, above, n 48, 13.

60 This concept is later explored in Chapter 5.

61 *Discrimination (Employment and Occupation) Convention* (C111) art 3(b).

62 Ibid. art 3(a).

63 CEACR, *General Report and Observations Concerning Particular Countries*, 99th sess, 2010 III (Part 1A) (ILO, 2010) 436 (emphasis added).

In conclusion, there must be a *legitimate* national policy. Libya tends to have policies; however, they tend to be too general and do not specify or utilise exact and well-defined terminology. For example, *Order No 258 of 1989*[64] uses phrases such as 'suitable job opportunities to women', 'suitable to women's nature and social conditions' and 'suitable to their psychological and physical make-up'.[65] Such phrases leave great room for discriminative and corrupt interpretation within legislation and regulations by government and delegated bodies, and in legislation and regulations (orders) by such persons as employers, supervisors and others.[66] Therefore Libya has been asked on countless occasions to fully explain its national legislation. For example, all the terms used and the implications for their use in regard to women must be defined and explained thoroughly to avoid discrimination that otherwise might occur.

Both the CEACR and the CEDAW Committee agree that 'it is not possible to speak of equal rights for women and yet to maintain a single sexual stereotype of the role of women exclusively as housewives'.[67]

Lack of data: an ongoing reporting issue

The lack of qualitative and quantitative data means that the real situation in Libya and the discrimination that employees (specifically the vulnerable group of working mothers) face would not be portrayed or unveiled. However, this study aims to do so.

The CEACR, as it has done countless times in the past, 'urges', 'requests' and 'pleads with' the Libyan Government to provide statistical data 'on the quantitative as well as qualitative position of [working] women',[68] for example. It also has requested the Government, in every way possible, 'to supply detailed information on the measures taken or envisaged to ensure effective application of the principle of equality of opportunity and treatment in employment'.[69]

The Libyan Government has not been faithful in its ratification. The CEACR seems to be continually pleading with the government to cooperate, starting many of its comments and observations with phrases such as 'It would be grateful'.[70] However, the government continues not to cooperate. At the same time, however, the CEACR continues to hope for every desired improvement, and provides the government with comments such as:

> The Committee trusts that the Government will make every effort to supply the information requested in order to allow the Committee to assess the effective application of the Convention.

---

64 *Order of the General People's Committee No 258 of 1989 on the Rehabilitation and Training of Libyan Women* (Libya).

65 CEACR, *Individual Observation – Libya* (2010) ILOLEX Doc No 062010LBY111), above n 49, 2 [3].

66 Chapter 4 investigates this issue in detail.

67 CEACR, *Comments Made by the Committee of Experts – Libya* (2009), above, n 48, 12.

68 Ibid. 8.

69 CEACR, *Individual Observation* (2001) ILOLEX Doc No 062001LBY111, above n 57, 1 [2].

70 CEACR, *Individual Observation Concerning Convention No 103, Maternity Protection (Revised), 1952 Libyan Arab Jamahiriya (ratification: 1975)* 1999, CEACR 1999, 70th sess, ILOLEX Doc No 062000LBY103 (ILO, 2000) 1 [2].

Conclusion and Further Comments in Regard to the Discrimination (Employment and Occupation) Convention (C111)

Since the Libyan Government simply repeats material that is, in the main, identical to that in previous reports, the CEACR also continues, in turn, to repeat requests and comments and plead with the government to provide data and information that have been requested countless times in the past.

The CEACR is required to assess, observe and make recommendations. However, at this rate and as in the past, the present and possibly the future (if Libya continues in this careless and inconsiderate manner), the CEACR will continue to urge, request and (hopelessly) hope that Libya will fulfil its duty. Article 9 of this convention states that:

> 1. A Member which has ratified this Convention may denounce it after the expiration of ten years from the date on which the Convention first comes into force, by an act communicated to the Director-General of the International Labour Office for registration. Such denunciation shall not take effect until one year after the date on which it is registered.[71]
>
> 2. Each Member which has ratified this Convention and which does not, within the year following the expiration of the period of ten years mentioned in the preceding paragraph, exercise the right of denunciation provided for in this article, will be bound for another period of ten years and, thereafter, may denounce this Convention at the expiration of each period of ten years under the terms provided for in this Article.[72]

Therefore, the Libyan Government has had the opportunity to denounce the Convention four times. However, it has not done so. This can indicate that either: (a) Libya is pleased with the progress it has made since its ratification; or (b) Libya is not concerned, nor is it taking this convention seriously. From the reports that Libya has submitted and from the pleadings of the Committee of Experts over the years, it can easily be seen that Libya leans more towards option (b). The ratification of C111 is more for Libya's image. Just like so many of Libya's many laws, the ratification of C111 is a 'ticket' or illusion rather than a reality. In the words of the CEACR, the ratification of C111 'remain[s] a dead letter'.[73]

Developing Countries and International Labour Standards

One reason often given regarding lack of progress, especially in developing countries, is that there is a notable distinction between the enforcement of labour standards in developed and developing countries. Developing countries assert that any trend towards international standardisation would result in a serious competitive disadvantage for their firms.[74] Various studies have suggested that it is reasonable to expect developing countries to show reluctance to support the same level of labour standards as developed nations.[75] Interestingly, however, many of the 183 ILO member

71 *Discrimination (Employment and Occupation) Convention* (C111) art 9(1).

72 Ibid. art 9(2).

73 CEACR, *Individual Observation* (2001) ILOLEX Doc No 062001LBY111, above n 57, 1 [2].

74 Stephen B Deloach, Jayoti Das and Lindsey Conley, 'Power Politics and International Labor Standards' (2006) 12 *International Advances in Economic Research* 51, 51.

75 Ibid. 60.

states are developing countries.[76] The question might, therefore, be put whether the ILO standards are 'aspirational' rather than actual in this context?

Countries such as Libya might indeed be overwhelmed by the amount of work required to meet the high expectations of institutions such as the ILO, which would raise labour standards far above their current position. The ILO should take into consideration Libya's situation and should not be focused on it being on the same level as other more developed countries (such as the US and China). Rather, the ILO should be focusing and dedicating its time to research and investigation regarding the best methods and approaches that should be taken to *improve* Libya's situation in a *realistic* manner, assisting the government 'step by step' along the way so that the Libyan Government would be motivated to do more than merely 'copy and paste' past reports.[77] It has also been argued that a substantial improvement in labour standards would require increased investment in legal enforcement and infrastructure; and the increased expenditure that would be required would, for developing countries like Libya, result in a reduction in social welfare.[78]

Having the same institutions as wealthier countries is nigh impossible for Libya, as the country not only has limited financial assets but also lacks the necessary professional persons or institutions. Given that concerted action in regard to higher labour standards in Libya would cause problems such as a 'reduction in social welfare', the ILO should take into consideration Libya's limitations and abilities when issuing its recommendations.[79] However, Libya should also take greater advantage of the various opportunities and international organisations that are willing to help it fulfil its obligations to the best of its ability.

Maternity Protection Conventions

This section of the chapter will explore, examine and evaluate maternity protection and its effects on the working mother. First, it will trace its history and background, before outlining the importance of maternity leave. The three major maternity protection conventions will also be discussed and analysed. Lastly, I will examine, compare and analyse Libya's response regarding these conventions. In the process, the role of the relevant ILO Committee (the CEACR) will be considered.

A History of Maternity Leave

In 1880, the first law relating to paid maternity leave was established by Bismarck as part of the invention and enactment of social insurance in Germany.[80] It represented a rather paternalistic approach and was very concerned with the mother and child's health, to the extent that it *prohibited* mothers from returning to work during the first six weeks after childbirth.[81] Because of the

76 Blanpain et al, above n 6, 56.

77 Deloach, Das and Conley, above n 74, 60.

78 Ibid.

79 Ibid.

80 Sheila B Kamerman, 'From Maternity to Parental Leave Policies: Women's Health, Employment, and Child and Family Well-Being' (2000) 55(2) *Journal of the American Women's Association* 96, 97.

81 Olena Nizalova, *The Economic and Social Consequences of Maternity Protection: A Cross-Country Analysis* (LLM Thesis, National University: Kiev-Mohyla Academy, 1999–2000) 2.

increased social unrest, the threat of three international movements[82] and also the vulnerability of the new German state, Bismarck had taken the initiative to enact social insurance law as a device for enforcing the rights of workers and other groups and reducing the possibility of agitation and unrest.[83] Thus, in 1883 factory workers acquired health insurance; in 1884 accident insurance was introduced; and finally, in 1889, the old-age pension scheme was passed. With the launch of Germany's new legislation other European countries followed suit. (Great Britain and Austria, for example, were heavily influenced and followed in Germany's footsteps.)[84]

Maternity leave can involve both unpaid and paid leave. Generally it involves a fairly minimal period of paid leave. Paid maternity leave, in particular, has benefits for the welfare of the mother, the child and broader society, as it enables women to recover emotionally, psychologically and physically following pregnancy as well as providing them with the opportunity to establish a good balance between family life and their forthcoming careers. It also allows for arrangements to be made regarding the baby's care and feeding regime.[85]

Maternity Leave as an Essential Right

Maternity leave is a necessity and a basic right. It is important as it involves various areas and groups, such as human rights, health, families, children, employers, governments and children.

Fundamental human rights

Maternity leave has benefits for everyone but especially protects the right of working mothers, allowing them to live free from discrimination, as it permits them to have career breaks to establish families without sacrificing job security.[86] It is also fundamental for the child. For instance, the right to breast milk is protected under international law and is, at least theoretically, firmly protected. It is included in the well-established and undisputed right to food, health and life. Further, it is recognised internationally as a right held by children, women and workers. Even though each of these grounds on its own is adequate to provide for the right to breast milk for children and the right of women to breastfeed, it has been mutually reinforced on different levels.[87]

All humans have the right to food, 'adequate food' to be exact, and the most obvious 'food' for infants is breast milk. Breast milk fits and fulfils all the criteria of adequate food according to the UN Committee on Economic, Social and Cultural Rights (CESCR). These six criteria are: quality,

82 These comprised Catholicism, socialism, and the growing public concern with the problem of low-wage workers: in Sheila B Kamerman, 'A Global History of Early Childhood Education and Care: Background Paper Prepared for the Education for All Global Monitoring Report 2007 Strong Foundations – Early Childhood Care and Education' (SBK GLOBAL HX ECEC 2007/ED/EFA/MRT/PI/19, UNESCO, 2006) 18.

83 Kamerman, 'From Maternity to Parental Leave Policies' above n 80, 97.

84 Jean H Quataert, 'Woman's Work and the Early Welfare State in Germany: Legislators, Bureaucrats, and Clients Before the First World War' in Seth Koven and Sonya Michel (eds), *Mothers of a New World: Maternalist Politics and the Origins of Welfare States* (Routledge, 1993) 159, 162–3.

85 Lisa Heap, *Maternity Protection ILO Convention No 183: A New Standard for the New Century* (International Confederation of Free Trade Unions (ICFTU), Public Services International (PCI) and Education International (EI), 2001) 12.

86 Ibid. 10.

87 Olivia Ball, 'Breastmilk is a Human Right' (2010) 18(3) *Breastfeeding Review* 9, 9.

quantity, safety, accessibility, acceptability and safety. Without breast milk these cannot exist, and this right cannot be exercised without maternity leave.[88]

There are a number of factors that impact on a mother's decision to stop (or not initiate) breastfeeding. These include a lack of proper education regarding the benefits of breastfeeding (to baby and mother), the unavailability of proper facilities (hospitals or within workplaces) and insufficient or non-existent maternity leave. These are all infringements of the rights of mothers and their children.[89]

Society and social justice

Mothers and their partners can make important decisions regarding the care of their baby post-birth where maternity protection is provided, as this removes possible discrimination and perhaps even the threat of forced redundancy. Women work in order to retain their economic independence, to support themselves and their families and, most of the time, because they want to work. Undoubtedly, working women play an important role in maintaining economic growth, so it is essential that their right to have children and raise families – also a very important social function – is protected for the overall benefit of the community.[90]

Health

Maternity leave that allows for women to remain at home for a few months following birth and to take care of their newborn will have considerable health benefits for both the mother and the child.[91] Enhancement of the mother's and baby's health is achieved through support and protection during and following pregnancy. Maternity protection allows for the improvement of the health of both the mother and child.[92] It has been discovered that longer maternity leave periods result in improved health outcomes for children as well as mothers. It allows women to recover from birth and to establish a good breastfeeding regime which can reduce the risk of various adverse health outcomes.[93]

Families

Maternity protection is also very helpful for families during and following pregnancy because it provides job and income security and, thus, allows families to experience a happy and healthy birth and children to enjoy early childcare by a parent in their home. Furthermore, it removes the financial and employment-related concerns for families contemplating pregnancy. Paid leave is necessary for achieving income security in the sensitive period following birth when both the mother and the baby are adjusting to a new schedule. And, as Heap observes, such rights have family-wide ramifications.[94] Maternity protection and benefits enable mothers not to be 'compelled by economic necessity to engage in labour to the neglect of their duties in the family's home'.[95] While this quote echoes a stereotypical perception of her role, it is also realistic in that the mother

88 Ibid. 10–11.

89 Ibid. 13.

90 Heap, above n 85, 10.

91 Lawrence M Berger, Jennifer Hill and Jane Waldfogel, 'Maternity Leave, Early Maternal Employment and Child Health and Development in the US' (2005) 115(501) *Economic Journal* F29, F32.

92 Heap, above n 85, 10.

93 Berger, Hill and Waldfogel, above n 91, F29.

94 Heap, above n 85, 10, 13.

95 Daniel Cere, 'Human Rights and the Family' (2009) 22(1) *Academic Questions* 63, 74.

is the most likely person to provide breastfeeding to an infant. It enables her to enjoy her right as a mother to nurture her child at this critical time.

The importance of family is also stressed in Article 16(3) ('The Marriage and the Family') of the UDHR, where it is stated that '[t]he family is the natural and fundamental group unit of society and is entitled to protection by society and the State'.[96] Care options immediately post-birth in the home and later elsewhere have profound impacts on women and their families, as can be seen in the results of a 2001 study. This study found that even though role overload had an impact on marital incompatibility for experienced mothers, this was not the case for first-time mothers, who were more affected by inconsistencies between their preferred and actual childcare options. It was also observed that the length of maternity leave was strongly correlated with other variables, and that if a short leave period was combined with another factor it would lead to significant personal and marital unease.[97]

Children

The most fundamental role of maternity leave is the protection of children through the provision of a healthy growth environment. This is highly valued by societies, and it is expected that through sufficient maternity protection women are given the opportunity to have income security while with their child in their home. Sufficient maternity protection would also extend the right to the mother to continue breastfeeding her baby after returning to work. This would ensure the ongoing welfare of the baby, as well as a healthy future generation, which is a valuable asset to any society.[98] There is also a reasonable association between the length of maternity leave and the developmental progress of children. Where women stayed home longer post-pregnancy, this reflected positively in the developmental outcomes of the children.[99] In developed societies, studies have also shown that maternity leave provision increases (rather than decreases) the likelihood of a woman returning to work after giving birth. This compares to circumstances where its unavailability forces women to choose between work and maternity rather than combining the two in a satisfactory manner that is made possible through maternity protection.

Employers

Maternity leave also gives employers a chance to retain their experienced and valued female staff. Employers who have a focus on ongoing employee development and regard their employees as a worthy investment will want to ensure their return to the workplace. Maternity protection also encourages new mothers to return to work, and this has a positive impact on business operations.[100] This is not to say that it is not a contested area. There are many different expectations at play, and often extensive negotiations have to be conducted to ensure the best outcome for mothers. Employer expectations of uninterrupted employment and certain scheduling possibilities collide with the reality of compulsory post-partum leave and the great desirability of longer maternity leave as well as children's need for care and infants' feeding schedules.[101] Fellow workers may also express concerns about the relative justice of pay increments to those not actively in the workforce.

96 *Universal Declaration of Human Rights*, art 16(3).

97 Janet Shibley Hyde et al, 'Maternity Leave, Women's Employment, and Marital Incompatibility' (2001) 15(3) *Journal of Family Psychology* 476, 476.

98 Heap, above n 85, 10–11.

99 Berger, Hill and Waldfogel, above n 91, F33.

100 Heap, above n 85, 10.

101 Meina Liu and Patrice M Buzzanell, 'Negotiating Maternity Leave Expectations: Perceived Tensions between Ethics of Justice and Care' (2004) 41(4) *Journal of Business Communication* 323, 324–5.

Government

Maternity protection that preserves the well-being of mothers and their babies and permits women to continue to contribute to Libya's economic growth is beneficial for the government. It also serves the government's interests by allowing the use of scarce resources in alternative places and by supporting the development of a healthy population.[102] Maternity leave is of great importance, as it ensures the health of women (who are of great importance to the economy) and children (the future generations).[103]

In conclusion, from a solely practical, economy-focused or public policy perspective, great value would be seen to be offered by increased maternity leave periods and breastfeeding rates. The former would lead to the retention of skilled labour, allowing women who would otherwise leave the workforce – perhaps not to return for a significant period (if at all) – to return and contribute their expertise. This would represent cost savings to the government and the economy, as the skilled labour of these highly educated women would continue to be able to be placed at the service of the country rather than having the nation rely on imported foreign labour (for example, in midwifery). It would also represent a return on the country's investment in the education of these women and lead to a higher standard of living for families. In regard to implementing improved provisions for breastfeeding working mothers, this would not only encourage an earlier return to work than would otherwise be the case, but it would also lead to significant savings in both short- and long-term health expenditure. For instance, breastfeeding is associated with lower allergy levels, lower asthma rates, fewer episodes of infant diarrhoea and lower rates of respiratory morbidity in infants,[104] as well as playing 'a protective role in several chronic diseases, including Type 1 diabetes, inflammatory bowel disease and allergic diseases'.[105] With public health expenditure in Australia topping AUD 2,300 million in 2008–09, and continuing real increases expected,[106] better maternity leave and breastfeeding provisions could make an important contribution to the Australian national economy, as indeed they would to that of Libya.

Background of the Maternity Protection Conventions

It was not until 1919 that the International Labour Organization established the right to maternity leave in the form of a convention – the *Maternity Protection Convention* (C3). The subject of working women, before and after childbirth – including the question of maternity protection (which 'safeguards the woman, her baby and her job')[107] – has been on the agenda of the ILO for almost

102 Heap, above n 85, 10.

103 Nizalova, above n 81, 5.

104 W H Oddy et al, 'Breast Feeding and Respiratory Morbidity in Infancy: A Birth Cohort Study' (2003) 88(3) *Archives of Disease in Childhood* 224, 224.

105 Australian Institute of Health and Welfare (AIHW), 'Australia's Health 2010: The Twelfth Biennial Health Report of the Australian Institute of Health and Welfare' (AIHW Canberra 2010) 106, citing the National Health and Medical Research Council, *Dietary Guidelines for Children and Adolescents in Australia, Incorporating the Infant Feeding Guidelines for Health Workers* (NHMRC, 2003). See also Ball, above n 95, 11.

106 Australian Government and AIHW, *Health Expenditure Australia 2008–09* (10 October 2011) <http://www.aihw.gov.au/publication-detail/?id=6442472450&libID=6442472431>.

107 Jane Paul, *Healthy Beginning: Guidance on Safe Maternity at Work* (International Labour Office, 2004) 1.

a century.[108] In addition to maternity leave, ensuring equal opportunities for working women is of fundamental importance. It is essential to recognise the contributions of women to the workplace post-pregnancy and how their right of motherhood can be maintained through public policy.[109]

In its first session in 1919, the ILO drafted its first *Maternity Protection Convention* (C3). In 1952 the revised *Maternity Protection Convention* (C103) came into existence. The latter aimed to protect working mothers before and after childbirth. In 2000 the ILO yet again 'revised' its previous conventions and created one much more advanced. This section aims to give a brief background to each convention, and touch on their faults and shortcomings.

Maternity Protection Convention 1919 (C3)

ILO *Convention 1919* (C3), which entered into force on 13 June 1921,[110] endorsed the principle that working women are entitled to maternity leave with pay. It was ratified by 29 States parties, including Libya.[111] This convention was intended to support working women both in the public and private sectors for health reasons and to ensure equal employment opportunities. Therefore, employed women had access to maternity leave for the first time, with a compulsory period of six weeks post-confinement and the 'right' to another six weeks pre-confinement. Article 3(a) and (b) states that:

> In any public or private industrial or commercial undertaking, or in any branch thereof, other than an undertaking in which only members of the same family are employed, a woman –
>
> (a) shall not be permitted to work during the six weeks following her confinement;
>
> (b) shall have the right to leave her work if she produces a medical certificate stating that her confinement will probably take place within six weeks[112]

Maternity protection was clearly acknowledged as a priority by the ILO 'from its earliest days'.[113] C3[114] was the first international instrument to address the issue of maternity protection,[115] and contained some significant provisions protecting the rights of working women, including a number that impact on the ability to balance work and motherhood.

As almost half of the labour market is composed of women, a collective withdrawal by them would have major implications for the economy at both the micro and macro level. This highlights the desirability for women to achieve a healthy balance between their careers and domestic life

---

108 International Labour Organization, *ILO Conference to Debate Maternity Protection Health and Safety in Agriculture* (ILO Media Release, Geneva, 29 May 2000), indicated that a report would be presented at the 88th session of the ILO's conference beginning the following day.

109 Joyce Yen Feng and Wen-Jui Han, 'Maternity Leave in Taiwan' (2010) 59 *Family Relations* 297, 307–8.

110 *Maternity Protection Convention* (C3), opened for signature 28 November 1919, ILO (entered into force 13 June 1921).

111 International Labour Organization, *Country Ratification the Maternity Protection Convention, 1919 C3* (14 September 2011) <http://www.ilo.org/ilolex/cgi-lex/ratifce.pl?C003>.

112 *Maternity Protection Convention* (C3) art 3(a) and (b).

113 Heap, above n 85, 18.

114 *Maternity Protection Convention* (C3).

115 Paul, above n 107, 6.

to facilitate their ongoing participation and the significant role that maternity leave can play in enhancing this balance, and thus their level of workplace participation.[116]

This convention also introduced to the working mother the right to breastfeed her child during her working hours. The purpose behind this was to protect, enhance and sustain the health of both child and mother. Article 3(d) states that a mother 'shall in any case, if she is nursing her child, be allowed half an hour twice a day during her working hours for this purpose'.[117]

Though this convention was the first instrument that provided maternity leave for working women, working mothers were still unable to participate easily in the workforce. The major flaw of this convention was the period it allowed for maternity leave. The period allowed is minimal and totals 12 weeks, of which six weeks comprise compulsory post-confinement leave. This allocation is inflexible and unnecessarily restrictive. The mother only qualifies for the pre-confinement leave if she is in possession of a medical certificate which states that confinement will 'probably take place within six weeks'.[118] The pre-confinement period of six weeks may or may not be needed due to the circumstances of the mother. Again this is inflexible and does not respond to the situation where a pregnant woman requires extended leave due to threatened miscarriage or where she anticipates a confinement involving more than one child. As well as this, the compulsory period of six weeks post-confinement is astonishingly short and contradicts the convention's main purpose of protecting and looking to the best interests of mother and child. Such a short period is inadequate and does not allow for such interests to be catered for. The mother's and child's health would be at risk. A study in 2004 (rare, as there are not many studies in this field) has proven that working mothers who have returned to work after a period of six weeks' maternity leave are more likely to suffer from depression (specifically from 11 to 15 per cent more likely) than those returning after eight or 12 weeks.[119]

C3 also did not specifically address maternity benefits for working women. It simply outlined procedures to be followed.

Maternity Protection Convention 1952 (C103)

Female employment has seen a dramatic increase since the 1950s. The number of women who have retained their employment while raising their families has also been on the rise. This has been achieved by a combination of effective progress in relevant law, acknowledgement of the rights of working women and significant changes in business culture. Nevertheless, uniformity of practice in this area is limited; in some countries some women enjoy numerous benefits while others elsewhere have none.[120]

In 1952 the ILO revised the *Maternity Protection Convention* (C3) and renamed it the *Maternity Protection Convention (Revised)* (C103).[121] It also advised member states to introduce measures that would protect working women before and after childbirth by providing 12 weeks'

116 Xuelin Zhang, 'Returning to the Job after Childbirth' (2008) 20(1) *Perspectives on Labour and Income* 20, 21.

117 *Maternity Protection Convention* (C3) art 3(d).

118 Ibid. art 3(b).

119 Pinka Chatterji and Sara Markowitz, 'Does the Length of Maternity Leave Affect Maternal Health?' (10206 JEL No I1, National Bureau of Economic Research, January 2004) 26–7.

120 See, e.g., International Labour Office, 'ILO Conference to Debate Key Issues: Child Labour, Maternity Rights on Agenda' *World of Work*, No 29, Geneva, April–May 1999, 7.

121 *Maternity Protection Convention* (C103), opened for signature 28 June 1952, ILO (entered into force 7 September 1955).

paid maternity leave.[122] C103 came into force on 7 September 1955. It was ratified by 28 States parties, including Libya.[123] Maternity protective policies for working women have been adopted by more than 100 developed and developing countries.[124]

One of the main features of C103 was that it contained a specific provision on maternity leave. Article 3(2) states that:

> The period of maternity leave shall be at least twelve weeks, and shall include a period of compulsory leave after confinement.

The Article expands on this, stating in paragraph 3:

> The period of compulsory leave after confinement shall be prescribed by national laws or regulations, but shall in no case be less than six weeks; the remainder of the total period of maternity leave may be provided before the presumed date of confinement or following expiration of the compulsory leave period or partly before the presumed date of confinement and partly following the expiration of the compulsory leave period as may be prescribed by national laws or regulations.[125]

According to some, this flexibility, which was not evident in the previous convention, must be noted and condemned.[126] C103 also provided some additional leave for working women. For example, Article 3(5) stated that:

> In case of illness medically certified arising out of pregnancy, national laws or regulations shall provide for additional leave before confinement, the maximum duration of which may be fixed by the competent authority.[127]

Cash benefits during maternity leave were discussed thoroughly in Article 4.[128] In addition to this, C103 offered working mothers the provision of nursing breaks (under Article 5). A recent ILO review found that 144 countries had provisions concerning maternity leave, either in their employment laws or as a completely separate law.[129] The review found that 81 of these countries already guaranteed women 100 per cent salary during maternity leave, and some even had on top of this 'partial compensation'.[130] Also, over 125 countries 'have some provisions or legislation guaranteeing employment security for pregnant women and women taking maternity leave'.[131]

Lastly, Article 6 made clear that it was prohibited to dismiss a woman during her maternity leave, stating that:

---

122 Marian Baird, 'Paid Maternity Leave: The Good, the Bad, the Ugly' (2003) 29(1) *Australian Bulletin of Labour* 97, 98.

123 International Labour Organization, *Country Ratification the Maternity Protection Convention (Revised) 1952 C103* (14 September 2011) <http://www.ilo.org/ilolex/cgi-lex/ratifce.pl?C103>.

124 Nizalova, above n 81, 10.

125 *Maternity Protection Convention* (C103) art 3(2) and (3).

126 Al-Talawy, above n 2, 375.

127 *Maternity Protection Convention* (C103) art 3(5).

128 Ibid. art 4.

129 Nizalova, above n 81, 10.

130 Ibid.

131 Ibid.

> While a woman is absent from work on maternity leave in accordance with the provisions of Article 3 of this Convention, it shall not be lawful for her employer to give her notice of dismissal during such absence, or to give her notice of dismissal at such a time that the notice would expire during such absence.[132]

Although C103 introduced a more flexible period of leave, cash benefits, breastfeeding breaks during working hours and protection from dismissal, it still had its flaws. For instance, the period of 12 weeks' leave is still inadequate. A recent study found that women who returned to full-time employment within 12 weeks were more likely to have children who suffered 'externalising behavior problems at age 4'.[133]

Therefore, C103 needed to be further revised, not only in light of changing patterns of women's workforce participation, but also in light of various developments related to employment protection in many countries. Different issues – such as understanding the critical issues of pregnancy; safe and healthy workplace standards; and other contemporary international standards and goals on issues such as breastfeeding, childcare and parenting – still needed to be taken into consideration. It was also important to develop relevant maternity protections and benefits based on the experience of other international instruments, such as the *European Pregnant Workers Directive* which was adopted in 1992.[134]

The ILO's governing body saw the necessity for revising C103 in 1997 for a number of reasons. The main factor was the acknowledgement of the increase in the number of women undertaking paid employment and raising families at the same time. Another reason was the positive changes in nations' recognition and support of working women over time. A fundamental consideration was the emphasis provided on maternity rights in several other international agreements, including the *International Covenant on Economic, Social and Cultural Rights* (1966) (ICESCR) and the *Convention on the Elimination of All Forms of Discrimination against Women* (1979) (CEDAW).[135]

The purpose of the new suggestions put forward for discussion is to develop mechanisms which will enable countries at various stages of development to improve their national maternity protection schemes, for instance by regulatory controls of the length of leave and extent of cash benefits they provide.[136]

Maternity Protection Convention 2000 (C183): Aims and Provisions

Consequently, new international standards regarding maternity protection were adopted at the 88th Session of the International Labour Conference (ILC) on 30 May 2000.[137] The Committee agreed to revise the 1952 *Maternity Protection Convention* (C103), and thus the *Maternity Protection Convention 2000* (C183) came into being.[138] It entered into force on 7 February 2002. To date,

132 *Maternity Protection Convention* (C103) art 6.

133 Berger, Hill and Waldfogel, above n 91, F45.

134 National Women's Justice Coalition (Australia), 'Submission to the International Labour Conference 87th Session, 1999, *Revision of the ILO Maternity Protection Convention (Revised) 1952 (No 103) and Recommendation 1952* (No 95)' 6.

135 International Labour Office, 'ILO Conference to Debate Key Issues', above n 120, 7.

136 Ibid. 10.

137 ILO, *ILO Conference to Debate Maternity Protection Health and Safety in Agriculture*, above n 108, 2.

138 *Maternity Protection Convention* (C183), opened for signature 15 June 2000, ILO (entered into force 7 February 2002).

just 22 States parties have ratified this convention.[139] Libya is not among them (nor, it must be said, is Australia). C183 helps defend the health of children and mothers and eliminate gender discrimination in the workplace.[140] Despite the low level of signatories to this convention (though many others are signatories to the earlier conventions), paid maternity leave is common among ILO member states, with over 80 per cent providing 12 weeks or more paid maternity leave and over 40 per cent providing 14 weeks or more.[141]

This convention aims to promote the equality of all employed women who are pregnant, nursing and returning to work, 'including those in atypical forms of dependent work'.[142] This includes 'home workers, part-time, temporary and casual workers'.[143] States parties are to develop maternity benefits under national laws and pursue the goal of eliminating discrimination in employment as a shared responsibility of government and society. The revisions of C183 took into consideration all of the human rights conventions concerning the protection of the rights of women, and also took into account the circumstances of women workers and the need to provide protection during and after pregnancy.[144] The provisions of this convention mostly target working mothers, for instance in the following areas.

Protection of the mother's and child's health

Article 3 of C183 states that:

> Each Member shall, after consulting the representative organizations of employers and workers, adopt appropriate measures to ensure that pregnant or breastfeeding women are not obliged to perform work which has been determined by the competent authority to be prejudicial to the health of the mother or the child, or where an assessment has established a significant risk to the mother's health or that of her child.[145]

These provisions are mainly in regard to occupational health and safety issues for the mother that may impact on her or her child, and on her right not to be asked to perform works prejudicial to either or both.

Length of maternity leave

C183 provides for 14 weeks of paid maternity leave.[146] This moderate extension of two weeks increases the rate of return to work and overall employment levels following childbirth.[147] While there are many reasons prompting the revision of the maternity leave provisions, the protection of the health of the working mother and her child is the main one. For that reason, maternity leave 'shall include a period of six weeks' compulsory leave after childbirth, unless otherwise agreed at the national level by the government and the representative organizations of employers and

139 International Labour Organization, *Country Ratification the Maternity Protection Convention, 2000 C183* (14 September 2011) <http://www.ilo.org/ilolex/cgi-lex/ratifce.pl?C183>.
140 Nizalova, above n 81, 21.
141 Heap, above n 85, 13.
142 *Maternity Protection Convention* (C183) art 2 (1).
143 Heap, above n 85, 11.
144 International Labour Office, 'ILO Conference to Debate Key Issues', above n 120, 10.
145 *Maternity Protection Convention* (C183) art 3.
146 Ibid. art 4(1).
147 Zhang, above n 116, 22.

workers'.[148] This improvement increases confidence among employed women, and helps women balance the competing demands of children and careers.

Sick leave
Article 5 of C183 offers another form of leave for working mothers before or after maternity leave – for sickness or injury arising during their pregnancy or during childbirth. Article 5 notes: 'The nature and the maximum duration of such leave may be specified in accordance with national law and practice'.[149]

Assistance: financial and other benefits
Article 6 of C183 provides for working mothers to whom this convention applies financial benefits during maternity leave. These may take the form of both cash benefits and medical benefits. Direct financial benefits are designed to protect the health of the mother and her child and maintain their ability to enjoy an appropriate standard of living. Cash benefits 'shall not be less than two-thirds of a woman's previous earnings'.[150] In addition, a working mother has the right to medical assistance for herself and the child including 'prenatal, child-birth and postnatal care, as well as hospitalization care when necessary'.[151]

Working mothers and non-discrimination
C183 addresses the relationship between maternity leave entitlements and the principle of non-discrimination. Article 8 (paragraphs 1 and 2) state that:

> It shall be unlawful for employers to terminate the employment of women during her pregnancy or absence on leave referred to in Articles 4 or 5 or during a period following her return to work to be prescribed by national laws or regulation, except on grounds unrelated to the pregnancy or birth of the child and its consequences or nursing. The burden of proving that the reasons for dismissal are unrelated to pregnancy or childbirth and its consequences or nursing shall rest on the employer.[152]

This is the enormous extent of the protection provided for working mothers by this convention. The previous convention (C103) protected working women from dismissal from their work within absences for maternity leave *only*.

> A woman is guaranteed the right to return to the same position or an equivalent position paid at the same rate at the end of her maternity leave.[153]

The right to breastfeed
When a mother returns to work after her maternity leave has concluded, C183 provides her with two breaks (each of half an hour duration) in her working hours to breastfeed her child. It also provides that 'these breaks or the reduction of daily hours of work shall be counted as working

148 *Maternity Protection Convention* (C183) art 4(4).
149 Ibid. art 5.
150 Ibid. art 6(1), (2), (3).
151 Ibid. art 6(7).
152 Ibid. art 8(1) and (2).
153 *Maternity Protection Convention* (C103) art 6.

time and remunerated accordingly'.[154] The purpose of such breaks is to protect the health of both the mother and child.[155]

Observations in Regard to the Recommendations of C183

Despite the improvement of international standards on maternity leave embodied in C183, most research shows that take-up rates remain very low for working women.[156] This is because there are many shortfalls in the Convention in relation to things such as the period of maternity leave and breastfeeding provisions, cash benefits and protection from discrimination. Often a number of issues interact. For example, in Australia (like non-signatory the United States) there was no compulsory paid maternity leave for women until very recently, and workplace-based provision for childcare that would allow for the maintenance of breastfeeding is exceedingly rare; nor is time officially allocated for expressing milk for a child in care. This forces women to choose between maintaining breastfeeding (at the level recommended by the Australian National Health and Medical Research Council) and employment. In Libya there are provisions for breastfeeding, but childcare availability remains poor. This hampers a woman's ability to exercise her right to return to work following the birth of a child and to maintain breastfeeding. Inadequate length of paid maternity leave hampers the maintenance of breastfeeding at the optimum level for the recommended period (six months exclusively), adversely affecting mothers and children. Thus, the issues are much interconnected. They are covered in greater detail immediately below.

The period of maternity leave: still inadequate

The period allowed for maternity leave is still inadequate for working women who desire to achieve a balance between career and motherhood. There are a number of important considerations which affect a woman's decision to return to work after pregnancy, particularly if she wishes to maintain breastfeeding. Key issues affecting a woman's decision to return to work is the availability and cost of childcare, and a reluctance to leave the child in others' care. Due to these concerns, women with a short period of maternity leave may prefer to stay at home and leave their employment. As a result they would have to look for new employment opportunities when they wish to re-enter the workforce, and might experience a period of unemployment. However, if maternity leave was to be for a moderate length of time, these issues can be overcome or minimised and return to work rates post-pregnancy would increase.[157]

Also, it has been proven that longer periods of maternity leave result in 'declines in depressive symptoms' among women of childbearing age, especially working mothers. With lower incidence and intensity of depressive symptoms in the mother, negative effects on the child would be reduced. Therefore, the length of maternity leave does affect maternal health – the longer the leave the more positive the outcome generally for both the child and the mother.[158] A distinct long-term advantage offered by extended maternity leave would be improvements in the child's health outcomes, as it

154 *Maternity Protection Convention* (C183) art 10(2).

155 For more information, see Michael Baker and Kevin Milligan, 'Maternal Employment, Breastfeeding, and Health: Evidence from Maternity Leave' (2008) 27 *Journal of Health Economics* 871, 873–4.

156 Laura Addati and Naomi Cassirer, 'Equal Sharing of Responsibilities Between Women and Men, Including Care-Giving in the Context of HIV/AIDS' (EGM/ESOR/2008/BP.2, Division for the Advancement of Women Department of Economic and Social Affairs United Nations, 19 September 2008) 2.

157 Zhang, above n 116, 22.

158 Chatterji and Markowitz, above n 119, 26.

would allow the mother to breastfeed her child for a longer period. Furthermore, mothers who stay home longer following pregnancy can maintain a close watch on the child's health and well-being and can respond to their needs more effectively. Research has shown that mothers with an extended period of maternity leave continue breastfeeding for longer compared to those who more rapidly return to work.[159]

Cash benefits

The cash benefits for working mothers – referred to in Article 6 of C183, and the right of mothers during maternity leave – should be increased to the level of the mother's full income to enable her to maintain not only her own health but also her child's, with an appropriate standard of living.

Protection of working mothers from discrimination

To protect the working mother from any kind of discrimination in the workplace during her absence due to pregnancy (or her absence due to any circumstance related to family responsibility or maternity leave), C183 provides that women must return to their former position or an equivalent at the same rate of pay.[160] The ILO has recommended that maternity leave be considered 'as a period of service for the determination of her rights', but as a recommendation this is not binding on signatories.[161] This is of great importance because some employers treat maternity leave as not contributing to the service undertaken by women in their employment, and so maternity leave taken adversely affects their promotion opportunities. This effectively ensures that any senior position in the workplace is only open to men (or women without familial responsibilities). This can prevent working mothers from achieving high positions. This is an injustice.[162]

Length of breastfeeding

Regarding the period of breastfeeding, Article 10 of C183 should be extended to meet the particular need to maintain the mother's and the child's health, according to the World Health Organization (WHO).[163] Therefore, evidence showing the imperative health benefits 'of exclusive breastfeeding' for both mothers and newborns has led UNICEF and WHO to recommend a minimum 16-week period of paid maternity leave. This was recently extended to 6 months by the World Health Assembly (WHA)[164] due to the advantages of breastfeeding for both child and mother. The benefit for the child is clear, both in childhood and later years, as 'breastfed babies are less likely to suffer from a range of serious illnesses and conditions such as gastroenteritis, respiratory illness and otitis media'.[165] There are distinct advantages also for the mothers, as 'breastfeeding promotes faster maternal recovery from childbirth and women who have breastfed have reduced risks of breast and ovarian cancers in later life'.[166]

---

159 Berger, Hill and Waldfogel, above n 91, F33.

160 *Maternity Protection Convention* (C183) art 8 (2).

161 R 191 *Maternity Protection Recommendation 2000*: Heap, above n 85, 40.

162 This is clearly evident in Chapter 5.

163 Feng and Han, above n 109, 299.

164 Heap, above n 85, 12.

165 Australian Health Ministers' Conference, 'Australian National Breastfeeding Strategy 2010–2015' P3–6238 (Australian Government, Department of Health and Ageing 2009) 3.

166 Ibid.

Shortcomings of C183

C183 refers to a number of vital issues that are important for working mothers if they are to obtain their rights under the Convention and enjoy their rights to work and to motherhood. However, it has many shortcomings, which will be identified and discussed below.

Provision of childcare facilities

Article 10(1) of the Convention states: 'A woman shall be provided with the right to one or more daily breaks or a daily reduction of hours of work to breastfeed her child'.[167]

A following paragraph of this Article, or even another Article in the Convention, should then outline how the enjoyment or expression of this right could be achieved; however, the Convention fails to do so. Article 10(1) is great in theory; however, it is impossible in practice. For instance, a woman has the right to daily breaks when she can breastfeed her child. If this break is, for example, half an hour long and if the child is cared for in the mother's home or at a childcare facility separate from her workplace, then this half hour necessarily must include travel time and breastfeeding time. Travelling to and from the venue where the child is located can be costly, time-consuming and inconvenient, and would certainly, in the vast majority of cases, make breastfeeding impossible. The Convention needs to deal with this problem, and find a solution. This can be done, for instance, by making it obligatory for each and every workplace to provide childcare facilities where there is a significant number of working mothers at that workplace. This would then be both convenient, time-saving and just for the working mother and her child. All working mothers have the right to breastfeed and all children have the right to develop in the most positive of environments. Childcare facilities help cater for such rights. It is only right then that workplaces and childcare facilities are places that 'empower mothers to continue breastfeeding'.[168]

Provision of parental leave

C183 was centred on maternity leave and its benefits for the mother. It reflected its time and place. It did not mention other provisions for leave that are beneficial to the mother and whether maternity leave affects these. One such beneficial leave is parental leave. Parental leave (also known as childcare leave) differs from maternity leave (taken by mothers) and paternity leave (taken by fathers). Parental leave can be taken by either parent following the period of maternity leave. As for the conditions, they vary depending on the country. The ILO *Workers with Family Responsibilities Recommendation 1981* (R165) specifies what parental leave is, its conditions and benefits.[169] Also, if a working mother, after the expiration of her maternity leave, finds herself unable to return to work and has no right to any other leave (for example, sick leave) then she has the right to parental leave, which would mean that she now can practise her right to motherhood and work.[170]

The goal of parental leave is 'to help women enter the labour market, in so far as it enables them not to have to choose between a career and caring for their children'.[171] It can be used to overcome (at least in the earliest stages of a child's life) a lack of childcare facilities or the availability of

167 *Maternity Protection Convention* (C183) art 10 (1).

168 'Australian National Breastfeeding Strategy', above n 165, 35.

169 Addati and Cassirer, 'Equal Sharing of Responsibilities' UN doc EGM/ESOR/2008/BP.2, above n 156, 14.

170 Heap, above n 85, 41.

171 'Perspectives: Parental Leave' (1997) 136(1) *International Labour Review* 109, 124, 125, 127.

costly childcare beyond the means of the mother/family, which 'tends to reinforce the exclusion of such women from the labour market'.[172]

Parental leave can have both positive and negative long-term and short-term outcomes. In the short run parental leave is beneficial for the child in its early stages of development. It is also beneficial for both the mother and father, and therefore the whole family. Many countries consider parental leave an easy and cheap way to avoid the provision of expensive childcare facilities, particularly for young infants. However, parental leave (as with any leave) can lead to a deterioration of the employee's skills and it is harder for employees to return to work after long periods of leave. Therefore, many countries now shorten parental leave entitlements 'to prevent long absences from the labour market and the resulting deterioration of skills'.[173]

However, these negatives can easily be overcome. For instance, on her return to work the mother can have a training course to update her on any new changes in protocols, technology or systems. This way she can be updated and ready to work to the best of her ability after a long and relaxing leave period that has been of such benefit to her child. Another feature of parental leave is that it is available to both parents. Sometimes both parents take parental leave (one after the other, not simultaneously), which allows them to maximise the benefit to the child and has the additional benefit of encouraging the father to better bond with the child and to accept a greater caring role, and thus reduce the length of time a mother might otherwise spend away from the workplace. However, the ability to do this is often affected by employment income disparities (often still favouring the father rather than the mother) which reduce uptake by males, workplace responsibilities and the attitude of the employer, co-workers and family as well as that of the spouse. Other factors affecting uptake of parental leave include the availability and affordability of childcare facilities and the level of the allowance or benefit paid for parental leave.[174] Nevertheless, a mother now truly does have an increased ability to enjoy her rights to motherhood and work.

Provision of adoption leave

Another inadequacy of C183 is that it does not provide for adoption leave for working women. Adoption leave has already been implemented in some countries. The New South Wales Teachers Federation in Australia, for example, has agitated for both paid and unpaid adoption leave for women employees, and this has been accorded by the major state education employer.[175] Where such provision does not exist, this effectively discriminates against an employed woman who is unable to give birth but who still wants to enjoy the right of motherhood through adoption. According to these conventions, there is no similar provision of adoption leave for such women. Therefore, if any working woman wants to adopt a child, she gains no support from the current international legislative regime in terms of leave entitlements.

Despite the existence of C183, gender discrimination is still a problem in reality in terms of equal employment opportunities in the labour force. In Australia, for example, according to annual reports by the Human Rights and Equal Opportunity Commission (HREOC), women with children face significant discrimination. Easteal cites the example of a woman who, after returning from 12 weeks' maternity leave, was offered a new position at a lower level than her previous post, and

---

172 Ibid.

173 Addati and Cassirer, 'Equal Sharing of Responsibilities' UN doc EGM/ESOR/2008/BP.2, above n 156, 15.

174 'Perspectives: Parental Leave ', above n 171, 124–5, 127.

175 New South Wales Teachers Federation, *Adoption Leave* (26 May 2011) <http://www.nswtf.org.au/TemporaryTeachers/adoption.html>.

was offered reduced working hours (part time) that were unsuitable for her. The woman lodged a complaint with HREOC, alleging that the working environment to which she had returned was not favourable for a woman employee who had returned from maternity leave, and that she had encountered some hostile behaviour in the workplace. Therefore, she felt she had to resign from her job.[176]

There remains a gap between the norms contained in C183 and women's experience of access to maternity benefits. For instance, one empirical study of the situation in Bangladesh found two results. First, nearly 60 per cent of the employers thought that women workers were less capable in terms of skills and in relation to jobs dependent upon physical strength. Gender-based assumptions are usually made, as strength is often an untested criterion for employment – hence a weak man may be more likely to be employed than a strong woman. The provision of paid maternity leave and the need to provide separate seating arrangements for women with children also discouraged some employers from recruiting women. Second, 40 per cent of the employers surveyed gave preference to those women employees who were submissive to their employer, and unaware of their rights in relation to trade union membership and laws.[177]

Libya and the Maternity Protection Conventions

Maternity leave was extended to women in member states, including Libya. All the International Labour Organization (ILO) conventions are legal instruments. Once a government has ratified a convention, the member state is obliged to bring its national law and practice into conformity with the provisions of that convention and 'to report periodically to the ILO on its application in both the law and in practice'.[178]

On 27 May 1971 Libya ratified C3;[179] four years later (19 June 1975) it ratified C103.[180] In 2000 the ILO introduced C183 to replace C103. Although C183 came into force in 2002, it has been ratified by a total of just 22 member states. Libya is not among these (despite the fact that Libya is an active member of the ILO).[181]

With the introduction of C183, C103 is no longer available for ratification; however, for those countries (such as Libya) that have already ratified C103 and have not yet ratified C183, the earlier convention remains applicable.[182]

176 Patricia Easteal, *Less than Equal: Women and the Australian Legal System* (Butterworths, 2001) 144.

177 Afroza Begum, *Protection of Women's Rights in Bangladesh: A Legal Study in an International and Comparative Perspective* (PhD Thesis, University of Wollongong, 2004) 127.

178 International Labour Office, 'Women's Employment: Global Trends ILO Responses, 49th sess of the Commission on the Status of Women ', above ch 1 n 38, 23.

179 International Labour Organization, *C3 Maternity Protection Convention, 1919: Ratified by Libyan Arab Jamahiriya on 27:05:1971* (24 September 2011) <http://www.ilo.org/ilolex>.

180 International Labour Organization, *C103 Maternity Protection Convention (Revised), 1952: Ratified by Libyan Arab Jamahiriya on 19:06:1975* (24 September 2011) <http://www.ilo.org/ilolex>.

181 This because the Libyan Government has ratified 28 ILO conventions: <http://www.ilo.org/ilolex/cgi-lex/ratifce.pl?Libyan>.

182 Maternity Protection Coalition, above n 10, 1.

The Libyan Government and the CEACR

This section aims to explore the 'relationship' between the Committee of Experts on the Application of Conventions and Recommendations (CEACR) and the Libyan Government in regard to the *Maternity Protection Convention* (C3 and C103). Reports made by both parties regarding the Convention are thoroughly examined and analysed. A number of substantive problems remain unresolved, and again poor reporting practices are noted. The more recent comments made by the CEACR on Libya's performance in regard to C103 have been repetitive and indistinguishable from earlier responses since Libya's ratification in 1975.

Issues Remaining

For instance, the comments and observations highlighted in the Direct Request of 1990 (60th Session) are still being repeated decades later, in 2009. In 1990 the main concerns highlighted remained those such as the period of maternity leave, cash benefits payable, the scope of the Convention and non-Libyan female officials. These will be further addressed below.

Length of maternity leave

The CEACR hoped that the Libyan Government would amend Article 43 of the *Labour Code Act*[183] for three main reasons. Firstly, Article 43 'provides for the granting of pre- and post-natal maternity leave of a total of 50 days', which conflicts with Article 3 of the Convention – which sets a minimum period of 12 weeks for such leave as well as mandating a compulsory six-week post-confinement leave. Secondly, Article 43 states that only once a woman completes at least six months with her employer is she eligible for entitlement to leave; however, the Convention does not contain such conditions. Finally, Article 43 'does not contain provisions, in accordance with Article 3, paragraph 4,[184] of the Convention'.[185]

Cash benefits

There are two issues raised in this area. Firstly, according to Article 25 of the *Social Security Act*[186] and Article 43 of the *Labour Code Act*, maternity benefits are the responsibility of the employer. This is contrary to Article 4 of C103, specifically paragraphs 4 and 8, which state that benefits must be provided either via means of public funds or social insurance and that such payments are not the employer's responsibility. Secondly, because Article 25 of the *Social Security Act* does not specify the provisions regarding benefits, then its regulations must, especially if the circumstances highlighted in Article 3(4) of C103 become an issue.[187] Article 3(4) and (8) states:

---

183 *Labour Code Act No 58 of 1970* (Libya) art 43.

184 *Convention No C103* art 3(4) states that: 'the leave before the presumed date of confinement shall be extended by any period elapsing between the presumed date of confinement and the actual date of confinement and the period of compulsory leave to be taken after confinement shall not be reduced on that account'.

185 CEACR, *Individual Direct Request Concerning Convention No 103, Maternity Protection (Revised), 1952 Libyan Arab Jamahiriya (ratification: 1975) Submitted: 1990*, CEACR 1990, 60th sess, ILOLEX Doc No 091990LBY103 (ILO, 1990) 1 [2].

186 *Social Security Act No 13 of 1980* (Libya) art 25.

187 CEACR, *Individual Direct Request* (1990), ILOLEX Doc No 091990LBY103, above n 591, 1[3]–2[1].

> The leave before the presumed date of confinement shall be extended by any period elapsing between the presumed date of confinement and the actual date of confinement and the period of compulsory leave to be taken after confinement shall not be reduced on that account.
>
> In no case shall the employer be individually liable for the cost of such benefits due to women employed by him.[188]

Failing to match the scope of the convention

Article 1 of the *Labour Code Act* does not mention and, therefore, does not cover workers such as 'domestic workers and persons in similar categories, women engaged in stock raising and agriculture and permanent or temporary public officials working in state administrations and public bodies'.[189] Again, this conflicts with Article 1 of C103.

Provisions for non-Libyan female officials

Article 2 of C103 states that:

> For the purpose of this Convention, the term '*woman*' means any female person, irrespective of age, *nationality*, race or creed, whether married or unmarried, and the term '*child*' means any child whether born of marriage or not.[190]

It is no surprise, therefore, that the CEACR in 1990 urged the government to 'indicate the number of non-Libyan female officials and the number of them who are registered under social security, if any'.[191] The Committee made this request because Article 5 of Libya's *Registration, Contributions and Inspection Regulations of 1982* allows registration of non-Libyan officials on a voluntary basis, unless there is a specific agreement between Libya and the official's country of origin.[192] (In 2009, these issues were still of major concern.)

Ongoing Substantive Problems and Reporting Issues

These same problems as those noted above were being raised in 1994 (64th Session)[193] and in 1995. In 1995, the Libyan Government failed to provide responses to the issues and queries raised by the CEACR's previous observations in 1994. It stated: 'The Committee notes that the Government's report contains no new information in reply to previous comments. It must therefore repeat its previous comments'.[194]

188 *Maternity Protection Convention* (C103) art 3(4), (8).

189 CEACR, *Individual Direct Request* (1990), ILOLEX Doc No 091990LBY103, above n 591, 2 [3].

190 *Maternity Protection Convention* (C103) art 2 (emphasis added).

191 CEACR, *Individual Direct Request* (1990), ILOLEX Doc No 091990LBY103, above n 185, 2 [4].

192 Ibid.

193 CEACR, *Individual Observation Concerning Convention No 103, Maternity Protection Convention (Revised), 1952 Libyan Arab Jamahiriya (ratification: 1975)*, CEACR 1994, 64th sess, ILOLEX Doc No 061994LBY103 (ILO, 1994).

194 CEACR, *Individual Observation Concerning Convention No 103, Maternity Protection (Revised), 1952 Libyan Arab Jamahiriya (ratification: 1975) 1995*, CEACR 1995, 66th sess, ILOLEX Doc No 061996LBY1032 (ILO, 1996) 1 [1].

Since 1995, the Libyan Government has failed to submit its reports; consequently the CEACR reports of 1997[195] and 1998[196] were repetitive in nature. In 1999, the CEACR noted 'with regret that the Government's report has not been received for the third consecutive time'.[197] During this lengthy time period, the CEACR continued to virtually 'copy and paste' its previous comments and 'urge' the government to reply.

In 2000, the Libyan Government finally submitted its overdue report; and, in 2003, in its 74th Session, the CEACR replied. The CEACR's observations were of no surprise; the same issues raised years earlier were yet again emphasised. It also clearly stated at the completion of the observations that Libya's next report was due in 2004.[198] In 2005, CEACR reported:

> The Committee notes with interest that in July 2005, an ILO technical assistance mission visited the Libyan Arab Jamahiriya to assist the Government in resolving difficulties in applying ratified social security Conventions, including Convention No. 103. The Committee hopes that with the Office's assistance, the Government will take the necessary steps to give full effect, in law and in practice, to the provisions of the Convention on which it has been commenting.[199]

Yet, following this introductory paragraph, the CEACR continued to repeat its previous comments.

In its 2007 report, the CEACR expressed its displeasure with the government, and the same requests were made yet again. The official technical assistance mission sent in 2005 had so far been of no effect. CEACR expressed its hopes again in 2005, and then it repeated these in 2007, stating:

> It expressed the hope that with the ILO's assistance, the Government would be able to take the necessary steps to give full effect, in law and in practice, to the provisions of the Convention on which the Committee had been commenting for many years.[200]

In August 2007 (just after the CEACR's report) the Libyan Government submitted to the ILO Office a draft of its new *Labour Code*. This draft, accordingly, took into account the observations of the 2007 CEACR report and 'was to be submitted to the General People's Congress before the end of 2008'.[201]

---

195 CEACR, *Individual Observation* (1998) ILOLEX Doc No 061998LBY103, above n 47.

196 CEACR, *Individual Observation Concerning Convention No 103, Maternity Protection (Revised), 1952 Libyan Arab Jamahiriya (ratification: 1975) 1998*, CEACR 1998, 69th sess, ILOLEX Doc No 061999LBY103 (ILO, 1999).

197 CEACR, *Individual Observation* (2000) ILOLEX Doc No 062000LBY103, above n 70, 1 [1].

198 CEACR, *Individual Observation Concerning Convention No 103, Maternity Protection (Revised), 1952 Libyan Arab Jamahiriya (ratification: 1975) 2003*, CEACR 2003, 74th sess, ILOLEX Doc No 062004LBY103 (ILO, 2004) 3 [4].

199 CEACR, *Individual Observation Concerning Maternity Protection Convention (Revised), 1952 (No 103) Libyan Arab Jamahiriya (ratification: 1975) 2005*, CEACR 2005, 76th sess, ILOLEX Doc No 062006LBY103 (ILO, 2006) 1 [1].

200 CEACR, *Individual Observation concerning Maternity Protection Convention (Revised), 1952 (No 103) Libyan Arab Jamahiriya (ratification: 1975) 2007*, CEACR 2007, 78th sess, ILOLEX Doc No 062008LBY103 (ILO, 2008) 1 [1].

201 CEACR, *Individual Observation Concerning Maternity Protection Convention (Revised), 1952 (No 103) Libyan Arab Jamahiriya (ratification: 1975) 2009*, CEACR 2009, 80th sess, ILOLEX Doc No 062010LBY103 (ILO, 2010) 1 [1].

The CEACR in 2008 then expressed 'the hope that the amending legislation will soon be enacted and asks the Government to send in a copy of it, once adopted'.[202] The CEACR's 2009 report, therefore, focused on the incoming report and outlined specifically what it wanted from the government. The CEACR was still waiting a further 12 months later. In 2010, in regard to the expected report and information, the CEACR noted:

> Serious failure to submit. The Committee asks the Government to provide the information requested concerning the submission to the competent authorities, within the meaning of article 19, paragraphs 5 and 6, of the ILO Constitution, of all Conventions, Recommendations and Protocols adopted at 12 sessions of the Conference held between 1996 and 2007 (83rd, 84th, 85th, 86th, 88th, 89th, 90th, 91st, 92nd, 94th, 95th and 96th Sessions). It urges the Government to take steps without delay to submit the pending instrument to the competent authorities.[203]

By 2011, the situation was no different and again (this time in regard to the expected 2011 report from Libya) the CEACR stated:

> Serious failure to submit. The Committee asks the Government to provide the information requested concerning the submission to the competent authorities, within the meaning of article … It urges the Government to take steps without delay to submit the pending instruments to the competent authorities.[204]

It can now be concluded from all the CEACR's comments (and from previous similar observations) that the Libyan Government, upon ratification of a convention, does not necessarily take into account its responsibilities – or simply neglects them. It is necessary that member states' domestic laws are in conformity with the convention. If the domestic legislation falls below the minimum convention standards, the member state is responsible for making the necessary amendments to its legislation in order to achieve uniformity.[205]

Conclusion in Regard to ILO Conventions

The lack of ratification by all member states reduces the effectiveness of even the most advanced international protection schemes. The extent of the application of these schemes is also significantly limited by the reservations made by ratifying states. Implementation and enforcement at a national level are also of serious concern, as many countries (such as Libya) have not taken adequate measures post-ratification. It is necessary that a unified approach with cooperation on both international and national levels is adopted in order to overcome discrimination against women.[206]

---

202 CEACR, *General Report and Observations Concerning Particular Countries*, 99th sess, 2010 III (Part 1A) (International Labour Office, 2010) 721–2.

203 CEACR, *Submission to the Competent Authorities, Libyan Arab Jamahiriya, 2010*, ILOLEX Doc No 102010LBY (ILO, 2011) 1.

204 CEACR, *Submission to the Competent Authorities, Libyan Arab Jamahiriya, 2011*, ILOLEX Doc No 102011LBY (ILO, 2011) 1.

205 Maternity Protection Coalition, above n 10, 1.

206 Li Weiwei, 'Equality and Non-Discrimination under International Human Rights Law' (Norwegian Centre for Human Rights, 2004) 25–6.

The subjection of the ILO conventions to a supervisory system attracts quite significant criticisms, as these systems operate on recommendations, reports and so on, and do not incorporate actual enforcement.[207]

In relation to the effectiveness of international conventions, it is essential that a country follows the ratification of an instrument with the establishment of relevant enforcement mechanisms on a domestic level. The rise of human rights ideology has been strongly influenced by legal concerns as well as political ones. Countries have often based the progress of their commitment to human rights on 'legal' factors even though political influences have often had a major impact on the motivation behind human rights development at both national and international levels.[208]

There are numerous issues of critical importance in relation to women and employment, and the particular focus of the current research is on working women with family responsibilities in Libya. While Libya has legal rules which prevent discrimination and encourage participation, this legal regime is severely limited by social and cultural expectations. The next chapter addresses the Libyan legal system.

207 Weichselbaumer and Winter-Ebmer, above n 1, 246.

208 Luke McNamara, *Human Rights Controversies: The Impact of Legal Form* (Routledge-Cavendish, 2007) 13.

Chapter 4
Equal Rights in the Workplace for Women under Libyan Employment Law

Libyan society has long considered women as an essential part of its structure. Their role has undergone significant change; they have moved from being solely housewives and mothers to qualified workers and business owners. Women were provided with their full legal rights, including the right to vote, in 1969. The government provides free education for girls and women, and women have been encouraged by government support to take their place in the workforce even after having children and becoming mothers. Since the early 1970s, the government has established childcare centres and provided women with cash incentives to encourage them to return to the workforce after having children. Moreover, equal payment for men and women in the same occupation was ensured through laws enacted by the government.[1] This in turn has led more women to become involved and active in the workplace (for example, as professional women; as educators, nurses, lawyers, charity workers; and even as soldiers in the Libyan army).[2]

The Libyan legal system derives from Italian and French civil law on one hand, and Islamic law on the other.[3] This chapter addresses aspects of both civil law and Islamic law in relation to their impact on the rights of Libyan women in the workplace. The tensions that arise between the two legal systems have a direct impact, limiting women's ability to work and also the type of work women can do.

This chapter begins by addressing the laws enacted to prevent discrimination against working women in Libya, before identifying discrepancies between Libyan domestic law and international human rights law. It reviews the historical changes that have occurred in Libyan society, and covers areas including maternity leave, family allowance, childcare facilities, returning to work payments, and women's rights and inclusion in the military and court system. The chapter concludes with a discussion that addresses the day-to-day realities of working women that limit their ability to participate fully in the workforce despite the existence of legislation supporting their participation.

History of Legislation that Aims to Prevent Discrimination

Since 1969, the Libyan Government has tried to encourage women to participate more actively in the economy. The position and role of women in the economy has become one of the focal issues during the last four decades. Even under the monarchy the government did not discriminate against women,[4] and some encouragement was given to women for greater involvement in the

---

1 For instance, *Labour Code Act No 58 of 1970* (Libya) and *Wage Scales for National Workers Act No 15 of 1981* (Libya).

2 Paul A Rozario, *Libya (Countries of the World)* (Gareth Stevens, 2004) 24.

3 Abdullahi A An-Na'im, *Islamic Family Law in a Changing World: A Global Resource Book* (Zed Books, 2002) 174.

4 'On November 21, 1949, the United Nations General Assembly passed a resolution stating that Libya should become independent before January 1, 1952. King Idris I represented Libya in the subsequent

broader society.[5] However, women did not have the skills, experience or the qualifications for most of the positions available. Often the positions vacant were salaried positions in the public service which required certain skills and experience that women generally lacked. Their participation was generally in areas that required 'minimum skill' and involved employment that 'could be performed in [gender] segregated areas'.[6] This included occupations such as agriculture, domestic service and office janitorial functions during the monarchical regime.[7]

Libyan legislation prohibits discrimination on the basis of gender. For example, the *Constitutional Declaration 1969*[8] provides that 'All citizens are equal before the law'.[9] Given this statement, this chapter reviews the status of working women as it changes with the introduction of various pieces of legislation and changes in policy. This legislation comprises:

- *Labour Code Act No 58 of 1970*
- *Social Security Act No 13 of 1980*
- *Great Green Charter of Human Rights 1988* (under its principle of equality)
- *Order of the General People's Committee No 164 of 1988 on Employment of Arab Libyan Women*
- *Right of Women to Assume Posts in the Judiciary Act No 8 of 1989*
- *Army Act No 3 of 1984*
- *Promotion of Freedom Act No 20 of 1991*
- *Charter of Women's Rights and Obligations in Republic Society 1997*
- Acts and Orders related to the provision of maternity leave, childcare facilities and access to training.

The Principle of Equality in Libyan Law

The status of women, their rights and responsibilities as both mothers and as workers, and the responsibility of society to ensure that these are not compromised, are especially highlighted in the *Great Green Charter of Human Rights*. This document ostensibly granted many rights to the people of Libya, including women; but in practice these were often abrogated or arbitrarily restricted. It is hoped that the newly formed National Congress will not only reiterate many of its progressive elements (see below) and ensure that they are better enforced, but – specifically in relation to the

UN negotiations. When Libya declared its independence on December 24, 1951, it was the first country to achieve independence through the United Nations and one of the first former European possessions in Africa to gain independence. Libya was proclaimed a constitutional and a hereditary monarchy under King Idris. On September 1, 1969 … [Libya has a] new regime, headed by the Revolutionary Command Council (RCC), abolished the monarchy and proclaimed the new Libyan Arab Republic': Bureau of Near Eastern Affairs, *Background Note: Libya* (16 June 2011) <http://www.state.gov/r/pa/ei/bgn/5425.htm>.

5 Mahmud Salih Al-Adly, 'Al-Bu'd Al-Ensany Lihq Al-Mr'ah fi Al-Aml wa Al-T'liym wa Mrdwduh Al-Eqtisady' (Paper presented at the Aqtsadiat T'liym wa Aml Al-Mr'ah fi Aljmahyriyh Al-Ozma, Bnghazy (Libya) Jami't Qarywnis, 10–12 March 1997) 15 [Trans: 'The Human Factor for Libyan's Women Education and Employment and its Economic Return' (Paper presented at Women's Education and Employment in Libya: An Economic Perspective, Benghazi)].

6 Amal Obeidi, *Political Culture in Libya* (Curzon Press, 2001) 173.

7 Ibid.

8 *Constitution Declaration of 1969* (Libya).

9 This is evident in *Constitution Declaration of 1969* (Libya) art 5.

issues covered by this volume – will also further enhance the position of women in Libyan society so that they are able to combine successfully their roles of motherhood and paid employment and so contribute to the development of the new Libya.

Article 11 of the *Great Green Charter of Human Rights in the Jamahiriya Era 1988* (GGCHR),[10] which was adopted by the Basic People's Congress, states:

> The Jamahiriyan society guarantees the right to work.[11] It is a right and a duty for everyone, within the limits of their personal ability, individually or in association with others. Everybody has the right to practise the work of their choice.

Also, Article 17 states that '[t]he members of the Jamahiriyan society reject any segregation between [human beings] due to their colour, race, religion or culture'. Article 21 of the GGCHR emphasises the principle of equality, and states that:

> The members of Jamahiriyan society, men or women, are equal in everything which is human. The distinction of rights between men and women is a flagrant injustice which nothing justifies.

Nevertheless, the family is viewed as the cornerstone of society, and a mother has the right (and duty) to bring up her child (and specifically to breastfeed her child). Article 20 of the GGCHR states that:

> The members of the Jamahiriyan society affirm the sacred right for [people] to be born into a coherent family, where motherhood, fatherhood and brotherhood are given to [them]. Fulfilment of the human being is only in compliance with [their] nature if it is assured by natural motherhood and feeding. The child must be brought up by its mother.

Indeed, the use of 'must' in this document indicates that the mother not only has a right to bring up her child and the child a right to be brought up by his or her mother, but that the mother has a duty to do so. This appears to align with injunctions in the *Qur'ān* in regard to young children, in particular those being nursed by the mother.[12] However, the Qur'ānic allowance for wet-nurses (upon the agreement of both parents), subject to equitable payment for the woman concerned, indicates that other arrangements may be acceptable if approved by the parents.[13] (It is worth noting that should such an arrangement be reached, 'no blame' attaches to the mother.)[14] The mother's responsibility for care is, however, clearly upheld.[15] Therefore, any participation in the workforce must accommodate this right.

The emphasis on gender equality is clear, and legislation has been progressively passed that facilitates greater participation in the workplace by women, including those with family responsibilities. The extent to which this is achieved is examined further below.

---

10 *Great Green Charter of Human Rights in the Jamahiriya Era 1988* (Libya).

11 The function of Jamahiriyan society is to be a Libyan society.

12 *Qur'ān* 46:15. Where the role of the mother in gestation and weaning is indicated to be a period to weaning is indicated as 30 months; 2:233, where two years is indicated.

13 *Qur'ān* 2:233, where a breastfeeding period of up to two years is indicated.

14 Ibid.

15 As is the principle of family decision-making in regard to women's participation in the workforce. Again, such arrangements contribute to the harmony of the household and the nation, and are often informally observed in working families around the world, irrespective of their faith or nationality.

The Growth of Equal Rights for Working Women

Equal rights for working women grew progressively, with the introduction of legislation such as: the *Order of the General People's Committee*[16] *No 164 of 1988 on Employment of Arab Libyan Women*; the *Promotion of Freedom Act No 20 of 1991* (gender equality); and the *Charter of Women's Rights and Obligations in Republic Society 1997*.

The Order of the General People's Committee No 164 of 1988 on Employment of Arab Libyan Women

The *Order of the General People's Committee No 164 of 1988 on Employment of Arab Libyan Women*[17] aims to support any employed woman who is able to work in any situation (except the police force[18] and customs,[19] which are covered by separate legislation). This is affirmed in Article 1. Article 2 entitles women to work in various occupations as well as undertake professional training. Equally significant, both part-time and full-time work is to be made available for women in the administrative services and the production sectors. Part-time work is to be able to be converted to full-time and vice versa in response to changing work demands and in accordance with the decisions of the GP Cttee in regard to the Civil Service. Furthermore, part-time working women are entitled to receive full family and housing allowances. Indeed, women working part time are subject to the provisions of the *Social Security Act* regarding maternity leave (see below).[20] Such provisions arguably encourage greater workplace participation by women.

The Promotion of Freedom Act No 20 of 1991

The *Promotion of Freedom Act No 20 of 1991*[21] protects the rights of all citizens in the workplace regardless of gender. Article 1 stipulates that 'Citizens of the Great Jamahiriya, male and female, are free and enjoy equal rights'. Article 28 acknowledges working women's right to work and to choose the kind of work that suits their needs: 'A woman has the right to the occupation that suits her, she shall not be placed in a situation where she is employed … which does not suit her nature'.[22] While this latter phrase is often 'code' for restricting a woman's employment to what are traditionally deemed areas that 'suit her [feminine] nature' (such as childcare, infant teaching, nursing of women), recent decades in Libya have shown that it has been far more loosely interpreted to include roles within the police and customs, the judiciary, academia and so on – including roles of great responsibility, such as membership of the Committee for Preparation of New Laws

16 The function of General People's Committee (GP Cttee) in Libya is to be the representative of the Libyan Government.

17 *Order of the General People's Committee No 164 of 1988 on Employment of Arab Libyan Women* (Libya).

18 *Police Force Act No 6 of 1972* (Libya).

19 *Customs Act No 68 of 1972* (Libya).

20 See *Order of the General People's Committee No 164 of 1988 on Employment of Arab Libyan Women* (Libya) arts 3, 4, 9, 11.

21 *Promotion of Freedoms Act No 20 of 1991* (Libya).

22 Ibid. art 28.

for Election for the National Assembly – and women have increasingly shown an interest in the nation's political struggles.[23]

The Charter of Women's Rights and Obligations in Republic Society 1997

The *Charter of Women Rights and Obligations in Republic Society 1997*[24] was released to provide further rights for women in the workplace. It states that women and men should have equal rights in the workplace. These rights are in relation to positions that may be held; equal treatment in the workplace; and recognition of workers' knowledge and experience as well as their abilities in performing their roles.[25] This is the equivalent in principle to the provisions found in Australia under the Commonwealth *Equal Employment Opportunity for Women in the Workplace Act*[26] and the Commonwealth *Sex Discrimination Act*.[27]

Legislative Changes Encouraging Increased Workplace Participation by Women: Equal Pay Provisions

Article 31 of the *Labour Code Act No 58 of 1970*[28] (*Labour Code*) proclaims and supports anti-discrimination for those covered by this Act.[29] Libyan law does not differentiate on the basis of gender in terms of salary.[30] The employer must ensure that, regardless of an employee's gender, they are paid equally if the nature and condition of the occupation are the same as those of another employee. The *Labour Code* guarantees that an employee is to receive no less than the minimum wage, also fixed by regulation in accordance with this code.[31] To ensure equal pay across the broader workplace, the *Wage Scales for National Workers Act No 15 of 1981* was enacted.[32] The purpose of this Act is to protect the equal pay provisions for *all* Libyan employees. Article 1 states

23 Professor Abeir Imneina: Nahla Al-Ageli, 'Libya's Elections: Women Getting On Board' *Libya Herald* 29 June 2012 <http://www.libyaherald.com/feature-libyas-elections-women-getting-on-board/>. Although a quota of seats has been rejected for the new parliament, women are participating and campaigning for election both for seats allocated for individuals and for parties. In addition, women form 40% of members of one party, the Libyan National Party, which lists a woman (Ibtisam Ben Amer) as its top candidate in Tripoli. In regard to other positions of responsibility – such as appellate court judges like Naima Mohamed Jebril – see Nohad Topalian, 'Change Takes Time, Libyan Judge Says', *Libyan Youth Movement Feb 17th* website, 20 January 2012 <http://feb17.info/news/change-takes-time-libyan-judge-says/>. The report contains an interview with her.

24 *Charter of Women Rights and Obligations in Republic Society 1997* (Libya).

25 Ibid. art 12.

26 *Equal Opportunity for Women in the Workplace Act 1999* (Cth). See also *Equal Employment Opportunity (Commonwealth Authorities) Act 1987* (Cth).

27 *Sex Discrimination Act 1984* (Cth).

28 *Labour Code Act No 58 of 1970* (Libya).

29 Ibid. art 1 'The provisions of this Code shall apply to all persons working under a contract of employment' except for a number of specific categories exempted by the Act (such as employer's family members, domestic employees and pastoral workers). Also, 'This Code shall apply to manual workers employed by Government and public bodies unless their status has been defined by special regulations made by the Council of Ministers': ibid.

30 Rozario, above n 2, 23.

31 *Labour Code Act No 58 of 1970* (Libya) art 31. Note 'wage' includes in cash and/or benefits in kind.

32 *Wage Scales for National Workers Act No 15 of 1981* (Libya).

that the reason for wage scales for national workers is to ensure equal wages for employees with the same responsibility and occupation without discrimination between female and male workers. The fourth periodic report from Libya to the Human Rights Committee for the *International Covenant on Civil and Political Rights* (ICCPR)[33] summarises the state's position:

> With regard to wages, the labour and civil service laws and the laws on private enterprise do not discriminate against women. The legislature treats civil servants, workers and entrepreneurs as human beings, based on purely objective criteria. Women are not denied the right to an equal wage or to promotion, rises and other benefits provided for in relevant laws.[34]

The introduction of equal pay provisions resulted in greater participation by women. The Libyan developments here echo that of other nations. For example, in Australia labour force participation by women has increased significantly since the equal pay determination by the Commonwealth Conciliation and Arbitration Commission in 1969,[35] a decision that was supplemented by the *Affirmative Action (Equal Opportunity for Women) Act 1986* (Cth) (later the *Equal Opportunity for Women in the Workplace Act 1999* (Cth)).[36] These contributed to an increase in women's participation from 43.5 per cent to 58.7 per cent in the period February 1978 to June 2009.[37]

Legislation Providing for Broader Workplace Participation by Women

Workplace participation by women has traditionally been limited to certain sectors, namely agriculture, domestic service and basic secretarial services. Following the foundation of the Republic in 1969, legislation was increasingly designed not only to ensure that greater numbers of women entered the workplace but also that they were eligible to enter far more fields of employment. Careers for women have opened up substantially.[38] For example, women are now nurses, customs officers, office workers, police officers, flight attendants and teachers. Access to such careers is affirmed by the *Order of the General People's Committee No 258 of 1989 on the Rehabilitation and Training of Libyan Women*.[39] While the court system was opened to women,

---

33 *International Covenant on Civil and Political Rights* (ICCPR), opened for signature 16 December 1966, 999 UNTS 171 (entered into force 23 March 1976).

34 United Nations Human Rights Committee (HRC), *Consideration of Reports Submitted by States Parties under Article 40 of the Covenant, Fourth Periodic Reports of States Parties: Libyan Arab Jamahiriya*, UN Doc CCPR/C/LBY/4 (UN, 10 May 2007) 6 [29].

35 Australian Government, Department of Foreign Affairs and Trade, *About Australia: Women – Towards Equality* (2 November 2011) <http://www.dfat.gov.au/facts/women.html>. See *Australian Meat Industry Employees Union v Meat and Allied Trades Federation of Australia (Equal Pay Cases)* (1969) 127 CAR 1142 (Moore and Williams JJ, Chambers Public Service Arbitrator and Gough C, Judgment, 19 June 1969).

36 *Equal Opportunity for Women in the Workplace Act 1999* (Cth).

37 Australian Bureau of Statistics, Labour Force Survey (ABS, 2009) cited in Australian Government, Department of Families Office for Women, Housing, Community Services and Indigenous Affairs, 'Review of the Equal Opportunity for Women in the Workplace Act 1999: Consultation Report' (January 2010) 5 [2.1.2].

38 Amal Obeidi, 'Tatwir Harakt Al-Mr'ah fi Al-Mujtam' Al-Liby Byn Al-Tmkiyn wa Al-Tf'iyl: Dirast Twthiyqiyh' (2003–04) 23 *Majlt Dirasat fi Al-Eqtisad wa Al-Tijarh* [Trans: 'The Evolution of the Libyan Women's Movement: A Quantitative Study' *Journal of Economic and Commerce Studies*] 1, 3.

39 *Order of the General People's Committee No 258 of 1989 on the Rehabilitation and Training of Libyan Women* (Libya).

few were appointed at higher levels. Both this and military service are areas of work previously strongly identified with males. These areas are covered in greater detail below.

Military Service

Military service had been previously limited to males; however, the Women's Military Academy (WMA) was established in 1979 to train highly qualified female military officers. Graduates were directly promoted to the position of lieutenant. From the beginning of the 1980s, more radical changes occurred. Under the *Army Act No 3 of 1984*,[40] if they were physically fit, all men and women aged from 18 to 35 were compelled to undertake some military training at secondary school, and later compulsory military service. There is supposed to be no discrimination between men and women in the military ranks according to Libyan laws. While women are trained separately, they can serve on the front line and work in the same type of military occupations as their male counterparts. They also have the opportunity to be promoted to the higher ranks.[41]

The Courts System

Women have been given extensive rights in the courts system over time. Such rights include the capacity to hold the position of judge, public prosecutor and case administrator. In the past women could not enter these careers, due to a combination of traditional views of women and specific legislative restrictions. For instance, Article 43 of the *Judicial System Act No 51 of 1976* stated that only men could enter the judicial system, while women could work only as lawyers.[42] Men traditionally occupied such posts as deputy prosecutor, judge, prosecuting attorney and legal counsellor. However, Article 43 of *Act No 51 of 1976* was repealed by the *Right of Women to Assume Posts in the Judiciary Act No 8 of 1989*.[43] The purpose of this Act is to prevent any discrimination between men and women. Its first Article states that: 'A woman may assume judicial posts, as well as the posts with the public prosecution and administration of justice under the same terms as for men'. In 2006 *Act No 51 of 1976* was repealed by a new Act – *Act No 6 of 2006*.[44] Article 43 of this new Act (which consolidated the gains of previous legislation) confirmed *Act No 8 of 1989* regarding female participation in the judicial system.

Legislation Facilitating Greater Participation in the Workplace by Women with Children

While the legislation outlined above provided greater opportunity for women generally, further provision needed to be made to ensure greater participation of women with children. The right to maternity leave and the provision of suitable childcare facilities are just two of the many areas that require attention, and are among those covered below.

---

40 *Army Act No 3 of 1984* (Libya).

41 Obeidi, *Political Culture in Libya*, above n 6, 175.

42 *Judicial System Act No 51 of 1976* (Libya).

43 *Right of Women to Assume Posts in the Judiciary Act No 8 of 1989* (Libya).

44 *Judicial System Act No 6 of 2006* (Libya).

Maternity Leave

Two pieces of legislation are particularly concerned with the rights of women in the workplace both prior to and after confinement. They are the *Social Security Act No 13 of 1980*[45] and the earlier, but no less relevant, *Labour Code Act No 58 of 1970*,[46] the provisions of which still apply to employees covered by that code. In addition, specific orders and/or policies may exist for employees in a particular industry or employed by a specific employer.

Social Security Act No 13 of 1980
Both rights – work and motherhood – are recognised by the *Social Security Act No 13 of 1980*.[47] It makes provision for working women covered by this Act to have special maternity leave before and after childbirth for a period of no more than three months in total with full salary.[48]

Working women covered by the *Social Security Act* receive LYD 3 per month during pregnancy, starting from the fourth month for a maximum period of six months. Therefore, after the expiration of the six-month period the working mother has no right to the LYD 3 per month.[49] A further amount of LYD 25 is payable after childbirth.[50] This benefit, however, will not be granted unless the mother is registered (that is, has been an employee of an entity which qualifies her for such benefits under the Act) for six months prior to childbirth and has been an active member (that is, has been contributing financially to the system) for at least four months. It is also imperative to note that this benefit applies to all childbirths and all children covered by the Act. For instance, if the mother gives birth to twins then she has the right to LYD 50. This benefit also applies whether the child is female or male, born alive or dead, healthy or with disabilities. The mother is eligible to receive the payment upon the birth of the child at full term or after at least six months of pregnancy.[51]

There is also provision for additional funds for *all* mothers. The *Order of the General People's Committee No 51 of 2007 on Social Assistance*[52] provides a 'one-off' payment of LYD 100 to be paid to the mother for any child born, regardless of whether the mother is working or is a housewife. Thus, a working mother will receive benefits under the *Social Security Act*, the *Labour Code* or relevant industry statute (depending on their employment) as well as this general payment under the *Order on Social Assistance*.

Labour Code Act No 58 of 1970
Article 43 of the *Labour Code* supports the prevention of discrimination against mothers. It aims to protect working women covered by this Act by providing them with maternity leave. Under this provision when a female employee has completed six months' continuous service, she is entitled to 50 days of maternity leave with half pay, as long as she provides a medical certificate to her employer stating the possible date of her confinement. Under the *Labour Code*, it is unlawful to oblige a female employee to work for 30 days after the confinement.

---

45 *Social Security Act No 13 of 1980* (Libya).

46 *Labour Code Act No 58 of 1970* (Libya).

47 *Social Security Act No 13 of 1980* (Libya).

48 Ibid. art 25(C).

49 Muhmmd Suliman Al-Kutbi, *Nhw Fhm Afdl Lltshriy'at Al-Dmanyyh: Wifq Al-Ejr'at Al-Munfdh Lha* (Jami't Qarywnis, 2009) 166 [Trans: *Towards Better Understanding of Social Security Legislations* (Garyounis University 2009)].

50 *Social Security Act No 13 of 1980* (Libya) art 27(A) and (B).

51 Al-Kutbi, above n 49, 168–9.

52 *Order of the General People's Committee No 51 of 2007 on Social Assistance* (Libya).

Working women covered by the *Labour Code* are also entitled to extend their leave due to any illness which arises from their pregnancy or confinement, by submitting a medical certificate. However, the total absence must not exceed a period of three months. The provision of maternity leave under both these pieces of legislation encourages women to remain in the workplace both during pregnancy and following confinement.

Industry-Specific Legislation

Specific orders or policies may provide for employees in a particular industry or working for a specific employer. At least one sector has obtained greater protection for women expecting a child. The *Order of the General People's Committee No 154 of 2007 on Medical Workers in Hospitals and Training Centres*[53] applies to those under a contract of employment in that sector. It provides maternity leave for a total of three months on full salary. This leave may be taken before and/or after childbirth, but must include a period of at least six weeks (42 days) after childbirth.[54] This is in line with the provisions of the International Labour Organization (ILO) *Maternity Protection Convention (Revised) 1952* (C103)[55] designed to protect the health of both mother and child.

The *Workers' Affairs Policy for Libyan Iron and Steel Company of 2008*[56] provides, in Article 64, maternity leave for working women. The maternity leave is three months on full salary, including the period before and after childbirth, subject to the employee providing the employer with the relevant medical certificate/s.

Resignation Rights and Termination Payments

The *Labour Code*[57] also provides that any female employee covered by the Code is entitled to a leaving indemnity (provided under Article 47)[58] if she leaves her job either due to her marriage or due to the birth of her first child[59] – if, after giving notice to the employer, she leaves her employment within a period of six months following the date of her marriage or within the three months following her confinement. This payment is on condition of having completed three years of continuous service with the same employer. However, if she has worked for a shorter period, then she is entitled to half of the leaving indemnity.

Right to Return to Work

Article 45 of the *Labour Code* recognises the rights of working mothers to continue their work after maternity leave. It states: 'The employer shall not dismiss a worker or terminate [their] contract

---

53 *Order of the General People's Committee No 54 of 2007 on Medical Workers in Hospitals and Training Centres* (Libya).

54 Ibid. art 25.

55 *Maternity Protection Convention* (C103) art 3(3). Also affirmed by art 4(4) of the *Maternity Protection Convention* (C183).

56 *Workers' Affairs Policy for Libyan Iron and Steel Company 2008* (Libya).

57 *Labour Code Act No 58 of 1970* (Libya).

58 Ibid. art 47 provides a leaving indemnity (termination payment) payable upon expiry of 'a seasonal or similar of contract, a fixed-term contract, or where a contract for an unspecified period is terminated'. This amounts to 'half a month's pay for each year of service up to five years, and one month's pay for each year of service thereafter'.

59 Ibid. art 55.

during any of the leave periods referred to in the foregoing sections' (with such leave periods including maternity leave).[60]

Article 159 also maintains the right of working women to not have their contract terminated during maternity leave, and sanctions for breaches of this provision are in place. Article 159 of the *Labour Code* imposes penalties for any employer who infringes Article 45 by dismissing a worker or refusing to reinstate them when directed. It states:

> A person who infringes the provisions of part II, Chapter I, concerning individual contracts of employment or any order made there under shall be liable to a penalty of not less than [LYD] 20 and not more than [LYD] 50. In cases where the employer refuses to obey a judge's injunction to refrain from dismissing a worker or a court order to reinstate a worker, the penalty shall be [LYD] 50. In all cases the penalty shall be multiplied by the number of workers in respect of whom the offence is committed.

Also, Article 162 provides further monetary penalties, specifically for a manager who fails to protect working women in the workplace. It does not impose one overall monetary penalty, but rather a fine that is multiplied by the number of persons in respect of whom the infringement is committed. In the event that the same offence is recommitted within the following year by the same person, the individual may be sentenced to a term of imprisonment not exceeding one month or required to pay an additional fine. In some instances compensation may be payable in the event of an unjust termination of a work contract.[61]

Rights for Nursing Mothers

The health and safety of working women and their children is also supported by Article 97 of the *Labour Code*, which states:

> For eighteen months reckoned from the date of her confinement a female worker who is nursing her child shall be entitled to two daily nursing breaks of half-an-hour each, in addition to normal rest breaks. These two additional breaks shall be included in the hours of work and shall not entail any reduction in wages.

In this provision the Libyan Government fulfilled the requirements of Article 5(1) and (2) of the ILO *Convention on Maternity Protection* (C103)[62] which states:

> 1. If a woman is nursing her child she shall be entitled to interrupt her work for this purpose at a time or times to be prescribed by national laws or regulations.
>
> 2. Interruptions of work for the purpose of nursing are to be counted as working hours and remunerated accordingly in cases in which the matter is governed by or in accordance with laws and regulations; in cases in which the matter is governed by collective agreement, the position shall be as determined by the relevant agreement.

60 Ibid. arts 38–43.

61 Ibid. art 162. See also Guido Boni, 'The Labour Market in the SEM Countries: A Legal Perspective' (European University Institute, 2009) 25.

62 *Maternity Protection Convention* (C103) art 5(1) and (2).

The 2000 revision of the *Maternity Protection Convention* (C183), not yet ratified by Libya, contains similar provisions in Article 10(1) and (2), which guarantee the right of a woman to take 'one or more daily breaks or a daily reduction of hours of work to breastfeed her child', with such breaks or reduction in hours to be determined by national law and practice, and to 'be counted as working time and remunerated accordingly'.[63]

Both the Libyan Government in its regulations and those framing the ILO conventions recognise the benefit of breastfeeding for the mother and the child. Research has shown that breastfeeding has benefits for the health of both. Several studies have found that women who had breastfed their children had a reduced risk of developing breast cancer, especially women who had longer periods of breastfeeding.[64] Research has also shown that breastfeeding protects against childhood obesity as well as obesity in later life.[65] The prevalence of obesity was found to be higher among children who were never breastfed compared to those who were breastfed, regardless of other socioeconomic factors.[66] Breastfeeding was relatively important during the first stages of life.[67] The effect of breastfeeding on reducing the risk of childhood obesity was evident regardless of maternal diabetes or weight status,[68] especially if the breastfeeding was prolonged.[69]

Provision of Childcare: Workplace-Based Childcare

The most important determinant (other than the provision of maternity leave) of whether women are able to maintain their participation or enter the workforce is the availability of suitable childcare. Here again Libya has begun to address the issue. The *Labour Code* made initial provision that every employer who employed more than 50 female workers in the same workplace *may* be required to provide childcare for their children. Article 98 stated:

> The Minister of Labour and Social Affairs may by order require every employer who employs fifty or more female workers in the same workplace to provide [a] nursery for their children. The order shall prescribe the conditions and specifications for such nurseries, the rules to be observed therein and the expenses to be borne by the female workers using them.
>
> In all cases the employer must provide seats in places where female workers are employed to enable them to rest if the nature of work so permits.

---

63 *Maternity Protection Convention* (C183) art 10(1) and (2).

64 Tongzhang Zheng et al, 'Lactation Reduces Breast Cancer Risk in Shandong Province, China' (2000) 152(12) *American Journal of Epidemiology* 1129, 1132; see also Laufey Tryggvadóttir et al, 'Breastfeeding and Reduced Risk of Breast Cancer in an Icelandic Cohort Study' (2001) 154(1) *American Journal of Epidemiology* 37, 39.

65 S Arenz et al, 'Breast-feeding and Childhood Obesity: A Systematic Review' (2004) 28 *International Journal of Obesity* 1247, 1254.

66 André Michael Toschke et al, 'Overweight and Obesity in 6- to 14-year-old Czech Children in 1991: Protective Effect of Breast-Feeding' (2002) 141(6) *Journal of Pediatrics* 764, 766.

67 Christopher G Owen et al, 'Effect of Infant Feeding on the Risk of Obesity across the Life Course: A Quantitative Review of Published Evidence' (2005) 115(5) *American Academy of Pediatrics* 1367, 1375.

68 Elizabeth J Mayer-Davis et al, 'Breast-Feeding and Risk for Childhood Obesity: Does Maternal Diabetes or Obesity Status Matter?' (2006) 29(10) *Diabetes Care* 2231, 2233.

69 Laurence M Grummer-Strawn and Zuguo Mei, 'Does Breastfeeding Protect Against Pediatric Overweight? Analysis of Longitudinal Data from the Centers for Disease Control and Prevention Pediatric Nutrition Surveillance System' (2004) 113(2) *Pediatrics* 81, 85.

The *Order of the General People's Committee No 164 of 1988* appears to further support working mothers by providing for childcare services in the workplace. Article 12 states:

> A special area *may* be set aside, at the work place, for the care of the children of working women or for a children's day care service, whether these women are employed in the administrative, service or production sectors where a *sufficient* number of women are employed, such places may be equipped with the required installation to provide such care. The employer authority shall set up & equip such areas and care services in cooperation with the working women. The secretariats of the civil service, social security, education and scientific research shall provide the necessary advice and assistance.[70]

Therefore, this Order provides – at least theoretically – more opportunity for mothers to engage in paid work, as it repealed the minimum number of working mothers required to be employed in a workplace to trigger the possible provision of childcare.

However, the Order now merely states that employers 'may' provide care where a 'sufficient number of women' are employed.[71] The employer has the discretion to make a decision on whether provisions such as childcare facilities are made available for the working mothers depending on their number. The Order also highlights the broad consultative process involved in service provision where the employer chooses to provide such services. Such provision enables working mothers to continue working and know that they do not have to stress themselves with finding childcare services as they are arranged by the employer. Without childcare facilities, women may not be able to continue to exercise their right to work and their rights as mothers.[72]

The introduction of the *Child Protection Act No 5 of 1997*[73] and further amendment of the *Labour Code* has ensured further development of the provision of childcare in Libya. Again, this serves to encourage women's participation in the workforce.

The broader availability of quality childcare facilities has been ensured by the *Child Protection Act No 5 of 1997*. Article 11 of this Act states that where new areas are settled or new businesses are created, such areas must include children's playgrounds and gardens, and childcare services for working women. This appears to be a requirement, not an option for the employer.

Similarly, the *Amendment Act No 7 of 1997 of Some Provisions of Act No 58 of 1970 Concerning Labour*[74] confirms the right to childcare facilities in larger workplaces (50 or more female workers). This Act is an amendment of Article 98 of *Act No 58 of 1970* (mentioned above). It has been amended to read as follows:

> Childcare facilities for the children of female workers employed at factories and productive units where fifty or more [female] workers are employed. Conditions and regulations relating to such facilities will be fixed by a decision of General People's Committee in addition to the fees to be paid for such services.

---

70 *Order of the General People's Committee No 164 of 1988 on Employment of Arab Libyan Women* (Libya) art 12 (emphasis added).

71 Al-Adly, above n 5, 20.

72 Majidh Mahfwz, 'Musharkt Al-Mr'ah fi Al-Aml wa Al-Entaj' (Paper presented at the Aqtsadiat T'liym wa Aml Al-Mr'ah fi Aljmahyriyh Al-Ozma, Bnghazy (Libya) Jami't Qarywnis, 10–12 March 1997) 14 [Trans: 'Participation of Women in Work and Production' (Paper presented at Women's Education and Employment in Libya: An Economic Perspective, Benghazi)].

73 *Child Protection Act No 5 of 1997* (Libya).

74 *Amendment Act No 7 of 1997 of Some Provisions of Act No 58 of 1970* (Libya).

The *Order of the General People's Committee No 88 of 1998 on the Requirements for Childcare Facilities for Working Mothers*[75] further confirms the right to childcare facilities. This Order defines 'all workplaces' as including factories, industry, offices and workplaces for trade or non-profit with more than 50 women employed (Article 1) and includes both the public and private sectors. Article 2 states that such workplaces should be provided with a childcare facility for the children of female employees, while Article 3 outlines conditions to be followed, including hours of service (day long) and a requirement that the child be aged four months or over for enrolment.

Detailed requirements for working mothers are contained in Article 5, and include their having to provide the child's food and any items which are necessary for the child (such as clothes). It also provides funding guidelines that split the cost between employer and employee.

The division of the cost as outlined in the provisions must further act as encouragement for workplace participation by mothers. Article 5 is very supportive of the working mother, and encourages her to exercise both her right to work and to motherhood, as working mothers have to pay a relatively low contribution of LYD 10 towards the monthly funding of care, with the remainder paid by their employer.

The *Order of the General People's Committee No 10572 of 2009 on the Female Worker Who is Nursing her Child for Eighteen Months*[76] emphasises that it is necessary for employers to provide or establish a childcare facility in the workplace with the same requirements as in Articles 97 and 98 of the *Labour Code*.

Provision of Transport

Order No 164 of 1988[77] offers particular support in relation to the provision of transport for working women, specifically those employed in workplaces nominated under the two systems to which the Order refers (namely the *Labour Code* and the *Civil Service Act No 55 of 1976*).[78] *Order No 164* requires the employer to 'whenever possible provide [a] means of transport to and from work' (Article 13). This is supported in Article 7 of *Order No 258 of 1989 on the Rehabilitation and Training of Libyan Women*,[79] which states that the workplace has to help working women by providing transport to and from the workplace. The rationale behind these Orders is to support working women who wish to exercise their right to work but require transport to and from work in order to exercise that right.

These Orders also give working women the opportunity to choose to work in many sectors of the workplace, not just within a limited 'traditional' range, such as, for example, the education sector. Previously, Libyan women's ability to choose employment was limited by the lack of suitable available transport. Many chose to work in the education sector as school teachers for two main reasons: firstly, because of the sector's flexible hours (due to the availability of a position in either a morning or afternoon teaching period); and secondly, because the proximity of such employment often meant no transport was needed.[80] Access to transport has been an impediment

75 *Order of the General People's Committee No 88 of 1998 on the Requirements for Childcare Facility for Working Mothers* (Libya).

76 *Order of the General People's Committee No 10572 of 2009 on the Female Worker Who is Nursing Her Child for Eighteen Months* (Libya).

77 *Order of the General People's Committee No 164 of 1988 on Employment of Arab Libyan Women* (Libya).

78 *Civil Service Act No 55 of 1976* (Libya).

79 *Order of the General People's Committee No 258 of 1989 on the Rehabilitation and Training of Libyan Women* (Libya).

80 Mahfwz, above n 72, 14.

to the full participation of Libyan women in the workplace. One study, which was carried out in 1997, indicated that 18 per cent of Libyan working women could not exercise their right to work because of a lack of transport.[81] In Libyan society women who use taxis or those who drive to work are looked down upon, particularly in rural areas. The main barrier is neither a legal nor an Islamic obstacle, but instead a traditional cultural view, one that looks down on families that allow their women to drive or use any private transport (alone or with other females) to go to work or any other place. This traditional factor prevails over any right granted by the legal system. As Niaz Shah has observed:

> One cannot fairly address women's position in pre-Islamic Arabia without an understanding of the tribal system. For it was the tribal structure and customs that had the greatest impact on women's rights.[82]

Fortunately, this restrictive view is gradually changing for the better. However, it remains the case that a woman is expected to obtain permission to drive from her *wali*[83] – who can be either her husband if she is married, or her father or older brother if she is single – and particularly when the workplace is far from where she resides. The intention is to protect women and girls. This action is also part of the concept of *wilaya* (guardianship). *Wilaya* is the 'accountability and responsibility' that male family members have towards female family members. Examples of *wilaya* would be the responsibility fathers and brothers have towards their mothers and sisters, and husbands towards their wives. *Wilaya* does not mean 'superiority or control',[84] but rather the task of males to take care of female relatives. The concept of *wilaya* is derived from *Shar'iah*. *Shar'iah* is Islamic law and is a part of the Libyan legal system;[85] therefore, *wilaya* is a recognised legal term. The provision of safe transport permits male relatives to fulfil their responsibilities and women to exercise their rights to work.

Provision of Healthcare

The ideology that every Libyan has the right to be treated free of charge is embodied in Article 1 of the *Health Act No 106 of 1973*.[86] Under this Act all Libyans have the right to full health cover,

---

81 Jibryl Al-Jrwshi, Mnswr Al-Zghynyn and Raby'h Al-Zydani, 'Al-Mr'ah Byn Al-Kullyh wa Al-Byt Fi Msratah' (Paper presented at the Aqtsadiat T'liym wa Aml Al-Mr'ah Fi Aljmahyriyh Al-Ozma, Bnghazy (Libya) Jami't Qarywnis, 10–12 March 1997) 11 [Trans: 'Women Between College and Home in Mesrta' (Paper presented at Women's Education and Employment in Libya: An Economic Perspective, Benghazi)].

82 Niaz A Shah, *Women, the Koran and International Human Rights Law: The Experience of Pakistan* (Martinus Nijhoff, 2006) 29.

83 Which, according to Abdullahi A An-Na'im, is 'a benefactor, companion, protector, governor, the legal guardian of a minor, woman or incapacitated person': Abdullahi A An-Na'im, *Cultural Transformation and Human Rights in Africa* (Zed Books, 2002) 311. Needless to say, some women reject the concept of their being placed in the same category as a minor or person with disabilities and thus being considered as one 'fewer and lesser abilities', particularly reasoning powers; however, others would argue that the provision acknowledges the vulnerability of women and, rightly used, can be an asset rather than a liability. Cf. Human Rights Watch, *Perpetual Minors: Human Rights Abuses Stemming from Male Guardianship and Sex Segregation in Saudi Arabia* (Human Rights Watch, 2008). It has implications in regard to transport, medical treatment, and work participation.

84 Aziza Abdel-Halim, *Did You Know? Refuting Rigid Interpretations Concerning the Position of Women in Islam, and Muslims' Interactions with Non-Muslims* (Northmead, 2008) 45.

85 An-Na'im, *Islamic Family Law*, above n 3, 174.

86 *Health Act No 106 of 1973* (Libya).

and therefore are treated free of charge both inside and outside the country. However, this depends on the health report given by the Government Health Committee (see further below). Article 50 supports Article 1 of the Act as it affirms the equal right of all Libyan people to health services.[87] It states that all citizens have the right to health services in hospitals, medical centres or any other health institutions established by the country's government.

Another order specifically created for civil service employees is the *Order of Executive Rules of Civil Service Act 1978*.[88] Article 20 states that free health cover is a right for every employee and should be provided or available at or through any medical institution within Libya. Article 21 makes provision for free access to health services other than those within Libya. It states that an employee has the right to full health cover outside Libya from the Libyan Government, subject to one of the following provisos being met:

- if the employee's well-being or life is at risk and their situation or state cannot be treated within Libya;
- if the necessary assets needed to treat the employee (for example, equipment) are not available within Libya.

Article 22 outlines the procedure needed to be followed in order to allow an employee to be treated outside Libya with full health cover from the government. It states that a recommendation from the medical institution where the employee is currently being treated is needed and must state that the institution is incapable of treating this patient. As well as this, the employee must receive approval from the Health Committee. If approval is received, it is then the Health Committee's responsibility to nominate the appropriate country where the employee can be treated. Article 23 states that the Health Minister makes the final decision on the treatment of an employee outside Libya.

Article 24 of this Order defines the term 'health cover' and what is actually covered for members of the Civil Service. According to this Article, aspects such as travel expenses, funding in regard to the treatment of the illness (for example, medicine, surgery), hospital accommodation expenses and so on are all included in the health cover.

In addition to the above, another relevant regulation for women and children is the *Order of the General People's Committee No 214 of 2002 Regarding the Health and Social Security Needs of Public and Private Hospitals of Child Care and Gynaecology*. Article 10 of this Order states that the health service's target is to meet all the necessary health requirements and needs of patients – specifically women and children.[89]

Concluding Comments

Overall, women in Libyan society have significant opportunities in employment, but they still face substantial difficulty in taking advantage of the opportunities available. Lack of necessary revision of the legislation – as well as a lack of enforcement of existing legislative provisions for childcare, transport, health care and so forth – undermines their effectiveness. Indeed, as the United Nations Development Programme (UNDP) Programme on Governance in the Arab Region (POGAR) has noted: while '[m]en and women are guaranteed equality under the law …

87 Ibid. art 50.

88 *Order of Executive Rules of the Civil Service Act 1978* (Libya).

89 *Order of the General People's Committee No 214 of 2002 Regarding the Health and Social Security Needs of Public and Private Hospitals of Child Care and Gynaecology* (Libya) art 10.

lack of enforcement has led to continued social inequality'.[90] The generational shift that has been observed to be underway in relation to women's participation would be accelerated – and greater participation by older women encouraged – if the existing legislative provisions were adequately enforced.

In terms of the formal law, there is no discrimination against working women in Libyan society. In practice, however, the involvement of working mothers in the workplace is still limited in almost every area of work, especially in the political system and public affairs. The main barrier is the difficulty of managing family and work responsibilities. This difficulty is exacerbated by: the relative brevity and inconsistency of maternity leave set out in legislation;[91] a lack of part-time occupations; the unavailability of flexible working hours; and the absence of childcare facilities in the workplace. Although most of these issues have – at least in part – been addressed by positive changes in Libyan law, these improvements have not been translated from theory into practice.

Discrepancies between Libyan Domestic Law and International Human Rights Law

When here referring to 'gaps', it should be noted that there are two distinct areas. The gap evident in theory is the difference between Libyan domestic law and international human rights law, whereas the gap evident in practice is the gap between domestic law and its practice in Libya due to lack of enforcement. The 'gap in theory' between Libyan legislation and international human rights law will be discussed specifically in this section, and the gap between Libyan law and its practice will be explored in Chapter 5.

The lack of practical application of Libyan legislation results in a number of critical gaps between domestic law and international human rights law. Indicators of the existence of such gaps are:

- a lack of women in the political system;
- shortfalls in the provision of maternity leave;
- the issue of medical benefits (both in terms of medical insurance and health care) for working mothers;
- the lack of childcare facilities;
- insufficient family allowance for working mothers; and
- the absence of flexible working hours.

Shortfalls are complicated by inadequate sanctions for breaches of legislation designed to support women in the workplace, and also by cultural and attitudinal factors that affect women's participation.

---

90 For a general example, see section under sub-heading 'Conditions of Women' in Programme on Governance in the Arab Region (POGAR), *Libya in Brief* (4 November 2009) <http://gender.pogar.org/countries/theme.aspx?t=4&cid=10>.

91 Information on the provision and duration of maternity leave for many countries can be found at International Labour Organization, *Maternity Protection* (30 October 2009) <http://www.ilo.org/travaildatabase/servlet/maternityprotection>.

Lack of Women in the Political System

Women only participate in the political system of Libya to a limited extent. Women have had the right to vote since 1969; but, 40 years later, there are few female parliamentarians, and fewer in ministerial positions. In the period from 1977 to 1999, no more than five women were elected or selected to higher political office: the General People's Congress (GPC) Secretariats and the General People's Committee (GP Cttee).[92] In the period 1999–2006, there were no more than three female ministers in the GPC, compared to 129 males.[93] Moreover, only three women (as opposed to 129 men) were selected for the GP Cttee in the period 1969–2006.[94] Estimates of participation in the GPC range from approximately 4 per cent (from the International Service for Human Rights)[95] to 8 per cent (from the Inter-Parliamentary Union). In 2007, women held 4.7 per cent of the seats of Libya's National Parliament.[96] According to the latter, overall just 36 (or 7.69 per cent) of the members of the GPC in 2009 were women.[97]

There are correspondingly very few women in senior political positions, or in public affairs, compared to their numbers in other fields.[98] This is despite the greater numbers of women taking advantage of secondary and tertiary education in more recent decades.[99] It may reflect perhaps a certain reluctance to place women in positions perceived to be of political power, and particularly a reluctance to place women in positions where they may exercise, or where they

---

92 Four were elected to the Secretariats of the General People's Congress (GPC), Libya's legislative body (all in the area of Women's Affairs), and one elected/selected to the General People's Committee (GP Cttee): Obeidi, *Political Culture in Libya*, above n 6, 175.

93 One woman as the Minister for Social Affairs, the other for Women's Affairs: Amal Obeidi, 'Bawadir Al-Eslah Al-Siyasi wa Athruh Ala Siyasat Tmkyn Al-Mr'ah fi libya: Dirash Estkshafih' (Paper presented at the Al-Siyasat Al-Ammh, Bnghazy (Libya), 12–14 June 2007) 361 [Trans: 'Political Reform in Libya and its Impact on Women: A Discovering Study' (Paper presented at the conference Public Policies, Benghazi)].

94 For education, culture and media: Amal Obeidi, 'Political Elites in Libya Since 1969' in Dirk Vandewalle (ed), *Libya Since 1969: Qadhafi's Revolution Revisited* (Palgrave Macmillan, 2008) 105, 121.

95 International Service for Human Rights (ISHR), 'Committee on the Elimination of All Forms of Discrimination against Women, 43rd sess, Libyan Arab Jamahiriya, 2nd–5th' (Treaty Body Monitor, ISHR, 29 January 2009) 4.

96 United Nations Economic and Social Commission for Western Asia (UN-ESCWA), *The Millennium Development Goals in the Arab Region 2007: A Youth Lens*, UN Doc E/ESCWA/EAD/2007/3 (UN-ESCWA, 2007) 46.

97 As at 30 September 2009, Libya ranked 114th in the 136 rankings of 187 countries on the proportion of women parliamentarians (using figures for the lower house of bicameral parliaments or for the single chamber of parliament of a unicameral system based on figures supplied to the Inter-Parliamentary Union (IPU), *Women in National Parliaments* (11 November 2009) <http://www.ipu.org/wmn-e/classif.htm>. It is worth noting that just one country reportedly had a greater proportion of female than male parliamentarians (Rwanda); just seven countries had between 40 and 49.9% (among them Sweden, South Africa and Cuba); 16 between 30% and 39.9% (including Angola, New Zealand, Nepal, Germany, Belarus); 41 between 20% and 29.9% (including Switzerland, Peru, Australia, Pakistan, United Arab Emirates, Canada, China); 70 between 10% and 19.9% (including the UK, Bangladesh, Indonesia, the USA, Syria, Japan, India); 28 between 5% and 9.9% (including Turkey, Ukraine, Libya, Sri Lanka); and 22 <5% (including Lebanon, Egypt, Papua New Guinea (with 9 at 0%, among them Saudi Arabia, Belize and the Solomon Islands). The figures do not add up to 187, but 185 countries as some appear to have supplied no figures.

98 Murad Al-Ra'wbi, *Huqwq Almr'ah Al-Arbiayh* (Al-Mrkiz Al-Qwmy Lldirasat Al-Qanwnyh wa Buhwth Huqwq Al-Ensan, 2000) 17 [Trans: *The Rights of Arabic Women* (National Centre for Studies)].

99 According to the most recent Libyan CEDAW report, women comprise 70% of all graduates: ISHR, Committee on CEDAW 43rd sess, above n 95, 4.

may be perceived to be exercising, authority over men – or it may simply be that women choose not to pursue careers in such areas.[100]

The poor rate of female participation in the GPC shows the significant gap between Libyan domestic laws and their objects and the practice of these laws.

Many Libyan laws provide for freedom and equality for all citizens, particularly in relation to the nation's political life. For instance, Article 2 of the *Promotion of Freedom Act No 20 of 1991* states that:

> Every citizen has the right to exercise authority, to self-determination at Peoples Congresses [PCs]; citizens may not be deprived of membership or nomination to secretariats if they fulfil the required conditions.[101]

However, the reality is, and as figures for women selected for the secretariats of People's Congresses clearly demonstrate, in practice not all citizens enjoy equality in this area. While participation by women has risen, their further successful nomination as representatives to the national GPC and to senior positions in legislative bodies and the parliamentary executive is sorely lacking.

Women have the 'right to exercise authority' under the Act; however, they are not given the opportunity – except on rare occasions and usually in fields related to women. Again, the higher the level of responsibility, the lower is the participation by women. The discrepancy also highlights the gap between Libyan domestic law and objects of international human rights law relating to full participation in political processes and positions.

The gap between the expectations generated by international law and the reality of domestic practice can also be found in many other areas, particularly where Libya ratifies conventions but never puts them into practice to their full extent. One such convention is the *Convention on the Elimination of All Forms of Discrimination against Women* (CEDAW) (see Chapter 2). Article 7 there states that it must 'eliminate discrimination against women in the political and public life of the country and, in particular, shall ensure to women, on equal terms with men' a number of rights – namely, the right to vote in elections and referenda and to be candidates for 'all publicly elected bodies'[102] and the right:

> (b) To participate in the formulation of Government policy and the implementation thereof and to hold public office and perform all public functions at all levels of government.
>
> (c) To participate in non-governmental organizations and associations concerned with the public and political life of the country.[103]

---

100 One author, Fatma Ghandour, refers to a study that found that 85% of women described 'significant advancement within their profession as either impossible or difficult'. Women themselves also may have difficulty seeing themselves as competent workers: another study found 77% thought women 'inherently weak, necessitating men to take charge and make decisions on their behalf'. See Fatma Ghandour, *Women's Status in Libya: Breaking the Cultural Shackles* (11 November 2009) <http://www.alarabonline.org/english/print.asp?fname=2008/07/07–17/zfeaturez/971.htm>.

101 *Promotion of Freedoms Act No 20 of 1991* (Libya) art 2.

102 *CEDAW* art 7(a).

103 Ibid. art 7(b), (c).

While women are eligible to vote and do so, it is at a lower rate than men.[104] Their participation is theoretically possible at all levels of political life, but they are not eligible for election 'on equal terms with men' in practice. All citizens are eligible to attend Basic People's Congresses, but usually the majority of those attending are male. Some women are reluctant to attend as they feel they will not be able to achieve their goals.

The arrangements for the new National Congress are quite complex and comprise 120 seats for individuals and 80 for parties, with no quota for women, though this was discussed during deliberations. However, the Election Commission did decide that for seats reserved for parties to contest, 'the names on the lists submitted by them had to alternate between men and women'. As a result, there are 625 women candidates, 540 of whom are being presented by the 130 political parties on the ballot list, and 85 women among the 2,500 candidates contesting the 120 seats reserved for individuals.[105]

In addition, there is a further gap between Libyan domestic law and international human rights law. Article 8 of CEDAW clearly states that:

> States Parties shall take all appropriate measures to ensure to women, on equal terms with men and without any discrimination, the opportunity to represent their Governments at the international level and to participate in the work of international organizations.[106]

If this Article of CEDAW is used to measure the practices in Libya, it will be found that the number of women working at the international level, even in relatively recent years, is quite low. For the period 1998–2002, for example, in relation to the position of the ambassador there were 52 men and two women, and in relation to consular level positions only 20 women, while consular secretaries comprised 78 men but just four women, and consular officers 16 men and nine women. However, when the lower-placed role of officer assistant is considered, some 24 men occupied the position compared to 36 women.[107] The number of women employees in this occupation is greater than the number of men because it is neither a professional nor high-status position; rather, it is just a matter of typing or maintaining correspondence and does not involve decision making.[108]

Similarly, the task of being a government representative to international bodies is mostly given to men, with this opportunity hardly ever given to women. For instance, there were just nine women participants in the sessions of the General Assembly of the United Nations from 1992 to 1997 of cycle of sessions 47 to 52,[109] while in 1998–2002 women participants totalled 58 as opposed to 275 men.[110] Although one could argue that this shows a degree of progress in terms of

---

104 Om Al-Ez Al-Farisi, *Al-Mr'ah wa Al-Musharkh Al-Siyasyyh fi Libya (1977–2005)* (Mrkiz Al-Hdarh Al-Arabiyh, 2008) 230 [Trans: *The Woman and Political Participation in Libya* (The Arabic Civilisation Centre)].

105 Al-Ageli, above n 23. Only the election results will indicate whether change permitted by such an arrangements actually secures greater female representation.

106 *CEDAW* art 8.

107 Al-Farisi, above n 104, 230.

108 Ibid. 231.

109 CEDAW Committee, *Consideration of Libya's Second Periodic Report*, UN Doc CEDAW/C/LBY/2 (15 March 1999), above ch 1 n 58, 21. This document contains a statistical report on male and female attendance at the Basic People's Congresses during the two ordinary sessions of 1995 and 1996, and on the participation of Libyan women in leadership positions.

110 Al-Farisi, above n 104, 231.

female participation, it also reveals the distance still to be travelled to achieve anything like equal representation at this level.

This inadequate participation continues despite the Libyan Government's ratification of CEDAW. One of the main purposes of this convention is to balance the position of men and women where they are to 'represent their Governments at the international level and to participate in the work of international organisations' without any discrimination.[111]

Lack of participation in upper management and at similar levels in governmental and parliamentary bodies reflects to some extent a belief that women are not capable of managing organisations.[112] Despite the growing number of highly educated women – women comprise 70 per cent of all graduates[113] – most top-level positions are offered to men.[114] Many believe that men have more efficient problem-solving skills than women, and this makes males more 'successful managers'.[115] The disproportionate level of males occupying higher-status positions and more generally in the workforce indicates that there is a gap between international human rights law and the practice of domestic law. In Libyan society, working women cannot gain equal employment opportunities in the workplace, particularly at higher levels in governmental or parliamentary bodies or at international representative level.

The CEDAW Committee, in its most recent concluding observations on the Libyan Government's second periodic report, noted that it remained 'concerned that women continue to be underrepresented in political and public life, particularly in decision-making bodies, including the executive branch of Government, and the diplomatic and public service'.[116]

Women's employment continues to be concentrated in lower-status positions and in the areas of health and education (see below). Employment may be regarded as 'shameful' by family members and discouraged not only by male relatives, whose approval may be sought before obtaining employment, but also by other women within the family.[117] Attitudinal change is therefore an important precursor for change in workplace participation by women, both in terms of general workplace participation rate and in distribution across levels of responsibility or authority.[118]

Unequal Treatment for Working Women under the Statutes: Maternity Leave

There are a number of important discrepancies and indeed gaps in Libyan domestic law in respect to maternity leave, and also in relation to international provisions for such leave. Relevant matters include the conditions under which such leave is provided, including length of service and/or social security insurance contributions, and even the type of employment (which may determine which Act and its relevant maternity leave provisions applies to a particular employee). Other

---

111 *CEDAW* art 8.

112 Al-Farisi, above n 104, 228.

113 ISHR, Committee on CEDAW 43rd sess, above n 95.

114 Shannon Klie, 'Family Responsibilities, Finances Prevent Women from Getting MBA' (2006) 19(13) *Canadian HR Reporter* 3, 5.

115 Dana Bible and Kathy L Hill, 'Discrimination: Women in Business' (2007) 11(1) *Journal of Organizational Culture, Communication and Conflict* 65, 66.

116 CEDAW Committee, *Concluding Observations – Libya*, UN Doc CEDAW C/LBY/CO/5 (6 February 2009), above ch1 n 58, 7 [29].

117 Sameena Nazir and Leigh Tomppert, *Women's Rights in the Middle East and North Africa: Citizenship and Justice* (Freedom House, 2005) 174.

118 CEDAW Committee, *Consideration of Libya's Combined 2nd–5th Reports*, UN Doc CEDAW/C/LBY/5 (4 December 2008), above ch 1 n 58, 5.

inconsistencies and gaps exist in relation to the duration of maternity leave, to whether maternity leave is paid or unpaid and, if paid, at what level.[119]

Conditions for access to maternity leave

Two Acts are the main sources of maternity protection for Libyan women: the *Social Security Act No 13 of 1980* (*Social Security Act*) and the *Labour Code Act No 58 of 1970* (*Labour Code*). The former deals primarily with the period of maternity leave. The latter Act deals with salary benefits.

The *Social Security Act* provides maternity leave subject only to the provision of a medical certificate for the confinement. Paid maternity leave under this Act is, however, subject to four months' social security insurance contributions,[120] while the *Labour Code* provides for paid maternity leave under certain conditions, including the completion of six months' continuous service, and is also subject to the provision of a medical certificate giving the 'presumed date of confinement'.[121]

Such a condition creates a discrepancy between Libyan domestic law and the standards contained in ILO conventions, because the *Maternity Protection Convention* provides maternity leave for working women without it being subject to *any* conditions, other than the production of a medical certificate,[122] in order to promote equality of all working women in the workforce and to prevent discrimination against them. The ILO Committee of Experts on the Application of Conventions and Recommendations (CEACR) has stated that as Libya's *Labour Code* makes maternity leave conditional upon six months' consecutive months of service with an employer – a requirement not authorised by the Convention – the Committee hoped that the requirement would be eliminated 'in the near future' when section 43 of the *Labour Code* is amended.[123]

Duration of maternity leave

A discrepancy exists regarding the period of maternity leave accorded to women employees under the *Labour Code* and the *Social Security Act*. Their provisions are also not entirely compliant with applicable international conventions.

If any woman applies for leave under the *Labour Code*, she is entitled to 50 days of maternity leave following confinement. Yet under the *Social Security Act* working women are eligible for special maternity leave before and after childbirth. This includes a compulsory 28-day post-confinement leave with provision for up to a maximum of three months' maternity leave – including leave taken both prior to and after confinement (Article 25(c)).

Working women thus qualify for the particular length of leave depending on which Act applies to their employment. The CEACR points out 'the incompatibility' between *Act No 13 of 1980 on Social Security* and the *Labour Code Act of 1970*.[124] This discrepancy between the provisions

119 This volume does not address in detail the situation for non-Libyan workers employed in Libya. These workers are covered by the terms of their employment contracts. Given the large number of non-Libyan employees in Libya, this is worthy of further study and consideration of the establishment of at least minimum provisions applicable under domestic law.

120 Under the Implementing Regulations for the *Social Security Act No 13 of 1980* (Libya) art 25.

121 *Labour Code Act No 58 of 1970* (Libya) art 43. For more information, see Al-Kutbi, above n 49, 168.

122 *Maternity Protection Convention* (C103) art 3(1) states that: 'A woman to whom this Convention applies shall, on the production of a medical certificate stating the presumed date of her confinement, be entitled to a period of maternity leave'.

123 CEACR, *Individual Observation* (2000) ILOLEX Doc No 062000LBY103, above ch 3 n 70, 2 [3].

124 CEACR, *Individual Observation* (2008) ILOLEX Doc No 062008LBY103, above ch 3 n 200, 2 [2].

of the two Acts introduces a level of inconsistency in how the same needs of women who work in different capacities are addressed, effectively creating two 'classes' of working women in the one society.

Neither the *Social Security Act* nor the *Labour Code* fully complies with the provisions of the ILO *Maternity Protection Convention* in terms of length of leave. The Convention[125] provides six weeks (42 days) compulsory leave (Article 3(3)) compared to the *Labour Code*'s 30 days compulsory maternity leave and the *Social Security Act*'s 42 days. Under the *Social Security Act*, leave may include both prenatal and postnatal leave (at the woman's discretion), but generally most mothers choose to take the leave after childbirth. However, if a woman chooses to utilise some of the maternity leave before childbirth, this shortens the period of leave after childbirth.[126] The CEACR pointed out that Libya's provisions for maternity leave contravened the Convention:

> [Article] 43 of the Labour Code provides for the granting of pre-and post-natal maternity leave of a total of 50 days whereas, in accordance with Article 3, paragraphs 2 and 3, of the Convention, the period of maternity leave shall be at least 12 weeks and shall include a period of six weeks' compulsory leave after confinement.[127]

Also, Article 43 of the *Labour Code* fails to provide prenatal leave as required under Article 3(4) of the *Maternity Protection Convention.*[128] The CEACR once again points out that:

> Prenatal leave must in all cases be extended until the actual date of confinement, and that the period of compulsory leave to be taken after confinement shall not be reduced on that account.[129]

Nor do either of the Libyan statutes discussed contemplate the need for longer periods of maternity leave that may be necessary for women who have twins or more complicated deliveries. Drafts have been completed that contemplate extensions for multiple births. In the revision, leave of 90 days is extended to 100 days in the event of a multiple birth under the draft 2001 Labour Code, and from 14 weeks to 16 weeks in the 2004 draft. These changes were proposed in draft form for some years and appeared to have been dropped from the agenda.[130] New legislation was, however, finally enacted in 2010 and is theoretically in force, but then it has lain idle – mere 'paper law' that has yet to be enforced.[131]

---

125 *Maternity Protection Convention* (C103) art 3(3).

126 A more recent version of the Convention (2000) contains provision for an even longer period of maternity leave, for 14 weeks: art 4(1). This has not been ratified by Libya.

127 CEACR, *Individual Direct Request* (1990), ILOLEX Doc No 091990LBY103, above ch 3 n 185, 1.

128 *Maternity Protection Convention 1952* (C103) art 3(4) states that: 'The leave before the presumed date of confinement shall be extended by any period elapsing between the presumed date of confinement and the actual date of confinement and the period of compulsory leave to be taken after confinement shall not be reduced on that account'.

129 CEACR, *Individual Observation* (2006) ILOLEX Doc No 062006LBY103, above ch 3 n 199, 2 [4].

130 Ibid. 1 [4].

131 In Libya, major Acts such as this one are required to have Executive Rules which further explain the conditions and grey areas of the Act. Without these Executive Rules the Act shall not be enforced. This Act's Executive Rules have not yet been issued. The Revolution of 17 February 2011 has also played a major role in this lack of enforcement. Therefore, previous legislation is still in force until the enforcement of this Act. This legislation will be discussed (specifically those Articles relating to the working mother) in Chapter 6, under 'Recommendations to the Libyan Government'.

Other changes the ILO wants to see adopted involve: the removal of the qualifying period for maternity leave; the adoption of a provision that maternity leave may be taken when necessary prenatally (or due to medical necessity or an error in the estimated confinement date) without shortening the postnatal leave; and the organisation of cash benefits payable under the *Social Security Act* 'in a manner consistent with the Convention'. The ILO CEACR, in its 2007 report, again expressed the hope that such changes would be adopted 'very shortly'.[132]

Adoption leave

These Acts dealing with maternity leave[133] do not provide for adoption leave,[134] but only for children born to the working mother. This militates against best possible childcare practice for a child that has been 'fostered' (in Arabic, *Kafalah*)[135] as it discriminates between a woman who (perhaps unable to bear children) takes an infant born to another woman into her care and a situation where a woman cares for a child she herself has borne. This indicates a clear gap between the needs of working women and their children (both own born and fostered) and the provisions made by Libyan legislation. While adoption leave is not currently the subject of an international convention, it is an area of law that Libya – and other countries – should address.[136]

Paternity leave

Mention should be made that there is no provision of paternity leave. However, paternity leave and parental leave (non-gender discriminatory) is an increasing concern in international forums, including the ILO and, as is shown by their legislation, in some countries.[137] Such leave offers women the possibility of greater support during pregnancy and following childbirth. Further international demands on Libya in this area are to be expected, and also in regard to 'reconciling professional and family responsibilities and promoting equal opportunities and treatment between men and women'.[138]

---

132 CEACR, *Individual Observation* (2008) ILOLEX Doc No 062008LBY103, above ch 3 n 200, 3.

133 For instance, *Labour Code Act No 58 of 1970* (Libya) and *Social Security Act No 13 of 1980* (Libya).

134 In Libya, 'adoption', as western countries understand it, does not exist. Under *Shar'iah* law (based on the *Holy Qur'ān* 33:4–6), a child may be fostered (*Kafalah*). This is an accepted form of alternative care: *Convention on the Rights of the Child* (CRC) art 20. For more details, see Ali Omar Ali Mesrati, *The Best Interests of the Child: International Child Law as Interpreted in the Libyan High Court Jurisdiction* (PhD Thesis, University of Wollongong, 2009) 28.

135 Such a child retains parents even if s/he is physically separated from them by distance or death. For example, if the sister of a working woman died (a widow) and the working woman and her husband are prepared to take on the care of their relative, that child is not considered 'adopted' but 'fostered'. The child remains the child of the woman's sister and her deceased husband. The child does not lose his or her name or heritage.

136 Australia is one of the countries that offer adoption leave. See NSWTF, *Adoption Leave*, above ch 3 n 175.

137 *Council Directive 2010/18/EU of 8 March 2010 on Implementing the Revised Framework Agreement on Parental Leave Concluded by BUSINESSEUROPE, UEAPME, CEEP and ETUC and Repealing Directive 96/34/EC* [2010] OJ L 68/13 Preamble [3]; see also UNICE et al, 'Framework of Actions on Gender Equality First Follow-Up Report' (UNICE, UEAPME, CEEP, ETUC, 2006) 21.

138 *BUSINESSEUROPE, UEAPME, CEEP, ETUC Framework Agreement on Parental Leave* (Revised) 18 June 2009, Preamble.

Level and source of maternity benefit payable

Here again there is a discrepancy between the provisions of the *Labour Code* and the *Social Security Act*, and the provisions of at least one international convention. The *Labour Code* prescribes half pay and the *Social Security Act* full pay for their respective terms of maternity leave (the former 50 days, the latter up to three months), resulting in a variation in the salary benefits of the two groups of working women. Again, this effectively creates an inconsistency between two groups of working women living in the same society.

Three issues are raised in regard to the discrepancies between Libyan law and the international conventions, and the internal inconsistencies within Libyan law. First, they contravene Article 11(1) of CEDAW, which states that: 'States Parties shall take *all appropriate measures* to eliminate discrimination against women in the field of employment'.[139] In this regard, legislators need to be aware of the definition of discrimination provided by Article 1 of C111, which states:

> For the purpose of this Convention the term 'discrimination' includes:
>
> (a) any distinction, exclusion or preference made on the basis of race, colour, sex, religion, political opinion, national extraction or social origin, which has the effect of nullifying or *impairing equality of opportunity or treatment in employment or occupation*;
>
> (b) any other distinction, exclusion or preference which has the effect of nullifying or impairing equality of opportunity or treatment in employment or occupation as may be determined by the Member concerned after consultation with representative employers' and workers' organisations, where such exist, and other appropriate bodies.[140]

The Convention does recognise, however, that '[a]ny distinction, exclusion or preference in respect of a particular job based on the inherent requirements thereof shall not be deemed to be discrimination'.[141] A strict examination and delineation is needed of what comprises 'inherent requirements' that preclude a working mother's participation. Otherwise, this phrase may be abused as a 'catch-all' for roles that a woman or mother could reasonably be expected to perform. This includes executive roles which are not beyond the ability of well-educated women who are mothers. The use of such a phrase may allow the adoption of an approach that varies from employer to employer. The variation in the policies regarding maternity leave across industry and between employers or under two separate Acts with different requirements could not be permitted by an appeal to this provision. Therefore, a lack of uniform approach to benefits payable to women in the course of their employment could be considered a type of discrimination, as would a failure to ensure recognition of their maternity in calculations of period of service or insisting on a conditional period prior to leave being applicable.

Second, Article 43 of the *Labour Code Act* and Article 25 of the *Social Security Act* dictate that the cash benefits for maternity leave are the responsibility of the employer, which conflicts with paragraphs 4 and 8 of Article 4 of C103. The CEACR confirmed that:

> the Convention, in Article 4, paragraphs 4 and 8, provides that maternity benefits shall be provided either by means of compulsory social insurance or by means of public funds, and that in no case

139 *CEDAW* art 11(1) (emphasis added).

140 *Discrimination (Employment and Occupation) Convention* (C111) art 1(a) and (b) (emphasis added).

141 Ibid. art 1(2).

> shall the employer be individually liable for the cost of such benefits due to women employed by him.[142]

C103 has reasons for this. It allows for the use of compulsory social insurance, so eliminating the costs to the employer and thus protecting working women from discrimination in terms of hiring policies and also during employment (where, once married, they may be vulnerable to their position being terminated). This also recognises that the processes and responsibilities involved with organising, monitoring and providing cash benefits can be financially demanding and an unwanted burden for the employer.[143]

Third, while the full-pay entitlement accorded under the *Social Security Act* is consistent with the level of payment prescribed by the ILO *Maternity Protection Convention*, the Committee states that '[Article] 25 of Social Security Act No. 13 of 1980 does not contain provisions on the subject'.[144] The half-pay entitlement under the *Labour Code* conflicts with Article 4(6) of C103, which states:

> Where cash benefits provided under compulsory social insurance are based on previous earnings, they shall be at a rate of *not less than two-thirds* of the women's previous earnings taken into account for the purpose of computing benefits.[145]

Nor are the cash benefits provided by the *Labour Code* 'at a level which ensures that a woman can maintain herself and her child in proper conditions of health and a suitable standard of living', as required by Article 4(2) of the ILO *Maternity Protection Convention*. Article 4(5) further supports a woman's entitlement to adequate income during maternity leave, notwithstanding her period of employment or other qualifications required for benefits. It states that:

> Women who fail to qualify for benefits provided as a matter of right shall be entitled, subject to the means test required for social assistance, to adequate benefits out of social assistance funds.[146]

In regard to cash benefits (as provided by paragraphs 1, 4 and 8 of Article 4 of the *Maternity Protection Convention*),[147] the CEACR has been drawing the Libyan Government's attention to 'the need to take all necessary steps [to bring the relevant Article] into conformity with the [foregoing] provisions of the Convention by organizing the provision of cash benefits in a manner consistent with the Convention'.[148]

Women working in hospitals or training centres under a contract of employment as well as those employed in the Libyan Iron and Steel Company, however, do receive three months' maternity leave with full salary, subject to no conditions other than the supply of an appropriate medical certificate. These generous provisions, which are in line with the ILO Convention, contrast with those accorded to other women in Libya. Working women in Libya deserve equal treatment under the law – they are working in the same society.

---

142 CEACR, *Individual Direct Request* (1990), ILOLEX Doc No 091990LBY103, above ch 3 n 185, 2 [1].

143 Al-Talawy, above ch 3 n 2, 376.

144 CEACR, *Individual Observation* (1998) ILOLEX Doc No 061998LBY103, above ch 3 n 47, 2 [2].

145 *Maternity Protection Convention* (C103) art 4(6) (emphasis added).

146 Ibid. art 4(5).

147 Ibid. art 4(1), (4), (8).

148 CEACR, *Individual Observation* (2001) ILOLEX Doc No 062001LBY111, above ch 3 n 57, 3.

Shortfalls in Healthcare for Pregnant Women and Working Mothers

The *Executive Rules of Health Act No 106 of 1973* states that it is the government's responsibility to ensure that medical treatment and health cover is the right of every Libyan citizen.[149] The *Health Insurance Act No 20 of 2010* provides that compulsory health insurance contributions be paid by employers unless the person is a widow or orphan or otherwise disadvantaged person (including a person with no income or a person with 'limited income'), in which instances the government will contribute the full health insurance payment.[150]

However, it is evident that what is enacted in law is not necessarily a reality. Legislation in this area is not enforced, which is the great downfall of Libya's health system and the health care of its citizens.[151] By the government overlooking these laws and its failure to enforce them, many citizens (including employees, among whom are pregnant women and mothers) are being robbed of their rights (see below).

There is also a significant gap between health care available in urban and rural areas in Libya. Within urban areas there are health facilities such as private hospitals, specialists and so on; however, in rural areas the health system is poor, there is a shortage of medical staff and specialists, and the medical institutions are poorly managed and monitored. This has been attributed to 'absence of central guidelines on correct [staff] ratios or control over appointment'.[152] Many rural areas lack the facilities needed to support women's health in regard to pregnancies, childbirth and so on.[153] This gap between rural and urban areas within Libya exacerbates another gap – that between international law and Libyan law in this particular matter.

Article 12(1) of CEDAW clearly states that: 'States Parties shall take all appropriate measures to eliminate discrimination against women in the field of health care'.[154] In addition, paragraphs 1 and 2 of Article 14 of CEDAW state that:

149 *Executive Rules of Health Act No 106 of 1973* (Libya) art 1.

150 *Health Insurance Act No 20 of 2010* (Libya) arts 1, 3.

151 Salih Muftah Al-Zwy, 'Dawr Al-Qanwn fi Tnfydh Al-Siyasat Al-Amm' (Paper presented at the Alsiyasat Al-'Ammh, Bnghazy (Libya), 12–14 June 2007) 84 [Trans: 'The Role of Law in Executing Public Policies' (Paper presented at Public Policies, Benghazi)].

152 Eastern Mediterranean Regional Health Systems Observatory (EMRHSO), *Health System Profile: Libya* (WHO, 2007) 53. According to this profile, falling standards have been said to be one of the costs of the strain of trying to rapidly increase the number of medical staff: at 12. Neither has the government paid sufficient attention to the provision of other medical workers. This contrasts with the claims made by the government in the 2010 Human Rights Council Working Group on the Universal Periodic Review (HRCWG), 9th sess, Geneva, 1–12 November 2010, National Report Submitted in Accordance with Paragraph 15(a) of the *Annex to Human Rights Council Resolution 5/1: Great Socialist People's Libyan Arab Jamahiriya* UNGA UN Doc A/HRC/WG.6/9/LBY/1 (24 August 2010) 13 (HRCWG, *Libyan National Report* (2010) UN Doc A/HRC/WG.6/9/LBY/1).

153 Fathi Muhmmd Al-B'jh, 'Malm Yntbih Elyh Tqwym Al-Tnafusyh Fi Al-Jmahyriyh: Nzrh Fi Al-Hkmaniyh wa Siyasat Al-Tmkyn' (Paper presented at the Al-Siyasat Al-Ammh, Bnghazy (Libya), 12–14 June 2007) 320 [Trans: 'What Has Not Been Considered by the Competitiveness Calendar in Libya: An Insight into Governance and Empowerment Politics' (Paper presented at Public Policies, Benghazi)]. For example, numbers range from 6.3 doctors per 100,000 in Jdbaya to 28.5 per 100,000 in Benghazi; and from 19.4 per 100,000 in Mizrata to 275.8 per 100,000 in Ghat: EMRHSO, *Health System Profile: Libya*, above n 152, 53.

154 *CEDAW* art 12(1).

> 1. States parties shall take into account the particular problems faced by rural women … and shall take all appropriate measures to ensure the application of the provisions of the present Convention to women in rural areas.
>
> 2. States Parties shall take appropriate measures to eliminate discrimination against women in rural areas … In particular, shall ensure to such women the right: …
>
> (b) To have access to adequate health care facilities, including information, counselling and service in family planning.[155]

It can be shown that Libyan laws do not provide sufficient medical benefits (health care) for women (among whom are working mothers), in contravention of Article 4(3) of the *Maternity Protection Convention,* which states that: 'Medical benefits shall include pre-natal, confinement and post-natal care by qualified midwives or medical practitioners as well as hospitalisation care where necessary'.[156] Besides this, Article 12(2) of CEDAW contends that:

> States Parties shall ensure to women appropriate services in connection with pregnancy, confinement, and the post-natal period, granting free services where necessary, as well as adequate nutrition during pregnancy and lactation.[157]

Libya has made great strides in health care (reflected in life expectancy statistics to rival many western nations).[158] However, according to the World Health Organization (WHO), Libya still lacks adequate health services (preventive, curative and rehabilitative) and nutritional resources that are essential for life-long health.[159] Particularly relevant is the failure to provide high-standard health services for Libyan women during pregnancy, childbirth and post-partum. Also particularly relevant is the shortage of nurses and midwives in Libya that are needed to ensure the health of expectant women, mothers and babies.[160]

There is a huge discrepancy between the law and its practice in this area. Paragraph 2 of Article 367 of the *Executive Rules of Health Act No 106 of 1973*[161] states that the minimum level of staffing for nurses in hospitals is one nurse per two beds. This staffing level, however, is not even available in private hospitals.[162] International and national statistical sources indicate that in Libya there are 13 doctors, 48 nurses and 34 beds for every 10,000 citizens.[163] While this is said to be about average for the region, this does not mean that it is acceptable or should continue at that level rather than improve.

---

155 Ibid. art 14(1) and (2).

156 *Maternity Protection Convention* (C103) art 4(3).

157 *CEDAW* art 12(2).

158 Life expectancy for males (m) is 70 years and for females (f) 75 years; see World Health Organization, *World Health Statistics* (WHO, 2009) 38. This compares favourably to earlier figures of 70 years (m) and 75 (f) in 2006 and 67 years (m) and 70 years (f) in 1990: obtained from a WHO database using the 'whosis' search <http://apps.who.int/whosis/data/Search.jsp> at 26 October 2009.

159 World Health Organization, 'Country Cooperation Strategy for WHO and the Libyan Arab Jamahiriya 2005–2009' (EM/ARD/009/E/R, Regional Office for the Eastern Mediterranean, WHO, 2006) 17.

160 Ibid. 19–20.

161 *Executive Rules of Health Act No 106 of 1973* (Libya).

162 Al-Zwy, above n 151, 86.

163 Al-B'jh, above n 153, 320.

In regard to Article 20 of the *Order of Executive Rules of Civil Service Act*, every employee has the right to health services free of charge, while Article 21 states that any employee has the right to free health cover in a foreign country if they cannot be treated inside the country as the necessary prerequisites for adequate treatment are unavailable (for example, highly sophisticated equipment or particularly specialised expertise). However, in reality the GP Cttee is incapable of enforcing this Order. In 2005 the GP Cttee and the GPC failed to include an amount for foreign health care in Libya's annual budget, excusing their inaction by saying they needed to further organise and analyse this matter. By failing to cooperate with the Executive Power and by taking this course of action, the GP Cttee and the GPC created conflict between their decision and the enforcement of the provisions of the *Order of Executive Rules of Civil Service Act 1973*. This course of action is unlawful, as laws are not to be neglected or ignored unless there is a new law which states that the particular legislation or section of legislation has been repealed or is superseded. Therefore, not only has the GP Cttee acted contrary to the law but it has also prevented Libyan citizens and employees from exercising their right to obtain foreign health care where necessary. This poor judgment not only prevents people exercising their rights but also results in many people's lives being put at risk (and even lost).[164]

Medical benefits as a right for all working women have also been partly addressed by Libyan law and practice. Article 4(4) of the *Maternity Protection Convention* indicates that:

> The cash and medical benefits shall be provided either by means of compulsory social insurance or by means of public funds; in either case they shall be provided as a matter of right to all women who comply with the prescribed conditions.[165]

A woman can attend a clinic provided by the government for her pregnancy (or in regard to any other matter of her health) if she chooses or cannot afford private treatment. Nevertheless, under-resourced clinics may charge for tests (for example, blood tests) or other treatments. Those choosing to see a private physician must pay from their own pocket. There is no cash benefit in relation to such consultations.

Although the attendance of 'skilled personnel' at birth has increased from 65.7 per cent in 1976 to almost 99 per cent, such personnel are not typically midwives.[166] Libyan hospitals may lack many necessary assets, especially midwifery staff. Midwives contribute substantially to the social, emotional and physical health of both the mother and child. Research has shown that having a midwife throughout pregnancy comforts and encourages pregnant women, and that miscarriage rates (before 24 weeks' gestation) are lower, as are the rates of medical interventions at the birth, while labour tends to be spontaneous, the duration of hospitalisation shorter and breastfeeding rates higher. For lower-risk pregnancies, midwife-led models of care have much to recommend them.[167]

Hospitalisation (for childbirth, for instance) is available at no charge to the patients at public hospitals, but service provision is not consistent across the country (being particularly low in rural areas); nor is the standard of care consistent.[168] In common with the experience in many other countries, services have suffered at underfunded hospitals. Limited funding limits training and

---

164 Al-Zwy, above n 151, 85.

165 *Maternity Protection Convention* (C103) art 4(4).

166 EMRHSO, *Health System Profile: Libya*, above n 152, 20, 62.

167 Marie Hatern et al, 'Midwife-led Versus Other Models of Care for Childbearing Women' (2008) 4 *Cochrane Database of Systematic Reviews* 1, 2.

168 Al-B'jh, above n 153, 320.

restricts services in this area. Private hospitals can offer superior care – but at a price not all women and their families can afford (and there is no medical insurance scheme available to reduce costs of such private care). All pharmaceuticals (at both private and public hospitals) are at the patient's expense.

In their 2009 Concluding Comments in response to Libya's second and combined third to fifth periodic report, the CEDAW Committee requested improved data for services related to pregnancy and the postnatal period for women in both rural and urban areas. The failure by Libya to provide disaggregated statistics has been the subject of repeated criticism, as the extent and equality of access by women in different areas to services cannot be determined without such figures.[169] Although on a nationwide basis Libya has a maternal mortality rate (MMR) of 'less than 100 per 100,000 live births in 2000', the lack of disaggregated data means that a differential mortality rate (rural:urban) cannot be ascertained. It should be noted that some Gulf Cooperation Council countries have an MMR of less than 10 per 100,000.[170] This must be the aim for Libya.

Shortfalls in the Provision of Childcare Facilities

A further gap between Libyan domestic law and international human rights law is the unavailability of childcare facilities in the workplace for working mothers. Libya has ratified some important international conventions that support the provision of such facilities; however, its legislative provisions appear inadequate to secure their provision on a routine basis in practice. Often it has been assumed that the broader family can meet such needs. This is increasingly not the case across the world, including in developing countries. As Addati and Cassirer observe:

> In many developing countries it is often assumed that almost all workers can solve care problems by appealing to traditional family solidarity and finding a relative who can help ... In reality, dramatic social changes mean that many women cannot rely on traditional family supports for help with their care responsibilities. Urbanization, internal and international migration have ruptured extended family support networks.[171]

The *Convention on the Rights of the Child* (CRC)[172] was ratified by the Libyan Government on 15 May 1993.[173] Although a supportive government policy is reflected in *Act No 58 of 1970* (Article 98)[174] and in *Order No 88 of 1998* (Article 1),[175] the obligation to provide a nursery for the children of female workers in the workplace only applies to workplaces with 50 women or more. This condition does not seem reasonable considering that very few workplaces have this number of

---

169 CEDAW Committee, *Concluding Observations – Libya*, UN Doc CEDAW C/LBY/CO/5 (6 February 2009), above ch 1 n 58, 8.

170 UN-ESCWA, UN Doc E/ESCWA/EAD/2007/3, above n 96, 56.

171 Addati and Cassirer, 'Equal Sharing of Responsibilities Between Women and Men, Including Care-Giving in the Context of HIV/AIDS' (EGM/ESOR/2008/BP.2, Division for the Advancement of Women Department of Economic and Social Affairs United Nations, 19 September 2008) 5.

172 *Convention on the Rights of the Child* (CRC) opened for signature 20 November 1989, 1577 UNTS 3 (entered into force 2 September 1990).

173 OHCHR, *Status of Ratifications of the Principal International Human Rights Treaties 2006*, above ch 1 n 64, 7.

174 *Labour Code Act No 58 of 1970* (Libya) art 98.

175 *Order of the General People's Committee No 88 of 1998 on the Requirements for Childcare Facility for Working Mothers* (Libya) art 1.

female employees; and, in reality, in Libyan society it is difficult to find 50 or more mothers working in the same workplace. As a result, few working mothers in Libya enjoy the benefit of this provision. The CEDAW Committee, in its concluding observations following Libya's 1994 report to CEDAW, agreed, noting that:

> [e]mployers with a workforce of over 50 women were required to provide child-care facilities; members said that in effect it prevented the opening of child-care facilities because only few enterprises had more than 50 working women.[176]

However, CEDAW refrained from giving any guidelines as to what members thought was an acceptable number to trigger childcare in the workplace.

The *Order of the General People's Committee No 164 of 1988 on the Employment of Arab Libyan Women*[177] attempted to provide a solution to this shortfall for women working in workplaces of less than 50 employees by stating that an employer with a 'sufficient' number of women in the workforce 'may' decide to provide childcare facilities.[178] While this theoretically opens the way for employers of fewer than 50 female employees to provide childcare, it also leaves it open to employers to decide whether or not to provide their women employees with childcare facilities. The problem with such an option is that different employers have different opinions and some could choose to provide it while others may not. This leads to discrimination in terms of service provision for working mothers in the same country who have the same need for childcare but are working in various locations and types of employment.[179] That its provision is restricted to Arab Libyan women introduces a further possible element of discrimination between working women in Libya.

Although Article 11 of the *Child Protection Act No 5 of 1997*[180] made it compulsory for local councils developing 'green-field sites' to provide childcare facilities for working women in those areas, unfortunately no similar provision was made for existing businesses or areas. So childcare availability is based not on need but on where the mother lives or works.

Act No 7 of 1997[181] on the amendment of some provisions of the *Labour Code* amended Article 98. Under this provision, childcare facilities are to be provided for 'children of female workers employed at factories and productive units where 50 or more workers are employed'. Conditions and regulations regarding such facilities (and including matters such as fees) were left to the GP Cttee.[182]

Problems remained despite the amendment – it simply restated what had been expressed previously in the first part of Article 98. In other words, it added nothing new nor deleted any part of paragraph 1. It can be clearly seen that the same idea or thought was repeated,[183] yet it

176 United Nations, GAOR 49th sess, Supp No 38 (CEDAW Committee, Report, 13th sess (17 January–4 February 1994) UN Doc A/49/38, (1994) (*Concluding Observations – Initial Report – Libya*) [164]. For the entire *Concluding Observations of the Committee on the Elimination of Discrimination against Women: Libyan Arab Jamahiriya (Initial Report)*, see [126]–[185] of UN Doc A/49/38.

177 *Order of the General People's Committee No 164 of 1988 on Employment of Arab Libyan Women* (Libya).

178 Ibid. art 12.

179 Al-Adly, above n 5, 20.

180 *Child Protection Act No 5 of 1997* (Libya) art 11.

181 *Amendment Act No 7 of 1997 of Some Provisions of Act No 58 of 1970* (Libya).

182 Ibid. art 1(2).

183 'Child care facilities for the children of female workers employed at factories and productive units where fifty or more workers are employed. Conditions and regulations relating to such facilities will be fixed

repealed paragraph 2, removing the requirement that employers provide 'seats in places where female workers are employed to enable them to rest if the nature of work so permits'.[184]

The requirement for a workplace to have a minimum of 50 female employees for such childcare provisions to come into effect necessarily limits its application to only the largest workplaces and afforded no assistance to female employees in smaller workplaces.

Again the need for the revision of childcare provisions is clear. Smaller workplaces may not be able to fund suitable workplace-based care. In such cases, community-based care centres could perhaps be jointly funded by employees, employers, communities and the broader community who benefit from an increase in workplace participation by women, which in turn reduces household poverty and increases national productivity and wealth. Such centres would be particularly suited for children who are past nursing. Adequate financial support for mothers in their homes to enable them to nurse their children to that age may also facilitate longer-term workplace retention of female employees.

Without childcare in the workplace (or immediately adjacent), nursing mothers are unable to feed their children, and both mother and child cannot enjoy the benefits that research has shown would be theirs if breastfeeding had been able to occur (for example, lower childhood obesity rates[185] and lower breast cancer rates).[186] Women are unable to exercise their rights guaranteed by the ILO *Maternity Protection Convention* unless a suitable childcare facility is accessible. Such centres need to be on-site or nearby, as otherwise the nursing break is insufficient to allow a mother access to her child.

The Order of the General People's Committee No 88 of 1998 on the Requirements of Child Care Facility for Arab Libyan Working Mothers[187] has some gaps in its provisions for childcare facilities in the workplace for working mothers. A condition imposed by Article 3 of this Order effectively prevents working mothers from exercising both rights – work and motherhood. Article 3 creates a significant gap in care provision between that provided by this Order and that provided by other domestic Acts in Libya. Under this Article children may not be enrolled in childcare until they have attained four months of age. Yet under *Act No 13 of 1980*, the working mother enjoys only three months' maternity leave.[188] Thus there is a one-month gap in terms of care provision between maternity leave and childcare availability for a working mother if she is fortunate enough to have such care provided at her workplace. Traditional reliance on informal care may not be adequate, and nor should it be relied upon. Childcare for the working mother's child should be her entitlement.

Also, under the *Labour Code Act* the working woman has maternity leave of 50 days,[189] and under this Act she cannot return to her job or send her child to the childcare facility until he or she attains four months of age (120 days). Thus an even longer 'gap' period between maternity leave and childcare provision exists in these circumstances, again preventing the working mother from enjoying both her rights – that of work and of motherhood.

---

by a decision of the General People's Committee in addition to the fees to be paid for such services': art 1.

184 *Labour Code Act No 58 of 1970* (Libya) art 98(2).

185 Mayer-Davis et al, above n 68, 2233.

186 Tryggvadóttir et al, above n 64, 39.

187 *Order of the General People's Committee No 88 of 1998 on the Requirements for Childcare Facility for Working Mothers* (Libya).

188 See *Social Security Act No 13 of 1980* (Libya) art 25.

189 See *Labour Code Act No 58 of 1970* (Libya) art 43.

Not only do the Acts and Orders regarding childcare provision mentioned above not apply uniformly across all workplaces, but they also only apply in very few sections of the labour force.[190] In practice, they too are not enforced.[191] So, substantial obstacles remain to working mothers who wish to exercise both rights, that of work and of motherhood.[192]

There is a clear gap between Libyan domestic law and international human rights law in relation to childcare provision. Article 11(2)(c) of CEDAW, for example, states that States parties are to take measures:

> To encourage the provision of the necessary supporting social services to enable parents to combine family obligations with work responsibilities and participation in public life, in particular through promoting the establishment and development of a network of child-care facilities.[193]

Also, Article 18(3) of the CRC affirmed that:

> States Parties shall take all appropriate measures to ensure that children of working parents have the right to benefit child-care services and facilities for which they are eligible.[194]

The gap between Libyan domestic law and international human rights law is obvious when the two are compared. CEDAW 'encourages' service provision and support for parents, while the CRC states the responsibility for member states to provide childcare more strongly, stating that 'States Parties shall take all appropriate measures to ensure that [working parents] have the right to benefit [from] child-care services ... for which they are eligible'.[195] Here childcare facilities are the *right* of working parents.

Such provisions exist in international law and increasingly across the globe because it has been found in developed countries that good-quality childcare can increase working women's participation in the workplace and promote equal opportunity in employment by helping women to return to work as soon as possible after the child is born. This not only improves the level of maternal employment but also reduces family poverty, enhances parenting skills and strengthens family and community unity.[196] Libya needs to follow the steps of countries whose experiences have been highly favourable in this field (for example, Sweden, France, New Zealand and the United Kingdom), enhancing the quality of childcare and, as a result, working women's lives by allowing them to exercise their rights without adverse effects on their families.[197]

The importance of childcare availability is evident in the literature. For instance, in an Australian study participation by married women in the workforce has been found to be significantly affected by the presence of young children in their family. Although the study admitted that this participation might be subject to other factors (such as a mother's choices), the association between women's participation in the workforce and the accessibility of affordable

---

190 Such as the one in Garyounis University (now the University of Benghazi), Libya.

191 Al-Ra'wbi, above n 98, 95.

192 Mahfwz, above n 72, 14.

193 *CEDAW* art 11(2)(C).

194 *Convention on the Rights of the Child* (CRC) art 18(3).

195 Ibid.

196 UNICEF, 'The Child Care Transition: A League Table of Early Childhood Education and Care in Economically Advanced Countries' (Innocenti Research Centre (UNICEF), 2008) 11.

197 Ibid. 10–11.

and high-quality childcare could not be excluded as a key factor.[198] It has also been observed that 'marital status, gender, and the presence of children did interact in significant ways to influence perceptions of discrimination'.[199]

As '[i]nternational law exists in treaties and sometimes [in] customary practice agreed between nations [but] ... broad terms, it is not enforceable in the same way national laws can be enforced'.[200] This gives Libya the opportunity to avoid completely and honestly fulfilling what is required of it under the international instruments to which it is party. Enforcement relies upon other bonds. As Ball observes, '[i]nternational law is binding, but the cords that bind nations to comply are, by and large, political and moral'.[201] And, it could be said, the effectiveness of such bonds in encouraging countries to comply with their obligations may vary significantly in strength according to the other parties' own commitments and understandings. Indeed they may share the viewpoint of the recalcitrant member.

Insufficient Family Allowance for Working Mothers

There is a significant lack of sufficient allowances for family, pregnancy and childbirth to help support Libyan working families financially. Although there are some family allowances provided under Libyan law, such allowances are extremely low. For instance, the *monthly* payment of LYD 4 for every wife and LYD 2 for each child, as provided under Article 24 of the *Social Security Act*, is extremely low[202] when it is taken into account that AUD 10[203] is the equivalent of LYD 11.3.[204] The minimum private sector wage is set at LYD 250 per month.[205] While the cost of fuel is a mere LYD 0.2 per litre, housing costs appear high, as does the cost of food;[206] and the Libyan family allowance, even in combination with the working wage, is a very inadequate amount for a parent or a husband who works and has responsibility for a family. The amounts paid are insufficient to meet their needs. Such a low rate of family payment, however, would certainly act as an incentive for women to return to work. The level of these allowances demonstrates a gap between Libyan domestic law and international human rights law. Article 27(2) and (3) of the CRC indicate that:

---

198 Lixin Cai, 'Work Choices of Married Women: Drivers of Change' (Productivity Commission, Canberra, 2010), 50.

199 Elizabeth Hirsh and Christopher J Lyons, 'Perceiving Discrimination on the Job: Legal Consciousness, Workplace Context, and the Construction of Race Discrimination' (2010) 44(2) *Law and Society Review* 269, 289.

200 Olivia Ball, 'Breastmilk is a Human Right' (2010) 18(3) *Breastfeeding Review* 9, 9.

201 Ibid.

202 The cost of powdered milk formula for a baby is about LYD 5 per week. (LYD is the accepted international abbreviation for the Libyan dinar.) Compared to Australian provisions 'Family Tax A and B' (formerly 'family allowance' or 'child endowment'), the amount is tiny.

203 AUD is the accepted abbreviation for the Australian dollar.

204 CoinMill.com, *The Currency Converter* (23 October 2009) <http://coinmill.com/AUD-LYD.html>.

205 Boni, above n 61, 24. See also Bertelsmann Stiftung, 'BTI 2010: Libya Country Report' (BTI 2010, Bertelsmann Stiftung and Center for Applied Policy Research (CAP), Munich University, 2009). Note: social pensions are from LYD 90 to LYD 130 for people without dependants; LYD 180 for two-member families; and LYD 220 for three-member families or above (2007): at 16.

206 Rent per month for a two-bedroom unit is LYD 350 per month, while a three-bedroom unit may cost LYD 550. Yet the private sector minimum is LYD 250 per month. In relation to food, meat may be LYD 12–15/kg: personal communications (October 2009).

> The parent(s) or others responsible for the child have the primary responsibility to secure, within their abilities and financial capacities, the conditions of living necessary for the child's development.
>
> States Parties, in accordance with national conditions and within their means, shall take appropriate measures to assist parents and others responsible for the child to implement this right and shall in case of need provide material assistance and support programmes, particularly with regard to nutrition, clothing and housing.[207]

Under the *Social Security Act*, a working mother is entitled to receive LYD 3 per month from the beginning of her fourth month of pregnancy.[208] This payment ceases once she has given birth (or suffered a miscarriage). The low level of support offered by this provision hardly encourages working women to become mothers while employed. Furthermore, another provision of this law states that working women are entitled to LYD 25 after giving birth (a 'one-off' maternity payment).[209] The low level of this payment gives women a choice of either being a mother or an employee – but not both. A working woman, if she becomes a mother, needs more support than this to raise the child, and for the care of the child during working hours. Add to that medical costs and transport costs to and from work, and women may feel that the costs and strain of continuing to work are too high and choose to leave the workforce.

The amounts paid are considered very low. They were set in 1980 when the Act was passed and have never been increased in the 30 years since. They have not kept pace with consumer price movements (which in the last seven years alone have varied from a minimum per annum increase of 1 per cent in 2003 to 10.4 per cent in 2009),[210] considerably eroding the value of maternity and child payments. They are not suitable for the current circumstances. Such deterioration leads to a gap in terms of adequacy of payment between Libyan provision under the law and what could be expected under international human rights laws ratified by Libya.[211]

In Kuwait, under *Act No 1 of 1990 to Increase the Family Allowance* the corresponding allowances are far more generous.[212] The monthly allowance per child is Kuwaiti dinar (KWD) 50.[213] This is equivalent to AUD 174.05 per month, compared to the figures for the Libyan monthly family allowance per child of LYD 2, or approximately AUD 2 per child per month (see above).[214]

Domestic legislation in Libya also fails to be amended regularly to counterbalance deterioration due to inflation or other causes, in contravention of international provisions. Article 11(3) of CEDAW states that:

---

207 *Convention on the Rights of the Child* (CRC) art 27(2) and (3).

208 *Social Security Act No 13 of 1980* (Libya) art 27(A).

209 Ibid. art 27(B).

210 Index Mundi, *Libyan Inflation Rate (Consumer Prices)* (23 May 2011) <http://www.indexmundi.com/libya/inflation_rate_(consumer_prices).html>. For a detailed breakdown, see Central Bank of Libya, 'Economic Bulletin for the Second Quarter of the Year 2009' (2009), Table 30 'Cost of Living Index' and 'Consumer Price Index' 2004–2009'. See also Al-Masraf Al-markzy Al-Lybya, *Al-Namw Baswal Al-Bonwk Al-TJarea Al-Lybya fy Al-Rba Al-Thany* (4 June 2011) <http://www.moheet.com/show_news.aspx?nid=301056&pg=3> [Trans: Central Bank of Libya, *Economic Bulletin for the Second Quarter of the Year 2009*].

211 E.g., *Convention on the Rights of the Child*, *CEDAW* and the *Maternity Protection Convention.*

212 *Act No 1 of 1990 to Increase the Family Allowance* (Kuwait).

213 Ibid. art 2.

214 Exchange Rates for Kuwaiti Dinar, *Convert Kuwaiti Dinar to Australian Dollar* (2 November 2011) <http://themoneyconverter.com/KWD/AUD.aspx>.

> Protective legislation relating to matters covered in this article[215] *shall* be reviewed periodically in the light of scientific and technological knowledge and shall be revised, repealed or extended as necessary.[216]

This Article needs to be incorporated in Libyan law to address the problems working women face, particularly in relation to childcare provision and maternity leave/social support provisions.[217] Increasing the amounts payable to a level that would clearly support women in their dual role as mother and employee would contribute to a woman's ability to fund maternity leave adequately, thus protecting her health and the health of her unborn child. Adequate family and maternity payments could be further protected by the introduction of indexation provisions to protect their value automatically (thus reducing the need to return for legislative amendments).

Women cannot enjoy both their right to work and motherhood if laws are not revised and made relevant to the times and conditions in the workplace that now exist. In order for laws to move forward and provide for equality for women in the workplace, especially working mothers, they need to be reviewed and amended. Libya has not fulfilled its commitment under CEDAW in relation to working women.

Some attempt has been made to increase payment, and indeed to ensure there is no discrimination between mothers in the workplace and mothers in the home. The new *Order of the General People's Committee No 51 of 2007 on Social Assistance* states that when a new child is born a sum of LYD 100 is available upon successful application.[218] This Order created assistance for any child born, regardless of whether the mother was employed outside the home or not.[219] Together with the other payments mentioned above (family allowance, maternity leave), the amount remains insufficient to meet the needs of the child. Also, they represent a gap between Libyan domestic law and international human rights law. According to Article 26(1) and (2) of the CRC:

> States Parties shall recognize for every child the right to benefit from social security, including social insurance, and shall take the necessary measures to achieve the full realization of this right in accordance with their national law.
>
> The benefits should, where appropriate, be granted, taking into account the resources and the circumstances of the child and persons having responsibility for the maintenance of the child, as well as any other consideration relevant to an application for benefits made by or on behalf of the child.[220]

Current Libyan legislation has no regard for the income of the parents or children involved. Thus, it is in contravention of the provisions of the international legislation. In addition, Article 27(1) of the CRC affirms that:

> States Parties recognize the right of every child to a standard of living *adequate* for the child's physical, mental, spiritual, moral and social development.[221]

---

215 *CEDAW* art 11(1) and (2), particularly 2(b) and (c).
216 Ibid. art 11(3) (emphasis added).
217 Al-Ra'wbi, above n 98, 64.
218 *Order of the General People's Committee No 51 of 2007 on Social Assistance* (Libya).
219 Ibid. art 2.
220 *CRC* art 26(1) and (2).
221 Ibid. art 27(1) (emphasis added).

Such a provision requires research into what is required in terms of income and income support to ensure an adequate standard of living for all children in Libya, and a determination on the part of the government to ensure that this can be met in terms of the *Labour Code* and *Social Security Act*. This necessarily includes the provision of funded maternity leave and adequate family allowances.

The Libyan Government has acknowledged that '[while] no one [in Libya] ... suffers from extreme poverty and hunger ... this is not to deny ... that limited-income families need State assistance to exist'.[222] Some 24 per cent of all Libyan households are considered to fall within this category,[223] and while some measures have been adopted in an attempt to increase their familial income, these measures remain inadequate.[224]

Increased workplace participation by women could be expected to raise the familial income and standard of living for such families in particular. Healthy wage levels for women have a positive effect on women's workforce participation and their availability for work, as has been documented in Australia.[225] Ensuring that their rights are protected as mothers and workers will assist that transition in Libya. This includes income supplementation to enable women to combine maternity and employment at crucial times in their lives without suffering significant falls in income. This could be expected to encourage their continued participation in the workforce rather than their withdrawing completely from it. The earlier mentioned provision of affordable workplace-based childcare will similarly assist their continued workforce participation and increase family income. Thus, support at crucial times could result in longer-term family income rises that remove a number of limited-income families from this category, decreasing the need for social support over the lifetime of the family members.

The Absence of Flexible Work Hours

The last gap concerns the absence of work hours' flexibility, which prevents working mothers' full participation in the workplace. Yet it has been shown around the world that if workplaces become more responsive to the needs of workers with families, there are benefits that accrue for both parties. These can include retention of skilled labour and decreased labour turnover for employers, and increased workplace participation over time by women, with resulting increased familial income and decreased reliance on social benefits. As Addati and Cassirer observe:

> Working time measures can help make the workplace more responsive to the needs of workers with family responsibilities, while also increasing productivity and expanding equal opportunity.[226]

Greater equality of opportunity in the workplace and greater degree of shared caring in the home are two desirable outcomes that can be facilitated by a family-friendly workplace. A shift in role perceptions could also be expected over time, one that would further enhance opportunities for women in the workplace and increase the willingness of male family members to take on greater caring responsibilities in the home, to the benefit of the entire society.

---

222 HRCWG, *Libyan National Report* (2010) UN Doc A/HRC/WG.6/9/LBY/1, above n 152 [68].

223 Ibid.

224 For instance, families recorded as of limited income have been allocated since 2006 a state (Economic and Social Development Fund) administered investment fund which, it is claimed, paid out an average of LYD 2,200 per family in 2007, rising to approximately LYD 3,400 in 2009: ibid.

225 Cai, above n 198, 50.

226 Addati and Cassirer, 'Equal Sharing of Responsibilities' UN doc EGM/ESOR/2008/BP.2, above n 171, 19.

Until comparatively recently, under the *Labour Code* the working week for both women and men in Libya was 48 hours, comprising a six-day week of eight hours per day, with the legal maximum of 66 hours per week.[227] The working week was reportedly reduced by the government in 2006 to 40 hours per week.[228] There is no reference to part-time or casual work in the *Labour Code*; nor does reference to the possibility appear in other Acts such as the *Civil Service Act No 55 of 1976* (which governs public sector employment),[229] or in Acts relating to private employment contracts (for teachers and nurses for example).

While *theoretically* part-time work (not casual) exists under the *Order of the General People's Committee No 164 in 1988 on Employment of Arab Libyan Women*,[230] in reality this is far from the experience of Libyan women. One of the biggest problems is that, practically speaking, there is no such thing as part-time work for both men and women in Libya (apart from some – very few – private employment contracts for seasonal work, for example in agriculture or in private sector employment, which often offers little security or may not offer benefits such as maternity leave).

There is very limited opportunity for part-time employment for educated women, other than a few limited positions in private employment – again without any of the protections afforded by law (for example, maternity leave, sickness benefits, termination payment). No part-time or casual employment opportunities exist in the public sector.

Essentially, part-time and casual work opportunities are not made available by employers, both public and private. Again this creates a barrier as it forces women to 'choose' between being a full-time employee or a mother.[231] This is obvious even in the most flexible occupation for Libyan working mothers – teaching in primary schools, which in Libya (unlike Australia) has the potential for flexibility offered by the two teaching periods (senior school in the morning or primary school in the afternoon). However, if a teaching mother works in the morning period and her young children study in the afternoon period, she will not be at home to take care of them before they leave after school. Any childcare provision is at the instigation of the teachers themselves and not provided by the employer. In many other occupations, however, there may be no possibility of offsetting children's schooling and mothers' working hours as the working day falls across all or part of the school day. This factor may be one of the reasons that have contributed to the experience of working women where they are deprived of the opportunity to exercise both their right to work and their right to motherhood simultaneously.

Despite the many international and national conventions, Acts and regulations, 'Women still participate in the labour force on an unequal footing'.[232] Even developed countries such as Australia are faced with this fact.[233] However, it is more evident in developing countries such as Libya.

---

227 *Labour Code Act No 58 of 1970* (Libya) art 69. See Boni, above n 61, 24.

228 Boni, above n 61, 24.

229 *Civil Service Act No 55 of 1976* (Libya).

230 *Order of the General People's Committee No 164 of 1988 on Employment of Arab Libyan Women* (Libya) arts 3–11.

231 Mufidh Al-Zaquzi, 'Al-Mr'ah wa Al-Aml wa Ta'dud Al-Awar wa Tadarubha' (Paper presented at the Aqtsadiat T'liym wa Aml Al-Mr'ah Fi Aljmahyriyh Al-Ozma, Bnghazy (Libya) Jami't Qarywnis, 10–12 March 1997) 8 [Trans: 'The Woman and Work: A Conflict of Multiple Roles' (Paper presented at Public Policies, Benghazi, published 12–14 June 2007)].

232 Sharan Burrow, 'An Unequal World' (2004) 27(3) *UNSW Law Journal* 884, 886.

233 Ibid.

Nevertheless, the overall participation of women in the workplace in Libya has risen from 4 per cent in 1964[234] to 14.5 per cent in 1995 to 32.2 per cent in 2004.[235] This indicates that women are increasingly able to utilise the qualifications that they have gained through their growing access to education. In regard to the latter, it is perhaps worth citing the dramatically increased literacy rate for women over 15 (rising from 53 per cent in 1990 to 73 per cent in 1995 and 81.3 per cent in 2004) while cutting illiteracy among female youth from 39 per cent in 1980 to less than 7 per cent in 2000.[236] Modern Libyan women, in fact, have a higher level of education than their male contemporaries.[237] In higher education the percentage of females to males has risen from 79.05 per cent in 1995 to 112.8 in 2006.[238] The challenge remains to ensure that this investment reaps the reward intended for society.

There remains a strong inverse relationship between having a job and having family responsibilities for women in Libya. A 1988 study found that the proportion of women working decreases significantly with marriage. At that date, only 27 per cent of working women were married, while 73 per cent of working women were unmarried.[239] As recently as 2000, of the North African countries Libya continued to have the largest economic activity gap, but the trend is towards a narrowing of that gap.[240] In subsequent years that figure could have been expected to have further improved somewhat, yet the proportion of working women still remains low compared to advanced nations; and, somewhat surprisingly (after so many years of socialist revolutionary activity), Libya (together with Algeria) remains at the lowest rate of economic activity by North African women.[241] This is a situation that persists across their working lifetimes.[242] Indeed, 'participation across lifetime' figures clearly indicate that when women reach the age of marriage and enter their years of childbearing, participation falls. Libyan women, after an initial flurry of activity, soon fall to the lowest rate of participation in North African countries.[243] This is not something a new and ambitious nation can sustain if it wishes to fulfil its potential. As the United Nations Economic Commission for Africa (UNECA) observed in its 2005 report commenting on the paradox that North Africa presents, despite rising female activity levels:

> [O]n the one hand, the region has the lowest rates of women in employment in the world … yet on the other hand, its rates for women's access to education are equivalent, if not superior, to those observed in other developing countries.[244]

---

234 Amal Obeidi, *Al-Mrah wa Al-Bhth Al-Almy fy Aljmalt Allybya: Drash Thlylyh Letjahat Alrsal Alalmyh fy Klyt Algtzad* (1990–2009) (15 November 2011) <www.finstonconsulting.com/…/Arabic%20 Paper%20by%20Amal%20Obeidi.pdf> [Trans: *Women and Scientific Research in Libyan Universities: Analysis of Trends in School* for Thesis in the Faculty of Economics, Garyounis University (1990–2009)].

235 EMRHSO, *Health System Profile: Libya*, above n 152, 14.

236 Ibid.

237 Ibid.

238 HRCWG, *Libyan National Report* (2010) UN Doc A/HRC/WG.6/9/LBY/1, above n 152 [69].

239 Zynb Muhmmd Al-Zahri, *Al-Mr'ah Al-Amilh Fi Al-Mujtama' Al-Arabi Al-Liby Al-Mu'asr* (Mnshwrat Jami't Qarywnis, 1988) 97 [Trans: *The Working Woman in Contemporary Libyan Society* (Garyounis University, 1988)].

240 United Nations Economic Commission for Africa (UNECA), *Economic and Social Conditions in North Africa Part III: The Economic Participation of Women in North Africa*, 20th mtg of the Intergovernmental Committee of Experts (Tangier, Morocco 13–15 April 2005) UN Doc ECA-NA/TNG/ICE/XX/3/III/Rev.1 (March 2005) 4 [3].

241 Ibid. 3 [1], 4 [2], 5 [4].

242 Ibid. 9 [7].

243 Ibid. 8 [6], 9 [7].

244 Ibid. 6 [21].

The authors of that report claimed that North African women 'do not face any legal barrier to their access to economic activity'. However, as has been clearly observed in this research, barriers to participation can be far more subtle and comprise contradictory legislation, failure to enforce legal rights, and often far more powerful, cultural expectations. Education has significantly increased, and contraceptive use among women has grown significantly (even in rural areas), indicating an increased desire to limit overall fertility or space children.[245] Yet participation at significant levels (30–40 per cent) has not extended far beyond the age of 29, but rather follows the traditional pattern of a rather steep decline, levelling off only during the period 45–50 years of age.[246] This has been recognised as an underutilisation of a valuable resource in terms of labour for the country as whole, and as a poor return on an investment in women's and girls' education:

> The investment in girls' education made by families and governments, and the fall in fertility rates, should have had a more rapid and more powerful impact on women's activity. This has not been the case. North Africa thus has an unexploited potential of human capital in its educated women, which leads to losses of economic growth, jobs and wellbeing for the families and society as a whole.[247]

Given the withdrawal of female labour from the workforce, it could be anticipated that married working women who are also mothers form a group that is even less well represented in the workforce. This could be by their own desire, the pressures of increased family responsibilities and the demands of parenthood – traditional expectations (their own, their spouses' and those of employers). Employment prospects could also be affected by employer concerns about the possibilities of future pregnancy,[248] the funding of periods of maternity leave, the possibility of family leave requests and so on, even if it is not legally permitted to take such matters into consideration:

> Even if women are as skilled, clever and talented as men, competitively placed employers will rationally prefer male to female workers if they expect that women, and not men, experience a productivity decline due to childbirth.[249]

As regards those in paid employment, Libyan women are highly represented in the services sector as opposed to industrial or agricultural sectors.[250] This includes education and nursing. Women's occupations are highly concentrated in certain sectors. The highest percentage of working women (35.5 per cent) comprises those who were primary and secondary school teachers.[251] The reasons

245 EMRHSO, *Health System Profile: Libya*, above n 152, 57.

246 UNECA, *Economic Participation of Women in North Africa*, UN Doc ECA-NA/TNG/ICE/XX/3/III/Rev.1 (March 2005), above n 240, 9.

247 Ibid. 6 [21].

248 Despite observations such as, 'Pregnancy is not an illness, many women work through most of their pregnancy and return to work after childbirth': Jane Paul, *Healthy Beginning: Guidance on Safe Maternity at Work* (International Labour Office, 2004), 9.

249 Addati and Cassirer, 'Equal Sharing of Responsibilities' UN doc EGM/ESOR/2008/BP.2, above n 171, 9.

250 UNECA, *Economic Participation of Women in North Africa*, UN Doc ECA-NA/TNG/ICE/XX/3/III/Rev.1 (March 2005), above n 240, 10 [9].

251 Zynb Muhmmd Al-Zahri and Salih Ali Al-Zyn, *Al-Mr'ah Al-Arabiyh Al-Libyyh Fi Eshriyn Aam 1969–1989* (Mnshwrat Jami't Qarywnis 1989) 43 [Trans: *The Libyan Women in 20 Years: 1969–1989* (Garyounis University)].

behind this career selection by a relatively large proportion of Libyan women are the three-month maternity leave provided by the occupation[252] and the flexibility of two teaching periods (morning and afternoon).[253] For these reasons 75 per cent of the total female college enrolment is in the education sector.[254] In regard to nursing opportunities, statistics have indicated that a large proportion of nursing graduates are not actively registered for work.[255] This again may represent the withdrawal of women from the workplace as familial responsibilities increase with marriage and children. As UNECA so succinctly puts it:

> Studies of women's activity unanimously agree that the major obstacle to women's work is their family responsibilities. They have far more difficulties than men in striking a balance between work and family responsibilities; they therefore make concessions in their work, being less mobile, doing fewer hours of work, taking on fewer responsibilities and progressing less far in their careers, leaving and returning to the labour market more frequently and even giving up work.[256]

In a country where part-time work is not an option, where childcare (where available) is inadequate, where appropriate transport for women is an enduring issue and where other matters remain undecided or unfavourable for women, withdrawal becomes the alternative.

This continues to be reflected in workplace participation rates. Participation appears to be increasing, but on a lower trajectory than some could have anticipated. The number of working women has increased, but they are still not fully participating in the workplace. A 1995 study conducted in Libya showed that the number of women in the workplace was 200,800 and the number of men 831,800. Although women in Libyan society have reached 49 per cent of the total active economic population (that is, they are aged between 15 and 65 years),[257] they represented just 19.4 per cent of those in the workplace, according to statistics of the Libyan Ministry of Population.[258] United Nations statistics revealed that by 2006 this proportion had increased, but only to 27.78 per cent of the labour

252 *Social Security Act No 13 of 1980* (Libya) art 25(C).

253 Abudl Hameed Sa'eed Hasn, 'Etijahat Al-Mr'ah Al-Libyyh Al-Amilh fi Al-Aml' (Paper presented at the Aqtsadiat T'liym wa Aml Al-Mr'ah fi Aljmahyriyh Al-Ozma, Bnghazy (Libya) Jami't Qarywnis, 10–12 March 1997) 21 [Trans: 'The Directions of the Working Women in Libya' (Paper presented at Women's Education and Employment in Libya: An Economic Perspective, Benghazi)].

254 Muhmmd Ramadan Bu Z'kwk and Muhmmd Kaybh, 'Al-T'liym wa Msahmat Al-Mr'ah Al-Lybyh fi Suwq Al-Aml' (Paper presented at the Aqtsadiat T'liym wa Aml Al-Mr'ah fi Aljmahyriyh Al-Ozma, Bnghazy (Libya) Jami't Qarywnis, 10–12 March 1997) 7 [Trans: 'Education and the Contribution of Libyan Women in the Labour Market' (Paper presented at Women's Education and Employment in Libya: An Economic Perspective, Benghazi)].

255 It has been estimated that approximately 30% of registered nurses are inactive: EMRHSO, *Health System Profile: Libya*, above n 152, 54.

256 UNECA, *Economic Participation of Women in North Africa*, UN Doc ECA-NA/TNG/ICE/XX/3/III/Rev.1 (March 2005), above n 240, 9 [26].

257 Abdullh Muhmmd Shamiyh, Shafiyh Salim Bu Shwiyqyr and Marym Muhmmd Awhydah, 'Waq' Al-Mr'ah Al-Amilh fi Madint Bnghazy: Dirast Halh' (1997) 8(1–2) *Mrkiz Al-Buhwth Al-Eqtisadyh* 164, 168 [Trans: 'The Working Woman in the City of Benghazi: A Case Study' *Research Centre for Economic Sciences*].

258 Al-Hy'h Al-Watniyh Llm'lumat wa Al-Twthyq, 'Al-Sukkan wa Al-Quwa Al-Amilh wa Al-Aujwr wa Al-Entajiyh fi Libya' (Amant Al-Tkhtit, 1989) 10 [Trans: 'Population, Labour, Wages and Productivity in Libya' (National Commission for Information and Documentation)].

force.[259] However, according to the World Bank, in 2008 female participation in the labour force actually decreased slightly, to 21.89 per cent.[260] Therefore, women are still playing a less than optimal role in the workplace, in terms not only of numbers but also the roles they play.

Current Libyan laws do not acknowledge the need for working women to balance work and motherhood. Their situation could be substantially improved if they were given access to part-time work. In recent studies it has been proven that part-time work enhances individual well-being, provides greater life satisfaction and gives individuals the luxury of managing their time more freely.[261] Further research has shown that part-time work offers many other benefits: for instance, the 'retention of skilled and valued employees, reduced absenteeism, higher productivity of part-time employees, easier recruitment and retention by adopting "family friendly" policies'.[262] Part-time work helps working mothers to balance work and motherhood. For instance, working mothers are able to spend more time caring for their children and family than is possible with full-time work. This allows increased family income without a mother being as anxious about her family and its care, thus providing for a happier and healthier family life for all concerned. Part-time work reduces the 'collision' between work and family, and therefore there are fewer 'sacrifices' to be made by the working mother.[263]

On a society-wide level, productivity is increased and equal opportunity expanded.[264] Working mothers with heavy family responsibilities seek more flexible working hours, and for them therefore permanent part-time work is a popular choice. Just as this is the case in Australia, the same could be predicted for women in Libya who also need a higher income to meet the financial aspects of those responsibilities and yet need the time to meet the physical and caring, emotional aspects of those responsibilities. Part-time work can give them the luxury of balancing their working and family responsibilities.[265] In conclusion, part-time work allows women to combine motherhood and work. However, reliable childcare to suit such employment is critical.[266]

This evidence shows that working women in Libya still cannot easily exercise both rights –the right to work and the right to motherhood – simultaneously. Even if the number of women increases in the judiciary,[267] such an increase will not necessarily improve the legal circumstances of women. Laws are generally made by the GPC and by branches of the executive empowered to do so (such as the General People's Committee, which issues Orders, and government ministers who issue Decrees); not by the judiciary, whose role it is to uphold and apply the laws.

However, greater participation by women in the courts system and more broadly in policy and administrative sectors, and roles that include aiding the formulation of legislation, may assist in

---

259 United Nations Development Programme, *Libya: Labor Force, Female (% of Total Labor Force)* (5 November 2008) <http://www.undp-pogar.org/countries/morestats.asp?cid=10&ind+188>.

260 Trading Economics, *Labor Force: Female (% of Total Labor Force) in Libya* (24 June 2011) <http://www.tradingeconomics.com/libya/labor-force-female-per cent-of-total-labor-force-wb-data.html>.

261 Christopher Higgins, Linda Duxbury and Karen Lea Johnson, 'Part-Time Work for Women: Does it Really Help Balance Work and Family?' (2000) 39(1) *Human Resource Management* 17, 29.

262 Association of Professional Engineers, Scientists and Managers, Australia (APESMA): Professional Women's Network, *Work and Family (Access to Part-Time Work)* (24 June 2011) <http://www.apesma.asn.au/women/work_and_family.asp>.

263 Higgins, Duxbury and Johnson, above n 261, 29.

264 Addati and Cassirer, 'Equal Sharing of Responsibilities' UN doc EGM/ESOR/2008/BP.2, above n 171, 19.

265 Burrow, above n 232, 887.

266 Charlene Canape, *The Part-Time Solution: The New Strategy for Managing Your Career while Managing Motherhood* (Random House, 1990) 167.

267 Obeidi, 'Political Reform in Libya and its Impact on Women', above n 93, 361.

altering perceptions that may – despite the great leaps forward made by Libya – still persist in the minds of many and influence the framing of legislation and its enforcement.

Particularly problematic is the gap between the theory expressed in existing employment laws and their practice. While many laws exist to protect and support working mothers in Libya, their enforcement is lacking.[268] This continues to be a major source of problems faced by Libyan working women, particularly expectant women and mothers. Chapter 5 will address this issue more closely.

Limits of Sanctions

While sanctions are imposed where there are breaches of Libyan laws relevant to working women's rights (such as the right to return to work), they are not sufficient to deter such breaches. If an employer dismisses an employee contrary to the rights guaranteed under the *Labour Code*, that employer is liable to be fined. However, the penalties contained in Articles 159 and 162 are very low – not less than LYD 20 (approximately AUD 20) and not more than LYD 50 (AUD 50).[269] A term of imprisonment is possible for employers guilty of repeated offences. Article 162 states that 'if the employer commits the same offence more than once within that year he *may be* sentenced to a term of imprisonment *not exceeding* one month' (emphasis added). So if the employer does commit the same offence within the *same* year there is a possibility of being imprisoned, but if so it will be for no more than a month; and if the employer commits the same offence but in the following year, they only receive a very low fine. Although there are penalties in place, it is arguable that, given the small fine payable and the possibility of a short (and not certain) imprisonment, these would not provide much of a deterrent for employers if they were to be inclined to carry out such actions.

Concluding Comments

Research by Luke McNamara revealed that there is a great variation in the legal nature and implications of human rights values in different countries, regardless of the claim of 'universality' of human rights as they are embodied in the various international human rights instruments.[270] This research explores the dimensions of this intersection of international human rights instruments and Libyan practice in regard to working mothers and as revealed in Libyan law and practice. As he rightly observes:

> [T]here is a qualitative difference in the extent to which, in practice, individuals and groups in different states enjoy the human rights in question, and/or are able to use human rights law as a vehicle to achieve particular social justice goals.[271]

It is not acceptable to expect individual women to manage their family and work responsibilities unaided. In fact around the globe, in terms of women in the workplace and in their families, women comprise 'nearly half of the world's workforce, women supply the main financial support for 30

268 Ibid. 363.

269 *Labour Code Act No 58 of 1970* (Libya); see above, subheading 'Right to Return to Work' re arts 159 and 162.

270 Luke McNamara, *Human Rights Controversies: The Impact of Legal Form* (Routledge-Cavendish, 2007) 4.

271 Ibid.

per cent of the world's homes, [and] by 2010 70 per cent of women will be employed during their childbearing years'.[272]

The government has a responsibility to ensure that the transition to combining these two responsibilities is successful and benefits both society as a whole and the individual families whose mothers are workplace participants. Current Libyan laws do not adequately acknowledge the reality that half of the potential workforce – women – have a dual role to play in society as successful mothers and as efficient workers in the building of their society.[273] This is exacerbated by the government's failure to enforce what provisions do exist to support women, and especially those women who are mothers, in the workforce. The government has a role in making it possible for working mothers to combine these competing roles. Part of the problem has stemmed from the slow-moving process of legislative change. Although change is fast-paced by some – particularly highly conservative – estimates, a growing section of Libyan society has come to believe it is not fast enough. The government has failed to revise and amend legislation in a timely manner to accommodate the increasing demands being made on women by the need to further develop and build Libyan society in a manner in which they can fully contribute as both mothers and workers. A lack of literature relating to legal studies of women's rights in the workplace compounds the problems as they remain essentially 'below the horizon' of the nation's policymakers.[274]

Individuals are not responsible for fixing the problems that have been created by the system. It should be the responsibility of government to review laws and provide more equal opportunities for women in the workplace, so that they can play an effective role in Libyan society.

From what has been revealed regarding Libyan domestic law in relation to working women, and from all that has been discussed and highlighted regarding the gap between international and national law, it is now time to discuss and explore the gap between the theory and practice of Libyan law. The following chapter will explore this gap by reporting on qualitative interviews conducted with working women in Libya.

272 Paul, above n 248, 6.

273 Fwzyih Muhmmd Abu Alsyd, 'Mu'wiqat Aml Al-Mr'ah wa Turuq Muwjhtaha' (Paper presented at the Aqtsadiat T'liym wa Aml Al-Mr'ah Fi Aljmahyriyh Al-Ozma, Bnghazy (Libya) Jami't Qarywnis, 10–12 March 1997) 6 [Trans: 'Women's Employment in Libya: Obstacles and Solutions' (Paper presented at Women's Education and Employment in Libya: An Economic Perspective, Benghazi)].

274 Saliha Sanqr, 'Ghyab Al-Bhth Al-'Elmy An Qadaya Al-Mr'ah' (Paper presented at the Al-Mr'ah Fi Al-Mujtm' Al-Arabi, Bnghazy (Libya) Jami't Qarywnis, 28–31 March 1989) 4 [Trans: 'The Absence of Scientific Research Concerning Women's Issues' (Paper presented at Women in Arab Society)].

Chapter 5
The Rights of Working Mothers in Libyan Law – In Practice

The previous chapter detailed the support for working mothers' rights in Libyan legislation, but also described the discrepancies between Libyan and international law. The aim of this chapter is to examine the extent to which those rights that exist in Libyan law and policy to protect the rights of working mothers are enjoyed *in practice*. In order to achieve this aim, interviews were conducted with working mothers from the most common fields of work in Libya in both the public and the private sectors. This method of data collection was one of the four steps to be taken (as outlined in Chapter 1) to find answers to the questions that underpin this volume. Empirical data of this sort is valuable because it enables an exploration of what is actually occurring 'on the ground'.

Interview Format

The interviews were semi-structured; that is, each interview was guided by a standard list of mostly open-ended questions which (unlike a standardised interview or questionnaire) gave respondents the opportunity to express their opinions.[1] It also gave them considerable freedom to focus and expand on issues of greatest importance to them. The format is designed to reveal 'existing knowledge in a way that can be expressed in the form of answers and so become accessible to interpretation',[2] with the qualitative data derived from interviews able to provide rich and in-depth understandings of the issues being investigated.[3] In qualitative research the interview is the main tool used to access the 'ultimate facts'.[4] It enables researchers to access an individual's own practices and knowledge, 'the rich and complex processes that comprise an individual's life experience'.[5]

Working mothers were interviewed to compare the extent to which the theory of their rights actually matched the practice of those rights within the circumstances of the multifaceted daily lives of work and motherhood as represented in the responses of those women interviewed. As Marshall and Rossman have noted:

> One cannot understand human actions without understanding the meaning that participants attribute to those actions – their thoughts, feelings, beliefs, values and assumptive worlds; the researcher therefore needs to understand the deeper perspectives captured through face to face interaction.[6]

1 Uwe Flick, *An Introduction to Qualitative Research* (Sage, 2nd ed, 2002) 74.
2 Ibid. 84.
3 Beverley Hancock, *An Introduction to Qualitative Research* (Trent Focus Group, 1998) 9; see also Terry Hutchinson, *Researching and Writing in Law* (Lawbook, 3rd ed, 2010) 107.
4 Robert E Stake, *The Art of Case Study Research* (Sage, 1995) 64.
5 Cassandra E Sharp, *Becoming a Lawyer: The Transformation of Student Identity Through Stories* (PhD Thesis, University of Wollongong, 2006) 73.
6 Catherine Marshall and Gretchen B Rossman, *Designing Qualitative Research* (Sage, 3rd ed, 1999) 57.

In the present context, data of this type is especially valuable because this study is the first of its kind in this field of law in Libya.

Depth and breadth of insights is also facilitated by the condition of anonymity on the basis of which the interviews were conducted. It freed women to describe reality as they experienced it.

Before conducting interviews, approval was obtained from the relevant ethics committee of the university under whose auspices the research was conducted,[7] and individual interviewees received an information sheet that described the project, detailed their rights and assured them of the confidentiality of the research and the anonymity of the participants. After they had read the participant information sheet, every interviewee who was contacted for this project decided to participate and signed the consent form.[8]

In order to ensure anonymity, respondents' names and individual workplaces have been replaced by a system which only broadly identifies the type of occupation by a group number – (G 1: teachers; G 2 doctors; G 3: workers within the court system (whether lawyers, prosecutors or judges); G 4: administrative sector – and by assigning a participant number to each woman within that group. For example, a respondent who is a member of the teaching profession has neither her name nor school disclosed, but is simply identified as G 1.7. Pinpoint references to a particular page of the interview transcript are represented by an additional number, such that page 14 of the English translation of the transcript of the interview with that same teacher would be referenced as G 1.7.14.

Who Was Interviewed and Why: Sample Selection

The interviewees were working women from the most common fields of work for women in Libya in both the public and private sectors. The interviewees numbered 40 and fell into four categories, each composed of 10 persons. Each category comprised a specific type of employment in Libya: namely, education, medicine, the court system (that is, lawyers, prosecutors and judges) and government administration. Single women and married women without children were excluded as they did not have children and this was a prerequisite for eligibility for the interviews as this research is about the experience of working mothers.

The interviews with the working mothers were generally conducted on an individual basis; however, a few (due to their time constraints) were conducted in a group situation. Most of the women were able to participate during their lunch-break at work.[9] They selected this time because after work the mother's full focus is on her house and children. I accepted their condition that the interviews be conducted at their workplace because it was a familiar surrounding for the interviewees and there would be no external interruptions. This, in effect, leads to a positive outcome for the interview by making it a comfortable procedure.[10]

These interviews were conducted with mothers who have been working for 3–34 years. This broad span facilitated access to a range of perspectives in terms of experience, as well as offering insights about changes over time.

---

7 The Human Research Ethics Committee approval number is HE09/317.

8 All forms used were approved by the relevant ethics committee. The consent form for the interviews and the participant information sheet are included as Appendix B and C.

9 Finding a suitable time to conduct interviews with the working mothers was the sole problem encountered and hinged on the limited time frame to collect the data and the degree of difficulty members of the various groups had in scheduling the interview session.

10 Barbara W. Sommer and Mary Kay Quinlan, *The Oral History Manual* (Rowman & Littlefield, 2nd ed, 2002) 61.

Educational Sector

The first group consisted of mothers working in the education sector as teachers of elementary, intermediate and secondary classes in both the private and public sectors. The study included six schools from different regions: four schools from the public sector and two from the private sector.

Interviews with this group were conducted because a study in Libya found that 35.5 per cent of Libyan working women belong to this group.[11] Libyan women have a substantial presence in the sector. In 2002–03, for example, women comprised 77 per cent of primary level teachers and almost 65 per cent at secondary level.[12]

The main reason for this choice of occupation is the flexible working hours that are available. These hours give women a choice between two teaching periods (either morning or afternoon), which allows them to arrange their households more easily than do the working hours of other occupations. Among other reasons is the three-month maternity leave provided. Another reason, generally speaking, is that a father or husband will strongly encourage his daughter/wife to follow this career as there is no real mixing with any males, rather just with other female teachers and staff. So a woman will easily get permission to obtain employment in this field. Also, in Libyan culture it is much more acceptable for a woman to work in the education sector. Hence up to 85 per cent of staff in this sector (administration as well as teaching) are female.[13]

Health Sector

The second group consisted of mothers working in the public and private health sectors as doctors. Some of these interviews were conducted with a group of women doctors working in the biggest public maternity hospital; some interviews were with women doctors working in a private maternity hospital; other interviews were with doctors working in the largest public hospitals that deal with accidents; and the rest were with women doctors working in four clinics located in different regions.

There has been an increase in the number of working mothers among doctors, and so this group of women was chosen to conduct interviews with. The high percentage of women graduates has also boosted the number of female medical staff available.[14] In Libyan culture and in Islam it is also

---

11 Zynb Muhmmd Al-Zahri and Salih Ali Al-Zyn, *Al-Mr'ah Al-Arabiyh Al-Libyyh Fi Eshriyn Aam 1969–1989* (Mnshwrat Jami't Qarywnis 1989) 43 [Trans: *The Libyan Women in 20 Years: 1969–1989* (Garyounis University)], 43.

12 'In 2002/03 there were 188,552 teachers at the basic education level (of whom 77% were women) and 47,268 teachers at the secondary level (of whom 64.7% were women)': United Nations Educational, Scientific and Cultural Organization (UNESCO), *World Data on Education: The Socialist People's Libyan Arab Jamahiriya* (27 October 2010) <http://www.ibe.unesco.org/Countries/WDE/2006/index.html>.

13 Al-Hy'h Al-Ammh Llm'lumat, 'Taqrir Al-Tnmiyh Al-Basharyh: Tmkiyn Al-Mr'ah Al-Libyh wa Qdaya Al-Nw' (Al-Hy'h Al-Watniyh Llm'lumat wa Al-Twthyq, 1999) 139 [Trans: General Information Authority, 'Human Development Report: Empowering Libyan's Woman and Gender Issues' (National Commission for Information and Documentation)].

14 For the academic year 1995/96, women comprised 44% of students in the School of Medicine, 65% in the School of Dentistry and 64% in the School of Pharmacology: CEDAW Committee, *Consideration of Libya's Second Periodic Report*, UN Doc CEDAW/C/LBY/2 (15 March 1999), above ch 1 n 58, 25. By 2006/07, women comprised the majority of students in faculties of higher education: CEDAW Committee, *Concluding Observations – Libya*, UN Doc CEDAW C/LBY/CO/5 (6 February 2009), above ch 1 n 58. 'The number of students in colleges of health, technology, medicine, law, and industry in 2006–2007 totalled 9133, including [sic] 2916 males and 6217 females'. Women and girls also outnumbered males at

more acceptable for a female to see a female doctor rather than a male doctor; this has contributed to the rise. (It is also perhaps worth noting that, in terms of women occupying positions requiring higher education, women outnumbered men in dentistry and pharmacology as early as the mid-1990s, and in these and other faculties the number of women continued to rise.)[15]

As most people are aware, however, being a doctor is one of the most difficult jobs, so the research was done to see whether the law helps and encourages the working mother to be able to balance her role as a mother and as a doctor, which is very demanding. Does she enjoy her legal rights as a doctor and as a mother? Or does the failure to accommodate her specific needs (as well as residual prejudice and resulting discrimination) result in the growing student numbers not being reflected in workplace participation levels?

Employees within the Legal System

The third group consisted of mothers working in the court system, in both public and private capacities. The public occupations were judges,[16] prosecutors[17] and defence lawyers.[18] The mothers who were interviewed were chosen from both the Northern Court and the Southern Court. Public employees in the legal system (in contrast to those in the private sector) fall under the *Judicial System Act No 6 of 2006*.[19] The private sector members of this group were lawyers.

This sector was chosen because in Libya the entry of women into the judicial sector as judges and prosecutors is a recent development. As this is the case, the research aimed to see whether the working mother is enjoying her legal rights in her career as well as her legal rights as a mother. Since the judge is the one that enforces the law, are the women in this sector able to enforce their rights? In addition to their experiences in the workplace, particularly in relation to maternity leave and other parenting related issues, these women will add a further dimension. This group, as legal practitioners, will be able to contribute a legal perspective, particularly in relation to the comprehensiveness and usefulness of Libyan maternity leave legislation – and as to whether the

specialised secondary schools (basic, social, economic, engineering, biological and legal sciences, and the Arabic and English languages), where they comprised 136,928 of the 242,271 students: CEDAW Committee, *Consideration of Libya's Combined 2nd–5th Reports*, UN Doc CEDAW/C/LBY/5 (4 December 2008), above ch 1 n 58, 27.

15 Majlis Mujamm 'Al-Fiqh Al-Islami Al-Dawly, 'Mudawat Al-Rajul Llmr'ah' (1994) 8(3) *Mujamm 'Al-Fiqh Al-Islami* 9, 9 [Trans: Council of International Islamic Jurisprudence Academy, 'Medical Treatment of Women by Men' (1994) 8(3) *Islamic Jurisprudence Academy 9*].

16 It was difficult to schedule interviews with judges with their limited time and various duties. Although they have specific days on which they work, and on these days they may attend court and, once court is in recess, meet with the other judges to discuss the case and then they make a collective decision and deliver a deliberation. Thus, a scheduled interview could (and would) be cancelled at the last minute as a judge's time in court would have taken longer than planned and family needs had then to be attended to.

17 Prosecutors found scheduling interviews the most difficult as they are available in the office all day, and being continually contacted by police about new crimes. Prosecutors then take time to decide whether to place suspected criminals on remand or release them on bail and so on. They also visit the jail cells several times and even go out to crime scenes regularly, all in order to complete an investigation. It is almost impossible for such employees to find free time.

18 Scheduling interviews was also difficult in relation to defence lawyers. They are frequently meeting with defendants, researching in the court library or attending sessions in court, so they too found it a struggle to find time to meet.

19 *Judicial System Act No 6 of 2006* (Libya).

phenomenon under study is the result of an absence of suitable laws or a problem primarily of implementation and enforcement.

Administrative Sector

The fourth and final group consisted of mothers occupying different administrative positions where they – in common with primary and secondary teachers and medical employees in the public sector (but not the private sector) – fall under the *Civil Service Act No 55 of 1976*[20] and its rules of application, as well as the *Social Security Act No 13 of 1980*.[21] Personal interviews were conducted with mothers occupying administrative positions in the Social Security Department, the Department of Administrative Monitoring, the National Library and Garyounis University (the 'mother university' in Libya),[22] as well as in an engineering consultancy, the banking sector and lastly a government-owned company.

The purpose of the involvement of this group was to see whether these mothers were able to exercise their legal rights despite the challenges they face with the lack of flexibility that is typical in the field of administration. Working hours usually extend from 7:00am to 3:00pm (for some, 4:00pm), and this poses difficulties for women with young children due to the children's hours of schooling. Another obvious challenge is the limited availability of part-time employment in this sector, which further reduces choice and adds stress.

The Transcription Process

Interviews were conducted in Arabic, as previously indicated, and audio recorded;[23] the resulting recordings were then transcribed. A translator was engaged to translate the transcript from Arabic to English. The author then reviewed the translation to ensure accuracy, for when translation is involved the task is doubly difficult, as a researcher has to ensure answers have been translated (in this case from Arabic to English) truthfully and without losing the original meaning. It is important that the nuances and the emotions (here contained in the Arabic text) are conveyed in the translation. Once this was completed, the transcript was further revised by eliminating any typographical errors and verified by comparing it to the original Arabic text, making sure that it was a reliable translation.

Coding the information was necessary to lead to the categorisation of concrete evidence within the text. This facilitates the extraction of relevant data and subsequent deductions or conclusions

---

20 *Civil Service Act No 55 of 1976* (Libya).

21 *Social Security Act No 13 of 1980* (Libya). Note *Social Security Act* art 31 covers only those people who are employed by the government and its authorities etc. This includes universities, government schools (not private schools), government health centres (not private ones). Also, it does not cover those in private employment (unless these persons make contributions under the *Social Security Act* in a type of self-insurance) and it does not apply to not privately employed persons who are not citizens of Libya (such as foreign labourers etc.).

22 Following the Revolution of 17 February 2011, Garyounis University reclaimed its original name: Benghazi University.

23 Using a tape recorder has many benefits. Firstly, it helps the interviewer engage and fully communicate with the interviewee. This in turn helps the interviewee both relax and feel more at ease. Secondly, it helps in the process of translation further on. Therefore, using a tape recorder is both convenient and practical. See Chris Barker, *Cultural Studies: Theory and Practice* (Sage, 2000) 30.

based on that evidence. Thus this has to be done very precisely. The data can also be more closely examined, which will lead to a clearer interpretation. Here the content of the individuals' statements become evident, rather than an assumed shared view/opinion.[24] Coding revealed the important issues that working mothers encounter in their struggle to combine or balance their rights at work as well as their rights of motherhood. In the research here referred to, a number of keywords were identified relating to the themes being investigated (for example, maternity leave, breastfeeding and so on).

Responses could be rapidly located and then categorised (for example, whether the mother was able to breastfeed at work or was unable to breastfeed at work). For maternity leave, key words included 'benefits' and 'period'. Some of the important questions that were asked of the working mothers were related to:

(i) the existence or otherwise of maternity leave (its length, benefits payable and so on);
(ii) the availability of prenatal and obstetric care
(iii) the availability of childcare facilities in the workplace;
(iv) the existence (or otherwise) of discrimination between them and their colleagues (including both male and women without children);
(v) whether the mother was able to exercise her right to the time allowed by law for breastfeeding;
(vi) the availability of transport;
(vii) their experiences as a working mother; and
(viii) their suggestions for improved enforcement of existing legislative provisions and also their suggestions for legislative change.[25]

The main themes that emerged from the interviews with working mothers were that:

(i) they experienced discrimination on the basis of gender generally, and specifically on the basis of motherhood;
(ii) childcare facilities were generally lacking or their provision was inadequate;
(iii) the provision of maternity leave (including payment of benefits and so on) varied according to employer and workplace;
(iv) provisions for breastfeeding also varied depending on the workplace, type of employment and the manager's views;
(v) the provision of maternity allowance and baby bonus also varied, despite Libyan women's legal entitlements;[26]
(vi) the provision of transport necessary for women to be able to work is generally poor; and
(vii) women generally found prenatal and obstetric care expensive and its provision not universal.

---

24 Kathy Charmaz, 'Qualitative Interviewing and Grounded Theory Analysis' in Jaber F Gubrium and James A Holstein (eds), *Handbook of Interview Research Context and Method* (Sage, 2001) 683–4.

25 See Appendix A for a copy of the interview questions as presented to the interviewees.

26 Provision of maternity allowance and baby bonus entitlements is almost universal. It applies to Libyan working mothers; however, non-citizens working under contract are excluded. Any benefits to be received are those specified in their contracts with their employers. Again, given the large number of non-Libyan employees in Libya, this is worthy of further study and the establishment of at least minimum provisions applicable or acceptable under domestic law. As such employees would be ineligible for government social security type payments, consideration could be given to such workers being provided with equivalent payments by private employers, or perhaps such minimums as might be established under legislation.

These areas will be explored in greater detail below. The interviews reveal the huge gap between theory and the practice with regard to the rights of working mothers in Libya. Reasons for this will be then suggested.

The Main Themes that Emerged from the Interviews

General Discrimination

As outlined in Chapter 4, employers in Libya are prohibited from discriminating against mothers in the workplace or against women in the workplace more generally.[27] The interviews revealed that, in practice, the situation diverged considerably from that supposedly guaranteed by law.

Many of the working mothers interviewed revealed that they had been discriminated against, even though Libyan law states that there should be no gender-based discrimination and that equality of men and women should be guaranteed in the workplace.[28] When asked if they faced discrimination in relation to their rights at work, the majority of respondents stated that they did face discrimination, both in general as a woman and more specifically as a mother (see below).

Gender Discrimination

Many respondents reported discrimination that they attributed to a general discrimination against women. Indeed, 30 of the 40 respondents (75 per cent of interviewees) stated that they encountered discrimination in the workplace. Such discrimination was reported as affecting their income, training and promotion. One working mother, a teacher, stated that:

> I didn't receive any encouragement or bonus. … in 2009, not one of my students failed in year 9 in the subject of Physics, even though I used to teach four classes which totalled 120 students. Even with this I never even received recognition in 2009, [yet] it was my right to receive level 11 in teaching and this is what is stated in the law.
>
> This is because the principal does not like me and he is biased against female teachers, especially one that demands her rights. I never used to surrender my rights and this used to upset him. The Libyan society is male dominated and so the woman can't do anything except to obey, even if she is an educated woman.
>
> I was denied … these bonuses because the condition for receiving [them] is a report … [from both] the director and the principal. So in 2009, my annual report from the director was excellent but from the principal, it was poor. This is the reason why I was [denied] … my bonus and receiving the bonus is very important in my profession.[29]

Women may feel pressured not to complain about their situation in the workplace even when they are fully entitled to do so.

---

27 See Chapter 4, under 'History of Legislation that Aims to Prevent Discrimination'.

28 For instance, see the *Charter of Women Rights and Obligations in Republic Society 1997* (Libya) art 12.

29 G 1.9.24–5.

> In 2008, the principal wrote a report that I was away for 2 days, so they deducted 25 dinars from my wages for a period of 6 months. When I knew about this, I was shocked and when I checked my record I realised that I was actually at school on the days that he said that I was away.
>
> When I complained to the principal [asking him] to fix this mistake, he told me that you have to accept this administration error because otherwise the school will be judged badly by the Ministry of Education for this error. So what can I do? I had to keep quiet and accept this decision because if I said anything then the principal will make my job more difficult. The right of the teacher is not recognised, so I'm thinking of resigning due to poor treatment.[30]

This respondent felt further discriminated against when she took sick leave for access to reproductive technology, a move that has had lasting effects on her career to date. She said:

> On another issue, I cannot conceive naturally. My second child was 7 years and I couldn't fall pregnant again without IVF. So when a specialist came to Libya in October 2009 and I underwent fertility treatment, one of the conditions was that I [would] need extreme medical attention for 2 weeks and I had a letter from the doctor about this issue.
>
> But even with this valid excuse, I was not allowed to stay in my job … their reason being that I was on sick leave and cannot be working. The decision came from the Ministry of Education. I appealed this decision before the court and up until now, I'm still waiting to get my job back, after being in this job for 25 years and giving all my time for education continuously with pleasing results for our students with success on a high scale. So I demand recognition for the teachers' honour.[31]

Some working mothers find that they are routinely expected to work unpaid overtime. There is no consideration of their domestic responsibilities.

> I work in an important specialised job and almost daily I even have to work when I get home. After completing meeting all the demands of my children and putting them to sleep, I open all my work files and I work for up to 3 hours daily without any pay. Imagine this and we are not given any encouragement or monetary bonus for our valued service. For your information, the head of the prosecutors always thanks and mentions the commitment of the working mother, compared to the men.[32]

Another of the working mothers also highlighted discrimination in terms of the lack of equality in her workplace between herself and her male colleagues regarding teaching roles, workloads and

---

30 G 1.9.25. Many more cases highlight the fact that if the situation were the same but a male employee was involved, then the treatment would have been handled differently, such as is testified to by G 1.5.14:

'With regards to discrimination in treatment within the workplace, yes there is a clear gap between the treatment of a female employee and male employee, in regards to supervision, examination or absenteeism with or without an excuse. My fellow male employees do not get questioned and pressured if they are late or if they are absent. Whereas, we, female employees are pressured and if for example I was absent due to a sick child at home and I provide all the necessary medical documents as proof I get questioned and I risk my job'.

31 G 1.9.26.

32 G 3.1.62.

access to further teacher training, even though the law states that there should be equality of rights and work conditions.

> With regards to discrimination, there is discrimination between males and females: … the male teachers are not responsible for exam supervision and marking. This is with regards to the school. With regards to teaching in general, there was a training course outside of the country, about teaching skills and about specialisation in special areas. We (female staff) didn't know anything about it except through the television. When we saw it on television, we realised that only men were allowed to participate.
>
> I have a female colleague who works in another school and the principal told her about the training on the same day, in the morning, even though she has been a science teacher for the past 20 years. She told him that she would like to participate in the training and asked for the details, such as where at and when. He then told her that the exam [had] already started. She asked him why he had not told her earlier and why he had just told her right then even though she is at the school every day. His answer was that this is how it is.[33]

This is representative of the discrimination that women generally face in the education workplace. It also clearly demonstrates the entrenched attitudes to women's access to further training on an equal footing to their male colleagues, despite women's increased penetration of the workplace and access to (and success in) tertiary education.

Evidence of general broad discrimination is also found in regard to employees in the courts/legal system (lawyers, prosecutors, judges). Every interviewee from this field stated that she had not been initially aware of English courses that had been offered to male colleagues but not to them. One of them stated that:

> With regards to discrimination, yes I do notice this. For example, there was an external English course, outside Libya and we didn't know about it [but] … 70 male members from the legal system were sent. Some were judges and others were members of the court system. This is discrimination, because the women were denied this opportunity, without justification.[34]

Another working mother in the courts confirmed this, saying:

> Regarding discrimination, yes I notice it. For example, they were sending men from the legal sector to Britain to learn English, but they didn't tell the women that are in the same sector about it. All the people that were sent to Britain were male.[35]

Discrimination is also perceived as being based on grounds other than gender.

> Also, the people who are working in the Southern courts, they did a computer course and each one of them got given a computer, but the people working in the Northern courts, received nothing. Even though we are under the same law, living in the same country, so I don't know what the issue is behind this discrimination.[36]

33 G 1.6.16–17.
34 G 3.3.66.
35 G 3.8.80.
36 G 3.8.80.

Women in the judiciary also feel discriminated against in ways that affect their income.

> There is another point. Each female lawyer has 3 cases per month and it is necessary for her to complete these cases. Personally, I face 2 problems. Firstly, the director, depending on his mood … on how happy he is with me, some months he will give me 2 cases and sometimes he will give me 3 cases. This affects my yearly allowance and any promotion because I didn't complete 3 cases in the month.[37]

Discrimination can affect further education and also hamper day-to-day working activities.

> Secondly, I need a reviewer to check my case. The reviewer is the one that helps me to finish my cases, which are placed in my hands. I am specialised in civil cases. There is a book, regarding civil law, that is very important and this book is kept in the courts storage. But the director doesn't want to give the book to the lawyers, [he lends it to male not female lawyers] even though it's available in the court library. However, the books that are available in the library are many and everyone works according to these books, but in my profession, I can't find any other book that suits me so I went and bought it from my own money, so that my work doesn't stop.[38]

Attitudes shown can also make a woman feel very vulnerable in the workplace.

> Another point is [that] one day I went to my director and asked if there was anything new? He told me, 'What do you want? We already provide you with a car and an office'.[39] So I said to him that I'm not asking about a car or about an office, but I'm asking about a course to update our knowledge in the law and also for [a] computer course. Until now, we don't know how to use a computer and we need to improve our knowledge in the law. So when the director told me that our cars are provided, [when] we all bought our cars with our private money and we don't even have any suitable desk to do our work on. We miss even a chair to sit down to have a rest, but despite all this, we love our work and usually 90% of the job is being done by working women.
>
> So when his answer was like this I became scared and so I kept quiet. If he gets angry towards me, it will mean that I will lose my job, with regards to his annual report to the head supervisor. By Allah, we have been discriminated against as women. We want to work in peace without rights. Unfortunately, we are the ones who defend those whose rights are denied. The another funny thing is, when you need a pencil or any other item of stationery to complete our job, the director will ask us to sign the invoice, and truly that is disrespectful.[40]

Another kind of discrimination that is faced by working mothers, and women generally, is that, even though a woman may demonstrate the highest quality in her work and works to the best of her ability, she will never be promoted to higher positions in the workplace although she has earned it. This was confirmed by most of the working mothers in all the different career paths that were investigated. This can be seen from the following (a working mother in the legal system):

---

37 G 3.8.80.

38 G 3.8.80.

39 In relation to the purchase of the car, those employed in the public legal system can buy their cars at a slightly reduced cost due to a government subsidy.

40 G 3.8.80–81.

> The working mothers in the legal system have reached the level [where they are eligible] for the position of the Head of Prosecutors and the Head of the Court. However, they were not given any of these positions as they were given to males, without any justification provided.[41]

This was also verified by another working mother (also in the legal system) who stated that:

> Regarding the working mother … even though she is a working mother, [and] she has reached the level of Head of Prosecutors and Head of the Court in the legal systems, even though she is qualified for this position, she has never been given this position. Also, I would like to say that some of the male members of prosecutors and lawyers were sent to Britain to study English but no women were sent. When we spoke about this, nothing was been changed. Truly, the serious issues in Libya are changed with political decisions and not by legal ones.[42]

Her training had been affected by a bias against women. This also occurs in other fields of employment. The experience of another working mother (a banking employee) testifies to the existence of a more general discrimination against women:

> I didn't get to do any of the training courses that occurred overseas or even inside my country. The ones that were offered this training are men, all less experienced and with less knowledge. I didn't get to reach any high position in the bank. Even though there were men that became the head of the bank or the assistant bank manager … they are less knowledgeable and experienced than me in this bank. A woman could be offered the [position of] president of any other department … [but not that of becoming] the manager of the bank.[43]

Another working mother exposed strong discrimination in her workplace in terms of benefits offered to female as opposed to male employees:

> With regards to discrimination, yes I did notice this from different aspects. For example, a man is given a mobile phone even though he is not a professional like me. Also, the men will get a car and the workplace will cover all of the expenses of the car, but this right was not given to any of the women. Also, the training sessions offered inside and outside Libya, will be offered mainly to the men. This is the situation of the women and we always know that [women are] … the victim.[44]

Further evidence indicates that discrimination is widespread:

> With regards to discrimination, yes I did notice it very strongly. When I was the manager of my section, I didn't receive any special benefits like the other male managers. For example, I should be given a mobile phone with credit every month as well as a car from the workplace, to be able to supervise the other sections. Also, for your information there is a special bonus every month and extra work every month, I never took my job lightly and I never left my work before the official closing time even though I was entitled to leave 1 hour early. This was because I was the manager. … After a male took my … position, believe me in one month he received all of

41 G 3.3.66–7.
42 G 3.9.84–5.
43 G 4.2.90.
44 G 4.4.96.

> the privileges, such as a car, mobile with credit and monthly bonuses. This is the worst kind of injustice between male and female.[45]

Specific Discrimination on the Basis of Motherhood

In addition to the general discrimination experienced by women in the workplace, there is also discrimination that more specifically affects working mothers. One such area is a failure by employers to follow maternity leave provisions. In the following instance, a deduction was taken from a woman's wage during maternity leave. Such a deduction from the wage of this working mother (a prosecutor) violates the *Social Security Act*:[46]

> Maternity leave was 3 months according to the law, however what happened to me was that 60% was deducted from my wage during my maternity leave. Even until now, I still don't know the reason why this was done, as it is documented in the law that you are entitled to your full wage while on maternity leave. When I appealed the deduction in my wage, there was still no change.[47]

This does not appear to be an isolated incident. Another working mother stated that:

> Maternity leave with all my children was 3 months, but what confuses us is that we know that the maternity leave should be for 3 months with full payment. What happened once, about 3 years ago, for maternity leave was that the first month and a half was with full pay and then the other month and a half was without any allowance and this has a big impact on the full wage.[48]

Yet another working mother, a teacher, affirmed that such practices are not limited to any specific field of employment:

> during maternity leave, when you receive your income, it is incomplete as one of the components of your income, the teaching allowance – this is given to teachers for their hard effort, is taken out.[49]

Women who have children may also find their opportunities to work become limited. Working mothers may be prevented from working at private schools, for example, if they are pregnant despite the law guaranteeing their continued employment at all workplaces:[50]

> [I]t was well known, that a pregnant woman could not work at this particular school. The school's policy only allows woman who are single or elderly to work there.[51]

The experience of one working mother was that while the law regarding her right to resume work was respected, she could not maintain her position at its existing level without a struggle. Her

45 G 4.9.108–9.

46 *Social Security Act No 13 of 1980* (Libya).

47 G 3.1.60–61.

48 G 3.9.81–2.

49 G 1.9.22.

50 There is no exemption (including in education) to the legislation regarding employment of women during pregnancy. A woman may, however, be medically certified as unable to work in an occupation during her pregnancy for health reasons (e.g., threatened miscarriage).

51 G 1.8.20.

experience more generally clearly demonstrates that there is little equality in the workplace in regard to conditions:

> With regards to discrimination, yes I did notice it very strongly … when I took maternity leave, a decision was made to exchange me for someone who was less qualified and I was moved to another position. But when I came back to work, I appealed this irresponsible transfer and I sent my complaint to the head of the Supervisors of Management. Then they accepted my complaint and gave me back my old job. However, in reality, when I thought about my old job and the long hours I did without any bonus and for your information I miscarried due to climbing stairs many times a day and nothing was presented to me, I accepted my new job.
>
> I was transferred without any reason [being supplied], just because I contradicted the manager regarding things that he wanted to be done that are against the law and the instructions that were given to us. Do you know that it's necessary that the women in the workplace shouldn't say 'no', because this is considered to be disrespectful to the male. The manager considers that anything that I challenge him [in] … regards to what he wants, is to be wasting his time …[52]

There are other examples of ways in which employers may seem to be following the law, but actually circumvent its intentions. For example, a woman was severely discriminated against by her employer who did not permit a high grading for workplace performance to be given to those who take (compulsory) maternity leave. Without such a grading ('excellent'), the employee cannot qualify for a long-service bonus. This represents a clear example of discrimination on the basis of motherhood.

> [T]here was something created that wasn't legal. This was that the maternity leave will prevent the working mother from receiving 'excellent' in her annual report. Imagine an employee working in the bank for 25 years and his/her annual report is excellent, so it's his/her right to receive 2,000 dinars as a reward for his/her experience. So I was denied this because of maternity leave … [though] my annual report was good. So I said to the management that the reason that I took my maternity leave as it is compulsory for me to take it as I am in need of this natural necessity. So I told them, that I have 2 children now and what happens if I have more children.[53]

Another working mother reports that:

> [D]uring sick leave, for which I get a doctor's report, I get punished for this in my annual promotion report, because I wouldn't get a promotion if the manager finds that I have been away due to sick leave and maternity leave. If I don't get excellent in my annual report, I will not receive a promotion and this is discrimination, as men don't need maternity leave and this is discrimination against the working mothers. We are denied promotion as we are working mothers and here this shows that we are punished as we are mothers.[54]

---

52 G 4.9.108–9.
53 G 4.2.90–91.
54 G 4.1.88.

Discrimination can also occur when employers cancel breastfeeding hours – which are guaranteed by law.

> [T]he manager cancelled the breastfeeding hours as he decided that every working mother can leave work 1 hour earlier than their official shifts end. But when he realised that there would be a shortage of staff he decided to cancel this. This is discrimination because I am a breastfeeding mother. I was denied the pleasure of this right because the manager denied this hour.[55]

A further statement made by another working mother indicates that employers may manipulate the time allocated by law or even ignore the provision regarding breastfeeding.

> [T]he manager of the bank used to give permission to the breastfeeding working mother to leave work at 2:30pm instead of 3:30pm. This was like being given your 1 hour breastfeeding. The truth is my baby didn't benefit from my breast milk, as he couldn't get it at the time he needed it ... The manager started complaining later, when the working mothers kept taking this early leave, as the working mother leaves at 2:30pm. He said, 'There is no more breastfeeding hour after today'. So he cancelled it without any legal ruling.
>
> But what can I do? If we complain, we will get punished and the punishment will be that there is no satisfaction from the manager. For example, I will have a weak annual report given to me and that will deny me from getting any bonus, because I complained about the manager's decision.[56]

It is evident from the individual interviews that discrimination against women in the workplace and against mothers in particular is endemic, despite the existence of legislation prohibiting such discrimination.

Provision of Childcare Facilities in the Workplace

As outlined in Chapter 4, Libyan laws[57] and many of the Orders from the General People's Committee emphasise that it is necessary for employers to provide or establish a childcare facility in the workplace.[58] The interviews reveal, however, that such provision is rare; and where provision exists, it is often not of an appropriate standard. Of the 40 interviewees, just 25 per cent (or 10 women) had access to childcare in their workplace.[59] Of those 10 respondents, none considered the provision adequate. None of the workplace childcare centres were seen by the respondents as fulfilling the necessary requirements for healthy and safe childcare for children.

The interviewees reported provision of childcare facilities in the teaching and health sectors as well as in universities. However, the respondents also noted that these fell short of the requirements necessary to protect the welfare of children. With regard to the provision of childcare centres, only

55 G 4.2.91.

56 G 4.1.86–7.

57 For example, *Labour Code Act No 58 of 1970* (Libya); *Amendment Act No 7 of 1997 of Some Provisions of Act No 58 of 1970* (Libya); *Child Protection Act No 5 of 1997* (Libya).

58 *Order of the General People's Committee No 164 of 1988 on Employment of Arab Libyan Women* (Libya); *Order of the General People's Committee No 10572 of 2009 on the Female Worker Who is Nursing her Child for Eighteen Months* (Libya); *Order of the General People's Committee No 88 of 1998 on the Requirements for Childcare Facility for Working Mothers* (Libya).

59 Of the six centres, three were located in schools, one in a hospital and two in medical centres.

that provided at the university was fully established by the university management (the employer), who provided both space and staff. As for the childcare centres provided in the teaching and health sectors, these were established by the dedication of the working mothers. The childcare workers are paid by the working mothers, who also furnished the centres. Workplaces gave permission for the centres to be established but would only provide the empty room and nothing else.

One working mother in the education sector observed that although she did have access to childcare facilities in the workplace, the standard was poor:

> This childcare centre consists of only a room which is approximately 3 by 3 metres, with one small window. Where the children can rarely leave the room, and the carer has no experience or knowledge about a child's needs. This centre was established by us the female teachers who cleaned the room, brought in some furniture and signed a contract with the carer whose salary is paid by the female teachers as well. The only thing the principal did was allowing us to establish it; and we are thankful for that.
>
> However I am not happy with it at all. First of all it is located in the school's yard where in winter there is no protection for the children. Secondly, the bathroom that is next to the centre is not clean, and the principal didn't agree to close one of the four toilets, so, and out of necessity, we cleaned a toilet located on the second floor so it would be hygienically ready for a child to use it. However, when a child wants to go to the toilet, the carer has to leave the other children unattended. I am very worried about this situation, where no other choice is available.[60]

The childcare facilities provided in the health sector also do not meet what most mothers would consider health and safety requirements. Unfortunately, no regulations or standards exist in the legislation regarding childcare provision. Thus staffing levels, the staff–child ratio and training are unregulated; nor are there any guidelines for care or accommodation dependent upon the age of the children or infants in care. The legislation only provides that an employer must create a childcare facility in the workplace, without placing any further demands on employers in the legislation or associated regulations/orders.

The opinion that such centres are inadequate is confirmed by many of the doctors that were interviewed. One of the doctors said:

> [T]here is childcare in my workplace, but I prefer not to put my child in it because firstly the childcare centre is like a little room, secondly it has 30 kids in it, whose mothers work at the same clinic, thirdly there is only one person who's looking after these children and she thinks that she can control and protect these children. My child is only 4 months old so I'm not willing to sacrifice the health of my child. Fourthly, there is a possibility that if I put my child in the room with these children that he could get a contagious disease from other children. The solution was to put my baby with my sister so that my child could get better protection.[61]

Even though there are childcare centres provided in the education and health sectors, they fall short of the needs of the mothers. Childcare centres are mainly provided in some primary schools, and then only for the morning sessions. Working mothers employed in the afternoon session or in high schools are not provided with any childcare facilities.

60 G 1.1.2–3.

61 G 2.3.35.

In the absence of adequate workplace childcare facilities, it is necessary for working mothers who have young children to solve their own problems by placing their children in private childcare, leaving them home alone or leaving them with relatives or neighbours. Their willingness to do this depends on their financial situation (for example, whether they can meet everyday living expenses) or their level of enthusiasm about continuing to work. One teacher stated:

> I worked [the] afternoon shift and there was no childcare in the afternoon, [though] … there was childcare provided in the morning, so my solution was to leave my children with my mother.[62]

Another working mother who teaches in a high school stated that:

> There was no childcare at the school and we (the teachers) asked about having a childcare [facility] in our workplace and our female principal said that it was very unusual to have childcare facilities in a high school. My solution was to put my baby daughter with my mother-in-law, so she could look after her and I used to leave my 8-year-old son home by himself.[63]

Another teacher reported that:

> There is no childcare in the school where I work and when we told the principal that we want childcare, he said that the education system is under no obligation to provide childcare. He said that he is still not convinced that childcare is necessary in the school. So, I leave my eldest child in a private childcare that costs me 450 dinars and I leave my youngest child with my neighbour.[64]

From the individual interviews that were conducted with the teachers, it was evident that not all the primary schools have childcare facilities. Most of the teachers found themselves forced to leave their children at home by themselves if they were to continue to work. In one extreme example, a working mother explained her arrangements as follows:

> There was no childcare in the school where I worked, so I used to leave my first child with my parents, but with my second child it became difficult for me to transport two children to my parents' house and then go to school. So I used to leave my oldest child – aged 1 year and nine months – with my youngest child by themselves. One day I came home to find my youngest baby crying and her sibling tried but failed in making her quiet so he decided to get out of the room and close it and waited for me to return. I came back and found her still in tears.[65]

This mother was placed in a desperate situation: without her working the family would lack the necessities of life (including formula for the baby and sufficient food). She provided as best she could by leaving water, formula (which the elder child fed to the younger, four months old), biscuits and fruit for the children. She was very distressed about the situation but could see no other way out in the absence of workplace-provided childcare.

Childcare facilities are more widely available in the health sector, but many respondents did not regard them as safe for the children. In addition, childcare facility opening hours are not compatible with the working hours of those working in the medical sector. Some of the doctors that

62 G 1.5.13.
63 G 1.6.15.
64 G 1.10.27.
65 G 1.9.22.

work in hospitals are on shift work, with schedules that are continually changing. All the doctors interviewed who work in hospitals struggle to find a balance between work and motherhood. One doctor confirmed that:

> Yes, there is a childcare centre in the hospital but I prefer not to put my children there after my maternity leave is finished. This is because it is a small room that falls short of all of the standards of child protection from all points of view. Even if we assume that this childcare centre meets all of the requirements of a childcare centre and a mother feels content in placing her child there, the issue is also that the childcare centre only operates in the morning.
>
> To be specific, I sometimes work the morning shift but sometimes I work the afternoon shift and twice a week I even do the night shift. I know that a number of the other gynaecologists also complain about this issue and the fact that in Libya we do not have a single childcare [centre] that operates at night. So, the solution that I reached is to leave my children with my poor mother to look after them.[66]

As for the working mothers in the administration sector of the university, initially there were no childcare facilities available in the workplace. Even though the number of working mothers had long (and by far) exceeded 50 (the number of working mothers required by law to have a childcare centre established),[67] there was previously no childcare centre established in the university, although this is mandated by law.[68] Working mothers continually asked for this service at meeting after meeting, until in 2007 the first childcare facility was established in the university. Before then, however, the situation was dire:

> There was [initially] no childcare centre in the work place. Imagine the biggest university in Libya has around 500 female workers in the administration and academic sections and the majority of them are working mothers. There has been a demand for a childcare centre but this demand didn't get any consideration and that's what makes me have a lot of trouble regarding my return to work.
>
> I tried to find a private childcare outside my workplace that is suitable for my 3 baby girls but I didn't find any childcare suitable that will make me feel safe about my children. I suffered depression and I was confused between my job and my children. Truly I am in need of paying the living expenses because my husband can't do it by himself. So the solution for me was that I made a special order of 3 beds, each one of them can fit a big person and is quite high so that the baby can't get out of it (like a cot).
>
> In the night I used to keep them awake until late at night and wake them at 5:00am, give them a bath, feed them and then leave them playing in their beds. I would leave them home by themselves and go to work at 7:30am until 12:00 and then go back home before the official working time, which is 2:00pm. This was because of the breastfeeding hour and also the manager gave me another hour considering my situation.[69]

---

66 G 2.8.51.

67 *Labour Code Act No 58 of 1970* (Libya) art 98.

68 According to statistics from Garyounis University in Libya, the number of female staff members reached 520 employed within the university campus. Outside the campus a further 177 were employed.

69 G 4.7.101.

It is worth noting that this is the situation that still prevails for working mothers who lack access to such facilities.

Another working mother in a university described the conditions for mothers and their children before a childcare centre was established, and spoke of the various approaches adopted by mothers. In passing, she reveals the poor standard of care at some contemporary centres – and the fatal consequences this had for one of her children:

> There is no childcare centre at the workplace. For your information the number of the female staff is more than 500. The solution was to leave my 1st, 2nd and 3rd children with my mother-in-law [but] after my husband's family left and went to live far away I had another … baby, so I was forced to leave her in a public childcare centre.
>
> But this childcare centre was not in good condition and not suitable for my child. No childcare worker had any qualification so this childcare was not clean and not safe. When I would leave my work and go to pick up my baby I would find her still in her old nappy from the morning, even though I used to bring spare nappies for my baby and … the nappies that I had placed in her bag would be missing. Also, the number of children was too many and the place was always dirty. … The furniture was brought by the mothers as the centre did not have any furniture. I had no other solution other than this childcare, as it was close to the university.
>
> Unfortunately, my baby contracted an infection [there] … and was taken to hospital and regrettably she died, because of the childcare centre. … this childcare [centre] is still operating … There was a nurse in this childcare, but she didn't come every day. My baby needed a penicillin injection every day, because her health was in a bad condition and my work denied me any carer's leave. So what I did was to go to the nurse by myself as she was related to my mother-in-law. I asked her to give my baby an injection every day. But sadly, the sickness/disease didn't give my baby any chance and unfortunately she passed away. After a while, I had another baby and after my maternity leave, I left him with my relative because she lives near my house. This is what happened with the rest of my children.
>
> … [N]ow, a childcare centre has been established in the last 4 years and also, a pre-school, but after long suffering by the working mother. This was only because we used to ask at every meeting for a childcare centre. So the manager used to say, 'I know that and I know what you want', and I used to say 'If you want me to be at work, provide us with childcare, we beg you because we are suffering'.[70]

The childcare facility was finally established in the university after persistent demands from the working mothers. However, it still does not fulfil the requirements most parents believe are necessary for a childcare centre, such as trained staff, although from a health point of view it seems to be better than other childcare centres. There is no requirement in Libyan legislation or regulations for childcare workers to have specific qualifications or any experience of working with children prior to hiring. I visited this centre personally and I found that it has no resources, equipment, toys or anything that you would expect in a childcare facility. The children are not allowed to go outside and play, as they share the grounds with a primary school and there is no

70 G 4.8.104–5.

specific playground for them. For this reason, approximately 30 children of various ages spend all day locked up together in the one room.

As for the courts, the number of working mothers in this field in particular locations also exceeds the number needed to trigger the legal requirement for the establishment of a childcare centre. Yet there has been no childcare centre established. This was confirmed by the following statement from a prosecutor:

> There is no childcare centre in my workplace and this … makes me think about changing my workplace to case management. Even though there also is not a childcare centre there but still the work load is less even though it's the same pay. So after my maternity leave, I left my child with my family and my husband's family. After my mother's death, I opted for private childcare. We did ask for a childcare centre in our workplace, but our demand was made fun of. The director asked us, 'Could you imagine a childcare centre in a court house?'
>
> For your information, the percentage of working mothers in this court house comprises about 80% of the employees. In the workplace, the working mother is dealt with like a male without any consideration given to her personal situation. There is no responsibility or help given in the workplace and we don't have any right to demand it even though this right is documented in the law.[71]

This situation was also evident from the interviews with the lawyers. All 10 lawyers, prosecutors and judges interviewed expressed dissatisfaction with the total lack of workplace-provided childcare facilities. One lawyer stated:

> The person that used to take care of my children after I went back to work was my mother. This is due to the fact that there is no childcare in my workplace. For your information, the Public Corporate Administration of Lawyers has close to 300 female lawyers and even with this, there is no childcare centre available in my workplace.[72]

One of the judges interviewed responded to the questions on childcare availability as follows:

> There is no childcare centre in this court or any other place linked to the legal system, even though there is a demand for it. Our demand was denied, even though the [number of] working mothers in the legal system reaches over 70 … in this court alone. So the solution for me was to leave my child with my mother. My work used to be case administration, 3 days per week and sometimes every day … depending on the work load.[73]
>
> Even though the law states that there should be a childcare centre in the workplace and we demanded it, regrettably we weren't able to apply this law even though we are the ones that apply all the other laws. As the saying says, 'The door of the carpenter is always broken!' I only have one child, so I can find a solution to my problem, but I have a friend who can't work on Saturdays, so if she is forced to come to work, she comes very quickly and for a short time and then she goes back

71 G 3.9.82.
72 G 3.6.75.
73 G 3.3.64.

> home. This is due to the fact that schools in Libya don't open on Saturdays and her husband works and she can't leave her little children alone.[74]

With regard to the interviews that were conducted with working mothers in the administration sector, it was found that there was no childcare facility in any of the workplaces except the university. This leaves the working mother with few options: namely privately provided or public childcare. If she is seeking childcare, it can be assumed that the option of relatives or neighbours is already untenable for some reason; this leaves public childcare. Thus, the remaining alternative is a public childcare centre. This usually is not suitable on two counts: firstly, centre opening hours are severely limited, being only from 8:00am until midday; and secondly, they usually fail to meet even the most basic health and safety provisions that a parent would like to see implemented.[75]

In the absence of workplace childcare provision, some mothers mix their care options between private and public or simply leave their children home on their own. The alternative may be threatened unemployment. This was seen in the interview with one of the working mothers in the administration sector when she stated that:

> There are no childcare centres in the workplace and [when] we demanded it, our demand was denied and the manager told us that he can't imagine a childcare [facility] in the workplace. When we told him at our meeting that we are suffering, he told us 'get divorced, or leave your job'.
>
> The solution was that when my child reaches an age that I can be comfortable about, I placed him in pre-school, but it was very costly. With my 2nd and 3rd children, I use[d] to leave them home by themselves from 8:00am until 1:00pm. One day, I came back home and I found my baby had vomited and he was lying down on his face, so I was scared that something had happened to him. I lifted him up, gave him a hug and I started to cry and I cried for the injustice that I face, myself and my baby. Not because of anything, but only to be able to live with dignity, myself and my children. This situation forces us to choose between motherhood and work. There are no rights mentioned.[76]

It can be seen from all the previous information and the interviews that, with regard to childcare availability in the workplace, there is little or no provision made to meet the requirements laid down by law. In addition, the law itself is revealed as lacking detail in terms of the nature of the service to be provided by employers (for example, the standard of training for staff at such a centre, its furnishings, dimensions of the room provided and so forth), although one order outlines fee schedules for the mothers and the necessity for them to provide food for the children being cared for[77] and another specifies that a number of secretariats provide advice and assistance in regard to such centres.[78] The research undertaken has not uncovered any general guidelines issued in relation to such matters.

---

74 G 3.3.65.

75 Again, it should be recalled that no guidelines for the quality of a centre or its staff have been issued.

76 G 4.10.110.

77 *Order of the General People's Committee No 88 of 1998 on the Requirements for Childcare Facility for Working Mothers* (Libya).

78 *Order of the General People's Committee No 164 of 1988 on Employment of Arab Libyan Women* (Libya) art 12.

Provision of Maternity Leave

As outlined in the previous chapter, mothers working under the *Social Security Act No 13 of 1980* have the right to maternity leave for a period of three months (a single period that includes leave occurring both before and after birth and totalling three months) on full salary.[79]

Thirty-six of the 40 respondents worked in positions covered by the *Social Security Act*.[80] All mothers working in the public sector, when asked the length of their maternity leave, replied 'three months'. However, discrepancies emerged during the individual interviews.

The law clearly states that maternity leave is three months to be taken by the mother before and after giving birth at her own discretion and with full salary, or to be taken after giving birth. The law allows the working mother to make the decision regarding leave, depending on her personal situation. No employer can force her to take leave in a way that suits the employer.

However, respondents stated that they were forced to take leave to suit the employer or on the employer's terms, at the employer's discretion, not the employee's. In one case a mother was compelled to take one and a half months' leave before giving birth and a further one and a half months after giving birth (albeit on full salary). This compulsion is contrary to the law but occurs in practice. The mother stated:

> I took 3 months maternity leave, but I was forced to take 1.5 months leave before I gave birth and 1.5 months leave after giving birth. This is not what is legally [required]. With this situation, the law states that the working mother makes this decision and should not be forced. I told my manager, this is forbidden and cannot be done. He told me this is my rule, and all I could do was to take extra leave (after delivery) without pay and he agreed to this. I was not able to go back to work straight away as I had a caesarean delivery.[81]

Employers also flouted the requirement that maternity leave be on full pay. One teacher did not receive some of the components of her income, so her income was reduced. Another mother stated that:

> Maternity leave is 3 months but the leave is not enough for me as I had caesarean delivery. The other problem is during maternity leave, when you receive your income, it is incomplete as one of the components of your income (the teaching allowance – this is given to teachers for their hard effort) is deducted.[82]

Another mother stated regarding maternity leave:

> Maternity leave was 3 months according to the law; however, what happened to me was that 60% was deducted from my wage during my maternity leave. Even until now, I still don't know the reason why this was done, as it is documented in the law that you are entitled to your full wage while on maternity leave. When I appealed the deduction in my wage, there was still no change.

79 *Social Security Act No 13 of 1980* (Libya) art 25(C).

80 These being all 10 in administrative positions, 8 of the 10 in schools, 9 of the 10 in the courts and 9 of the 10 in the medical profession.

81 G 4.6.99.

82 G 1.9.22.

> To my knowledge, there was no deduction in my wage with my second child and … I still don't know the reason behind this.[83]

This clearly contravenes the law, as allowances and so forth are included in 'full pay'; the income of the mother is substantially reduced if these are not included, and her capacity to meet everyday expenses during the period of her maternity leave is likewise curtailed.

Respondents reported many such contraventions of the maternity leave provisions. One mother took three months' maternity leave; however, she received full income for one and a half months and a partial income for the other one and a half months. When asked about her maternity leave, she stated that:

> Maternity leave with all my children was 3 months, but what confuses us is that we know that the maternity leave should be for 3 months with full payment. What happened once, about 3 years ago, for maternity leave was that the first month and a half was with full pay and then the other month and a half was without any allowance and this has a big impact on the full wage.[84]

Again, the approach of removing components of pay was adopted by the employer, contravening the law.

In another case, a working mother was denied some of her income while on maternity leave, thereby effectively denying her the full maternity leave to which she was legally entitled. Her circumstances were such that she was forced – by the lack of adequate remuneration during the first one and a half months – to return to work prematurely. She stated:

> I was forced to go back to work after one month and a half because the other month and a half [would be] without any allowance, [and] I was in need of [my] full wage because I have a lot of responsibilities. I tried to pursue the person responsible for the deduction to my wage without any legal reason … [but] what can we do when the decision has been made by the Head of the Prosecutors or the Minister of Justice. So when we appeal, we usually appeal in front of these people. They are the ones that made this [initial] decision against you.[85]

In terms of adequacy of the length of leave provisions under the law, over 80 per cent of all the working mothers interviewed (both public and privately employed) believed that the length of maternity leave given is not enough to protect the health of both the mother and the baby. When a mother gives birth to more than one baby, her need for leave is greater and so the mother is forced to take more leave without any pay. Such a mother may struggle because without pay she cannot meet her daily expenses, and a return to work after only three months may be too difficult. One mother so affected stated:

> The maternity leave was 3 months but what happened to me was that I had triplets in my first labour so it was difficult to go back to work after 3 months. So I was forced to take 1 year's leave without pay … [T]his affected our expenses because there were 3 children. Imagine the wage of my husband was spent totally on the nappies, food and clothes for the babies. With my second

83 G 3.1.60–61.
84 G 3.9.81–2.
85 G 3.8.78–9.

> delivery I took 6 months' leave without pay. Also after the labour I had health problems and I nearly died, so I took sick leave because my health was very bad.[86]

Maternity leave is also not long enough as sometimes there is no suitable childcare for newborn to three-month-old infants, whether in the private or public sector. As one mother stated:

> Maternity leave was 3 months with all my children and in reality this is not enough, especially because we are missing childcare centres in the workplace.[87]

Also, another mother stated that:

> The maternity leave that I had with all my children was 3 months each. And in fact, it is not enough, because the baby at that time is still very young to go to childcare since it is not designed for that age.[88]

As for the working mothers in the private sector, they do not receive any maternity leave. When these working mothers from all four sectors (education, medicine, judiciary and administration) were interviewed, of the four persons in private employment just one respondent (in a private school) was given maternity leave with pay, and that working mother received just one month's maternity leave on full salary. If a mother needs more than a month's leave at that workplace, she can take it – but without any pay. This was clearly stated by one of the working mothers, who said:

> I received 1 month paid maternity leave. If a working mother needs more maternity leave, she can take leave without pay. We know this school is the only school that gives 1 month's maternity leave with full salary.[89]

The working mother in this school has an entitlement (accorded by the employer) to one month's maternity leave with full salary.[90] However, if the working mother returns to work after one month, then this contravenes the *Maternity Protection Convention*[91] – an international convention ratified on 19 June 1975 by Libya,[92] and one which clearly states that maternity leave should be three months. This term was decided upon for the protection of the health of both mother and baby. Thus it is clear that the private sector's lack of provision of maternity leave or inadequate leave provision contrasts with Libyan domestic provision for teachers in the public sector and is contrary

86 G 4.7.100–101.

87 G 4.10.110.

88 G 1.2.5.

89 G 1.7.17.

90 Such payment is not guaranteed by law. Private schools in Libya are able to grant their employees paid maternity leave. The school above has adopted such a policy. Others are reported to not employ women who are mothers, or even women who are married and may bear children.

91 *Maternity Protection Convention* (C103), opened for signature 28 June 1952, ILO (entered into force 7 September 1955).

92 Libya ratified the 1919 *Maternity Protection Convention* on 27 May 1971. It ratified the 1952 revision on 19 June 1975. International Labour Organization, *List of Ratifications of International Labour Conventions Libyan Arab Jamahiriya* (7 April 2011) <http://webfusion.ilo.org/public/applis/appl-byCtry.cfm?lang=EN&CTYCHOICE=1520>.

to Libya's obligations under international law, as Libya ratified the first (1919) and then second (1950s) version of the *Maternity Protection Convention* in 1971 and 1975 respectively.

The interviews revealed disturbing cases of discrimination in the private teaching sector, despite the principle of anti-discrimination embedded in Libyan law. Some of the private schools refuse to employ married women because the schools do not want to give any maternity leave, even unpaid, and this was clearly stated by one of the teachers employed in a private school, who said that:

> [There is] no maternity leave at all in the private sector. It was well known, that a pregnant woman could not work at this particular school. The school's policy only allows woman who are single or elderly to work there ...[93]

No paid maternity leave is generally given in the private sector, and such payment is not guaranteed by law. Respondents also commented that the majority of the mothers in the private sector receive just one month *unpaid* maternity leave and after this month's leave, mothers return to work straight away.

Nor are women in the public sector exempt from pressure to take leave at their employer's discretion or from pressure to return to work before they are physically ready. One woman was asked why she did not take maternity leave longer than the month unpaid leave given by her employer after the birth of her child as she had used her paid leave prior to the birth, also at her employer's direction. She replied that she wished that she could take more leave but she 'was in need of full wage because I have a lot of responsibilities'.[94]

Lack of social security provision makes working mothers particularly vulnerable to exploitation in such circumstances. A working mother may sacrifice her health and that of her baby in order to maintain the family income. Libya falls short of the standards set by relevant Australian law and policy in terms of the provision of family support for families with children.[95] It should be noted, however, that Australia has lagged far behind Libya in terms of provision for compulsory *paid* maternity leave, with the implementation of such a policy only anticipated in announcements by both the federal government and the Opposition during 2009–10 and enacted by the Labor Government in 2010 to come into effect in 2011.[96] However, yet again, the gap between provisions *in law* and their effective implementation in Libya restricts the provision of effective paid maternity leave and equality in the workplace in practice. The interviews revealed that there is a difference

93 G 1.8.20.

94 G 3.8.78.

95 For quite a number of years, a 'family allowance' or benefit has been payable in Australia to families with dependent children. More recently, it has become known as 'Family Tax Benefit Part A' and 'Family Tax Benefit Part B' and is payable to those who satisfy particular income and assets tests. These parents are entitled to receive a fortnightly benefit based on number of children to help meet daily expenses. They may also qualify for an amended form of 'baby bonus' (spread over a number of months) that also assists new parents on limited incomes. For more details see House of Representatives Standing Committee on Family and Human Services, *Balancing Work and Family: Report on the Inquiry into Balancing Work and Family* (CanPrint Communications, 2006) 45–9.

96 Prior to that, compulsory but unpaid maternity leave provisions existed, while leave with pay only existed for some employees as a result of negotiations with employers (with length of such paid leave varying and usually subject to a number of conditions). Until the policy was enacted in legislation, Australia and the United States had the dubious honour of being the only two nations of the developed world lacking provision of compulsory paid maternity leave. See *Paid Parental Leave Act 2010* (Cth).

between the theory of the law and the actual practice with regard to maternity leave and the struggles of the working mother when she has a child.

Provision of the Breastfeeding Hour

In the previous chapter it was noted that Article 97 of the *Labour Code Act No 58 of 1970* states that a working mother is entitled to breastfeed her baby from when the baby is born until the baby reaches 18 months old. A mother is entitled to two breastfeeding sessions per day for half an hour each time, in addition to her normal breaks. These breastfeeding sessions are included within the regular work hours and the mother's working day is not extended to compensate for time lost.[97] Such provisions appear to indicate recognition by the Libyan legislature of the importance of natural breastfeeding for both the baby[98] and the mother.[99]

However, from the individual interviews with working mothers, it was confirmed that the breastfeeding hour enshrined in law is not provided in every workplace, though the reasons given varied. One reason supplied by interviewees is the lack of childcare facilities in the workplace (making access for breastfeeding impossible). Another reason supplied by interviewees was that in some workplaces the manager makes provision in accordance with his own interpretation of the law, or in accord with his own personal opinion. Unfortunately, the provision of breastfeeding in practice is not generally in accordance with Libyan legislation; nor is its provision routinely enforced via workplace inspections and the like.

With regard to the first reason that the working mother does not enjoy her right to the breastfeeding breaks, namely the lack of a workplace-based childcare facility, it is very inconvenient for an employee to leave her workplace and go and breastfeed her baby elsewhere due to difficulties with transport, traffic and time taken. The breastfeeding time to which she is entitled would be wasted on transport if she attempted to access her child at a childcare facility located other than in her workplace. This was confirmed by many of the mothers when asked if they enjoyed their breastfeeding hour. According to one mother attempting to juggle the roles of nursing mother and employee:

> I didn't enjoy my breastfeeding hour that was provided for me at work, however. Because I was home in the morning, I was able to breastfeed, as I was home until 12 midday. When I used to come home after work at 5pm, my baby would have been crying continuously until I got home because it is difficult for a breastfed baby to go without milk for this amount of time and she refused to take any other milk. For sure, this is due to the fact that there is no childcare in the workplace.[100]

97 'For eighteen months reckoned from the date of her confinement, a female worker who is nursing her child shall be entitled to two daily nursing breaks of half-an-hour each, in addition to normal rest breaks. These two additional breaks shall be included in the hours of work and shall not entail any reduction in wages': *Labour Code Act No 58 of 1970* (Libya) art 97.

98 The effect of breastfeeding on reducing the risk of childhood obesity was evident regardless of maternal diabetes or weight status. See Elizabeth J Mayer-Davis et al, 'Breast-Feeding and Risk for Childhood Obesity: Does Maternal Diabetes or Obesity Status Matter?' (2006) 29(10) *Diabetes Care* 2231, 2233.

99 Several studies have found that women who had breastfed their children had a reduced risk of developing breast cancer, especially women who had longer periods of breastfeeding. See Tongzhang Zheng et al, 'Lactation Reduces Breast Cancer Risk in Shandong Province, China' (2000) 152(12) *American Journal of Epidemiology* 1129, 1132.

100 G 1.5.13.

Another mother also stated (somewhat rhetorically):

> [H]ow can I enjoy the breastfeeding hour that is my legal right, if there is no childcare centre in the school?[101]

A mother who works in the health sector stated that:

> I didn't enjoy my breastfeeding hour, which is a right given to me, because there is no childcare centre in my workplace.[102]

A doctor confirmed this, as she stated that:

> There is no childcare available in my workplace with good health conditions and consequently because of this my milk used to dry up in my breast so I am unable to breastfeed my baby.[103]

Another doctor also stated:

> How can I enjoy my breast feeding hour that is documented in the law, without the existence of childcare centres in the workplace? With my first children, I used to work the morning shift and I used to leave my children with my mother. When I used to finish work and come back home, my breasts used to hurt me as they were full of milk and my baby will be crying as he would want to feed. So I used to feed him but there is suffering between work and motherhood.
>
> But with the rest of my children, I worked in the hospital and my work was very hard as they use to always change my shifts … sometimes day shift, sometimes afternoon shift and sometimes night shift. Once a week, I have to stay all day. The solution that I reached is to breastfeed, as I am a doctor and I know the benefit of breastfeeding, but without the existence of safe childcare in the workplace, I used to bring my baby with me to work. I put him in a room close to my room. When I have a break, I used to breastfeed him but when he started to face some health problems, I knew that this was because he is with me in the hospital. This forced me to give him baby formula.[104]

Those mothers working in the courts also confirmed that they too were not able to exercise their right to the breastfeeding hour. One of them stated:

> I didn't enjoy my breastfeeding hour that is provided by the law for many reasons. The first reason is because there is no childcare in my workplace. Secondly, there is no transport to take me from my workplace to the place where my child is and finally because my daily working hours are from 8:30am until 2:00pm.[105]

Another mother in the court system stated:

---

101 G 1.10.27.
102 G 2.1.30.
103 G 2.7.48.
104 G 2.9.55.
105 G 3.1.61.

> How can I enjoy my breast feeding hour that I am entitled to by the law, when there is no childcare centre available in my work place? I suffered because of this shortage and both my child and I suffered.[106]

Another mother in the same sector also stated:

> I couldn't benefit from the breastfeeding hour due to there being no childcare centre and a lack of transportation. Also with the difficulty of the workload in the courts and the working hours that are from 8:30am until 1:30pm and at times until 2:30pm depending on the workload. During my maternity leave I was dedicated to my breastfeeding; however, after my maternity leave my only solution was to use baby formula.[107]

The working mothers in the administration sector had the same thoughts. One of them stated:

> The truth is I could have enjoyed this hour, if there was a childcare centre in my workplace or somewhere nearby. But because of the unavailability of this service, I didn't enjoy this hour.[108]

Another mother in the same sector also stated:

> I used to enjoy my breastfeeding hour by leaving work an hour earlier than my working time and that was hard for the baby and reduced my milk supply. There are 2 reasons for this. Firstly, you are not allowed to leave work in the middle of your working shift and the second reason being the unavailability of childcare centres in the workplace …[109]

Also, another statement:

> I didn't enjoy the breastfeeding hour that is documented in the law, due to there not being a childcare facility in my workplace.[110]

The other reason why mothers were unable to exercise their right to the breastfeeding hour provided by law was (as stated earlier) that managers interpret the law in any way they choose, without any reference to the legal position or any apparent consideration being given to the baby's and mother's health. This was evident in many interviews.

For example, some of the managers insisted that the right to breastfeed does not exist, and argued that it is not stated in the law. When some of the interviewees were asked about their ability to exercise their right to breastfeed, their response was that their managers were not aware that such a right is given to the mothers and that they were sure that such a law does not exist. As one of the working mothers in the education sector testified:

> The principal told me that the right of breastfeeding does not exist in any of the schools and even if it does exist, there is definitely no childcare. If we assume that the breastfeeding hour is given, yet there is no childcare in the workplace, then we still can't enjoy this right as there would be no

106 G 3.7.77.
107 G 3.9.83.
108 G 4.1.86.
109 G 4.2.89.
110 G 4.3.92.

easy access to our children due to lack of transport and in this time the breastfeeding hour would be finished (that is by the time a mother is to find transport, then get home, then feed her baby sufficiently, then eat and then find transport to go back to school). We would therefore also have problems with the principal.[111]

She was not alone in her experience. A teacher in another school also stated her belief that this right of breastfeeding was not approved either in public or private sector education, when she stated:

Honestly, there is no right at all for breastfeeding in schools, whether they are private or public.[112]

Also, a number of doctors confirmed the apparent reluctance of hospital administrators to provide for breastfeeding breaks mandated by law. One doctor stated:

No, I didn't enjoy my breastfeeding hour that is legally documented in the law. Here in the workplace, they do not recognise this.[113]

A doctor in a different workplace stated that the director of staff there also denied the working mother's right to breastfeeding breaks:

The director is very strict and quick to say no and my working hours are from 8:00am until 2:00pm, so he didn't allow me to enjoy this right. Imagine, I leave my work at 2:00 in the afternoon and then go to my sister's to pick up my child and then go home and so I arrive at 3:00 in the afternoon and I find my breast full of milk. This truly makes health problems for the mother and also this will make the breast milk dry. So the people responsible truly don't have any idea about this reality.[114]

There are some managers whose provision of breastfeeding breaks depends on their interpretation. For instance, some allowed the breastfeeding hour, but it was only given to the mothers in the last hour of their work (that is, not split into two equal sessions as stated by law) and it was given to all working mothers, whether they breastfed or not, so long as they had babies. This was made clear by the working mothers at the university, one of whom stated:

Yes, I did enjoy the breastfeeding hour that is documented in the law and that was with the help of my manager. He allowed all mothers, regardless of breastfeeding or not, to leave work an hour earlier than the official closing time.[115]

A manager in a bank also combined the two half-hour breaks into a single break of an hour's duration to be taken in the last hour of the working day for all working mothers, not just breastfeeding mothers. This one-hour shorter working day was allocated initially to breastfeeding mothers:

[T]he manager of the bank, used to give permission to the breastfeeding for all working mother, to leave work at 2:30pm instead of 3:30pm. This was like being given your 1 hour breastfeeding.[116]

111 G 1.9.22–3.
112 G 1.8.20.
113 G 2.2.33.
114 G 2.3.35.
115 G 4. 9.107.
116 G 4.1.86.

Further evidence from another working mother indicates the adoption of such a policy:

> I used to enjoy my breastfeeding hour by leaving work an hour earlier than my working time (the manager made this decision).[117]

The Human Resources Department of the university and the bank manager had also concluded that as it was very beneficial for the working mother who does not breastfeed to also get 'an early mark' and go home earlier to see her children, so all working mothers were leaving work an hour earlier. However, while this may initially appear advantageous (especially for those women no longer nursing their infants), it does not fulfil the legislation about breastfeeding rights, as the legislation specifically provides for two breaks in order to accommodate the natural interval between feeds for infants and young children. By combining the two breaks into a single hour at the end of the day not only does the baby suffer by having to wait such a long time for a feed (perhaps encouraging supplementary feeding and/or premature and ill-advised weaning of an infant), but the mother may also experience health problems such as mastitis as a result. Timing was an issue for many mothers:

> The truth is my baby didn't benefit from my breast milk, as he couldn't get it at the time he needed it.[118]

Another mother bore witness to the problems that could result from combining the breaks into a single hour:

> I used to enjoy my breastfeeding hour by leaving work an hour earlier than my working time and that was hard for the baby and reduced my milk supply. There are 2 reasons for this. Firstly, you are not allowed to leave work in the middle of your working shift …[119]

One of the working mothers interviewed spoke of the benefits for both the baby and the mother of natural breastfeeding given to the baby on demand:

> I know that natural breastfeeding protects the baby from diabetes that is now widespread amongst young children and also it protects women from breast cancer. It also protects the child from changing environmental conditions and also provides other benefits for the child and the mother.[120]

The working mothers in the bank agreed to accept the combined hour only because they had no other choice. The arrangement was brief, for the bank manager realised that with all the working mothers leaving at the same time, there was a shortage of tellers to serve the customers, as all the tellers are females. Most of the office staff was also women, further reducing the bank staff in the afternoon. His solution was simple. He completely cancelled the breastfeeding hour for all mothers, including those who actually breastfed. The problem had been created by the bank manager himself and not by the law, as it was his decision to allow all working mothers to leave early and not just breastfeeding mothers. The cancellation of this hour caused extreme suffering for the breastfeeding mothers and their babies and was not legally acceptable. As one of the mothers stated:

---

117 G 4.2.89.
118 G 4.1.86.
119 G 4.2.89.
120 G 2.6.45.

> [T]he manager cancelled the breastfeeding hours as he decided that every working mother can leave work 1 hour earlier than their official shifts end. But when he realised that there [would be] a shortage of staff he decided to cancel this. This is discrimination because I am a breastfeeding mother. I was denied the pleasure of this right because the manager denied this hour ...[121]

Here, we see that the bank manager, instead of enforcing the law regarding breastfeeding rights and giving the rights to the breastfeeding mothers, first extended it in a corrupted form to all working mothers and then cancelled it for all mothers, including nursing mothers, which is in clear breach of the law. He could have solved the problem by allowing the nursing mothers to have their two half-hour feeding times and leave work at their regular hours and by not giving any concessions to the mothers who were not breastfeeding.

Alternatively, if the bank manager was insistent on not following the law as it stands, he could have adopted another approach to avoid the consequences of his actions (of combining the two breaks and granting it to all working mothers, not just breastfeeding ones). Instead of cancelling the breastfeeding time, he could have managed a roster system whereby the mothers leave at different times so as to minimise impacts on customers. But none of these solutions were adopted; instead, by cancelling the breastfeeding time for nursing mothers, the manager acted in breach of the law and showed a disregard for both the babies and the working mothers. The law is made for all to follow and not for individual employers to 'adapt' it to suit their needs or adopt it wherever or whenever convenient.

From the evidence above it can be seen that although the law gives breastfeeding rights to working mothers who nurse their babies, in reality there is a big difference between theory and practice. This became evident in the interviews. It is clear that managers also have great power and authority in executing their decisions and in following or refusing to follow the law in regard to breastfeeding as well as in regard to issues related to maternity leave. There are a few avenues that a working mother can appeal to with regard to the breach of the law.[122] However, the process is often so long and difficult that they do not access this service. It is not easy for women to assert this right.

Provision of Maternity Allowance and Baby Bonus

As outlined in the previous chapter, the law states that every working mother employed by the government (and its authorities) is entitled to the maternity allowance and the baby bonus as documented in Article 27 of the *Social Security Act No 13 of 1980*. During the interviews it became obvious that the law is enforced differently from one workplace to another. Often its correct enforcement depends on the employees at the particular office of the Social Security Department where the person applies and on the degree of individual employee awareness of their entitlements.

During the interviews with the working mothers from the university, it was clear that all had received the baby bonus and maternity allowance without any struggle. This is because the university specifically employs someone who has experience with dealing with the Social Security Department to completely look after the payments of the allowances for the university employees.

121 G 4.2.91.

122 For example, many workplaces have internal review offices where a request regarding entitlements may be lodged. However, matters may be expedited if one has a 'contact' in the office; otherwise a request or complaint may languish untouched for months, sometimes years.

In this way, working mothers receive their legal entitlement without any difficulty. As one of the administrative employees stated when asked about access to entitlements:

> Yes, I did receive the baby bonus and maternity allowance which is documented in the law. This is because the university has a special employee to do all the applications regarding welfare, so this didn't give us any problems with the welfare administration or in delaying our application.[123]

However, some of the working mothers from the different sectors were not even aware of their right to such entitlements. Such women were only told of their work obligations and not of their entitlements. Although highly educated, they were completely oblivious to the fact that they were entitled to receive a baby bonus and maternity allowance. One teacher stated:

> No, I didn't know about this right at all … we receive at our workplace … only leaflets that state our duties … no legal rights are mentioned.[124]

Another teacher also was ignorant of her entitlements: 'I didn't receive the maternity allowance and baby bonus and I had no idea about this allowance'.[125] Mothers from the health sector were also unaware of their entitlements. One doctor stated:

> With regards to the baby bonus and maternity allowance, I swear by Allah that this is the first time I have ever heard about it.[126]

Another doctor also only became aware of her entitlements through the interviews being conducted. But upon being informed of the level of remuneration, she noted that the benefit would not even cover the daily necessities of a baby. She said:

> No I didn't get any of this allowance as I didn't know about it except from you personally. Even still, this allowance does not cover anything even though this benefit is to encourage the working mother. It's not enough and it doesn't cover anything.[127]

Somewhat surprisingly, not even those in the legal sector were all aware of the entitlements.[128] This is due to a lack of training and awareness-raising in the workplace – not just in the education and administrative sectors but also in the legal/courts sector. This lack of awareness was confirmed by one of the mothers in the courts sector who stated:

> [U]nfortunately I couldn't access these bonuses, the reason being that I didn't know about them. … thank you for telling me as I am now pregnant and I will try and demand this bonus.[129]

---

123 G 4.7.102.

124 G 1.1.3.

125 G 1.9.23.

126 G 2.1.30.

127 G 2.3.35.

128 This came as somewhat of a surprise. Most would expect that those administering the law or working in the courts would be aware of the law because they enforce the law. But from the interviews conducted, this is apparently not the case.

129 G 3.1.61.

It is telling that she refers to her now going to 'try and demand' the allowance and bonus, although these are in truth her legal entitlements.

The degree of knowledge about entitlements varies. Some have become aware of them over time, such as the following mother from the administration sector:

> I had absolutely no knowledge about these bonuses. I only found out about the last bonus which is 100 dinars.[130]

However, another working mother in the same sector was in total ignorance of the allowances and bonus until questioned about her access to them in the course of the interviews conducted by this researcher. She stated that: 'With regards to the baby bonus and maternity allowance, I was not aware of this'.[131]

There were *some* mothers from different sectors who were aware of the law but did not try to access the benefit, due to two reasons: the first being the difficulty in the process, including the length of time involved and the number of visits required to a Social Security Department office; the second reason being the low level of the benefit, so low some thought that it was not worth the effort involved. This is evident from the following statement:

> I am aware of these allowances but I didn't try to get it as the amount is so little, it doesn't cover anything. So I don't apply for it because of the difficulties in trying to get it and I don't have time to waste, neither does my husband, in trying to get this little amount.[132]

Another mother was of the same opinion:

> No, I didn't try to apply to get these allowances because the application process is very time consuming. As I am always busy with my job, I don't have time to apply and go through the process.[133]

Here a mother from the judiciary sector gives her reasons for not applying:

> I didn't receive my baby bonus or maternity allowance as I didn't apply for it. Because the amount of money is so small, it's insulting. Why should I waste my time with my paperwork and then follow it up?[134]

Another mother from the same sector agreed:

> No, I didn't try to access this as it is such a small amount that is worthless to the right of the mother and the baby.[135]

The same opinion was stated by another mother:

---

130 G 4.4.95.
131 G 4.5.97.
132 G 2.4.38.
133 G 2.7.48.
134 G 3.3.65.
135 G 3.4.69.

> With regards to the maternity allowance and the baby bonus that is documented in the law, I know about it and due to the fact of the difficulty in administration and that it's not worth anything, so I didn't ask for it.[136]

This view was shared by another mother from the administration sector who said that:

> It was very difficult to ask for the maternity allowance and baby bonus because of the difficult administration process. So I didn't ask for it, especially as the amount is not worth it.[137]

Nevertheless there were some mothers who did think it worth the trouble to apply. They knew about the entitlements and they applied to receive them, but did not receive the maternity allowance or the baby bonus due to problems with or within the Social Security Department itself. This became evident from the interviews. One mother from the education sector stated:

> I couldn't get my maternity allowance and baby bonus because of the bad administration in welfare services.[138]

Another mother from the court system sector also commented:

> I applied for the allowance but I didn't receive the maternity allowance or baby bonus that I am entitled to by law and my daughter is now 5 years and I still haven't been able to receive it.[139]

Another mother from the same sector also stated:

> I couldn't receive the baby bonus and maternity allowance for my children that I applied for ...[140]

The husband of a mother from the administration sector applied for the benefits when they became aware of their existence, but this couple's experience too was unsatisfactory:

> My husband applied for it, but as my baby is already 2 years, we still haven't received it. The reason being is that we don't know anyone in the social security centre.[141]

There is strong evidence of ill-informed staff incorrectly administering the legislation, as two working mothers in the exact same situation experienced different outcomes. Both were entitled to the same benefit and both of them applied; however, one of them received the benefit and one of them did not, and without any apparent reason being given. The law gives this right to the mothers without any conditions (other than their being an employee of a government entity). One of the mothers stated:

> In the beginning, I had no idea about the baby bonus and maternity allowance, but some time later, I found out, after giving birth to all of my children. I had a relative who worked in the social

136 G 3.6.75.
137 G 4.2.89.
138 G 1.4.11.
139 G 3.8.79.
140 G 3.9.83.
141 G 4.4.95.

> security centre and she told me about the bonuses. I gave her my application and surely, I received the complete bonus.[142]

Here it is evident that this mother received her right even after a long delay between the birth of the children and the application for the maternity allowance and baby bonus for each child. The reason given was that she had a relative who worked in the Social Security Department who not only informed her of the availability of the benefits but also may have helped her with the process. The reason given was not that it was her legal entitlement but that her relative was able to help her in the process.

A second mother, in the same situation, applied but her application was denied with no legal reason supplied for the refusal. The mother stated:

> With regards to the baby bonus and maternity allowance, I was not aware of this and when I did find out my children were of school age. I tried to apply for it but I was rejected.[143]

Another example is of a mother who applied and met all the requirements to receive her entitlement, but was not able to access the benefit for any valid reason. She stated:

> I couldn't get it, because when the special employer took the application papers, the Social Security Office burnt down and my baby's papers were burnt and so I didn't get it. When I came back to ask for it, I was told that my baby is now 1 year old and so his right was denied, even though the reason was that his paperwork was burnt in the Social Security office. But what can we say or do … nothing, but be patient.[144]

There is another type of illegal action that was uncovered in the interviews. Some working mothers applied for their maternity allowance and baby bonus and submitted all the necessary paperwork, only to be told that while they can receive the baby bonus, they were denied the maternity allowance, but were often given no reason. There has never been an amendment of the legislation relating to the maternity allowance. One of the working mothers, when asked about receiving her entitlement, stated:

> Yes, I did receive my maternity allowance and baby bonus, but with my 5th child, I only received 25 dinars, which was the baby bonus only and when I asked for the maternity allowance, they told me that it [doesn't apply to me].[145]

Another mother also confirmed the misinformation about the existence of the maternity allowance. She stated:

> Maternity allowance and baby bonus: I couldn't receive the maternity allowance because it had been denied, but I did receive the baby bonus, which was only 25 dinars and this was only after a lot of difficulty and time.[146]

---

142 G 4.3.93.

143 G 4.6.99.

144 G 4.8.105. There is in fact no requirement that the person apply before the child reaches his or her first birthday. See also note 147 and corresponding text (G 1.5.13) where a child 1.5 years old qualified.

145 G 4.8.105.

146 G 4.1.87.

Those applying often face lengthy delays and problems with their application, as one mother said:

> Yes I know this, but I didn't get any maternity allowance although I did receive my baby bonus, which was 25 dinars. Even this was very difficult to receive as my husband applied for it many times before we actually received this bonus. That was the situation with my first child. With regards to my 2nd child, I received my baby bonus when my baby was one and a half years old.[147]

The misinformation was widespread, as mothers across several workplaces and types of employment reported similar stories. One woman in administration stated:

> Yes, I did get the baby bonus but the maternity allowance was denied because the government cancelled it ...[148]

From the above, it is evident that there is a great deal of inconsistency in the application of the relevant legislation on the maternity allowance and baby bonus. The staff (and even those at managerial level) at Social Security Department offices appear to make ill-informed decisions. In one instance a mother who actually worked in a division of the department itself was refused her entitlements by a senior officer.[149]

Implementation depends on their knowledge (or lack of it) and their willingness to process applications (which sometimes appears to depend on whether the mother has a 'contact' in the particular office), and not on the needs of the working mothers. It could be suggested that in many instances a lack of knowledge of the legislation, or overwork, may lead to unintended errors. However, the interviewees also indicate that officers may expedite or delay decisions based on personal acquaintance or familial relationship with the claimant, notwithstanding the provisions of the legislation. Familial loyalty is valued in the Libyan community, and offers extended family members opportunities in terms of access to employment, continued care for ageing family members and care of children (as demonstrated by the provision for breastfeeding breaks); however, it also carries an obligation to help family before others. Thus, an applicant who is a family member may have her application processed while others wait far longer.

In regard to the baby bonus and maternity allowance, the interviews repeatedly uncovered illegal actions undertaken by some departmental officials in relation to working mothers. The law clearly states that every mother is entitled to these benefits without her being subject to any conditions. The interviews revealed an inconsistent approach being taken by the Social Security Department. In some instances conditions were applied. One of the mothers interviewed described how her application for entitlements was rejected, the initial reason given being that she had accessed the private health sector during her pregnancy and so was not entitled to apply. This is completely incorrect. Her evidence was:

> With regards to the baby bonus and maternity allowance, I couldn't get it because of the hard application process from the welfare office. For your information, they told us that [my application for] the maternity allowance was [denied]. At the beginning, we were told that because you use the health private sector, you are not entitled to this right and so I said to them that I can't go the

147 G 1.5.13.

148 G 4.9.107. The interviewee here means that she was told her application was rejected because such an allowance no longer existed. This advice was false – the maternity allowance did exist, as did her entitlement.

149 G 4.9.107.

> public sector for 2 reasons. Firstly, because of the unavailability of complete services and secondly, because of the operating hours being only in the morning. This is what forced me to stop going there because if I leave, I will be warned and then reported as absent and I will be dismissed from my job. So how can I fix this problem? So the Social Security office reached a solution to cancel the allowance and instead they said they will provide more services in the public sector.[150]

However, accessing the private health system is not a basis for rejecting an application for the baby bonus or the maternity allowance, and in this instance the woman was denied both.

In addition to the maternity allowance and baby bonus referred to above, there is another one-off payment of 100 dinars which is given to all women who give birth, whether they are working or not, as provided in the *Order of the General People's Committee No 51 of 2007 on Social Assistance*.[151] Again many women are unaware of their entitlement and fail to apply. However, even when mothers applied for this assistance, many never received it. Again, access seemed often to depend more on 'contacts' with those administering the process than on following correct procedure. One of the mothers commented that:

> In 2007, a decision was made for me to be given a bonus of 100 dinars – that is the only time I have got one. However, my husband tried 10 times to get that bonus for me from the social security office, and I only received it when my child was 2 years of age; despite the fact that one of my friends got it after 2 months since the decision was made, and that was because her husband knew the worker at the social security office.[152]

Other mothers are deterred from applying by the difficult administration process involved and the length of time it takes to go through that process and be able to actually access this benefit. One of the mothers never even applied for the provision, having been dissuaded from applying for a different reason:

> I only knew of the last allowance [baby bonus] and it was an amount of 100 dinars to be given to every mother and I haven't applied for it as I heard from all of my colleagues that to receive this benefit is very difficult indeed.[153]

Another mother was of the same opinion. Although she applied for the allowance, her experience was far from satisfactory. She said:

> the new bonus that has recently been registered, which is 100 dinars, I didn't get it because there are a lot of hassles in the process and it is very hard to access it due to the bad administration in Libya. Imagine that my child is nearly 2 years old and I still didn't receive it yet.[154]

In conclusion, it was evident from the interviews that there is a great difference in reality, between the theory and practice of the law, with regard to the right of the working mother accessing the maternity allowances and baby bonus provided by law. It is also obvious that most mothers experienced difficulty in trying to access the benefits – the most important things seemed to be 'who

---

150 G 4.10.110–11.

151 *Order of the General People's Committee No 51 of 2007 on Social Assistance* (Libya).

152 G 1.2.5.

153 G 1.10.27.

154 G 2.9.55–6.

you know' and (unlike the usual expression) 'what you know'. The employees' lack of knowledge of their rights combines with the apparent dependence on 'contacts' to thread an application through the discouragingly difficult and time-consuming processes required in any attempt to access even minor benefits (benefits that may apparently be withheld almost on a whim). Accessing a legal *right* has been degraded into something that depends on the will of (and knowledge held by) others. This is highly discriminatory. Unfortunately, it appears that women's access to their basic rights in regard to maternity allowances and the baby bonus is not enforced equally for all working mothers.

Provision of Transport

The previous chapter explained the importance of the availability of transport for working mothers in Libya. Article 13 of *Order No 164 of 1988*[155] and Article 7 of *Order No 258 of 1989*[156] were specifically framed to facilitate women's participation in the workplace by encouraging the provision of transport to and from work for women. It is crucial in the Libyan context. There is often no public transport available, and the use of the private bus services is generally culturally unacceptable as this involves travel on often crowded, mixed-gender buses, which poses a danger to women's health and safety.[157] Addati and Cassirer observed:

> For women, transport can be more difficult than for men, and travel time can often be longer. Women's access to a number of forms of transport is restricted because of social and cultural rules. Generally, women do not have access to private vehicles and are more dependent than men on public transport. In addition, in some societies, men traditionally board buses first, with the consequence that women often do not get on. Using public transport can also be unsafe for women and in some places it can be socially difficult for women to share crowded public transport with men.[158]

The use of private taxis (with male drivers unrelated to the woman) is also unacceptable as it exposes unaccompanied women to risks to their own and their family's reputation. The cost of taxis is also prohibitive. As for working mothers driving themselves to work, there are two main problems: firstly the cost of acquiring and running a second vehicle for a family may be too great; and secondly, permission to drive to work may not be forthcoming from a working woman's husband.[159]

When suitable public transport is not available, women may feel they have no option but to use private transport buses, which is generally culturally unacceptable for a number of reasons (including those outlined above), or, alternatively, to cease working – hence the importance

155 *Order of the General People's Committee No 164 of 1988 on Employment of Arab Libyan Women* (Libya).

156 *Order of the* General *People's Committee No 258 of 1989 on the Rehabilitation and Training of Libyan Women* (Libya).

157 Working women struggle with small crowded buses with smoking (and often male) passengers who they would not normally mix with, and in the event of a breakdown of an unreliable vehicle a woman may be stranded alone. In terms of other risks, potential tourists, for example, are warned that driving in Libya is known to be hazardous; there is a high accident rate and little traffic enforcement despite poor driving standards and heavy traffic volumes. Windblown sand adds a further hazard. See Australian Government, Department of Foreign Affairs and Trade, *Travel Advice: Libya* (9 June 2011) <http://www.smartraveller.gov.au/zw-cgi/view/Advice/Libya>.

158 Addati and Cassirer, 'Equal Sharing of Responsibilities' UN Doc EGM/ESOR/2008/BP.2, above ch 1 n 39, 4.

159 Such permission is required in Muslim families in Libya and conservative states elsewhere.

of transport that is acceptable being provided by the government or the workplace. The above legislation was framed to make transport available from the workplace, to enable working mothers to exercise their right to work (without the struggle and costs that arranging suitable private transport would involve).[160]

Unfortunately, it was evident from the interviews that transport was not made available by some of the workplaces. For example, in the educational[161] and medical sectors, employer-supplied transport was not available at all. This was confirmed by both the doctors and the teachers. One teacher faced a number of problems due to the lack of availability of transport and tried a number of solutions:

> Transport to work was not available in the workplace, so I faced many problems with transport because the school is very far from my home and usually I was always late 5 minutes due to the private transport not being on time. The principal would make a note that I was late. Also, on the way home, I would be late in getting home and I would find my children waiting for me in the street. Therefore the only solution for me in getting to school and home on time is to catch a taxi, which is very costly in the morning and in the afternoon. There is no public transport available.[162]

Service provision has altered over the years, with cheap public transport giving way to expensive (and uncomfortable) private mini-buses. The same woman's observations go some way to testifying to the cultural reasons for women being reluctant to use such buses:

> In the past there was public transport and it was cheaper. All transportation now is private and it's expensive to access all the time.
>
> The other problem with accessing private transport is that if a woman uses the mini bus – which is cheaper, it will be very uncomfortable as many different people from all walks of life will be on the same bus. There will be people smoking, people using inappropriate language, even the way people look at you becomes a problem. All these things and more make it very uncomfortable for a woman to use the mini bus.
>
> As very few women use the mini bus it is commonly looked down upon when you see a woman catching the bus and especially if she is alone. This is part of the Libyan culture. Even her reputation can change. So unless she is really desperate, a woman will rarely catch the bus.[163]

But the alternative of a taxi is clearly regarded as no alternative for the vast majority of women in Libya:

> There is no transport from my work and this causes lots of trouble for me and suffering. For example, catching a taxi becomes a lot more expensive if you want to catch it to work and back home. You will not even be able to cover the cost daily with your wage. However if you catch it with a group of people, then the cost becomes cheaper and again, it is not culturally or religiously acceptable to see a woman alone with a car load of men.

---

160 Another obstacle is having a relative suitably qualified, fit, able and willing to drive the woman to and from work each day. Taking a taxi would be out of the question for most working women.

161 'There is no transportation available in any workplace in the teaching sector': G 1.8.21.

162 G 1.9.24.

163 G 1.9.24.

> So what then is the solution to transport? Taxis are unaffordable, a mini bus is not a good option and few women drive. How does a woman get to work on time if there is no transport provided from her workplace? This proves to be a big dilemma for most working mothers and a solution needs to be found.[164]

One of the doctors was of the same view with regard to the lack of availability of transport supplied by the workplace, and she stated that:

> No, there is no transport from my workplace even though workplace laws are insistent that your workplace must provide transport for you, but in all truthfulness, we are on one side and our law is on another side.[165]

As for the courts, this sector does not currently provide transport – though it has in the past. The experience of women working in that sector was not without difficulties. After the court sector began to import cars at a low price for their employees, the transport that had been previously provided was cancelled; but obviously not all women (and their families) had the means to purchase cars, or the desire to drive them. This was confirmed by all the working mothers in this sector. One of them commented:

> At the beginning of my work, transport was available, but after the legal system imported cars from overseas, the transport system was cancelled and they said that you can buy a car, for a set price, lower than the market price.
>
> But sadly, there are women that can drive and others that can't, especially some of those whose parents refuse to let them drive the car by themselves and this is very harsh. So they are forced to hire a private bus to transport them to work, but as for myself, I drive my car.[166]

Another mother from the same sector also complained about the lack of transport availability from the workplace:

> No, transport is not accessible from my workplace, even though it should be provided. But the law, especially with regards to the women in Libya, is on hold and put away and this is a critical negligence. So a few of my friends have been forced to use the public transport and pay from their pocket. This is a dangerous thing. The judge and the prosecutor should reduce their contact with the people because this affects his ability in his job, as he is a human being too.
>
> The pressure of the workload, doesn't give us a chance to ask for our right. The answer, even if we asked the question, is 'write and the cure comes from Allah'. We are sure that there will not be any change. All we can do is be patient.
>
> The answer from the people will be that this is the women's situation – who told you to get married – you must choose work or stay home.[167]

---

164 G 1.6.16.
165 G 2.8.52.
166 G 3.3.66.
167 G 3.4.70.

As for the administration sector, there were differences from one workplace to the other with regard to transport availability. For example, a mother from the university enjoyed the availability of transport from her workplace, but she said that it was 'because the university is far from the city'.[168]

Another mother, also from the administration sector (but from a different workplace), mentioned that there was transport availability from her work but that the employee's right to access it depended on the employee living a certain distance from the workplace. She also disclosed that the service provided was inadequate for the number of employees, very disorganised and unreliable.

> Yes transport is available from my workplace but I'm not entitled to it because I live close to my workplace.
>
> … the female employee is helpless and she is at the mercy of the driver. Sometimes the driver will come and pick her up and sometimes he won't, so she has to find her own way. When she asks the driver, 'What happened, I was waiting for you?', he will answer her, 'The bus was too crowded today', or sometimes 'There was a lot of traffic and I couldn't get to your house'.
>
> … we find that the workplace provides transport, but it's not enough to satisfy the number of female employees that work in this administration.[169]

One mother, also from the administration sector, commented that initially there was transport availability from her workplace but then it was cancelled after she made the 'mistake' of purchasing a car.

> Before, transportation was available, but when the bank purchased some cars from overseas, I took one and paid from my personal account. Then the transport service ceased. Personally, I suffer with transport as I can't drive by myself and this is unjust. We bought cars from our private accounts and [then] we were denied the workplace transportation that is guaranteed by law. I [now] use a private transport service.[170]

Another mother from the same sector commented:

> There is no transport available from the workplace and this causes great suffering and it is expensive to use the private transport.[171]

From all the evidence provided by the interviews with working mothers from all four sectors working in the same country under the same laws, it was evident that the legislation is not enforced equally from sector to sector. The right of the working mother to transport is dependent on the approach adopted by the manager at her workplace.

Again, the situation regarding transport (in common with that for the provision of childcare, maternity leave and breastfeeding times as provided by law) is often not the result of ignorance on the part of employers and managers, especially in the public sector. Every government entity workplace is aware of the law and has a special legal department to implement it; however, in reality they fail to do so. Nor is there any government authority that has to monitor whether the

168 G 4.6.99; see also G 4.7.101: 'Yes, in all honesty there is transport available from the university'.
169 G 4.3.93–4.
170 G 4.1.87–8.
171 G 4.10.111.

actions of the manager (in either the public or private sector) accord with the legislation. Thus a great discrepancy exists between the theory and practice of the law relating to transport for female employees.

Provision of Health Services

As outlined in Chapter 4, every Libyan has the right to be treated free of charge under Article 1 of the *Health Act No 106 of 1973*.[172] Libya's ratification in 1995 of the *Convention on the Elimination of All Forms of Discrimination against Women* (CEDAW) prompted further developments. Under CEDAW Libya promised to provide health services to all mothers in order to protect the mother and the baby.[173] *Order No 214 of 2002* states that health services are to be available specifically for the health needs of childcare and gynaecology.[174]

The interviews revealed, however, that the health services differed from one medical centre to another. This also depended on the manager of the medical centre and how the medical centre is run, as a number of the mothers from all the four groups made clear during the interviews when they were asked whether they accessed the public or private sector during pregnancy.

The answers from the women of all four sectors were very similar – they had accessed both the public and private sectors. The reasons for this were the same for all mothers. While cost could affect the choice of whether a mother accessed private sector services, public sector services could also involve particular costs; while accessing private health sector services inevitably involved higher additional outlays.

> To tell you the truth, during my pregnancy I used the public sector for two reasons; the first one was because the private health sector is very expensive, and the second one was because an excellent female doctor from the public sector worked in a clinic near my home. But I still pay for the ultrasounds an amount of 10 dinars for each; and for the pathology tests and medication [for which] I use the private sector. And that is because our income cannot cover all the costs in the private sector ...[175]

Another mother from the same sector reasoned similarly, with recourse to private sector services where specific services were lacking in the public sector. Compromises might have to be made, however, due to the higher cost of private service provision.

> During my pregnancy, I used to access the public health sector and whatever services were not available there, I used to try and get from the private health sector for example; pathology tests and treatment. However, giving birth in the private sector is expensive, so I access the public sector even though the service is not great.[176]

A doctor who accessed both the public and private sectors during her pregnancy and delivery stated:

172 *Health Act No 106 of 1973* (Libya).

173 *CEDAW* art 12(1) and (2).

174 *Order of the General People's Committee No 214 of 2002 Regarding the Health and Social Security Needs of Public and Private Hospitals of Child Care and Gynaecology* (Libya).

175 G 1.2.6.

176 G 1.6.15.

> With regards to health services, I used to access the public hospital during delivery. Because I'm a doctor and I have colleagues working in this hospital, I used to go to them to make sure that my health and my baby's health is okay. But this opportunity is not available to every working mother. I also access the private health sector because the services in the public sector are not completely available.[177]

Mothers from the courts sector confirmed the need to access both public and private services to ensure complete medical services:

> I used to access the public sector when I was pregnant and working as a lawyer and my work was not daily depending on the case. I heard of a public clinic that has all the services needed, so I accessed it but even still I needed to access the private sector.[178]

Mothers from the administration sector also noted the need to access the public sector (as well as the private sector) for some services during their time of pregnancy and delivery. One stated:

> Truly, I accessed both the public and the private sector. With regards to the public sector, it was necessary to go there for immunisations, as this is not available in the private sector. As for other services that were not available in the public sector, I needed to access the private sector, even though it was expensive.[179]

The working mothers from all sectors complained of the shortage of services in the public sector and stated that because of this they had little confidence in accessing public sector health services. Most also expressed doubts about the quality of the services provided. It was found that more than 50 per cent of the working mothers accessed the private sector, and most of them said that it was due to the same reason: the lack of services or fears for the quality of service provision in the public sector. This was evident during the interviews. Also evident was a reliance upon 'contacts' to guarantee service – whether this was in the public or the private sector. One of the teachers stated:

> I used to access the private sector during the entire period of my pregnancy including delivery, because I had to have caesarean births and truly all the health services are available in the private sector. There is also respect and appreciation in this sector, unlike the public sector where this does not exist.
>
> But, if you have strong contacts, like the head staff, in the clinics or have any family friends, you will benefit from all the services in the public sector. But without this, you don't receive any respect and even if you do find respect, the services are only available during the morning.[180]

The doctors shared the concerns expressed by the teacher about the quality of service provision in the public sector, but utilising private sector services access came with a substantial price-tag attached. One doctor stated:

---

177 G 2.1.31.
178 G 3.2.63.
179 G 4.3.93.
180 G 1.9.23.

> With regards to the health services, during my pregnancy and delivery I accessed the private sector. This is because the level of hygiene in the public health services is not good as it's unclean and crowded. I don't have time to wait around and also there is no equipment or pathology service and medicine is not readily available. Because with my 1st and 3rd babies I had caesarean delivery I had to go through the private sector and it was costly.[181]

Mothers from the courts sector also were of the same opinion regarding public sector health services provision for expectant and new mothers. One of them stated:

> The health services in the public sector [are] negligent and this is what forced me to access the private sector. Also the hours in the public sector are only in the morning session and private clinics operate in the evening.[182]

Another mother from the same sector also stated:

> Certainly, I used to access the private sector due to the lack of administration, the unavailability of necessary equipment for pregnant women and the overcrowding in the public sector. So I used to access the private sector and even now that my children are in pre-school, I still take them to the private sector for any health issue.[183]

An administration sector mother also said that she accessed private sector services due to a lack of service availability in the public sector:

> During my entire pregnancy and delivery, I accessed the private sector because of the lack of services in the public sector.[184]

Another mother from the same sector stated:

> I used to access the private sector as my pregnancy was very hard and I needed special care, whereas in the public sector sometimes I can find a doctor and sometimes I can't. Also, the operating hours in the public sector is only in the morning and I work in the morning. The services are also not complete in the public sector.[185]

Working mothers from all four sectors voiced similar complaints about access to health services. Working mothers employed within the health system confirmed that the problems are pervasive. One working mother in the biggest public maternity hospital drew attention to the services being severely overtaxed, resulting in care being less than optimal:

> I have been working at this hospital for 20 years continuously with lots of giving and care … Truly, the difficult thing that my colleagues and I face is that there are a lot of sick patients in our hospital. Sometimes I can receive up to 40 cases of pregnant women daily that are coming to give birth and I do about 4 caesareans per day. So, we spoke to the Department of Health, about the increase in

181 G 2.6.46.
182 G 3.4.69.
183 G 3.7.77.
184 G 4.5.97.
185 G 4.9.107–8.

> [the] number of patients and their answer to us was that they will open a new hospital with 1,200 beds. In all honesty, when they opened the new hospital, they took a big number of doctors from our hospital and that affected the number of doctors we had as the number of our patients didn't decrease. Sometimes there are 2 pregnant women in the same bed.
>
> Research shows that a mother needs to stay in the hospital for at least 2 days after giving birth so that she can be looked after, but because of the number of patients, sometimes she has to leave 2 hours after giving birth. This is very dangerous for the life of the mother and the baby and we are sick of talking about this issue, so the only solution we have is to look for our retirement age, so that we can have a rest. But research shows that no doctor working in the maternity ward will live to celebrate his 60th birthday. What we say, is that all of the doctors that work in this hospital are so exhausted and they don't have anything to offer anymore.[186]

A second doctor expressed similar concerns:

> I have been working in this hospital for 18 years and have never stopped … Imagine this hospital receives between 130 and 150 patients daily some of whom their cases include delivery, miscarriage, female diseases and also big operations. The birthing cases include about 70 deliveries per day … we asked for very important things for this hospital for the sake of the patients, but there was no response … The people responsible for the health sector are not qualified for this responsibility. This hospital was built in 1918 and until now, there hasn't been any changes not even addition of extra rooms or anything else. Imagine that![187]

While the doctor above noted the lack of infrastructure and resulting overcrowding and less than optimal care, a third doctor who has worked for eight years gave evidence of the difficulties facing medical staff and their patients in public health facilities, particularly in relation to equipment:

> I have been working as a doctor for 8 years … I … work … as a Gynaecologist … There is a lot of important equipment that is missing in the hospital and imagine that there is only one Cardiotocogram which is the baby heart monitor and this machine is very important to protect the life of the baby from death in its final month. This is a big hospital that receives between 130–150 female patients every day. One machine has to be shared by 3 departments: pre-natal unit, birthing unit and the emergency unit.
>
> So when I suggested to the head of the department that we get together and put some money in to purchase another machine, because it is very important in our work, to protect the baby and the mother, he told me how you can say that, as you will face questioning by a special department. This is forbidden and we asked the Department of Health for a machine but there was no answer and he told me to be patient and work with what we have.[188]

The threat of investigation (mentioned in the final paragraph) if necessary equipment is purchased gives an insight into a culture that one hopes is disappearing from the new Libya, to be replaced by

186 G 2.8.52–4.
187 G 2.7.49–50.
188 G 2.9.55–6.

one where such a request would be welcomed rather than seen as a veiled criticism and therefore an insult and a threat to the regime.

Working mothers testified to the conditions (scarcely sanitary) that prevail in the public hospitals. One in the courts sector said:

> Imagine with my 3rd child, after I gave birth, I was placed with another mother in the same bed, right after giving birth! All the other rooms had the same situation, 2 mothers per bed. Imagine I am haemorrhaging and the lady next to me is haemorrhaging. Facing a lot of diseases and after this experience and the lack of care about the patient, I decided with my 4th child to access only the private sector.[189]

From the individual interviews that were conducted, it is clear that there are struggles that the mothers face during their pregnancy and delivery due to the shortage of necessary services in the public sector, which forces them to access the costly private sector. There is no equality of access to quality care. Access and quality vary not only between the sectors but also between the various centres within each system and with individual practitioners. Access is further mediated by the financial situation of the mother and her family, and often compromises appear to be made. Again it is obvious that there is a difference in terms of the provision of quality health services for expectant working mothers and their children, that is, between what the legislation offers in theory and what mothers receive in practice.

Conclusion: Implementation and Enforcement are Problematic

From the interviews conducted with working mothers, it is evident that the enforcement of relevant Libyan laws is seriously uneven. This is so despite the fact that the legal rights of working mothers are very clear and do not need any further clarification or interpretation with regard to their implementation and enforcement in the various workplaces. Some of the reasons for the uneven implementation and enforcement of the law are legal, while others are administrative. This will be clarified in detail below.

Legal Reasons

There are several legal reasons that have led to a failure to enforce the law with regard to the rights of working mothers.

1. Monitoring the law and ensuring its implementation and enforcement remains a problem in Libya. Libya failed to grasp the opportunity offered when the High Court's power of review of legislation (a power it had held since its inception in 1953 but lost in 1982)[190] was re-established through *Act No 17 of 1994*.[191] Even though the Court's role was to review the executive power and the legislative power in Libya, the process became one of monitoring (rather than a genuine review), and such monitoring did not guarantee increased enforcement; rather, the use of

189 G 3.9.83.

190 *Re-establishment of the High Court Act No 6 of 1982* (Libya); see also Division for Public Administration and Development Management (DPADM), Department of Economic and Social Affairs (DESA), United Nations, *Great Socialist People's Libyan Arab Jamahiriya: Public Administration Country Profile* (4 October 2010) <http://unpan1.un.org/intradoc/groups/public/documents/UN/UNPAN023273.pdf>.

191 *Monitor the Executive Power and the Legislative Power Act No17 of 1994* (Libya).

legislative and executive power was merely documented. And so monitoring the law[192] *and* ensuring its implementation and enforcement remains seriously lacking in Libya. Thus, there is only limited internal monitoring of legislation and regulations or orders at their inception, in their drafting. Compliance with international obligations appears not to be considered at this stage. Rather, it is in the later reports to the relevant bodies that such matters come to the attention of the government.

The laws themselves fail to provide for monitoring of workplaces or, where such mechanisms exist for monitoring, departmental compliance with the laws' provisions is poor. Monitoring compliance on a workplace basis, therefore, is seriously lacking. In relation to maternity leave provision, childcare facilities, transport provision and breastfeeding breaks, for example, no inspectorate exists and few statistics are gathered. This remains a bone of contention for the international bodies to which Libya must report.[193]

Libya has, until the most recent Revolution of 2011, lacked a constitution in the conventional sense.[194] Consequently, its laws were not able to be enforced subject to the overarching provisions of a constitution. Where a constitution exists, there is an avenue for enforcing the law, as legislation enacted that is contrary to the provisions of a nation's constitution can often be challenged in a country's courts on the basis that legislation is not to be incompatible with the nation's constitution.[195] Having an effective modern constitution opens the way for a legislature to be censured for passing legislation contrary to the constitution. It could also be anticipated that legislation promoting the aims embodied in a constitution would be favourably received and the likelihood of their implementation and enforcement increased. If such a constitution embodied the rights of working mothers, their rights might be able to be better protected.

192 Salih Muftah Al-Zwy, 'Dawr Al-Qanwn fi Tnfydh Al-Siyasat Al-Amm' (Paper presented at the Alsiyasat Al-'Ammh, Bnghazy (Libya), 12–14 June 2007) 84 [Trans: 'The Role of Law in Executing Public Policies' (Paper presented at Public Policies, Benghazi)] 77–8; see also Fathi Muhmmd Al-B'jh, 'Malm Yntbih Elyh Tqwym Al-Tnafusyh Fi Al-Jmahyriyh: Nzrh Fi Al-Hkmaniyh wa Siyasat Al-Tmkyn' (Paper presented at the Al-Siyasat Al-Ammh, Bnghazy (Libya), 12–14 June 2007) 320 [Trans: 'What Has Not Been Considered by the Competitiveness Calendar in Libya: An Insight into Governance and Empowerment Politics' (Paper presented at Public Policies, Benghazi)] 328.

193 CEDAW Committee, *Concluding Observations – Libya*, UN Doc CEDAW C/LBY/CO/5 (6 February 2009), above ch 1 n 58, 8 [36].

194 The pre-revolutionary 1951 *Constitution of Libya* (amended 1963) was abolished by the Constitutional Declaration of 11 December 1969, and a provisional limited 'Temporary Constitution' adopted, to be replaced by a short document – *Declaration on the Establishment of the Authority of the People 1977* (Libyan) – under which the *Qur'ān* is listed as the constitution of the country (Article 2). Libya still awaits a legislated constitution as one would be commonly understood. The apparent discrepancy between the 1969 Temporary Constitution and the 1977 Declaration had not been addressed when the Transitional Government took control after the Revolution of 2011. The incoming government formulated a draft constitution which has yet to be formally approved. For the text, see *Draft Constitutional Charter for the Transitional Stage* (23 October 2011) <http://www.al-bab.com/arab/docs/libya/Libya-Draft-Constitutional-Charter-for-the-Transitional-Stage.pdf>. Currently there does not appear to be progress in creating a new constitution. Meetings of the body charged with formulating its wording had ceased at the time of writing in 2011.

195 For example, if a country's constitution contained a guarantee of equality of access to employment or education irrespective of gender or nursing mother status, implementation of legislation that effectively reduced such access could perhaps be appealed to a country's Supreme Court and overturned, necessitating further legislative change.

2. The instability seen in Libyan legislation with the rapid addition of new legislation and its continual change in terms of organisation and responsibility within sectors[196] causes great confusion in the different sectors, where those in charge of administering the legislation or putting its provisions into action are uncertain as to what is to be applied and when. This confusion leads to a degree of uncertainty in the application of legislation and even conflict which later leads to further instability. If the authorities themselves charged with administering legislation are in some doubt as to its correct implementation, how can their employees (working women) be expected to understand or know their entitlements?

Unfortunately, in such circumstances new legislation can lead to uncertainty regarding an issue rather than solving the problem. Indeed, as evident in Libya today, the old legislation may be a lot clearer than the new. This contradicts logic – the new law should be clearer than, and preferable to, the legislation it replaces. This is the norm of any society. Unfortunately, this is not the case in Libya.[197]

3. The amendment or the repeal of Libyan laws, either with or without clear justification, results in the non-enforcement of these laws.[198] For instance, *Act No 7 of 1997*[199] amended Article 98 of *Act No 58 of 1970*.[200] However, this 'amendment' was no improvement. It simply restated paragraph 1, but repealed paragraph 2 – a paragraph that was very important to the working mother.[201] There was no progress in relation to women's rights as mothers in the workplace.

4. Another factor ostensibly related to the law, and one that influences the non-enforcement of the law, is that different administrators interpret the law or regulation (or order) in different ways. This leads to the law being neglected by the majority of both individuals and workplace administrative bodies. Therefore, the law is either put into practice or not, depending on the interpretation of the legislation by the relevant head of administration. If implemented, such implementation will differ from workplace to workplace, again depending on the head of administration's opinion on the matter. It also differs depending on the type of work done.[202] The result is an appearance that Libya is divided into many regions and that these regions have 'different' laws. In reality, however, Libya has only one system of law that should be applicable throughout the country.[203]

It was discovered during the interviews that there were many cases of such 'misinterpretations'. For instance, there was a clear difference between many working mothers in regard to aspects such as their right to the baby bonus and maternity allowance. For example, one woman was prevented from exercising both these rights (baby bonus and maternity allowance) because she gave birth in a private hospital.[204] This is an 'exemption' clearly not mentioned in law. Another case that was evident with many women was the fact that while many women did have three months' maternity leave, they had access to it only under strict conditions.[205] Such conditions included taking half of

---

196 For example, under one Act all sectors of education may be treated as a unit, while under another, each section is treated as a separate unit. Such arrangements may fluctuate with each successive piece of legislation.

197 Al-Zwy, 'The Role of Law', above n 192, 133.

198 Ibid. 76.

199 *Amendment Act No 7 of 1997 of Some Provisions of Act No 58 of 1970* (Libya).

200 *Labour Code Act No 58 of 1970* (Libya).

201 See in detail Chapter 4, under 'Shortfalls in the Provision of Childcare Facilities'.

202 For privately employed persons, access to some benefits also depends on their contributing to a social security scheme: *Social Security Act No 13 of 1980* (Libya) art 31.

203 Al-Zwy, 'The Role of Law', above n 192, 81.

204 G 4.10.110–11. See text above n 150.

205 See above in the current chapter, under 'Provision of Maternity Leave'.

it before the anticipated date of birth of the child and half after the birth. Such conditions are not mentioned in the law and are clearly, again, a 'misinterpretation'. From these and other examples, it can be concluded that not only is there a large gap between the experience of women in different workplaces but also that many of these women do not enjoy their rights – as these rights are either ignored or modified, depending on the head of administration of their particular workplace.

5. Libyan workforce administrators also struggle with the issue of the plethora of departmental offices and other bodies with which they have to deal, all of which are charged with monitoring various issues (for example, public sector employment issues, bribery or corruption and so forth). Some are created by law and others created by executive fiat; a number may handle the same cases simultaneously. For example, there is (or at least were prior to the 2011 Revolution) a 'Purification Office' and the 'Office of the Independent Monitor of the People' (both government offices within the Ministry for Justice); and non-government bodies (not created by legislation) such as the Convoys or Caravans Revolutionary and Revolutionising Committees[206] and various other bodies for administrative development. All may be involved in a case that arises, for example, from an instance of corruption. It will take time to establish the new legislative, administrative and judicial bodies. It is assumed that, at least in the interim, these bodies or equivalents may continue to exist. There is no guarantee – yet surely there is the hope – that a simpler, clearer administrative system can be constructed and legislation enacted and enforced that guarantees the rights of working mothers.

The problem to date (and probably for some time in the foreseeable future), however, has been that, firstly, in terms of processes of investigation, officials from different offices (independent of each other) may investigate a single case. This causes confusion in a workplace which is trying to respond to requests from different investigating bodies, with all the paperwork that entails. This wastes time and effort, and reduces the productive capacity of that workplace. This has led to discomfort in various workplace administrative offices.[207]

Secondly, at the investigative end (at the monitoring bodies), so many different people working on the same case is also an inefficient and wasteful use of time and resources. The monitoring bodies are overwhelmed with a confusion of 'paper trails' in relation to the many bodies which may have a stake in the matter and not focusing on their main goal, which is to enforce the law. Nor are they necessarily dealing with the problems forwarded by the workplace administrative offices to the monitoring offices for adjudication or advice. Many are only opened or noted but not actually concluded and solved.[208]

Monitoring offices are also created to settle disputes or disagreements in the workforce, for example, employee complaints.[209] It should be noted that truly independent bodies are almost unknown, as all such organisations must be approved in order to function. Hence there are a limited

---

206 English translation of the names of these organisations is difficult, but both were created by the government – by executive fiat not by specific parliamentary legislation.

207 Ahmed Al-Sadq Al-Jhany, 'Al-Ekhtisas Al-Jina'y Lljihat Al-Rqabyyh Ala Al-Edarh Al-Ammh' in Muhmmd Zahi Al-Mghiyrbi and Abdul Jalyl Adm Al-Mansouri (eds), *Al-Edarh Al-Ammh Fi Libya: Al-Waq' wa Al-Tumohat* (Mrkiz Buhwth Al-Auluwm Al-Eqtisadyh, 2004) 371, 384 [Trans: 'Criminal Jurisdiction for Governmental Agencies on Public Administration' in *Public Administration in Libya* (Research Centre for Economic Sciences)].

208 Ibid. 385.

209 It should be noted that employees can bring complaints firstly to their immediate superior and then, if that is unsatisfactory, to their legal office (in their government department or entity). However, if they are unsatisfied with the response at that level, they can then go directly to the appropriate monitoring body (that is, the one created by the law and related specifically to their field of employment). Administrators can also

number of government approved representative associations. The Women's Union and the Judges' Association, the Boy Scouts and the Libyan Red Crescent are some of the few organisations given the appropriate licence.[210] This necessarily reduces the capacity for independent critical evaluation of government policy and legislation, fosters a reluctance to criticise legislation and also contributes to its lack of enforcement.

6. Another factor that contributes to the failure by employers to put the law into practice (and also to employee ignorance of their rights) is the lack of appropriate legislation and/or regulation in certain areas. For example, the educational private sector has been allowed to flourish without its having been given set regulations governing the rights and conditions of its employees.[211] These are not protected; nor does there appear to be controlled supervision of the actions of members of the sector. For instance, during my interview with one particular woman who was employed at a private school, she revealed that to work at this school a woman must not be married. This clearly conflicts with Libya's anti-discrimination laws.[212] Another issue faced by employees in the private sector, generally, is that there may be no official, lawful contract between employee and employer. As a consequence, the employee has no rights and therefore can be discriminated against.

7. The interference of the executive in the legislative arm's work causes an overload in legislation which leads to dispute and conflict, which in turn results in legislation not being enforced.[213] This is clear in instances such as the provision of childcare facilities in the workplace. *Act No 58 of 1970* and *Act No 5 of 1997*[214] were both promulgated by the legislature, yet the executive promulgated three Orders on childcare facilities. These three Orders created repetition, difference and collision between the two Acts. The first Order states that there may be childcare facilities in the workplace; however, there should be a reasonable number of working women to do so.[215] The second Order sets out certain requirements that have to be met in order for a child to be enrolled in childcare.[216] The third, *Order No 10572 of 2009*,[217] restates the ideas regarding the establishment of childcare facilities to help the working mother contained in Article 98 of *Act No 57 of 1970* and Article 12 of *Order No 164 of 1988*. However, these statutes state different bases for the establishment of childcare centres in the workplace (the latter leaving the matter to the employer's discretion).

8. Even though many working women face many hardships and are greatly discriminated against in their workplace, they do not speak up; they do not complain or demand their rights. Feeling helpless, these women attempt to deal with these hardships or live with them. Even though

---

contact these bodies. If an employee is unhappy with the outcome, they can then go to the court – if they can afford it. This is impossible for most if not all working mothers.

210 Hanspeter Mattes, 'Formal and Informal Authority in Libya Since 1969' in Dirk Vandewalle (ed), *Libya Since 1969: Qadhafi's Revolution Revisited* (Palgrave Macmillan, 2008) 55, 61–2.

211 Attiah Al-Mhdi Al-Fytwri, 'Aqtisadyat Al-Edarh Al-Ammh' in Muhmmd Zahi Al-Mghiyrbi and Abdul Jalyl Adm Al-Mansouri (eds), *Al-Edarh Al-Ammh Fi Libya: Al-Waq' wa Al-Tumohat* (Mrkiz Buhwth Al-Auluwm Al-Eqtisadyh, 2004) 57, 65 [Trans: 'The Economics of Public Administration' in *Public Administration in Libya*], above, n 207.

212 See Chapter 4, under 'History of Legislation that Aims to Prevent Discrimination'.

213 Hussein Abdul Qadir, *Tawazun Al-Sulth fi Al-Dimuqratiyyh Al-Sh'biyh* (LLM Thesis, Jami't Qarywnis, 2002) 127 [Trans: *The Balance of Government in Libya* (Garyounis University)].

214 *Child Protection Act No 5 of 1997* (Libya).

215 *Order of the General People's Committee No 164 of 1988 on Employment of Arab Libyan Women* (Libya).

216 *Order of the General People's Committee No 88 of 1998 on the Requirements for Childcare Facility for Working Mothers* (Libya).

217 *Order of the General People's Committee No 10572 of 2009 on the Female Worker Who is Nursing her Child for Eighteen Months* (Libya).

the working woman in Libya faces hardship and discrimination in her workplace or cannot obtain her rights in the workplace, she does not seek to have her rights enforced by a court of law for a number of reasons both structural and cultural. Firstly, the Libyan judicial system is slow to handle any cases before it.[218] Secondly, a woman attempting to obtain her rights would be a subject of gossip (as would her family) rather than seen as someone seeking justice and what is rightfully hers. Succinctly put, her alternatives are simply to stay in the workplace and endure the situation or 'stay at home'. Despite their educational qualifications, their increasing workplace participation and a (very) slowly expanding area of activity, such a degree of assertiveness would be seen as culturally inappropriate, even 'shameful' by many. This must change for women to gain access to their rights.

Administrative Reasons

The second reason the law is not enforced is administrative. Again, there are many administrative reasons that lie behind failure to implement the law. The administrative reasons are:

1. The rapid and rushed change of the heads of administration at both the national and regional level, and their varying ethical and ideological standpoints in the workplace, results in an unpredictable administrative system. Its output tends to be unstable (varying according to whoever occupies a particular office rather than consonant with the legislation) and weak. This issue leads to an administrative system unable to fulfil its role, unable to take care of individuals and unable to function properly.[219]

2. The lack of top-rate personnel occupying important administrative roles, especially that of head of administration in most government departments, is one of the main reasons why the law is not enforced. In many cases the Libyan system selects administrative heads according to such aspects as purported allegiance to the government or on the basis of tribal loyalties (and perceived obligations) rather than selecting candidates based on their ability and skill. Today, selection on such illegitimate bases predominates, and risks hampering the country's development.[220] Loyalties to family and extended familial or tribal obligations may also affect appointment to lower positions or ease of access to legislated entitlements, as is demonstrated by a number of the interviews. Workplace employment policies must also be transparent and unbiased to achieve the best outcomes for women – and especially women who are mothers – in the workplace.

On the complexities inherent in the implementation of the Jamahiriya system, its impacts on administration and legislation, and the role played by broader tribal loyalties in the mix, it is worth repeating the observation of George Joffé, that '[t]he new institutions, despite their populist and egalitarian appearance, are … neopatrimonial in nature'[221] and (one could add) may manifest traditional patriarchal attitudes towards women in the workforce and their rights despite the existence of legislation to the contrary. The integrated structure has meant an absence of dissenting

---

218 Al-B'jh, above n 192, 329.

219 Salih Muftah Al-Zwy, 'Athr Al-Lamrkziyh Ala Ada' Al-Edarh Fi Libya' in Muhmmd Zahi Al-Mghiyrbi and Abdul Jalyl Adm Al-Mansouri (eds), *Al-Edarh Al-Ammh Fi Libya: Al-Waq' wa Al-Tumohat* (Mrkiz Buhwth Al-Auluwm Al-Eqtisadyh, 2004) 108, 132 [Trans: 'Decentralisation Impact on Libyan's Administration Performance' in *Public Administration in Libya*], above, n 207.

220 Abu-Bkr Mustfa Ba'yrh, 'Al-Siyast Al-Ammh Lltnmiyh Al-Edariyh' (Paper presented at the Al-Siyasat Al-Ammh, Bnghazy (Libya), 12–14 June 2007) 204 [Trans: 'Public Policies for Administrative Development' (Paper presented at Public Policies, Benghazi)].

221 George Joffé, 'Prodigal or Pariah? Foreign Policy in Libya' in Dirk Vandewalle (ed), *Libya Since 1969: Qadhafi's Revolution Revisited* (Palgrave Macmillan, 2008) 191, 201.

voices in what is essentially a one-party state where such 'values are either marginalized or absorbed into the unitary structure of the *jamahiriyya*'.[222] Independent voices may have great difficulty being heard. It is perhaps worth noting that there is no possibility of union representation in a workplace in relation to women or other workers, as 'freedom of association or of expression' are not guaranteed.[223] The unitary nature of the state is supposed to have accommodated implementation of rights and so forth, yet it is evident from the interviews conducted that this is not the case.

Baltmr lamented the disappearance of high-quality administrative systems, the inadequacy of the existing monitoring systems and the disappearance of the practice of employing the right person for the right place. It also seems that the strict and straightforward policies, goals, functions and regulations – which are the necessary foundations for a strong and unbiased administrative system – were also disappearing.[224]

3. Within administrative systems (at local, regional and national levels in various areas of the public sector, or in individual enterprises or system-wide in the private sector), there is often no management of training for employees.[225] Without training there will be no development within any administration.[226] There is also a lack of research and modification within such systems. Not only this, but the systems do not prioritise and expand their knowledge. All these factors lead to one conclusion – the Libyan administration system is not improving and developing to fulfil its role.[227] This is fundamental for public administration generally and crucial for their implementation of the rights of women in the workplace.

4. The unstable and consistent changes in the various workplace sectors without any planning, research and analysis leads to both employer and employee ignorance of the rights of employees. For instance, a ministry may be closed one day and then the next day may be re-opened and then closed again. This is repeated constantly, without any logical explanation or reason for doing so.[228] This factor has a great impact on the administration ministries; with the constant change of the workplace sectors the administration ministry has lost its efficiency and stability.[229]

5. The World Economic Forum has noted that the country's competitiveness continues to be affected by inefficient and corrupt administrative practices.[230] The practices detailed above have

222 Ibid. 200.

223 Ibid.

224 Ahmed Ali Baltmr, 'Kfa't Al-Qiyadat Al-Edariyh Mn Al-Muttlabat Al-Asasiyh Lejwdat Al-Qita' Al-Amm fi Libya' in Muhmmd Zahi Al-Mghiyrbi and Abdul Jalyl Adm Al-Mansouri (eds), *Mrkiz Buhwth Al-Auluwm Al-Eqtisadyh* (2004) 209, 216 [Trans: 'Efficiency of the Administrative Leadership of the Basic Requirements for the Quality of the Public Sector in Libya' in *Public Administration in Libya*], above, n 207.

225 Libya ranked 110th of 139 countries in extent of staff training: World Economic Forum (WEF), *Global Competitiveness Report 2010–2011* (WEF, 2010) 217.

226 Ba'yrh, above n 220, 203.

227 Baltmr, above n 224, 225.

228 Ba'yrh, above n 220, 208.

229 Muhmmd Zahi Al-Mghiyrb, 'Athr Al-Tghyyrat Al-Hykaliyh Ala Wd'a Al-Siyasat Al-Ammh wa tnfiydhha Fi Libya (1977–2003)' in Muhmmd Zahi Al-Mghiyrbi and Abdul Jalyl Adm Al-Mansouri (eds), *Al-Edarh Al-Ammh Fi Libya: Al-Waq' wa Al-Tumohat* (Mrkiz Buhwth Al-Auluwm Al-Eqtisadyh, 2004) 35, 39 [Trans: 'The Re-Structuring Impact on Public Policies in Libya' in *Public Administration in Libya*], above, n 207.

230 In 2006 Libya was 105th of 163 countries in the WEF's *Global Competitiveness Report* (2006): Ba'yrh, above n 220, 211, where the authors cite the WEF, *Global Competitiveness Report 2005–2006* (2006). Four years later, it still ranked 100th of 139 countries: WEF, *Global Competitiveness Report 2010–2011*, above n 225, 216–17. In 2009–10, WEF, *Global Competitiveness Report 2009–2010* (2009) 200. Libya ranked 88th, up from 91st in 2008–09, WEF, *Global Competitiveness Report 2008–2009* (2008) 218; but the

continued to affect competitiveness by impairing effective functioning and contributing to limited female workplace participation (where it ranked 133rd).[231] However, there is another factor clearly evident and cited as 'the most problematic factor for doing business' in Libya by Libyan businesses themselves: corruption.[232] (Unsurprisingly, inefficiency in government administration ranked second.)[233] Corruption is not simply the offering and accepting of bribes; it can be more subtle 'undue influence' regarding policies, contracts or employment, or continuing systems of patronage[234] that have survived into the modern world. Corruption is evident in the areas of both administration and finance[235] and 'remains a major skewing factor in the award and execution of international business contracts'.[236] This further impacts on competitiveness and the international reputation of the country.

6. Failure to implement the full requirements of the legislation in relation to mothers in the workplace is not uncommon and can stem from an unwillingness to do so or from ignorance. For example, during the interviews with the working mothers in the educational sector it became clear that there were differences in implementation. The principal of one school agreed to the establishment of a childcare facility while another refused.[237] Another aspect that was highlighted during the interviews was in regard to the one hour allowed for breastfeeding. Some schools allowed their employees to exercise this right while others refused to do so, maintaining that this was not even a right in the first place.[238] Such actions contribute to Libya's position of 111th out of 111 countries surveyed in the *Global Competitiveness Report 2005–06* in regard to the aspect of 'quality of management [in] schools'.[239] As a result, 'policies and practices remain inconsistent across the country, employers must consider their alternatives and examine their benefits plans. If plans discriminate against ... mothers they risk potential human rights complaints and/ or grievances'.[240]

7. Complex work procedures and the unorganised, unrevised administrative procedures serve the country and its citizens poorly. These, and the unrecognised importance of modification and development within the administration and the ministries, are among the reasons behind the slow, inefficient and unreliable administrative system in Libya.[241] A number of international studies and

---

overall ranking remains skewed by Libya's favourable macroeconomic environment (where it ranks 7th): 216. Nonetheless, it continues to face 'numerous challenges related to the inefficiency of [its] goods, labour and financial markets, as well as underdeveloped infrastructures and low levels of technological adoption, among others': 39.

231 WEF, *Global Competitiveness Report 2010–2011*, above n 225, 217.

232 Cited by 20.9% of respondents to the WEF survey: ibid. 216 [see Table].

233 Ibid.

234 See, e.g., International Bank for Reconstruction and World Bank, 'World Development Report: The State in a Changing World' (Oxford University Press, 25 June 1997) 13, 109.

235 Ba'yrh, above n 220, 209–10.

236 Ethan D Chorin, 'The Future of the U.S.-Libyan Commercial Relationship' in Dirk Vandewalle (ed), *Libya Since 1969: Qadhafi's Revolution Revisited* (Palgrave Macmillan, 2008) 153, 155.

237 See in details this chapter, under 'Provision of Childcare Facilities in the Workplace'.

238 See details this chapter, under 'Provision of the Breastfeeding Hour'.

239 Al-B'jh, above n 192, 319.

240 Natasha VandenHoven and Shelly Shapero, 'Maternity Leave and Employee Benefits' (2002) 26(5) *Benefits Canada* 9, 10.

241 Mas'oud Abdul Hafiz Al-Badri, 'Tqyym Al-Mashakl wa Al-Su'wbat Allti Tuwajih Al-Edarh Al-Maliyh Al-Ammh' in Muhmmd Zahi Al-Mghiyrbi and Abdul Jalyl Adm Al-Mansouri (eds), *Al-Edarh Al-Ammh Fi Libya: Al-Waq' wa Al-Tumohat* (Mrkiz Buhwth Al-Auluwm Al-Eqtisadyh, 2004) 282, 285 [Trans:

reports completed in this area indicate Libya's vulnerable position on any international comparison in regard to administration.[242]

From the above, it can be seen that due to continual changes in administration, as well as continual role changes in administration and changes in legislation, the law is not being enforced and current administrative procedures are time-consuming and inefficient.

Concluding Statement

Working mothers in Libya do not enjoy their rights in the workplace. In reality, the Libyan woman is very tolerant of her situation and asks for the minimum of her rights. What she complains of the most is not having any childcare facilities or, where these do exist, that she lacks *suitable* childcare facilities where she can leave her child and be confident that the child is comfortable and well cared for in adequate surroundings with suitably trained personnel. There are no guidelines, or inspectors, for building safety and hygiene. The government needs to prioritise these areas for women to be able to leave their children confidently in quality childcare centres in their workplace. It also needs to look at training for staff and, again, at the provision of inspectors to ensure that any regulations introduced related to working mothers are enforced.

It is clear from the interviews conducted that many of the working mothers leave their children with their family, neighbours or friends. Some of them, who have nowhere to place their children, have even resorted to leaving them at home by themselves, even from a very young age. This is what the working mothers complain most about, and some of them have had to leave work in order to look after their children as they have no one to help look after their children.

Due to these struggles, the number of women in the workforce in Libya is decreasing. With regard to female participation in the workforce, Libya has been ranked 133 out of 139 countries.[243] This reflects a very poor participation rate in comparison to that of other countries, yet in terms of secondary and tertiary enrolment rates, Libya is in the top 50 countries surveyed.[244] The subsequent low female employment participation rate represents an inefficiency that no nation can afford. If Libya is to continue to advance, it needs to deliver on the promise of an environment that fosters the employment of its talented and well-educated women, allowing them to combine both motherhood and employment. It is not enough merely to enact legislation that purports to do so.

Countries with good laws (and with appropriate bodies to monitor and enforce the law) that protect and ensure the rights of women, especially those of working women, are met are countries that will prosper with females in the workforce. A high number of females in the workforce has many benefits, including contributing to the wealth of the nation. Take Australia, for example: since the enactment of the *Sex Discrimination Act 1984*,[245] the number of women in the workforce 'has almost doubled'. This has led to Australia becoming a 'wealthy nation', its 'gross domestic

---

'Problems and Obstacles Facing the Public Financial Administration: An Evaluation' in *Public Administration in Libya*], above, n 207.

242 Amal Obeidi, 'Bawadir Al-Eslah Al-Siyasi wa Athruh Ala Siyasat Tmkyn Al-Mr'ah fi libya: Dirash Estkshafih' (Paper presented at the Al-Siyasat Al-Ammh, Bnghazy (Libya), 12–14 June 2007) 361 [Trans: 'Political Reform in Libya and its Impact on Women: A Discovering Study' (Paper presented at the conference Public Policies, Benghazi) 356.

243 WEF, *Global Competitiveness Report 2010–2011*, above n 225, 217.

244 Ibid.

245 *Sex Discrimination Act 1984* (Cth).

product doubling since 1981'.[246] Its participation rate still lags behind the Northern European states, but the recent enactment of the *Paid Parental Leave Act 2010*[247] is expected to assist women to maintain and increase their presence in the workforce. Measures to allow families to successfully combine parenthood and workplace participation stand to not merely increase a nation's financial wealth, but also the physical and mental well-being of its members. In Libya, as elsewhere, many women desire to contribute to the development of their nation while not forgoing childbearing or a degree of involvement in the rearing of their children. They do not wish their education to only be exercised in the confines of their homes and in their immediate family circle. Rather, they wish to contribute to the building of a new nation, with expanding developmental horizons and a better future for their children, particularly (it must be said) for their daughters.

It is a matter of justice. Constructing a just society, one that (among other things) recognises the contribution of women, particularly mothers, is the challenge that faces the new Libya.

246 Sharan Burrow, 'An Unequal World' (2004) 27(3) *UNSW Law Journal* 884, 885.
247 *Paid Parental Leave Act 2010* (Cth).

Chapter 6
Conclusion

> Where, after all, do universal human rights begin? In small places, close to home – so close and so small they cannot be seen on any maps of the world. Yet they are the world of the individual person; the neighbourhood he lives in, the school or college he attends; the factory, farm, or office where he works. Such are the places where every man, woman, and child seeks equal justice, equal opportunity, equal dignity without discrimination. Unless these rights have meaning there, they have little meaning anywhere. Without concerted citizen action to uphold them close to home, we shall look in vain for progress in the larger world.[1]

These wise words of Eleanor Roosevelt in her speech at the United Nations in 1958 were my inspiration for this volume.

This study undertaken facilitated the detailed discussion and exploration of the rights of the working mother in Libya. It explored the balance needed to ensure that both these rights (right to motherhood and work) were best able to be expressed and the factors that were preventing such a balance from occurring. The effects of international human rights law regarding working women on the domestic law of Libya have been investigated. Has Libyan law allowed the working mother to practise both her rights in the workplace? Has it provided her with what is required to ensure these rights are available not only in law but also in practice – that is, are her rights enforced? Does the Libyan working mother encounter equal opportunity and justice within her workplace? This volume has aimed to answer all these questions in six chapters.

Findings

In terms of international human rights law, it is still difficult for an international body to determine what can be (and has been) implemented in specific countries in regard to women and their rights of motherhood and work in the workplace. Indeed, information from non-governmental sources is welcomed as a way of gaining information on member state implementation from a source other than the government of the respective country. Formally, every one of the States parties concur with all the principles present in UN conventions, the *Convention on the Rights of the Child* (CRC) and the *Convention on the Elimination of All Forms of Discrimination against Women* (CEDAW), and with the specific Articles related to working mothers in the workplace. Although they may have entered a number of reservations, these (at least theoretically) should not contravene the spirit of the convention. The same can be said in relation to signatories to the International Labour Organization (ILO) conventions. Yet working women across the world still do not enjoy all their rights in the workplace. This particularly applies to working mothers in developing nations, who still face many obstacles in their bid to enjoy both rights, the right to work and motherhood.

---

1 Eleanor Roosevelt: speech made at the presentation of *In Your Hands: A Guide for Community Action for the Tenth Anniversary of the Universal Declaration of Human Rights*, to members of the UN Commission on Human Rights, United Nations 27 March 1958: quoted in Gary B Melton, 'Building Humane Communities Respectful of Children: The Significance of the Convention on the Rights of the Child' (2005) 60(8) *American Psychologist* 918, 918.

Female participation in the workplace depends on factors such as the number and age of a woman's children (if any), her marital status and the number of sick, disabled or elderly people in the household. Generally, the higher the level of responsibility at home, the lower is the workplace participation by women; and no matter her level of education or workload outside the home, a woman shoulders 'the lion's share' of household duties.[2] Her unpaid duties in the home, including childcare, affect her participation, but it is also critically affected by the degree to which her participation is facilitated by her society.

Although willing to sign a number of international human rights instruments, Libya's implementation in a number of areas remains problematic. Indeed, Libyan 'cultural relativism in relation to international human rights law is in itself problematic'.[3] Where women are considered in international human rights law as equal citizens (and, at least theoretically, in some places within Libyan law), cultural stereotypes in Libya, as elsewhere, portray a woman's place as 'in her home'. This influences interpretation of both international and domestic law and its implementation. In the workplace, there may be problems related to access (career initiation), maintenance and promotion (where the higher the level of responsibility, the lower the proportion of women may be found). These remain areas of concern for women, particularly working mothers, across the world.

In conclusion, working women both in Libya and around the globe today are finding it difficult to balance both their rights: their right to motherhood and their right to a career.

It has more recently been said that international legislation is being degraded, and now has lost its 'power'. It may be 'a significant symbolic tool, but ... a very weak device in reality to assist in improving the actual lives of women around the world'.[4]

Unsurprisingly, even the most widely accepted and best recognised conventions have no effect unless they are ratified by member states and then implemented – as originally intended – by those states. In terms of a lack of ratification, Libya has not had many incidents in this field; however, the same cannot be said for implementation and enforcement. Therefore, a convention that is not ratified or is over-'reserved' or not even practised to any great extent by the member state is of little benefit to those for whom certain rights and standards are sought to be guaranteed by its implementation. For international law to be effective, national policy must be in harmony with it, not in conflict – as is the case with Libya in regard to the majority of international human rights conventions that it has ratified.

Four major conventions that have the potential to have a substantial impact on women's rights as mothers and workers are the UN's CEDAW and CRC, the ILO's C111 and the (three) Maternity Protection Conventions. These were all ratified by Libya (with the exception of the *Maternity Protection Convention of 2000* (C183)), but Libya has thus far seriously failed in their implementation. All of the conventions highlighted deal with and affect the working mother in various ways. For instance, the Maternity Protection Conventions allow the mother the right to motherhood and employment. Although these conventions are well structured in theory, in practice Libya is not fulfilling its obligations. The periodic reports that Libya submits to the responsible committees are really never met with applause. The committee repeats that either Libya is merely 'copying and pasting' its previous reports or is not really understanding that committee's requests. Libya is negligent in the enforcement of these conventions. Institutions, organisations and groups

---

2 Neil Rees, Katherine Lindsay and Simon Rice, *Australian Anti-Discrimination Law: Text, Cases and Materials* (Federation Press, 2008) 333.

3 Ali Omar Ali Mesrati, *The Best Interests of the Child: International Child Law as Interpreted in the Libyan High Court Jurisdiction* (PhD Thesis, University of Wollongong, 2009) 221.

4 Adrien Katherine Wing, 'International Conventions' in Joseph Suad (ed), *Encyclopedia of Women and Islamic Cultures: Family, Law and Politics* (Brill, 2005) vol 2, 306.

are required to supervise the 'progress' of the particular convention, and Libya has not done so. Libya merely 'signs and forgets'. In such countries where official reports (if and when submitted) may not reflect what is occurring or provide only limited data, thus submissions by NGOs are often welcomed.

The human rights treaties that have been examined in this volume are powerful if practised so as to fulfil their potential. However, careful analysis of the implementation of each reveals that there are, unfortunately, significant shortcomings in relation to Libya's fulfilment of its obligations.

Women in Libyan society have significant opportunities in employment law, but they still face substantial difficulty in taking advantage of the opportunities available. Lack of necessary revision of the existing legislation as well as a lack of enforcement of existing legislative provisions for childcare and so forth undermine their effectiveness.

In terms of the formal law, there is no discrimination against working women in Libyan society. In practice, however, the involvement of working mothers in the workplace is still limited in almost every area of work, especially in the political system and public affairs. The main barrier is the difficulty of managing the responsibilities of family and those of work. This difficulty is exacerbated by the relative brevity[5] and inconsistency of maternity leave set down in legislation; and although most of these issues have – at least in part – been addressed by positive changes in Libyan law, these improvements have not been translated from theory into practice.

An examination of the primary materials collected from Libyan law and international law found that there were fundamental flaws in Libyan employment laws. One example is the varying provisions for maternity leave (varying from three months on full pay and subject to no conditions to 50 days on half pay and subject to a number of conditions). This creates two classes of working mothers, as does the lack of provisions for non-citizen working mothers. Other factors strongly affect women's participation and their exercise of the rights accorded to them in international and national law. These include: the absence of adequate childcare facilities in the workplace; a lack of part-time occupations; unavailability of flexible working hours; inadequate transport arrangements and healthcare and so on. This creates a significant gap between Libyan domestic laws and the objects of international law. For example, there are shortfalls in the Libyan provision of maternity leave in law and a lack of provision of adequate childcare as well as inadequate family allowance payable to working mothers and so on, yet their proper provision is required under international law. Libya has ratified the conventions applying to such matters and is, at least in theory (and also sometimes in domestic law), committed to making adequate provision.

Shortfalls are clearly complicated by inadequate sanctions for breaches of legislation designed to support women in the workplace, and also by cultural and attitudinal factors that affect women's participation.

Interviews conducted with working women in Libya suggested that there were two main types of reason why Libyan laws are seriously uneven; these are administrative and legal. Analysis of the empirical data showed a significant difference between the theory and practice of Libyan law. For example, working women (including those who are mothers) encounter discrimination in relation to opportunities for further education and training and promotion within the workplace. In relation to those women who are also mothers, there is a failure by employers to provide legislated leave, breastfeeding times and childcare facilities, and a failure to provide transport as is also required by law. Many women also do not receive the baby bonus and maternity allowance provided by law.

5 Programme on Governance in the Arab Region (POGAR), *Libya in Brief* (4 November 2009) <http://gender.pogar.org/countries/theme.aspx?t=4&cid=10>.

In conclusion, the working mother has not been able to practise both her rights, as the law is not amended where required to accord with the international conventions to which Libya is a party. In addition, the rights that are enshrined within the legislation are not adequately enforced.

Recommendations

This section will identify the central problems revealed by this research, and propose possible solutions.

International Law, International Labour Standards and International Bodies

The operation of international treaty-monitoring bodies is a subject of almost universal criticism. Such international systems are supervisory systems and so do not incorporate actual enforcement of their laws. They can issue sanctions; however, this is rare. If a member state is not abiding by the laws and regulations of conventions that it has signed, the responsible body has no power to 'punish' it; this particular issue is beyond its power. International systems operate on recommendations, reports and meetings. International treaties and conventions recommend a country act or follow a certain path but they cannot force the country do so, just as they cannot force a country to sign a convention, or even to report as that country had previously agreed.[6]

Consideration of the various diverse cultures, traditions, religions and laws of the world

International human rights law must be universal. Its power derives largely from that universality.[7] International human rights law must also be unbiased and neutral. It must, therefore, not only benefit from western traditions, for example, but also from the traditions and practices of humanity as a whole. Finally, international laws must be considerate of the diverse cultures, religions and laws of the world.

Treaty-monitoring committees, such as the CEDAW Committee, complain about the number of reservations and are critical of States parties. However, it is too simplistic to lay blame at the feet of States parties who have entered reservations without also interrogating the weaknesses of a convention itself. When a treaty attracts significant reservations a question must be asked whether it embodies the required degree of universality, or whether those who framed it have failed to take the concerns and views of a significant number of countries and their peoples into consideration. For example, the CEDAW Committee criticises *Libya's Law No 70 of 1973*, which criminalises 'extramarital sexual relations [which] may have a disproportionate impact on women'.[8] From a Libyan perspective, however, it is not Libya's law that must in this instance be criticised, but rather the Convention itself as it is insensitive to and ignorant of the morals and values of many cultures and peoples of the world. This specific law is in harmony with Islamic law (*Shar'iah*) which is the basis of Libyan law, and any request for the removal and repeal of this law conflicts with Libya's legal system. Libyan laws are based on French and Italian Civil Law and Islamic law. Many Islamic countries have entered reservations to Articles 2 and 16 of CEDAW. The issue of reservations was thoroughly discussed in Chapter 2.

6 Doris Weichselbaumer and Rudolf Winter-Ebmer, 'The Effects of Competition and Equal Treatment Laws on Gender Wage Differentials' (2007) 22 *Economic Policy* 235, 246.

7 Melton, above n 1, 919.

8 CEDAW Committee, *Concluding Observations – Libya*, UN Doc CEDAW C/LBY/CO/5 (6 February 2009), above ch 1 n 58, 5–6.

Labour standards – equal standards
Developed and developing countries enforce different labour standards, with developing countries often arguing that 'any movement towards harmonization of standards will put their firms at a comparative disadvantage'.[9] A number of researchers agree that 'less-developed countries should not be expected to support the same level of labour standards as their wealthier counterparts'.[10] A separate, yet related, issue is the level of enforcement of what labour standards do exist. In developing countries labour standards are often poorly enforced, if at all; and corruption may further affect the initiation or outcome of prosecution or use of other enforcement mechanisms. Similarly, the creation and enforcement of provisions for women in the workplace are part of labour standards, and some may fear that improving these conditions in comparison to those of other countries might put them at a disadvantage.

Countries such as Libya might also be overwhelmed by the work involved in complying with the high expectations of institutions such as the ILO in terms of raising labour standards. The ILO should take into consideration Libya's situation and should not expect the attainment of these standards to the same level and at the same rate as developed countries. Rather, it should focus on dedicating its time to research and investigation on the best methods and approaches that should be taken to improve Libya's situation in a realistic manner. It should accompany Libya 'step by step' with genuine assistance and at a pace that enables realistic progress to be made. This may encourage the Libyan Government to cease merely 'copying and pasting' past reports and actively engage with the task of treaty implementation.[11]

If countries such as Libya are forced to have labour standards equivalent to those of more developed countries, they will incur the higher 'fixed costs associated with legal enforcement and infrastructure', which would in turn affect the level of funds available for social welfare.[12] Having the same institutions as wealthier countries is nearly impossible for developing nations. Libya not only has limited financial resources but also lacks professional expertise in the areas required. It also lacks the necessary institutions. The ILO needs to consider both Libya's limitations and abilities.

Recommendations to the Libyan Government

Libyan Government and international law
Prior to any ratification of international conventions, the Libyan Government must consider its abilities, limitations and strengths in implementing a particular convention. It must study the convention from various viewpoints. Firstly, it needs to determine whether the particular convention is in harmony and agreement with domestic and national law; therefore, whether it is contradictory to, or is in any way in conflict with, Islamic *Shar'iah* law. Secondly, it needs to determine whether this convention is culturally acceptable. Thirdly, and most importantly, the government must consider whether Libya is capable of abiding with this convention's regulations and operating system. In this regard, the Libyan Government needs to determine, for example, whether it is able to report every two years, establish the institutions required, replace current operating bodies, programmes and systems in Libya and so on.

However, once Libya ratifies a convention then it should abide by its system and regulations. In its comments to the particular committee responsible, Libya must not merely 'copy and paste' from

9 Stephen B Deloach, Jayoti Das and Lindsey Conley, 'Power Politics and International Labor Standards' (2006) 12 *International Advances in Economic Research* 51.

10 Ibid. 60.

11 Ibid.

12 Ibid.

previous reports. It should not delay its submissions. Libya should provide the committee with the material requested, for example, statistical data.[13] Libya also must harmonise its national policies with the conventions to which it has become a State party. Libya must also bear in mind that if it is facing particular difficulties in regard to fulfilling its obligations, then there are organisations and personnel prepared to help at its request.

This recommendation cannot be implemented without the assistance of the 'civil society, in particular women's non-governmental organizations' and 'an independent national human rights institution in accordance with a wide mandate to protect and promote women's human rights'.[14] There is a shortage of such organisations in Libyan society.

Following recent events, the nation is now in a state of flux. The author hopes that the revolution of 17 February 2011 marks a national readiness for change and the beginning of the transformation of Libya. One eminently desirable change is the closing of the gap between law and practice when it comes to matters regarding the rights of the working mother. The author trusts that ground taken for greater human rights for women will not be surrendered, but rather expanded in the coming years as Libya truly enters the twenty-first century. It is to be hoped that the rights of working mothers (and those of their children) are increasingly recognised and protected as these women strive to fulfil their roles of mother and worker.

Libyan Government and domestic law

Libya must amend and repeal some of its national laws to achieve consistency with the various international conventions that the country has ratified. It does not just stop there, however. Libya must put these laws into practice.

Another issue of great concern is the difference between public and private sector laws. Public and private sector laws must be the same for all working women so that inconsistencies are prevented. Libya must consider the best interests of the working mother so that she may be able to balance both her rights: work and motherhood.

Issues to be Considered When Introducing New Legislation

In 2010, the *Concerning Labour Relations Act No 12 of 2010* was enacted. The intention behind the introduction of this Act was to place all employees in Libya (except those whose status falls under special laws and regulations) under one law. This Act, if enforced, will have many benefits for the working mother. However, 12 months later, the Executive Rules required for its enforcement were yet to be issued. This Act contains 183 Articles, two of which specifically concern the working mother, namely, Articles 25 and 26.

Article 25 extends maternity leave from 12 weeks under the previous Act[15] to 14 weeks, subject to submission of a medical certificate stating the expected date of delivery. This Act differentiates between provisions for multiple births and single-birth events. This Article specifically grants a

13 'The Committee calls upon the State Party to put in place a comprehensive system of data collection, including measurable indicators to assess trends in the situation of women and progress towards women's de facto equality over time. It invites the State Party to seek regional and international assistance, as necessary, for the development of such data collection and analysis efforts': CEDAW Committee, *Concluding Observations – Libya*, UN Doc CEDAW C/LBY/CO/5 (6 February 2009), above ch1 n 58, 9.

14 Ibid.

15 *Social Security Act No 13 of 1980* (Libya).

period of 16 weeks' maternity leave to working mothers who give birth to more than one child.[16] It also prohibits any employer from terminating an employee's contract during pregnancy or during an absence due to maternity leave, 'except where there are justifiable reasons' unrelated to 'pregnancy or maternity and birth complications or breast feeding'.[17] Lastly, Article 25 confirms Article 97 of the *Labour Code Act* on breastfeeding.

Article 26 reiterates Article 11 of the *Child Protection Act No 5 of 1997*. This means that any workplace employing women with children must provide a childcare facility for these children. This requirement is neither new nor recent in Libya's legislation; however, it is here confirmed.

For the major part of this new Act, however, the General Peoples Committee will be required to create and issue Executive Rules to clarify and further explain the Act. Such rules supply the details required for employers, employees and the courts to understand and fulfil the requirements of the Act. The Act requires Executive Rules to be issued.[18] These specify such things as: the supervisory powers of officials in emergency situations; the applicable Acts and controls (for example, conditions applying) in regard to organising all types of leave (including maternity leave); and details regarding a system to be put in place for women's part-time employment.

This new Act with all its great advantages has, however, many flaws and at times is unclear. For example, Article 2 of this Act is extremely difficult for the layperson to understand. It states:

> Until issuance of these rules and decisions stipulated by law, the work shall continue with rules and decisions applicable during execution of this law without contradicting its legislations.[19]

But what does this actually mean in terms of maternity leave, for example? Does it mean that no employer can remove or shorten the 12 weeks' maternity leave already guaranteed under previous legislation, but that the new maternity leave provision (of 14 weeks for a singleton birth or 16 weeks for those who have a multiple birth) cannot be enforced? The primary concern is that the delay in issuing the Executive Rules defers justice and improved conditions for working mothers. It may also lead to employers not realising that they still need to fulfil the earlier requirements in regard to childcare facilities.

Before introducing any new domestic legislation, Libya must address the following issues.

Firstly, it must consider whether the proposed new law will conflict with any international convention that Libya has ratified or with any other domestic legislation currently in force. Secondly, Libya must consider whether this new legislation can be put into practice (that is, whether it is realistic and whether the necessary assets required are accessible and available). Thirdly, before the introduction of such legislation, it must be assessed by a supervisory committee (a national government body) whose role is to examine and assess legislation from all different perspectives. It must take into consideration the best interests of the nation as a whole (and, therefore, the best

---

16 I hope the new Libyan Government enforces this Act as many Articles, such as Article 25, will benefit the working mother in many ways. However, many Articles must be amended. See Appendix D for further analysis and a detailed commentary on the *Concerning Labour Relations Act No 12 of 2010*.

17 *Concerning Labour Relations Act No 12 of 2010* (Libya) art 25(2).

18 These Executive Rules have not yet been issued (at December 2011).

19 Unofficial translation of *Concerning Labour Relations Act No 12 of 2010* (Libya) (titled 'Law No 12 for 2010 Concerning Labour Relations') available at <http://libyaninvestment.com>. Another unofficial translation reads: 'Pending the enactment of this regulation and decisions stipulated herein, current regulations in force and which do not contradict their terms, shall apply' (ILO Natlex <http://www.ilo.org/dyn/natlex/docs/MONOGRAPH/86041/101168/F1324209671/LBY86041%20pp.%201%20to%2061%20.pdf>).

interests of women, children, employees and so on). This can only be possible if professional experts, both women and men, are given equal opportunity to comment and make recommendations.

If the new legislation is concerned with and related to women, especially working women, then the majority of the examining committee must be women, as it is only women who can best understand the situation and hardships that other women (like themselves) encounter daily. It is only women who can relate to the difficulties women face and the imbalance they feel. Such a body could be comprised of representatives drawn from the nation's tertiary educational institutions, the judiciary and elected representatives. It could function somewhat like a Senate Committee does in the Australian Parliament (but with the addition of expert educational and judicial personnel). It would be able to comment on proposed legislation and also ask for comment from other relevant bodies prior to legislation being passed. Such an entity (composed of at least 50 per cent female representatives where matters proposed involve women and women's rights) would satisfy the *Shura* (consultation) requirement of Islam in regard to decision-making as well as assist the nation to progress towards the implementation of legislation more in line with its international obligations.

And, lastly, the final 'draft' of the proposed legislation should be examined by an external international and unbiased body that keeps the 'best interests' of women, especially working women, at heart. There is no more appropriate agency than UN Women – the UN Entity for Gender Equality and the Empowerment of Women, established in July 2010. This agency specialises in promoting and advocating for women's rights in all fields at the national level. Libya should become an active member of this agency and should rely on its advice and professional expertise.[20]

Supervision of Implementation

For legislation and regulations to be faithfully observed there must be non-government institutions (therefore, a third party) available to monitor, observe and ensure that the law is not being neglected, abused or misinterpreted. These institutions must be responsible for handling and resolving complaints. They must also be responsible for setting the procedures or steps that must be taken in the case of violation of legislation (for example, where an employer fails to provide employees with breastfeeding breaks) or a lack of enforcement due to lack of inspection or lack of action where a violation is detected.

Also, for legislation to be effective in practice, the parties concerned must be aware of it. They must be aware of their rights and the procedures to be followed if and when those rights are violated. In the case of working mothers and maternity leave, women must be educated about the period of leave allowed, its timing (before and/or after childbirth) and the benefits available during this period. Without educating the parties involved, how can employers be expected to fulfil their obligations or women be expected to complain and take their case to the right institution or body? The interview findings (Chapter 5) revealed that many working mothers were unaware of

---

20 General Assembly, *System-wide Coherence*, GA Res 64/289, UN GAOR, 64th sess, 104th plen mtg, UN Doc A/Res/64/289 (21 July 2010). For the text of the Resolution, see General Assembly, *Follow-up to the Outcome of the Millennium Summit, Draft Resolution Submitted by the President of the General Assembly: System-wide Coherence*, UN GAOR 64th sess, Agenda Item 114, UN Doc A/64/L.56 [49]–[90] (30 June 2010). 'Within countries that request its assistance, UN Women works with government and non-governmental partners to help them put in place the policies, laws, services and resources that women require to move towards equality. It draws on extensive knowledge and experience with which interventions work best in a given environment, and which do the most to unlock rapid national progress in attaining national and international commitments to women'. UN Women, *How We Work* (15 November 2011) <http://www.unwomen.org/>.

their rights, including (surprisingly) women working in the legal system. The CEDAW Committee agrees with this recommendation:

> The Committee recommends that educational programmes on the Convention, including its Optional Protocol and its jurisprudence, and programmes on women's rights be introduced for all legal professionals, including judges, lawyers, prosecutors and law enforcement personnel, as well as the public at large. It urges the state party to take special measures, including comprehensive legal literacy programmes, to enhance women's awareness of their rights so that they may be able to exercise them.[21]

Lastly, there must be a unified, organised and professional complaints system, where legal procedures are undertaken and where parties can find information, resources and advice regarding specific issues.

In conclusion, for a mother to practise and enjoy both her rights – motherhood and work – the Libyan Government is required to ensure that legislation benefiting and meeting the needs of working mothers is created; that working mothers are aware of such legislation; and that such legislation is not only theoretically beneficial but practically achievable.

Law Reform Proposals

The following recommendations should be applied to all working mothers, that is, those in both the public and private sectors. This will then prevent discrimination and allow the working mother to balance both her rights.[22]

Maternity leave

Maternity leave should be for a period of at least 16 weeks. The minimum period could vary in the event of multiple births: such that for those working mothers giving birth to one child (16 weeks minimum), twins (26 weeks), triplets or more (32 weeks). They must differ for those working mothers giving birth naturally (16 weeks) as opposed to by caesarean (which may vary from 26 weeks to a year or more, depending on the health of the mother) without being subject to any conditions except the submission of a medical certificate. This recommendation is in accordance with the ILO Maternity Protection Conventions.[23] Libya should look to Sweden, Norway and Denmark as great examples of countries with impressive maternity protection policies. These are among the top ten countries for paid maternity leave and length of maternity leave.[24]

---

21 CEDAW Committee, *Concluding Observations – Libya*, UN Doc CEDAW C/LBY/CO/5 (6 February 2009), above ch 1 n 58, 3.

22 Libyan laws regarding foreign (i.e. non-Libyan) workers fall outside the scope of this publication; however, it is an area of concern and I recommend further research be undertaken to examine the matter. It is a worthy subject for further investigation.

23 *Maternity Protection Convention* (C103) art 3(1) and *Maternity Protection Convention* (C183) art 4 (1).

24 Save the Children, 'Champions for Children: State of the World's Mothers 2011' (Save the Children, 2011) 30.

Cash benefits
The benefit must be 100 per cent of previous earnings for all working mothers in Libya (not just some, as is currently the case in existing legislation)[25] and not subject to any condition or limitation. This would enable the family income to continue to match expenditure (and savings remain the same) and so avoid negative economic, psychological and social effects on the mother and family. Funding such an initiative, however, should be the responsibility of the employer. If maternity leave were to be a government responsibility, this would make it more acceptable to employers.

Medical benefit:
This benefit should be provided for the working mother and her child and has to include:

> pre-natal, confinement and post-natal care by qualified midwives or medical practitioners as well as hospitalisation care where necessary; freedom of choice of doctor and freedom of choice between a public and private hospital shall be respected.[26]

As Article 4(4) of the *Maternity Protection Convention* (C103) states: '[C]ash and medical benefits shall be provided either by means of compulsory social insurance or by means of public funds'.[27] Such a regime that does not directly target the employer would lead to equal employment opportunities for working mothers, in particular those applying for jobs in the private sector.[28]

Childcare facilities
It must be compulsory for every region to have a reliable, safe and affordable childcare facility. Many working mothers are deprived of their rights and cannot balance work and motherhood because of a lack of childcare facilities or the inadequate standard of those available. Introducing standards of care and training for workers in the childcare industry would reassure mothers and make them confident of leaving their children in the care of others. The provision of adequate childcare facilities is also related to the issue of breastfeeding hours and breaks.

Breastfeeding hours and breaks
These should be increased so that the health of both the child and mother benefit and they are both able to reach their full potential. Length of hours and the number of breaks should vary with the age, health and circumstances of both the mother and child. It should be considered that the younger the child the more frequent the breaks, and therefore the longer the total time allowed for breastfeeding. However, a minimum of two hours is recommended for all.

Flexible working hours
Libya must introduce a system of part-time, casual and 'work from home' employment. These flexible arrangements allow the mother to balance her work and motherhood. Libya currently does not have this flexible system and, as highlighted in Chapter 4, the benefits of these flexible working periods for working mothers in particular (and families in general) are great, and benefits also flow through to the entire society.

---

25 This is according to *Social Security Act No 13 of 1980* (Libya) art 25(C).

26 *Maternity Protection Convention* (C103) art 4 (3).

27 Ibid. art 4(4).

28 This is the evidence highlighted during the interview when it was found that as part of school policy married women were not employed because of maternity leave.

Transport
Safe, culturally acceptable and affordable public transport must be available for working women to help them balance work with religion, culture and customs. Many working mothers neglect their career, as it may be unaffordable for them to catch a taxi twice a day every day or because it is culturally unacceptable for them to board a mixed-gender bus. Therefore, for the comfort of these women, gender-segregated transport must be made available and at an affordable price.

Baby bonus and family allowances
The amounts payable must be raised beyond the petty amount currently mentioned in the *Social Security Act*.[29] For the baby bonus, the Libyan Government should look to Australia as an example and follow in its footsteps. Therefore, the baby bonus must be raised by a significant amount. The Libyan Government should also look to Australia as an example regarding the payment of family allowances.[30]

Education
In addition, ignorance on the part of employers and employees as well as government bureaucrats in regard to women's rights in the workplace, and specifically in relation to the rights of working mothers, has also been shown to hamper women's employment and their enjoyment of benefits already provided in law. Women need to know their rights in order to assert them. An ongoing education campaign to alert women to their rights is required, as are programmes for employers and government officials. This is particularly important in the current context of change. A community-wide campaign by the government in consultation with women's organisations (and perhaps the UN Entity for Gender Equality and the Empowerment of Women) is recommended to assist the attitudinal change in the broader community that is so necessary for acceptance of the changes proposed.

Final Words

Libya stands at the beginning of a new journey. The paths that it can select to travel are many. The author hopes and prays that it will choose the path of justice and equality. A path chosen by the people, a path of the people, for the people – a people of justice; a people that recognise and respect the importance of international treaties; a people that together will close the gap and ensure that Libyan working mothers will not have to choose between a career and motherhood. I know and believe this journey will be long, tiring and difficult – but I also know and believe it is possible. The future seems brighter and the dark past is Libya's greatest teacher.

---

29 *Social Security Act No 13 of 1980* (Libya) arts 27(B) (baby bonus), 24 (family allowances).

30 For more details see House of Representatives Standing Committee on Family and Human Services, *Balancing Work and Family: Report on the Inquiry into Balancing Work and Family* (CanPrint Communications, 2006).

Appendix A

Interview Questions

Researcher: Naeima F.A. Al-Hadad
Research title: Working Women and their Rights in the Workplace: International Human Rights and its Impact on Libyan Law

1. Could you please tell me what are the main obstacles that face you in combining your family and work responsibilities?
2. In your opinion, what are the main reasons that make many working mothers take one-year leave after having three months' maternity leave?
3. According to conducted studies in Libya many working mothers choose to stay at home after giving birth to their second or third child. What are the main factors contributing to this issue in your opinion?
4. Who takes care of your children during the time you are at work?
5. Who can help you to solve the problem facing you during the work time?
6. How many hours do you spend at your work?
7. If you did take off your career or consider leaving your occupation, could you please say what factors would persuade you to do so?
8. What do you like the most about your career?
9. How many children did you give birth to during your career and why?
10. Usually maternity leave is three months. This right can be used either way before or after the delivery. Which way did you use it and why?
11. What is the financial support for working families; is it sufficient?
12. Are there any working women's rights that Libya should adopt, in your opinion?
13. How should the Libyan Government handle any future conflict between work and motherhood?
14. How optimistic are you about the next (ten) years, in terms of the both rights (work and motherhood)?
15. Do you want say anything else? Please do.
16. *Thank you for your time and frankness.*

Appendix B

Consent Form for Working Mothers

Researcher: Naeima F.A. Al-Hadad
Research title: Working Women and their Rights in the Workplace: International Human Rights and its Impact on Libyan Law

I have been given information about the project 'Working Women and their Rights in the Workplace: International Human Rights and its Impact on Libyan Law' by Naeima Al-Hadad, who is conducting this research as part of a PhD supervised by Prof. Luke McNamara in the Faculty of Law at the University of Wollongong in Australia.

I understand that the only burden associated with my participation in this research is the time involved in the interview. I have read the information sheet and have had an opportunity to ask Naeima Al-Hadad any questions I may have about the research and my participation.

I understand that my participation in this research is voluntary. I am free to refuse to participate and I am free to withdraw from the research before it is published. Also, neither my name nor my workplace will be used to identify my comments in the publications resulting from this study.

If I have any enquiries about the research, I can contact Naeima Al-Hadad or Prof. Luke McNamara or if I have any concerns or a complaints regarding the way the research is or has been conducted, I can contact the Ethics Officer, Human Research Ethics Committee, Office of Research, University of Wollongong.

By signing below I am indicating my consent to the use of the data for the research in the area of 'Working Women and their Rights in the Workplace: International Human Rights and its Impact on Libyan Law'.

I understand that the data collected from my participation will be used for the purpose of Naeima Al-Hadad's PhD thesis and related publications and I consent for it to be used in that manner.

Signed: Date / /
Name (please print):

Appendix C
Participant Information Sheet for Working Mothers

Researcher: Naeima F.A. Al-Hadad
Research title: Working Women and their Rights in the Workplace: International Human Rights and its Impact on Libyan Law

Purpose of the Research

The purpose of this research is to facilitate the enjoyment by working women of their rights as both independent workers and mothers, without requiring a choice of one over the other.

Investigators

1 Prof. Luke McNamara (supervisor of the research), Faculty of Law, University of Wollongong, Australia
2 Naeima F.A. Al-Hadad (PhD candidate), Faculty of Law, University of Wollongong, Australia

Methods and Demands on Participants

If you choose to be included, you will be asked to participate in a study about Working Women and their Rights in the Workplace: International Human Rights and its Impact on Libyan Law. You will be asked to answer questions about your career; the main difficulty facing you during the work time; financial support for working families; maternity protection; compatibility between work and motherhood responsibilities; current employment status; and hours spent at your work. The information will be recorded via audiotape. This is because the researcher will be able to concentrate on the discussion and it will help to gather accurate data. The interview may take 30 minutes of your time. You will receive a copy of the results after the study is completed if you wish so. If you have any questions regarding the research and its procedures, please do not hesitate to contact the researchers at any time on the contact details mentioned above.

If you would like to participate in this study please contact me on the phone number … and then we will arrange where and when to hold the interview.

Possible Risks, Inconveniences and Discomfort

The interview may take 30 minutes of your time to be conducted and it will be confined to one meeting only; we can foresee no risks for you. Your involvement in the study is voluntary and you may withdraw your participation from the study at any time and withdraw any data you have provided. Please do not answer questions that you are not comfortable with. Confidentiality will be assured and, also, you and your organisation will not be identified in any publications resulting from the research. Refusal to participate in the interviews will not affect your relationship with the employer.

Funding and Benefits of the Research

This study is funded by the Libyan Government in the form of a scholarship supporting the research student's enrolment as a PhD candidate at the University of Wollongong. The main benefit of this research is that it will identify reforms required to ensure that working mothers in Libya are able to enjoy both rights to work and motherhood. It will contribute to reduced discrimination in the workplace and increase working mothers' active participation in the economy. The information will be used solely for the purpose of this research. Findings from this study are subject to publication in the PhD thesis and in academic journals. Confidentiality is assured; your identity and the identity of your employer will not be identified in any part of the research as the responses will be coded.

Ethics Review and Complaints

This research has been reviewed by the Human Research Ethics Committee of the University of Wollongong. Any participant with concerns or complaints about the conduct of this research is invited to discuss these concerns with me, and if they remain unsatisfied with any aspect of the research, they should contact the University of Wollongong Ethics Officer.

Thank you for your time and interest in this study.

Appendix D
Concerning Labour Relations Act No 12 of 2010

During the three years of my PhD studies, I have been working with many Acts and Orders related to working women in Libya. One major Act is the *Labour Code Act No 58 of 1970*, which was recently repealed by Article 4 of the *Concerning Labour Relations Act No 12 of 2010.*[1] The Libyan legislature promulgated this Act with the intention of placing all employees in Libya under one law, except for those employees whose status falls under special laws and regulations[2] or those employees engaged in family activity (as couples, or in broader family arrangements).[3]

This Act has many benefits for working women. Some of its Articles in particular are specifically for working women and, even more specifically, the working mother. For instance, the provisions of this Act state that a labourer[4] or employee[5] is not permitted directly or indirectly to participate in any way or form in activities prohibited by law or policy or prevailing systems. This includes general prohibitions, such as working without permission of an employer[6] or accepting gifts.[7] This Article also specifically benefits working women by creating a penalty for the 'performance or incitement of any act ... considered as acts of sexual harassment'.[8]

Article 21 also confirms that there should be no discrimination in wages for work on the grounds of sex or religion or colour.

The many advantages for working women which have been conferred in the previous Acts and Orders are confirmed in Article 24. Again it is stated that there shall be no distinction in employment, treatment or wages on the basis of gender (equal opportunity and equal wages). However, women should not be engaged in employment considered unsuited to their nature; such employment is to be defined by a decision of the General People's Committee (GP Cttee).[9] In addition, it may be possible to reduce working hours for women in some professions (for example, in order to protect their health). Again, this must be decided by the GP Cttee. When making decisions and specifications, the GP Cttee is required to take into consideration the number of female and male employees and the demands of the workplace in that specified workplace. This will be governed by the Executive Rules of this Act.

---

1 Concerning *Labour Relations Act No 12 of 2010* (Libya).

2 For example, the employee in the judicial system, police force, customs, military service, lecture at university.

3 See Article 4 of the Introductory Section of Act No 12 of 2010.

4 This, as referred to in Article 5 of the Act, is '[a]ny normal person who performs effort under supervision and control of employer against share in production or financial amount'.

5 Article 5 of the Act states, '[p]erson who occupies one of the functions in administration's organization chart'.

6 *Concerning Labour Relations Act No 12 of 2010* (Libya) art 12 (1).

7 Ibid. art 12 (2). Other prohibitions include: removing documents without permission, art 12(9), and violating occupational health and safety provisions, art 12(11).

8 *Concerning Labour Relations Act No 12 of 2010* (Libya) art 12 (10).

9 These have yet to be issued (at 11 December 2011). They will be known as Executive Rules.

Article 25 puts into place a number of improved conditions for women as well as confirming a number of provisions already in previous and existing legislation. It extends maternity leave from 12 weeks under the previous Act to 14 weeks, subject to submission of a medical certificate stating the expected date of delivery. This leave includes at least a period of six weeks after birth. The Act differentiates between provisions for multiple birth and single-birth events:

> The woman has a right of maternity leave with pay for 14 weeks when submitting a medical certificate stating the expected date for maternity and this leave includes at least a period 6 weeks after birth and the leave is extended up to 16 weeks if more than one child is born.[10]

The grant of a period of 16 weeks' maternity leave to working mothers who give birth to more than one child is an important improvement in the Libyan law for working mothers. I also believe that Libya is the first Arabic country to grant a difference in the length of maternity leave for working mothers depending upon whether she gave birth to one child or multiple children (for example, triplets).[11]

Also under Article 25, the employment of working mothers may not be terminated during periods of pregnancy or during absence due to maternity leave, except when there are justifiable reasons which are unrelated to complications of pregnancy or breastfeeding or maternity and birth.

> Woman's work may not be terminated during pregnancy or absence during maternity leave except when there are justifiable reasons which are not related to pregnancy or maternity and berth complications or breast feeding.[12]

A working mother, as stated in Article 97 of the *Labour Code* on breastfeeding and later confirmed in the new Act, Article 25, has the right to breastfeed her infant over the next 18 months after delivery during her working hours for a minimum hour per day with pay.[13]

It confirms the right of breastfeeding mothers to a minimum one hour per day paid for breastfeeding, with that right enduring for 18 months after the birth of the child. Article 26 also confirms Article 11 of the *Child Protection Act No 5 of 1997*. It states that:

> Employers who employ women who have children should allocate places for children's custody; and more than one employer may allocate places for children's custody.[14]

This means that any workplace employing women with children must provide a childcare facility for these children. This ideology is not new or recent in Libya's legislation; however, it is here confirmed, indicating that the provision for childcare embodied in the previous Act is still encouraged and will be enforced.

Article 38 aims to protect the well-being of labourers and employees and their families. It states that employers should arrange the 'necessary insurance for their labourers and employees against

---

10 *Concerning Labour Relations Act No 12 of 2010* (Libya) art 25(1).

11 Vietnamese legislation provides maternity leave of at least 4 months on full pay and also offers an additional 30 days paid leave for each child after the first in multiple births (subject to service and insurance provisions): For full details, see ASEAN, Social Security Association *Social Security Country Profiles: Vietnam* (2007) ASSA <http://www.asean-ssa.org/CP_Vietnam.pdf>.

12 *Concerning Labour Relations Act No 12 of 2010* (Libya) art 25(2).

13 Ibid. art 25(3).

14 *Child Protection Act No 5 of 1997* (Libya) art 11.

diseases and occupational risks'. Employers must also ensure their employees and their families have access to healthcare and social security (the latter by facilitating payment by employees to the state for social security).

Article 54, covering women and men who are partners in business, states:

> Male and female partners are equal in rights and obligations considering a woman's rights during her period of pregnancy, child birth and maternity leave and others.

In an entirely new provision, Article 85 gives the working mother, in certain circumstances, permission to employ a domestic services worker/s. However, this is limited; for example, to instances where a household has more than seven persons or contains persons with disabilities (either child or parent who then cannot perform such duties). A working mother, if unable to perform her duties well or not at all in some situations, can be the recipient of such services. The Article states that:

> The house is served by … [the householder]; permission for practicing … [domestic] service for the family is not permitted, except in the following cases [such as] … if the woman works and she is not capable to take care.[15]

However, such a need would have to be established.[16]

The much-needed introduction of inspectors (referred to in Chapter 5) is embodied in Article 110 of the Act, which creates inspectors to inspect workplaces to monitor and enforce the provisions of this Act. Article 111 also enumerates the responsibilities of work inspectors. These include the enforcement of the provisions of this law and any related policies and orders issued; the submission of information and technical advice to employers and employees for the execution of this Act; the identification of shortcomings in the workplace in relation to the Act and putting forward recommendations for their amendment to the appropriate person/s within the workplace, and also in relation to the prevention of breaches; the reduction in the level of breaches of the legislation by highlighting the errors of the employers and taking the action required under the Act.[17] Inspectors must also submit annual reports on inspection visits on pro-forma reports.[18] It should be recalled in this regard that the scope of this Act includes the provision of childcare, maternity leave and the right to breastfeeding.

This Act enforces the rights of working women. It also ensures that these rights are protected and provides sanctions in the event of violations. For instance, paragraphs (1) and (2) of Article 121: paragraph 2 states that a penalty of a fine of at least LYD 500 and not exceeding LYD 1000 is to be issued in cases of a breach of Articles 13, 24,[19] 27, 28, 38 and 39 of this Act.

15 *Concerning Labour Relations Act No 12 of 2010* (Libya) art 85(4).

16 Awaiting promulgation of Executive Rules for details of application and approval processes.

17 *Concerning Labour Relations Act No 12 of 2010* (Libya) art 111(1) and (4).

18 Ibid. art 111(5).

19 Women should not be employed in works which are not familiar with woman's nature and specified by GP Cttee decision; and men should not be distinguished from women in treatment, employment and wages of equal value; and may reduce working hours for the women in some professions and works as specified by GP Cttee and to consider work requirements and number of employees from men and women as stated in the executive orders of this Act.

Paragraph 3 states that a fine of at least LYD 200 and not exceeding LYD 500 will be imposed on everyone violating Section (1) and (3) of this Act, Section 1 including Articles 12, 25 and 26. As mentioned above, these articles are very important for working women.

This new Act, with all its great advantages has, however, many flaws and at times is unclear. For example, this Act has two articles with opposing ideas (Articles 2 and 5). Article 2 even appears to combine that which cannot be combined. It states that:

> The executive rules of this law are issued by decision from GPC and include the executive legislations of this law ... Until issuance of these rules and ... [orders] stipulated by law, the work will continue with rules and ... [orders] applicable during execution of this law without contradicting to ... [the Articles of this Act].

This Article indicates that the Act cannot be functional or enforced unless the Executive Rules are issued by the General People's Committee (GP Cttee); rather, Libyan workplaces will continue to operate under the old Act and old Orders but 'without contradicting the new legislation'.

Thus, the GP Cttee is to create and issue the Executive Rules which are to clarify and further explain the rules and orders as demanded by this Act. Article 2 also states that until the GP Cttee decides to issue the Executive Rules for this Act, the old Acts and Orders are to still function and be enforced, with just one restriction: they must not oppose the new Act. This is clearly impossible[20] as the old Acts and Orders do oppose the new; the new were made for a reason: to improve and modify the old.

Article 5, however, states: '[t]his law will be published and applied from [the] date of publication'. This Act was published on 28 January 2010, but how can it be applied before the Executive Rules of this Act are issued by the GP Cttee? This Article clearly opposes Article 2, creating tension and confusion in the executive power and certainly among employers and employees.

Article 4 repeals *Labour Code Act No 58 of 1970*. The main purpose for this was to ensure that *all* employees in Libya have one Act that highlights all of their responsibilities and rights. However, Article 4 of the introductory section states that the Articles of this Act apply to all work relations in Libya, whether they are regulatory relations or contractual or with partnership and whether the entitlements are a proportion of economic activity or a cash amount – with the *exception* of employees whose status is organised by special Acts or regulations and also employees in family activity (couples, or business operated by extended family).

This exception reveals that discrimination exists or can occur between those women working under the new Act and those who are exempted from the Act, or who work under the various other Acts with different entitlements. For example, in regard to maternity leave, if a working mother is working under *Act No 12 of 2010*, she will be entitled a period of 14–16 weeks' maternity leave. On the other hand, if a working mother's employment falls under other Acts or is an exception, she will be entitled to a period of no more than 12 weeks' maternity leave as stated in the *Social Security Act*. As a consequence, discrimination remains between two women who are working in the same society.

Also, Article 25 states that working women have the right to paid maternity leave under this legislation, but the legislator has not specified or mentioned a required or minimum amount of pay. Thus it may be 25 per cent, 50 per cent, 75 per cent or 100 per cent of her income, or any fraction

---

20 For example, the old Act on maternity leave Social Security Act provides for 12 weeks maternity leave, while the new states 14–16 weeks. Does the Act mean follow the old Act unless the new Act has a different provision, then follow the new one?

thereof. By not indicating a specific amount of pay, the legislator is creating a huge problem; the legislator in this instance is allowing the employer to decide on the amount of pay for each individual employee. This action can lead to discrimination and inequity in pay. A great gap can now be found between individual working mothers. This Article constructs discrimination between working women who work under one Act and in the same country.

On the other hand, Article 25(c) of the *Social Security Act No 13 of 1980* states that the working mother has the right to maternity leave before and after childbirth for a period totalling three months on *full salary*. This Act is clear and leaves no room for individual interpretation. Even though this Act is a lot clearer than the new one, it still has its imperfections. For instance, it is also misinterpreted by many employers. This was evident during the interviews I conducted. It appears, however, that despite all its flaws, the old legislation is a lot clearer than the new in regard to the level of salary to be paid.[21]

In addition, Article 25 of the Act states that a working mother has the right to breastfeed her child during the 18 months subsequent to his/her birth. The breastfeeding period is for a minimum of one hour per day with pay, with work suspended (in one or more periods with a total of at least an hour per day) to allow for breastfeeding. This Article clearly supports Article 97 of the *Labour Code*. As a result, no amendment or improvement is evident; however, the fact that the earlier Act states more clearly its point of view cannot be ignored. According to the earlier Act the period of breastfeeding is stated as two daily nursing breaks of half an hour each. But the new one states 'period or periods', so here again it leaves the task of interpretation of the *period or periods* to the employer. This does not take into account the nursing needs of the child, for whom two half-hour breaks during the course of its mother's working day is generally far preferable. Again, this is another gateway for discrimination where women may be forced to take an hour's break at the end of a day to suit the employer (a practice that was revealed during the interviews). It does not introduce one appropriate standard across all employment; again, one woman will have a totally different experience to another, depending upon her employer.

Article 26 states that the workplace should establish childcare facilities for the children of working mothers and more than one workplace may allocate places for childcare services. This Act has not revised any of the old Acts and Orders; rather it supports the same idea – the only change was the action of taking away the *number* (50 or more working women) required to enforce the Act. This is stated in Article 98 of the *Labour Code*.

This Article also states that the conditions and regulations concerning the employment of working women will be subject to the Executive Rules of this Act, which will clarify the situation. This Article is aimed at childcare facilities in the workplace. Instead of appointing the Executive Rules to clarify the conditions and health and safety requirements concerning these childcare facilities, it merely drops the minimum 50 working women requirement. It fails to state the requirements for quality care that working women want for their children (child–carer ratio, qualifications, opening hours, physical surroundings, equipment and so forth). This is clearly a big mistake. This is a new Act but it represents such a missed opportunity, especially it seems in terms of providing childcare provision standards in the Executive Rules.

Article 121 of Chapter 7 (on 'penalties') states in paragraph 2 that a penalty of at least LYD 500 and not exceeding LYD 1,000 for contravening Articles 13, 24, 27, 28, 38 and/or 39 of this Act. Included under that penalty is Article 24, which focuses on many of the very basic issues for working women (equal employment, opportunity and treatment). The penalty is extremely low and

21 Al-Zwy, 'The Role of Law', above ch 4 n 151, 84.

scarcely one that will protect women's rights in the workplace. The penalty is incapable of serving as a deterrent to those who would ignore women's rights in the workplace.

Another major issue lies with paragraph 3 of the same Article, which states that a fine of at least LYD 200 and not exceeding LYD 500 will be imposed on those violating the other provisions of Chapters 1 and 3 of this Act. Chapter 1 includes Articles 12, 25, 26 and 38. Chapter 3 includes Article 111.

Article 12, mentioned above, aims to protect working women from sexual harassment by labourers and other employees. This Article has two inadequacies. The first is that the sexual harassment generally comes from the employer. The employer is often in a position of power in relation to the employee and feels able to exploit it, especially if the business is in the private sector[22] where women may be worried about not only losing their jobs but also their reputation if they make a complaint. This is true of highly educated women in well-paid employment as well as those less educated and in lower-paid positions. The second is that the penalty of between LYD 200 and LYD 500 is very low, and such a low-level fine is unlikely to deter those who would harass women and so is not an effective tool to defend the right of women to work in a secure environment.

Articles 25 and 26 of the new Act are the vital for working mothers. Article 25 in particular represents enhanced conditions for working mothers. However, the penalty for contravention of these Articles again is very low and would fail to protect working mothers' ability to exercise their rights in the workplace. Penalties under the old Act were commensurate (given the changing value of the LYD) and interviews with working mothers revealed that such penalties did not help guarantee the compliance of employers with the legislation.

Article 38 is very important to workers because under this Article the workplace must provide necessary insurance against disease and occupational risks. Also, it aims to provide healthcare and social protection for them and their families. This Article is essential in regard to the working woman; during the interviews, working mothers repeatedly raised the areas of healthcare and social protection as crucial concerns, and cited obtaining healthcare as a major struggle. Although there is potentially great benefit from this Article, the penalty provided for any breach is not enough to make this right be put into practice.

This Act contains 183 Articles, only two of which specifically concern the working mother (Articles 25 and 26). To apportion the working mother just two Articles of a possible 183 to address her rights – to protect and enforce them – clearly shows that the working mother is neither a priority nor a concern for the legislature. This does not give the working mother the opportunity to enjoy both rights, that of work and of motherhood.

22 Women in the public sector are more likely to feel secure in their employment and be less vulnerable.

Bibliography

Books

Abdel-Halim, Aziza, *Did You Know? Refuting Rigid Interpretations Concerning the Position of Women in Islam, and Muslims' Interactions with Non-Muslims* (Northmead, 2008).

Al-Farisi, Om Al-Ez, *Al-Mr'ah wa Al-Musharkh Al-Siyasyyh fi Libya (1977–2005)* (Mrkiz Al-Hdarh Al-Arabiyh, 2008) [Trans: *The Woman and Political Participation in Libya* (The Arabic Civilisation Centre)].

Al-Ghryani, Al-Sadq Abdul Rhman *Mudunt Al-Fqh Al-Maliky wa Ta'diylatuh* (Mu'sast Al-Ryan, 2002) [Trans: *Code of Maliki Jurisprudence and its Amendments* (Foundation Rayyan)].

Al-Khlyfah, Maryam Bent Hasan and Abdulkareem Alwan, *Moltqa Albhryn fy Hoquq Alnsln Wa Huryath Alasasyah* (Jameat Al-Bahryn, 2007) [Trans: *Forum in Bahrain Human Rights and Fundamental Freedoms* (University of Bahrain)].

Al-Kutbi, Muhmmd Suliman, *Nhw Fhm Afdl Lltshriy'at Al-Dmanyyh: Wifq Al-Ejr'at Al-Munfdh Lha* (Garyounis University, 2009) [Trans: *Towards Better Understanding of Social Security Legislations* (Garyounis University)].

Al-Ra'wbi, Murad *Huqwq Almr'ah Al-Arbiayh* (Al-Mrkiz Al-Qwmy Lldirasat Al-Qanwnyh wa Buhwth Huqwq Al-Ensan, 2000) [Trans: *The Rights of Arabic Woman* (National Centre for Studies)].

Alston, Philip and James Crawford, *The Future of UN Human Rights Treaty Monitoring* (Cambridge University Press, 2000).

Al-Talawy, Adnan Kalyl, *Al-Qanwn Al-Dawly Llaml: Shurwhat Limunzmt Al-Aml Al-Dwlyyh wa Al-Tshriy'a Al-Dwly Llaml 1919–2010* (Almrkz Al-Arabi Al-Swysry Libuhwth Al-Tshghiyl wa Huqwq Al-Ensan Fi Alaml – Geneva, 2011) [Trans: *International Labour Law: Explanations of International Labour Organisation and International Regulation 1919–2010* (Arabic Swiss Centre for Labouring Research and Human Rights in Employment)].

Al-Zahri, Zynb Muhmmd, *Al-Mr'ah Al-Amilh Fi Al-Mujtama' Al-Arabi Al-Liby Al-Mu'asr* (Mnshwrat Jami't Qarywnis, 1988) [Trans: *The Working Woman in Contemporary Libyan Society* (Garyounis University, 1988)].

Al-Zahri, Zynb Muhmmd and Salih Ali Al-Zyn, *Al-Mr'ah Al-Arabiyh Al-Libyyh Fi Eshriyn Aam 1969–1989* (Mnshwrat Jami't Qarywnis 1989) [Trans: *The Libyan Women in 20 years: 1969–1989* (Garyounis University)].

Amnesty International, *Human Rights Education Workshop for Non-Governmental Organizations* (Amnesty International, 2005).

Amnesty International, *The Duty of States to Address Violence against Women* (Amnesty International, 2004).

Amnesty International Australia, *Campaigning to Stop Violence against Women* (Amnesty International, 2004).

An-Na'im, Abdullahi A, *Cultural Transformation and Human Rights in Africa* (Zed Books, 2002).

An-Na'im, Abdullahi A, *Islamic Family Law in a Changing World: A Global Resource Book* (Zed Books, 2002).

Australian Human Rights Commission, *Women's Human Rights: United Nations Convention on the Elimination of All Forms of Discrimination against Women: CEDAW* (Commonwealth of Australia and the Human Rights and Equal Opportunity Commission, 2008).

Barker, Chris, *Cultural Studies: Theory and Practice* (Sage, 2000).

Berkovitch, Nitza, *From Motherhood to Citizenship: Women's Rights and International Organization* (Johns Hopkins University Press, 1999).

Blanpain, Roger et al, *The Global Workplace: International and Comparative Employment Law – Cases and Materials* (Cambridge University Press, 2007).

Bridgeman, Jo and Susan Millns, *Law and Body Politics: Regulating the Female Body* (Dartmouth, 1995).

Brown, David et al, *Criminal Laws: Materials and Commentary on Criminal Law and Process of New South Wales* (Federation Press, 5th ed, 2011).

Canape, Charlene, *The Part-Time Solution: The New Strategy for Managing Your Career while Managing Motherhood* (Random House, 1990).

Devesahayam, Theresa W and Brenda S A Yeoh, *Working and Mothering in Asia: Images, Ideologies and Identities* (NUS Press, 2007).

Dawy, Aly *Alqanwn Aldwly Alaam* (Dar Alkotop Alwatanyah, Bnghazy, 2nd ed, 2005) [Trans: *Public International Law* (National Library, Benghazi)].

Easteal, Patricia, *Less than Equal: Women and the Australian Legal System* (Butterworths, 2001).

Eastern Mediterranean Regional Health Systems Observatory, *Health System Profile: Libya* (World Health Organization, 2007).

First, Ruth, *The Elusive Revolution* (Penguin 1972).

Flick, Uwe, *An Introduction to Qualitative Research* (Sage, 2nd ed, 2002).

Gale, Maggie, *West End Women: Women on the London Stage, 1918–1962* (Routledge, 1996).

Gareis, Sven Bernhard and Johannes Varwick, *The United Nations: An Introduction* (Lindsay P Cohn trans, Palgrave Macmillan, 2005).

Hancock, Beverley, *An Introduction to Qualitative Research* (Trent Focus Group, 1998).

Heap, Lisa, *Maternity Protection ILO Convention No 183: A New Standard for the New Century* (International Confederation of Free Trade Unions (ICFTU), Public Services International (PCI) and Education International (EI), 2001).

Hiebert, Janet, *Charter Conflicts: What is Parliament's Role?* (McGill-Queen's University Press, 2002).

Holy Bible (Oxford University Press, 2nd ed, 1971).

House of Representatives Standing Committee on Family and Human Services, *Balancing Work and Family: Report on the Inquiry into Balancing Work and Family* (CanPrint Communications, 2006).

Human Rights and Equal Opportunity Commission, *Federal Discrimination Law* (HREOC, 2008).

Human Rights Watch, *Perpetual Minors: Human Rights Abuses Stemming from Male Guardianship and Sex Segregation in Saudi Arabia* (Human Rights Watch, 2008).

Hutchinson, Terry, *Researching and Writing in Law* (Lawbook, 3rd ed, 2010).

International Centre for the Legal Protection of Human Rights, *Non-Discrimination in International Law* (Interights, 2005).

International Labour Office, *ABC of Women Workers' Rights and Gender Equality* (International Labour Organization, 2nd ed, 2007).

International Labour Office, *Fundamental Rights at Work and International Labour Standards* (International Labour Organization, 2003).

International Labour Office, PRO 169 and the Equality Team, *Eliminating Discrimination Against Indigenous and Tribal Peoples in Employment and Occupation: A Guide to ILO Convention No 111* (International Labour Office, 2007).

James, Susan and Stephanie Palmer, *Visible Women: Essays on Feminist Legal Theory and Political Philosophy* (Hart, 2002).

Karolis, Robert, *The Convention on the Rights of the Child: The Making of a Deception* (Constitutional Heritage Protection Society, 1990).

Key, Ellen, *Barnets Århundrade* (Bonniers, 1900).

Krivenko, Ekaterina Yahyaoui, *Women, Islam and International Law: Within the Context of the Convention on the Elimination of All Forms of Discrimination Against Women* (Martinus Nijhoff, 2008).

Langwith, Jacqueline, *Human Rights* (Greenhaven, 2008).

Lewis, Paul M, *Ethnologue: Languages of the World* (SIL International, 16th ed, 2009).

Marshall, Catherine and Gretchen B Rossman, *Designing Qualitative Research* (Sage, 3rd ed, 1999).

McMahon, Martha, *Engendering Motherhood: Identity and Self-Transformation in Women's Lives* (Guilford Press, 1995).

McNamara, Luke, *Human Rights Controversies: The Impact of Legal Form* (Routledge-Cavendish, 2007).

Mercer, Ramona Thieme, *Becoming a Mother: Research on Maternal Identity from Rubin to the Present* (Springer, 1995).

Monaghan, Karon, *Equality Law* (Oxford University Press, 2007).

Nazir, Sameena and Leigh Tomppert, *Women's Rights in the Middle East and North Africa: Citizenship and Justice* (Freedom House, 2005).

Obeidi, Amal, *Political Culture in Libya* (Curzon Press, 2001).

Office of the United Nations High Commissioner for Human Rights, *Legislative History of the Convention on the Rights of the Child* (United Nations, 2007).

O'Leary, Zina, *The Essential Guide to Doing Research* (Sage, 2004).

Organisation for Economic Cooperation and Development, *Babies and Bosses: Reconciling Work and Family Life: A Synthesis of Findings for OECD Countries* (OECD, 2007).

Otman, Waniss and Erling Karlberg, *The Libyan Economy: Economic Diversification and International Repositioning* (Springer, 2007).

Paul, Jane, *Healthy Beginning: Guidance on Safe Maternity at Work* (International Labour Office, 2004).

Rees, Neil, Katherine Lindsay and Simon Rice, *Australian Anti-Discrimination Law: Text, Cases and Materials* (Federation, 2008).

Richards, Patricia, *Pobladoras, Indígenas, and the State: Conflicts over Women's Rights in Chile* (Rutgers University Press, 2004).

Ross, Stewart, *The United Nations* (Heinemann Library, 2002).

Rozario, Paul A, *Libya (Countries of the World)* (Gareth Stevens, 2004)

Shah, Niaz A, *Women, the Koran and International Human Rights Law: The Experience of Pakistan* (Martinus Nijhoff, 2006).

Sommer, Barbara W and Mary Kay Quinlan, *The Oral History Manual* (Rowman & Littlefield, 2nd ed, 2002).

Stake, Robert E, *The Art of Case Study Research* (Sage, 1995).

Steiner, Henry J, Philip Alston and Ryan Goodman, *International Human Rights in Context: Law, Politics, Morals: Text and Materials* (Oxford University Press, 3rd ed, 2008).

Tula, Maria Teresa, *Human Rights Activist of El Salvador* (Lynn Stephen trans, South End Press, 1994).
United Nations, *The Convention on the Discrimination against Women and its Optional Protocol: Handbook for Parliamentarians* (UN and Inter-Parliamentary Union, 2003).
Warren, Nagueyalti and Sally Wolff, *Southern Mothers: Fact and Fictions in Southern Women's Writing* (Louisiana State University Press, 1999).
Westwood, Sallie and Parminder Bhachu, *Enterprising Women: Ethnicity, Economy, and Gender Relation* (Routledge, 1988).
World Health Organization, *World Health Statistics* (WHO, 2009).
Yeo, Eileen Janes, *Mary Wollstonecraft and 200 Years of Feminisms* (Rivers Oram, 1997).
Yeo, Eileen Janes, *Radical Femininity: Women's Self-Representation in the Public Sphere* (Manchester University Press, 1998).
Ziring, Lawrence, Robert E Riggs and Jack C Plano, *The United Nations: International Organization and World Politics* (Thomson Learning, 3rd ed, 2000).

Book Chapters

Al-Badri, Mas'oud Abdul Hafiz, 'Tqyym Al-Mashakl wa Al-Su'wbat Allti Tuwajih Al-Edarh Al-Maliyh Al-Ammh' in Muhmmd Zahi Al-Mghiyrbi and Abdul Jalyl Adm Al-Mansouri (eds), *Al-Edarh Al-Ammh Fi Libya: Al-Waq' wa Al-Tumohat* (Mrkiz Buhwth Al-Auluwm Al-Eqtisadyh, 2004) 282 [Trans: 'Problems and Obstacles Facing the Public Financial Administration: An Evaluation' in *Public Administration in Libya* (Research Centre for Economic Sciences)].
Al-Fytwri, Attiah Al-Mhdi 'Aqtisadyat Al-Edarh Al-Ammh' in Muhmmd Zahi Al-Mghiyrbi and Abdul Jalyl Adm Al-Mansouri (eds), *Al-Edarh Al-Ammh Fi Libya: Al-Waq' wa Al-Tumohat* (Mrkiz Buhwth Al-Auluwm Al-Eqtisadyh, 2004) 57 [Trans: 'The Economics of Public Administration' in *Public Administration in Libya* (Research Centre for Economic Sciences)].
Al-Jhany, Ahmed Al-Sadq, 'Al-Ekhtisas Al-Jina'y Lljihat Al-Rqabyyh Ala Al-Edarh Al-Ammh' in Muhmmd Zahi Al-Mghiyrbi and Abdul Jalyl Adm Al-Mansouri (eds), *Al-Edarh Al-Ammh Fi Libya: Al-Waq' wa Al-Tumohat* (Mrkiz Buhwth Al-Auluwm Al-Eqtisadyh, 2004) 371 [Trans: 'Criminal Jurisdiction for Governmental Agencies on Public Administration' in *Public Administration in Libya* (Research Centre for Economic Sciences)].
Al-Mghiyrb, Muhmmd Zahi, 'Athr Al-Tghyyrat Al-Hykaliyh Ala Wd'a Al-Siyasat Al-Ammh wa tnfiydhha Fi Libya (1977–2003)' in Muhmmd Zahi Al-Mghiyrbi and Abdul Jalyl Adm Al-Mansouri (eds), *Al-Edarh Al-Ammh Fi Libya: Al-Waq' wa Al-Tumohat* (Mrkiz Buhwth Al-Auluwm Al-Eqtisadyh, 2004) 35 [Trans: 'The Re-Structuring Impact on Public Policies in Libya' in *Public Administration in Libya* (Research Centre for Economic Sciences)].
Al-Zwy, Salih Muftah 'Athr Al-Lamrkziyh Ala Ada' Al-Edarh Fi Libya' in Muhmmd Zahi Al-Mghiyrbi and Abdul Jalyl Adm Al-Mansouri (eds), *Al-Edarh Al-Ammh Fi Libya: Al-Waq' wa Al-Tumohat* (Mrkiz Buhwth Al-Auluwm Al-Eqtisadyh, 2004) 108 [Trans: 'Decentralisation Impact on Libyan's Administration Performance' in *Public Administration in Libya* (Research Centre for Economic Sciences)].
Baltmr, Ahmed Ali, 'Kfa't Al-Qiyadat Al-Edariyh Mn Al-Muttlabat Al-Asasiyh Lejwdat Al-Qita' Al-Amm fi Libya' in Muhmmd Zahi Al-Mghiyrbi and Abdul Jalyl Adm Al-Mansouri (eds), *Mrkiz Buhwth Al-Auluwm Al-Eqtisadyh* (2004) 209 [Trans: 'Efficiency of the Administrative Leadership of the Basic Requirements for the Quality of the Public Sector in Libya' in *Public Administration in Libya* (Research Centre for Economic Sciences)].

Bernstein, Stephanie, 'The Regulation of Paid Care Work in the Home in Quebec: From the Hearth to the Global Marketplace' in Judy Fudge and Rosemary Owens (eds), *Precarious Work, Women, and the New Economy: The Challenge to Legal Norms* (Hart, 2006) 223.

Buss, Doris E, '"How the UN Stole Childhood": The Christian Right and the International Rights of the Child' in Jo Bridgeman and Daniel Monk (eds), *Feminist Perspectives on Child Law* (Cavendish, 2000) 271.

Charmaz, Kathy, 'Qualitative Interviewing and Grounded Theory Analysis' in Jaber F Gubrium and James A Holstein (eds), *Handbook of Interview Research Context and Method* (Sage, 2001).

Chorin, Ethan D, 'The Future of the U.S.-Libyan Commercial Relationship' in Dirk Vandewalle (ed), *Libya Since 1969: Qadhafi's Revolution Revisited* (Palgrave Macmillan, 2008) 153.

Conaghan, Joanne 'Time to Dream Flexibility, Families, and the Regulation of Working Time' in Judy Fudge and Rosemary Owens (eds), *Precarious Work, Women, and the New Economy: The Challenge to Legal Norms* (Hart, 2006) 101.

Fottrell, Deirdre, 'One Step Forward or Two Steps Sideways? Assessing the First Decade of the Children's Convention on the Rights of the Child' in Deirdre Fottrell (ed), *Revisiting Children's Rights: 10 Years of the UN Convention on the Rights of the Child* (Kluwer Law International, 2000) 1.

Fredman, Sandra, 'Precarious Norms for Precarious Workers' in Judy Fudge and Rosemary Owens (eds), *Precarious Work, Women, and the New Economy: The Challenge to Legal Norms* (Hart, 2006) 177.

Gaudart, Dorothea, 'What Are the Origins of CEDAW? The History of the UN Convention on the Elimination of All Forms of Discrimination against Women' in Sylvia Kölbl (ed), *What is CEDAW? The UN Convention on the Elimination of All Forms of Discrimination against Women: The Human Rights of Women and What They Mean* (Federal Chancellery, Federal Minister for Women, Media and Civil Service, 2007) 12.

Hunter, Rosemary, 'The Legal Production of Precarious Work' in Judy Fudge and Rosemary Owens (eds), *Precarious Work, Women, and the New Economy: The Challenge to Legal Norms* (Hart, 2006) 283.

Joffé, George, 'Prodigal or Pariah? Foreign Policy in Libya' in Dirk Vandewalle (ed), *Libya Since 1969: Qadhafi's Revolution Revisited* (Palgrave Macmillan, 2008) 191.

Krasno, Jean E, 'Founding the United Nations: An Evolutionary Process' in Jean E Krasno (ed), *The United Nations: Confronting the Challenges of a Global Society* (Lynne Rienner, 2004) 19.

Lim, Hilary and Jeremy Roche, 'Feminism and Children's Rights' in Jo Bridgeman and Daniel Monk (eds), *Feminist Perspectives on Child Law* (Cavendish, 2000) 227.

Maternity Protection Coalition (MPC), 'ILO and the Ratification Process' in Lakshmi Menon (ed), *Maternity Protection Campaign Kit: A Breastfeeding Perspective* (World Alliance for Breastfeeding Action, 2003) 1.

Mattes, Hanspeter, 'Formal and Informal Authority in Libya Since 1969' in Dirk Vandewalle (ed), *Libya Since 1969: Qadhafi's Revolution Revisited* (Palgrave Macmillan, 2008) 55.

Norchi, Charles, 'Human Rights: A Global Common Interest' in Jean E Krasno (ed), *The United Nations: Confronting the Challenges of a Global Society* (Lynne Rienner, 2004) 79.

Obeidi, Amal, 'Political Elites in Libya Since 1969' in Dirk Vandewalle (ed), *Libya Since 1969: Qadhafi's Revolution Revisited* (Palgrave Macmillan, 2008) 105.

Quataert, Jean H, 'Woman's Work and the Early Welfare State in Germany: Legislators, Bureaucrats, and Clients before the First World War' in Seth Koven and Sonya Michel (eds), *Mothers of a New World: Maternalist Politics and the Origins of Welfare States* (Routledge, 1993) 159.

Rittich, Kerry, 'Rights, Risk, and Reward: Governance Norms in the International Order and the Problem of Precarious Work' in Judy Fudge and Rosemary Owens (eds), *Precarious Work, Women, and the New Economy: The Challenge to Legal Norms* (Hart, 2006) 31.

Sait, M Siraj, 'Islamic Perspectives on the Rights of the Child' in Deirdre Fottrell (ed), *Revisiting Children's Rights: 10 Years of the UN Convention on the Rights of the Child* (Kluwer Law International, 2000) 31.

Sills, Joe, 'The United Nations and the Formation of Global Norms' in Jean E Krasno (ed), *The United Nations: Confronting the Challenges of a Global Society* (Lynne Rienner, 2004) 47.

St John, Ronald Bruce, 'The Libyan Economy in Transition: Opportunities and Challenges' in Dirk Vandewalle (ed), *Libya Since 1969: Qadhafi's Revolution Revisited* (Palgrave Macmillan, 2008) 127.

Tertinegg, Karin, 'Women's Human Rights and Obligations for Austria' in Sylvia Kölbl (ed), *What is CEDAW? The UN Convention on the Elimination of All Forms of Discrimination against Women: The Human Rights of Women and What They Mean* (Federal Chancellery, Federal Minister for Women, Media and Civil Service, 2007) 19.

Vosko, Leah F, 'Gender, Precarious Work, and the International Labour Code: The Ghost in the ILO Closet' in Judy Fudge and Rosemary Owens (eds), *Precarious Work, Women, and the New Economy: The Challenge to Legal Norms* (Hart, 2006) 53.

Walby, Sylvia, 'Policy Strategies in a Global Era for Gendered Workplace Equity' in Heidi Gottfried and Laura Reese (eds), *Equity in the Workplace: Gendering Workplace Policy Analysis* (Lexington, 2004) 53.

Wing, Adrien Katherine, 'International Conventions' in Joseph Suad (ed), *Encyclopedia of Women and Islamic Cultures: Family, Law and Politics* (Brill, 2005) vol 2, 306.

Journal Articles

Abel, Emily K, 'Adult Daughters and Care for the Elderly' (1986) 12(3) *Feminist Studies* 479.

Anner, Mark and Teri Caraway, 'International Institutions and Workers' Rights: Between Labor Standards and Market Flexibility' (2010) 45 *Studies in Comparative International Development* 151.

Arenz, S et al, 'Breast-feeding and Childhood Obesity: A Systematic Review' (2004) 28 *International Journal of Obesity* 1247.

Baird, Marian, 'Paid Maternity Leave: The Good, the Bad, the Ugly' (2003) 29(1) *Australian Bulletin of Labour* 97.

Baker, Michael and Kevin Milligan, 'Maternal Employment, Breastfeeding, and Health: Evidence from Maternity Leave' (2008) 27 *Journal of Health Economics* 871.

Ball, Olivia, 'Breastmilk is a Human Right' (2010) 18(3) *Breastfeeding Review* 9.

Berger, Lawrence M, Jennifer Hill and Jane Waldfogel, 'Maternity Leave, Early Maternal Employment and Child Health and Development in the US' (2005) 115(501) *Economic Journal* F29.

Bible, Dana and Kathy L Hill, 'Discrimination: Women in Business' (2007) 11(1) *Journal of Organizational Culture, Communication and Conflict* 65.

Bowers, Katherine, 'Campaigning for Two' (2005) 43(11) *Boston Magazine* 94.

Brodmann, Stefanie, Gosta Esping-Andersen and Maia Güell, 'When Fertility is Bargained: Second Births in Denmark and Spain' (2007) 23(5) *European Sociological Review* 599.

Brown, Lorra M, 'Bringing Up Baby: The Impact of Motherhood on Career Advancement' (2008) 14(2) *Public Relations Strategist* 20.
Burrow, Sharan, 'An Unequal World' (2004) 27(3) *UNSW Law Journal* 884.
Buzzanell, Patrice M et al, 'The Good Working Mother: Managerial Women's Sensemaking and Feelings about Work-Family Issues' (2005) 56(3) *Communication Studies* 261.
Cere, Daniel, 'Human Rights and the Family' (2009) 22(1) *Academic Questions* 63.
Cohen, Cynthia Price, 'Implementing the U.N. Convention on the Rights of the Child' (1999–2000) 21 *Whittier Law Review* 95.
Cohen, Cynthia Price, et al, 'The United Nations Convention on the Rights of the Child' (1997) 91 *American Society of International Law* 74.
Cook, Rebecca J, 'Reservations to the Convention on the Elimination of All Forms of Discrimination Against Women' (1989–90) 30 *Virginia Journal of International Law* 643.
Craig, Lyn, 'Contemporary Motherhood: The Impact of Children on Adult Time' (2008) 23(1) (2007) *New Zealand Society* 113.
Cullingford, Elizabeth, '"Something Else": Gendering Onliness in Elizabeth Bowen's Early Fiction' (2007) 53(2) *Modern Fiction Studies* 276.
Curran, Laura, 'Feminine Women, Hard Workers: Foster Motherhood in Midcentury America (1946–1963)' (2006) 31(4) *Journal of Family History* 386.
Deloach, Stephen B, Jayoti Das and Lindsey Conley, 'Power Politics and International Labor Standards' (2006) 12 *International Advances in Economic Research* 51.
Dilts, David A and Samavati Hedayeh, 'Motherhood: Arbitral Thought on Employment Discrimination Based on Marriage and Pregnancy' (2005) 60(3) *Dispute Resolution Journal* 46.
Farhoumand-Sims, Cheshmak, 'CEDAW and Afghanistan' (2009) 11(1) *Journal of International Women's Studies* 136.
Fass, Paula S, 'A Historical Context for the United Nations Convention on the Rights of the Child' (2011) 633(1) *Annals of the American Academy of Political and Social Science* 17.
Federico, Annette R, 'George Gissing, the Working Woman, and Urban Culture' (2007) 49(4) *Victorian Studies* 703.
Feng, Joyce Yen and Wen-Jui Han, 'Maternity Leave in Taiwan' (2010) 59 *Family Relations* 297.
Fillion, Kate, 'Motherhood in the Age of Judgment' (2007) 80(5) *Chatelaine* 130.
Frohlick, Susan, '"Wanting the Children and Wanting K2": The Incommensurability of Motherhood and Mountaineering in Britain and North America in the Late Twentieth Century' (2006) 13(5) *Gender, Place and Culture* 477.
Graff, E J, 'The Opt-Out Myth' (2007) 45(6) *Columbia Journalism Review* 5.
Graham, Mary E, Julie L Hotchkiss and Barry Gerhart, 'Discrimination by Parts: A Fixed-Effects Analysis of Starting Pay Differences across Gender' (2000) 26(1) *Eastern Economic Journal* 9.
Grummer-Strawn, Laurence M and Zuguo Mei, 'Does Breastfeeding Protect Against Pediatric Overweight? Analysis of Longitudinal Data from the Centers for Disease Control and Prevention Pediatric Nutrition Surveillance System' (2004) 113(2) *Pediatrics* 8.
Hadfield, L, N Rudoe and J Sanderson-Mann, 'Motherhood, Choice and the British Media: A Time to Reflect' (2007) 19(2) *Gender and Education* 255.
Hall, Joshua C and Peter T Leeson, 'Good for the Goose, Bad for the Gander: International Labor Standards and Comparative Development' (2007) 28 *Journal of Labor Research* 658.
Hatern, Marie et al, 'Midwife-Led versus Other Models of Care for Childbearing Women' (2008) 4 *Cochrane Database of Systematic Reviews* 1.
Heilman, Madeline E and Tyler G Okimoto, 'Motherhood: A Potential Source of Bias in Employment Decisions' (2008) 93(1) *Journal of Applied Psychology* 189.

Higgins, Christopher, Linda Duxbury and Karen Lea Johnson, 'Part-Time Work for Women: Does it Really Help Balance Work and Family?' (2000) 39(1) *Human Resource Management* 17.

Hirsh, Elizabeth and Christopher J Lyons, 'Perceiving Discrimination on the Job: Legal Consciousness, Workplace Context, and the Construction of Race Discrimination' (2010) 44(2) *Law and Society Review* 269.

Hoq, Laboni Amena, 'The Women's Convention and Its Optional Protocol: Empowering Women to Claim their Internationally Protected Rights' (2001) 32 *Columbia Human Rights Law Review* 677.

Hyde, Janet Shibley et al, 'Maternity Leave, Women's Employment, and Marital Incompatibility' (2001) 15(3) *Journal of Family Psychology* 476.

Jivan, Vedna and Christine Forster, 'Challenging Conventions: in Pursuit of Greater Legislative Compliance with CEDAW in the Pacific' (2009) 10 *Melbourne Journal of International Law* 655.

Jones, Susanna, 'Exercising Agency, Becoming a Single Mother: Decision-Making Processes of Unmarried Women' (2007) 42(4) *Marriage & Family Review* 35.

Kahu, Ella and Mandy Morgan, 'A Critical Discourse Analysis of New Zealand Government Policy: Women as Mothers and Workers' (2007) 30(2) *Women's Studies International Forum* 134.

Kamerman, Sheila B, 'From Maternity to Parental Leave Policies: Women's Health, Employment, and Child and Family Well-Being' (2000) 55(2) *Journal of American Medical Women's Association* 96.

Keller, Linda M, 'The Convention on the Elimination of Discrimination Against Women: Evolution and (Non)Implementation Worldwide' (2004–05) 27 *Thomas Jefferson Law Review* 35.

Kelm, Mary-Ellen, 'Canadian Missionaries, Indigenous Peoples: Representing Religion at Home and Abroad' (2007) 76(1) *Church History* 221.

Kennelly, Ivy, 'Secretarial Work, Nurturing, and the Ethic of Service' (2006) 18(2) *Feminist Formations* 170.

Klie, Shannon, 'Family Responsibilities, Finances Prevent Women from Getting MBA' (2006) 19(13) *Canadian HR Reporter* 3.

Kohl, John, Milton Mayfield and Jacqueline Mayfield, 'Recent Trends in Pregnancy Discrimination Law' (2005) 48(5) *Business Horizons* 421.

Linstedt, Sharon, 'The Buffalo News, N.Y., Sharon Linstedt Column' (2006) *Knight Ridder Tribune Business News* 1.

Liu, Meina and Patrice M Buzzanell, 'Negotiating Maternity Leave Expectations: Perceived Tensions between Ethics of Justice and Care' (2004) 41(4) *Journal of Business Communication* 323.

Lovell, Peggy A, 'Race, Gender, and Work in São Paulo, Brazil, 1960–2000' (2006) 41(3) (23 August 2008) *Latin American Research Review* 63.

Majlis Mujamm' Al-Fiqh Al-Islami Al-Dawly, 'Mudawat Al-Rajul Llmr'ah' (1994) 8(3) *Mujamm' Al-Fiqh Al-Islami* 9 [Trans: Council of International Islamic Jurisprudence Academy, 'Medical Treatment of Women by Men' (1994) 8(3) *Islamic Jurisprudence Academy 9*].

Mama, Robin S, 'Needs, Rights, and the Human Family: The Practicality of the Convention on the Rights of the Child' (2010) 89(5) *Child Welfare* 177.

Mantilla, Karla, 'The Truth Behind the Mommy Wars: Who Decides What Makes a Good Mother?' (2006) 36(2) *Off Our Backs* 66.

Mathur-Helm, Babita, 'Equal Opportunity and Affirmative Action for South African Women: A Benefit or Barrier?' (2004) 20(1) (6 August 2008) *Women in Management Review* 56.

Mayer-Davis, Elizabeth J et al, 'Breast-Feeding and Risk for Childhood Obesity: Does Maternal Diabetes or Obesity Status Matter?' (2006) 29(10) *Diabetes Care* 2231.

McCrudden, Christopher, 'Using Public Procurement to Achieve Social Outcomes' (2004) 24(1) *Natural Resources Forum* 257.

McMillan-Capehart, Amy and Orlando Richard, 'Organisational Justice and Perceived Fairness of Hiring Decisions Related to Race and Gender: Affirmative Action Reactions' (2005) 24(1) *Equal Opportunities International* 1.

Melike, Sayil, Güre Aysen and Uçanok Zehra, 'First Time Mothers' Anxiety and Depressive Symptoms across the Transition to Motherhood: Associations with Maternal and Environmental Characteristics' (2006) 44(3) *Women & Health* 61.

Melton, Gary B, 'Building Humane Communities Respectful of Children: The Significance of the Convention on the Rights of the Child' (2005) 60(8) *American Psychologist* 918.

Merry, Sally Engle, 'Constructing a Global Law: Violence against Women and the Human Rights System' (2003) 28 *Law and Social Inquiry* 941.

Milkie, Melissa A and Pia Peltola, 'Playing All the Roles: Gender and the Work-Family Balancing Act' (1999) 61(2) *Journal of Marriage and Family* 476.

Millward, Lynne J, 'The Transition to Motherhood in an Organizational Context: An Interpretative Phenomenological Analysis' (2006) 79(3) *Journal of Occupational and Organizational Psychology* 315.

Mora, Claudia, 'The Meaning of Womanhood in the Neoliberal Age: Class and Age-Based Narratives of Chilean Women' (2006) 23(2) *Gender Issues* 44.

Obeidi, Amal, 'Tatwir Harakt Al-Mr'ah fi Al-Mujtam' Al-Liby Byn Al-Tmkiyn wa Al-Tf'iyl: Dirast Twthiyqiyh' (2003–04) 23 *Majlt Dirasat fi Al-Eqtisad wa Al-Tijarh* [Trans: 'The Evolution of the Libyan Women's Movement: A Quantitative Study' *Journal of Economic and Commerce Studies*] 1.

Oddy, W H et al, 'Breast Feeding and Respiratory Morbidity in Infancy: A Birth Cohort Study' (2003) 88(3) *Archives of Disease in Childhood* 224.

Ogawa, Naohiro, Robert D Retherford and Yasuhiko Saito, 'Caring for the Elderly and Holding Down a Job: How Are Women in Japan Coping?' (2003) 65 *Asia-Pacific Population and Policy* 1.

Owen, Christopher G et al, 'Effect of Infant Feeding on the Risk of Obesity across the Life Course: A Quantitative Review of Published Evidence' (2005) 115(5) *American Academy of Pediatrics* 1367.

'Perspectives: Parental Leave' (1997) 136(1) *International Labour Review* 109.

Pollitt, Katha, 'Desperate Housewives of the Ivy League?' (2005) 281(12) *Nation* 14.

Rabe, Marlize, 'Mother Matter; Motherhood as Discourse and Practice' (2005) 36(4) *Journal of Comparative Family Studies* 670.

Reisman, W Michael, 'Sovereignty and Human Rights in Contemporary International Law' (1990) 84(4) *American Journal of International Law* 866.

Scott, Amy M, 'Family Responsibility Discrimination' (2007) 62 (3 August 2008) *Employee Benefit Plan Review* 35.

Shamiyh, Abdullh Muhmmd, Shafiyh Salim Bu Shwiyqyr and Marym Muhmmd Awhydah, 'Waq' Al-Mr'ah Al-Amilh fi Madint Bnghazy: Dirast Halh' (1997) 8(1–2) *Mrkiz Al-Buhwth Al-Eqtisadyh* 164 [Trans: 'The Working Woman in the City of Benghazi: A Case Study' (1997) 8(1–2) *Research Centre for Economic Sciences*].

Sigle-Rushton, Wendy and Jane Waldfogel, 'Motherhood and Women's Earnings in Anglo-American, Continental European, and Nordic Countries' (2007) 13(2) *Feminist Economics* 55.

Toschke, André Michael et al, 'Overweight and Obesity in 6- to 14-Year-Old Czech Children in 1991: Protective Effect of Breast-Feeding' (2002) 141(6) *Journal of Pediatrics* 764.

Tryggvadóttir, Laufey et al, ‘Breastfeeding and Reduced Risk of Breast Cancer in an Icelandic Cohort Study’ (2001) 154(1) *American Journal of Epidemiology* 37.

Tucker Judith Stadtman, ‘The New Future of Motherhood’ (2006) 36(2) *Off Our Backs* 32.

Tydén, Tanja et al, ‘Female University Students’ Attitudes to Future Motherhood and Their Understanding about Fertility’ (2006) 11(3) *European Journal of Contraception & Reproductive Health Care* 181.

VandenHoven, Natasha and Shelly Shapero, ‘Maternity Leave and Employee Benefits’ (2002) 26(5) *Benefits Canada* 9.

Wagner, Cynthia G, ‘Progress Report on Discrimination against Women’ (2008) 42(3) *Futurist* 9.

Weaver-Zercher, Valerie, ‘Moms’ Malaise’ (2006) 123(3) *Christian Century* 29.

Weichselbaumer, Doris and Rudolf Winter-Ebmer, ‘The Effects of Competition and Equal Treatment Laws on Gender Wage Differentials’ (2007) 22 *Economic Policy* 235.

Whitehead, Diane, ‘Convention on the Rights of the Child’ (2009) 85(3) *Childhood Education* 178.

Wilson, Dolly Smith, ‘A New Look at the Affluent Worker: The Good Working Mother in Post-War Britain’ (2006) 17(2) *20 Century British History* 206.

World Alliance for Breastfeeding Action (WABA), ‘Mother Support Task Force (MSTF): World Alliance for Breastfeeding Action’ (2011) 9(1) *WABA MSTF: E-newsletter V9N1* 1.

Zhang, Xuelin, ‘Returning to the Job after Childbirth’ (2008) 20(1) *Perspectives on Labour and Income* 20.

Zheng, Tongzhang et al, ‘Lactation Reduces Breast Cancer Risk in Shandong Province, China’ (2000) 152(12) *American Journal of Epidemiology* 1129.

Ziss, Christy, ‘Employment Law Equal Opportunity-Accommodating Family Responsibilities’ (2000) (August 2000) *Austrian Company Secretary* 423.

Electronic Articles

Al-Ageli, Nahla, ‘Libya’s Elections: Women Getting On Board’ *Libya Herald* 29 June 2012 <http://www.libyaherald.com/feature-libyas-elections-women-getting-on-board/>.

Blades, Joan and Kristin Rowe-Finkbeiner, ‘The Motherhood Manifesto’ (2006) 282(20) *Nation* 11 <http://proquest.umi.com/pqdweb?did=1044513331&Fmt=7&clientId=20901&RQT=309&VName=PQD>.

Butler, Kelley M, ‘Wooing Women: Today’s Working Women Seek Mentors, Motherhood Transition’ (2006) *Employee Benefit News* 1 <http://proquest.umi.com/pqdweb?did=1014405271&Fmt=7&clientId=20901&RQT=309&VName=PQD>.

Carroll, Gigi, ‘Modern Motherhood’ (2007) 48(45) *Adweek* 13 <http://proquest.umi.com/pqdweb?did=1401053711&Fmt=7&clientId=20901&RQT=309&VName=PQD>.

Dobrow, Larry, ‘Parenting Newbie Cookie is a Friend to Upscale Moms’ (2007) 78(43) *Advertising Age* <http://proquest.umi.com/pqdweb?did=1378237061&Fmt=7&clientId=20901&RQT=309&VName=PQD>.

Eddy, Charmaine, ‘Women’s (Re)Production’ (2006) (190) *Canadian Literature* 122 <http://proquest.umi.com/pqdweb?did=1193591711&Fmt=7&clientId=20901&RQT=309&VName=PQD>.

Everingham, Christine, Deborah Stevenson and Penny Warner-Smith, ‘“Things are Getting Better all the Time?” Challenging the Narrative of Women’s Progress from a Generational Perspective’ (2007) 41(3) *Sociology: Journal of the British Sociological Association* 419 <http://proquest.umi.com/pqdweb?did=1301989871&Fmt=7&clientId=20901&RQT=309&VName=PQD>.

Hodson, Heather, 'Why Choosing Motherhood is in Fashion' (2006) (3532) *Harper's Bazaar* 309 <http://proquest.umi.com/pqdweb?did=991141991&Fmt=7&clientId=20901&RQT=309&VName=PQD>.

Kuchment, Anna, 'Moms Mean Business: Inspired by the Dot-com Boom, a Growing Number of Women are Dreaming up New Ventures while the Kids are Napping' (2006) 148(11) *Newsweek* 66 <http://proquest.umi.com/pqdweb?did=1129955651&Fmt=7&clientId=20901&RQT=309&VName=PQD>.

Louis, Lucille, 'Life as a Mother-Scientist' (2006) 53(15) *Chronicle of Higher Education* <http://proquest.umi.com/pqdweb?did=1204779551&Fmt=7&clientId=20901&RQT=309&VName=PQD>.

Make Every Woman Count, *Libya: Equal Participation of Women Vital for Building New Libya, Says UN Envoy*, 27 June 2012 <http://www.peacewomen.org/news_article.php?id=5069&type=news>.

Moses, Barbara, 'Successful Careers and Motherhood Don't Have to be Mutually Exclusive' (2007) 20(19) *Canadian HR Reporter* 31 <http://proquest.umi.com/pqdweb?did=1387415081&Fmt=7&clientId=20901&RQT=309&VName=PQD>.

Neff, Jack, 'How Tupperware Made Itself Relevant Again' (2007) 78(23) *Advertising Age* 19 <http://proquest.umi.com/pqdweb?did=1288304831&Fmt=7&clientId=20901&RQT=309&VName=PQD>.

Roffman, Rachel M, 'The Forced Prostitution of Girls into the Child Sex Tourism Industry' (1997) 3 *New England International and Comparative Law Annual* <http://www.nesl.edu/intljournal/vol3/childsex.htm>.

Smith, Rhiannon, 'Are Libyans For or Against Women's Rights?' *Libya Herald: The New Independent Libya Daily*, 30 June 2012 <http://www.libyaherald.com/are-libyans-for-or-against-womens-rights/>.

Topalian, Nohad 'Change Takes Time, Libyan Judge Says' *Libyan Youth Movement Feb 17th* website, 20 January 2012 <http://feb17.info/news/change-takes-time-libyan-judge-says/>.

Walker, Portia '10,000 Still Missing in Gaddafi's Killing Fields' *Independent* (UK) 1 July 2012 <http://www.independent.co.uk/news/world/africa/10000-still-missing-in-gaddafis-killing-fields-7901927.html>.

Ward, Celeste, 'Make Your Own Hours' (2005) 46(36) *Adweek* 29 <http://proquest.umi.com/pqdweb?did=902202311&Fmt=7&clientId=20901&RQT=309&VName=PQD>.

Win News, 'Women and Human Rights' (1993) 19(2) *Win News* <http://proquest.umi.com.ezproxy.uow.edu.au:2048/pqdweb?did=592574401&sid=10&Fmt=3&clientId=20901&RQT=309&VName=PQD>.

Cases

Australian Meat Industry Employees Union v Meat and Allied Trades Federation of Australia (Equal Pay Cases) (1969) 127 CAR 1142 (Moore and Williams JJ, Chambers Public Service Arbitrator and Gough C, Judgment, 19 June 1969)

Legislation

Libya

Amendment Act No 7 of 1997 of Some Provisions of Act No 58 of 1970 (Libya)
Army Act No 3 of 1984 (Libya)
Charter of Women Rights and Obligations in Republic Society 1997 (Libya)
Child Protection Act No 5 of 1997 (Libya)
Civil Service Act No 55 of 1976 (Libya)
Concerning Labour Relations Act No 12 of 2010 (Libya)
Constitution Declaration of 1969 (Libya)
Criminal Act 1953 (Libya)
Customs Act No 68 of 1972 (Libya)
Declaration on the Establishment of the Authority of the People 1977 (Libyan)
Executive Rules of Health Act No 106 of 1973 (Libya)
Great Green Charter of Human Rights in the Jamahiriya Era 1988 (Libya)
Health Act No 106 of 1973 (Libya)
Health Insurance Act No 20 of 2010 (Libya)
Judicial System Act No 6 of 2006 (Libya)
Judicial System Act No 51 of 1976 (Libya)
Labour Code Act No 58 of 1970 (Libya)
Marriage and Divorce Act No 10 of 1984 (Libya)
Monitor the Executive Power and the Legislative Power Act No17 of 1994 (Libya)
Order of Executive Rules of the Civil Service Act 1978 (Libya)
Order of the General People's Committee No 51 of 2007 on Social Assistance (Libya)
Order of the General People's Committee No 54 of 2007 on Medical Workers in Hospitals and Training Centres (Libya)
Order of the General People's Committee No 88 of 1998 on the Requirements for Childcare Facility for Working Mothers (Libya)
Order of the General People's Committee No 164 of 1988 on Employment of Arab Libyan Women (Libya)
Order of the General People's Committee No 214 of 2002 Regarding the Health and the Social Security Needs of Public and Private Hospitals of Child Care and Gynaecology (Libya)
Order of the General People's Committee No 258 of 1989 on the Rehabilitation and Training of Libyan Women (Libya)
Order of the General People's Committee No 10572 of 2009 on the Female Worker Who is Nursing Her Child for Eighteen Months (Libya)
Police Force Act No 6 of 1972 (Libya)
Promotion of Freedoms Act No 20 of 1991 (Libya)
Protection of Women's Right to Inheritance Act 1959 (Libya)
Re-establishment of the High Court Act No 6 of 1982 (Libya)
Right of Women to Assume Posts in the Judiciary Act No 8 of 1989 (Libya)
Social Security Act No 13 of 1980 (Libya)
Wage Scales for National Workers Act No 15 of 1981 (Libya)
Workers' Affairs Policy for Libyan Iron and Steel Company 2008 (Libya)

Kuwait

Act No 1 of 1990 to Increase the Family Allowance (Kuwait)

Australia

Equal Employment Opportunity (Commonwealth Authorities) Act 1987 (Cth)
Equal Opportunity for Women in the Workplace Act 1999 (Cth)
Paid Parental Leave Act 2010 (Cth)
Sex Discrimination Act 1984 (Cth)

Europe

BUSINESSEUROPE, UEAPME, CEEP, ETUC Framework Agreement on Parental Leave (Revised) 18 June 2009
Council Directive 2010/18/EU of 8 March 2010 on Implementing the Revised Framework Agreement on Parental Leave Concluded by BUSINESSEUROPE, UEAPME, CEEP and ETUC and Repealing Directive 96/34/EC [2010] OJ L 68/13

International Human Rights Treaties and Related Documents

Charter of the United Nations, opened for signature 26 June 1945 (entered into force 26 June 1945)
Convention against Torture and Other Cruel, Inhuman or Degrading Treatment or Punishment, opened for signature 10 December 1984 (entered into force 26 June 1987)
Convention on Consent to Marriage, Minimum Age for Marriage and Registration of Marriages, opened for signature 7 November 1962, 521 UNTS 231 (entered into force 9 December 1964)
Convention on the Elimination of All Forms of Discrimination against Women (CEDAW), opened for signature 1 March 1980, 1249 UNTS 13 (entered into force 3 September 1981)
Convention on the Political Rights of Women, opened for signature 31 December 1953, 193 UNTS 135 (entered into force 7 July 1954)
Convention on the Rights of the Child (CRC), opened for signature 20 November 1989, 1577 UNTS 3 (entered into force 2 September 1990)
Declaration on the Elimination of Discrimination against Women, GA Res 2263 (XXII) UN GAOR 22nd sess, UN Doc A/RES/2263 (7 November 1967)
Declaration of the Rights of the Child, LON (26 September 1924)
Declaration of the Rights of the Child, GA Res 1386 (XIV), UN GAOR, Sup No 16, UN Doc A/4354 (20 November 1959)
Declarations, Reservations, Objections and Notifications of Withdrawal of Reservations Relating to the Convention on the Elimination of All Forms of Discrimination against Women, UN Doc No CEDAW/SP/2006/2, 17–18 (*Libyan Arab Jamahiriya, Reservations*, 5 July 1995)
Declarations, Reservations, Objections and Notifications of Withdrawal of Reservations Relating to the Convention on the Elimination of All Forms of Discrimination against Women, UN Doc No CEDAW/SP/2006/2, 9 (Bahrain), 11 (Egypt), 14 (India), 15 (Israel), 17 (Lebanon)
Discrimination (Employment and Occupation) Convention (C111), opened for signature 25 June 1958, ILO (entered into force 15 June 1960)
Discrimination (Employment and Occupation) Convention (C111) *1958: Ratified by Libyan Arab Jamahiriya on 13 June1961*, ILOLEX Doc No 191961 LBY111
Division for the Advancement of Women, United Nations Department of Economic and Social Affairs, *Declarations, Reservations and Objections to CEDAW* (2007)

Eliminating Discrimination against Indigenous and Tribal Peoples in Employment and Occupation, opened for signature 29 February 2008 (entered into force 29 February 2008)
Employment Policy Convention (C122), opened for signature 9 July 1964, ILO (entered into force 15 July 1966)
International Convention on the Elimination of All Forms of Racial Discrimination (ICERD), opened for signature 21 December 1965, 660 UNTS 195 (entered into force 4 January 1969)
International Convention on the Protection of the Rights of All Migrant Workers and Members of Their Families (ICRMW), opened for signature 18 December 1990, 2220 UNTS 3 (entered into force 1 July 2003)
International Covenant on Civil and Political Rights (ICCPR), opened for signature 16 December 1966, 999 UNTS 171 (entered into force 23 March 1976)
International Covenant on Economic, Social and Cultural Rights (ICESCR), opened for signature 16 December 1966, 999 UNTS 3 (entered into force 3 January 1976)
International Labour Organization Constitution
Maternity Protection Convention (C3), opened for signature 28 November 1919, ILO (entered into force 13 June 1921)
Maternity Protection Convention (Revised) (C103), opened for signature 28 June 1952, ILO (entered into force 7 September 1955)
Maternity Protection Convention (C183), opened for signature 15 June 2000, ILO (entered into force 7 February 2002)
Minimum Age (Agriculture) Convention (C10), opened for signature16 November1921, ILO (entered into force 31 August 1923)
Minimum Age (Industry) Convention (C5) 1919, opened for signature 28 November1919, ILO (entered into force 13 June 1921)
Minimum Age (Sea) Convention (C7), opened for signature 9 July1920, ILO (entered into force 27 September 1921)
Optional Protocol to the Convention on the Elimination of All Forms of Discrimination against Women, opened for signature 6 October 1999, 2131 UNTS 83 (entered into force 22 December 2000)
Paid Educational Leave Convention (C140), opened for signature 24 June 1974, ILO (entered into force 23 September 1976)
Part-Time Work Convention, opened for signature 24 June 1994, ILO C175 (entered into force 28 February 1998)
Social Policy (Basic Aims and Standards) Convention (C117), opened for signature 22 June 1962, ILO (entered into force 23 April 1964)
Status of Ratifications of the Principal International Human Rights Treaties 2006 (Office of the United Nations High Commissioner for Human Rights)
Termination of Employment Convention (C158), opened for signature 22 June1982, ILO (entered into force 23 November 1985)
Universal Declaration of Human Rights (UDHR), GA Res 217A (III), UN GAOR, 3rd sess, 183rd plen mtg, UN Doc A/810 (10 December 1948)
Vienna Convention on the Law of Treaties (VCLT), opened for signature 23 May 1969, 1155 UNTS 331 (entered into force 27 January 1980)
Workers with Family Responsibilities Convention (C156), opened for signature 23 June 1981, ILO (entered into force 11 August 1983)

Reports

Addati, Laura and Naomi Cassirer, 'Equal Sharing of Responsibilities between Women and Men, Including Care-Giving in the Context of HIV/AIDS' (EGM/ESOR/2008/BP.2, Division for the Advancement of Women Department of Economic and Social Affairs United Nations, 19 September 2008).

Al-Hy'h Al-Ammh Llm'lumat, 'Taqrir Al-Tnmiyh Al-Basharyh: Tmkiyn Al-Mr'ah Al-Libyh wa Qdaya Al-Nw' (Al-Hy'h Al-Watniyh Llm'lumat wa Al-Twthyq, 1999) [Trans: General Information Authority, 'Human Development Report: Empowering Libyan's Woman and Gender Issues' (National Commission for Information and Documentation)].

Al-Hy'h Al-Watniyh Llm'lumat wa Al-Twthyq, 'Al-Sukkan wa Al-Quwa Al-Amilh wa Al-Aujwr wa Al-Entajiyh fi Libya' (Amant Al-Tkhtit, 1989) [Trans: 'Population, Labour, Wages and Productivity in Libya' (National Commission for Information and Documentation)].

Association for Childhood Education International and US National Committee of the World Organization for Early Childhood, 'Global Guidelines for Early Childhood Education and Care in the 21st Century' (ACEI-OMEP, 2000).

Australian Government Office for Women, Department of Families, Housing, Community Services and Indigenous Affairs, 'Review of the Equal Opportunity for Women in the Workplace Act 1999: Consultation Report' (January 2010).

Australian Health Ministers' Conference, 'Australian National Breastfeeding Strategy 2010–2015' (P3–6238, Australian Government, 2009).

Australian Institute of Health and Welfare, 'A Picture of Australia's Children 2009' (Cat No PHE 112, AIHW Canberra, 2009).

Australian Institute of Health and Welfare, 'Australia's Health 2010: The Twelfth Biennial Health Report of the Australian Institute of Health and Welfare' (AIHW Canberra 2010).

Boni, Guido, 'The Labour Market in the SEM Countries: A Legal Perspective' (CARIM Research Reports 2009/15, European University Institute, 2009).

Central Bank of Libya, 'Economic Bulletin for the Second Quarter of the Year 2009' (2, Central Bank of Libya, 2009).

Centre for Community Child Health and Telethon Institute for Child Health Research, 'A Snapshot of Early Childhood Development in Australia: Australian Early Development Index (AEDI) National Report 2009' (Australian Government, 2009).

Chatterji, Pinka and Sara Markowitz, 'Does the Length of Maternity Leave Affect Maternal Health?' (10206 JEL No 11, National Bureau of Economic Research, January 2004).

Committee of Experts on the Application of Conventions and Recommendations (CEACR), *CEACR: Individual Direct Request Concerning Convention No 103, Maternity Protection (Revised), 1952 Libyan Arab Jamahiriya (ratification: 1975) Submitted: 1990*, CEACR 1990, 60th sess, ILOLEX Doc No 091990LBY103 (International Labour Organization, 1990).

Committee of Experts on the Application of Conventions and Recommendations (CEACR), *CEACR: Individual Direct Request Concerning Convention No 111, Discrimination (Employment and Occupation), 1958 Libyan Arab Jamahiriya (ratification: 1961) Submitted: 1990*, 60th sess, ILOLEX Doc No 091990LBY111, International Labour Organization, 1990).

Committee of Experts on the Application of Conventions and Recommendations (CEACR), *CEACR: Individual Observation Concerning Convention No 103, Maternity Protection Convention (Revised), 1952 Libyan Arab Jamahiriya (ratification: 1975)*, CEACR 1994 64th sess, ILOLEX Doc No 061994LBY103 (International Labour Organization, 1994).

Committee of Experts on the Application of Conventions and Recommendations (CEACR), *CEACR: Individual Direct Request Concerning Convention No 111, Discrimination (Employment and Occupation), 1958 Libyan Arab Jamahiriya (ratification: 1961) Submitted: 1995, February*, 65th sess, ILOLEX Doc No 091995LBY1111 (International Labour Organization, 1995).

Committee of Experts on the Application of Conventions and Recommendations (CEACR), *CEACR: Individual Observation Concerning Convention No 103, Maternity Protection (Revised), 1952 Libyan Arab Jamahiriya (ratification: 1975) 1995*, CEACR 1995, 66th sess, ILOLEX Doc No 061996LBY1032 (International Labour Organization, 1996).

Committee of Experts on the Application of Conventions and Recommendations (CEACR), *CEACR: Individual Direct Request Concerning Convention No 111, Discrimination (Employment and Occupation), 1958 Libyan Arab Jamahiriya (ratification: 1961) Submitted: 1996*, 66th sess, ILOLEX Doc No 091996LBY1112 (International Labour Organization, 1996).

Committee of Experts on the Application of Conventions and Recommendations (CEACR), *CEACR: Individual Direct Request concerning Convention No 111, Discrimination (Employment and Occupation), 1958 Libyan Arab Jamahiriya (ratification: 1961) Submitted: 1997*, 67th sess, ILOLEX Doc No 091997LBY111 (International Labour Organization, 1997).

Committee of Experts on the Application of Conventions and Recommendations (CEACR), *CEACR: Individual Observation Concerning Convention No 103, Maternity Protection (Revised), 1952 Libyan Arab Jamahiriya (ratification: 1975) 1997*, CEACR 1997, 68th sess, (ILOLEX Doc No 061998LBY103 (International Labour Organization, 1998).

Committee of Experts on the Application of Conventions and Recommendations (CEACR), *CEACR: Individual Observation Concerning Convention No 103, Maternity Protection (Revised), 1952 Libyan Arab Jamahiriya (ratification: 1975)1998*, CEACR 1998, 69th sess, ILOLEX Doc No 061999LBY103 (International Labour Organization, 1999).

Committee of Experts on the Application of Conventions and Recommendations (CEACR), *CEACR: Individual Observation Concerning Convention No 103, Maternity Protection (Revised), 1952 Libyan Arab Jamahiriya (ratification: 1975) 1999*, CEACR 1999, 70th sess, ILOLEX Doc No 062000LBY103 (International Labour Organization, 2000).

Committee of Experts on the Application of Conventions and Recommendations (CEACR), *CEACR: Individual Observation Concerning Convention No 111, Discrimination (Employment and Occupation), 1958 Libyan Arab Jamahiriya (ratification: 1961) 1999*, 70th sess, ILOLEX Doc No 062000LBY111 (International Labour Organization, 2000).

Committee of Experts on the Application of Conventions and Recommendations (CEACR), *CEACR: Individual Observation Concerning Convention No 111, Discrimination (Employment and Occupation), 1958 Libyan Arab Jamahiriya (ratification: 1961) 2000*, 71st sess, ILOLEX Doc No 062001LBY111 (International Labour Organization, 2001).

Committee of Experts on the Application of Conventions and Recommendations (CEACR), *CEACR: Individual Observation Concerning Convention No 111, Discrimination (Employment and Occupation), 1958 Libyan Arab Jamahiriya (ratification: 1961) 2002*, 73rd sess, ILOLEX Doc No 062003LBY111, International Labour Organization, 2003).

Committee of Experts on the Application of Conventions and Recommendations (CEACR), *CEACR: Individual Observation Concerning Convention No 103, Maternity Protection (Revised), 1952 Libyan Arab Jamahiriya (ratification: 1975) 2003*, CEACR 2003, 74th sess, ILOLEX Doc No 062004LBY103 (International Labour Organization, 2004).

Committee of Experts on the Application of Conventions and Recommendations (CEACR), *CEACR: Individual Observation Concerning Maternity Protection Convention (Revised), 1952*

(No 103) Libyan Arab Jamahiriya (ratification: 1975) 2005, CEACR 2005, 76th sess, ILOLEX Doc No 062006LBY103 (International Labour Organization, 2006).

Committee of Experts on the Application of Conventions and Recommendations (CEACR), *CEACR: Individual Observation concerning Maternity Protection Convention (Revised), 1952 (No 103) Libyan Arab Jamahiriya (ratification: 1975) 2007*, CEACR 2007, 78th sess, ILOLEX Doc No 062008LBY103 (International Labour Organization, 2008).

Committee of Experts on the Application of Conventions and Recommendations (CEACR), *Comments Made by the Committee of Experts on the Application of Conventions and Recommendations (from 1990 to 2007) Discrimination (Employment and Occupation) Convention, 1958 (No 111): Libyan Arab Jamahiriya (ratification: 1961)*, 80th sess (International Labour Organization, 2009).

Committee of Experts on the Application of Conventions and Recommendations (CEACR), *General Report and Observations Concerning Particular Countries*, 99th sess, 2010 III (Part 1A) (International Labour Office, 2010),

Committee of Experts on the Application of Conventions and Recommendations (CEACR), *CEACR: Individual Observation Concerning Maternity Protection Convention (Revised), 1952 (No 103) Libyan Arab Jamahiriya (ratification: 1975) 2009*, CEACR 2009, 80th sess, ILOLEX Doc No 062010LBY103 (International Labour Organization, 2010).

Committee of Experts on the Application of Conventions and Recommendations (CEACR), *CEACR: Individual Observation Concerning Discrimination (Employment and Occupation) Convention, 1958 (No 111) Libyan Arab Jamahiriya (ratification: 1961) 2009*, CEACR 2009, 80th sess, ILOLEX Doc No 062010LBY111 (International Labour Organization, 2010).

Committee of Experts on the Application of Conventions and Recommendations (CEACR), *CEACR: Submission to the Competent Authorities, Libyan Arab Jamahiriya, 2010*, ILOLEX Doc No 102010LBY (International Labour Organization, 2011).

Committee of Experts on the Application of Conventions and Recommendations (CEACR), *CEACR: Submission to the Competent Authorities, Libyan Arab Jamahiriya, 2011*, ILOLEX Doc No 102011LBY (International Labour Organization, 2011).

Director-General, 'Time for Equality at Work: Global Report under the Follow-up to the ILO Declaration on Fundamental Principles and Rights at Work, 91st sess 1(B)' (International Labour Office, 2003).

General Assembly, 'System-wide Coherence', GA Res 64/289, UN GAOR, 64th sess, 104th plen mtg, UN Doc A/Res/64/289 (21 July 2010).

General Assembly, 'Follow-up to the Outcome of the Millennium Summit, Draft Resolution Submitted by the President of the General Assembly: System-Wide Coherence, UN GAOR 64th sess, Agenda Item 114, UN Doc A/64/L.56 [49]–[90]' (30 June 2010).

Human Rights Council Working Group on the Universal Periodic Review, 9th sess Geneva, 1–12 November 2010, 'National Report Submitted in Accordance with Paragraph 15(a) of the Annex to Human Rights Council Resolution 5/1: Great Socialist People's Libyan Arab Jamahiriya, UNGA UN Doc A/HRC/WG.6/9/LBY/1' (United Nations, 24 August 2010).

International Bank for Reconstruction and World Bank, 'World Development Report: The State in a Changing World' (Oxford University Press, 25 June 1997).

International Bureau for Children's Rights (IBCR), 'Making Children's Rights Work in North Africa: Country Profiles on Algeria, Egypt, Libya, Morocco and Tunisia' (IBCR, 2007).

International Labour Office, 'Women's Employment: Global Trends ILO Responses, 49th sess of the Commission on the Status of Women' (United Nations, New York, 28 February–11 March 2005).

International Service for Human Rights (ISHR), 'Committee on the Elimination of All Forms of Discrimination against Women 43rd sess Libyan Arab Jamahiriya, 2nd–5th' (ISHR, 29 January 2009).

Kamerman, Sheila B, 'A Global History of Early Childhood Education and Care: Background Paper Prepared for the Education for All Global Monitoring Report 2007 Strong Foundations – Early Childhood Care and Education' (SBK GLOBAL HX ECEC 2007/ED/EFA/MRT/PI/19, United Nations Educational, Scientific and Cultural Organization, 2006).

Library of Congress Federal Research Division, *Country Profile: Libya* (Library of Congress, 2005).

Productivity Commission, 'Disability Care and Support', Draft Inquiry Report (Australian Government Productivity Commission, February 2011).

Save the Children, 'Champions for Children: State of the World's Mothers 2011' (Save the Children, 2011).

Stiftung, Bertelsmann, 'BTI 2010: Libya Country Report' (BTI 2010, Bertelsmann Stiftung and Center for Applied Policy Research (CAP), Munich University, 2009).

UN Refugee Agency (UNHCR) and Economic and Social Commission for Western Asia (ESCWA), 'Protecting the Rights of Women in the ESCWA Region through the Proper Use of UN Resolutions and International Protocols on War and Armed Conflict, E/ESCWA/ECW/2009/1' (United Nations, 22 July 2009).

UNICE et al, 'Framework of Actions on Gender Equality First Follow-Up Report' (UNICE, UEAPME, CEEP, ETUC, 2006).

UNICEF, 'The Child Care Transition: A League Table of Early Childhood Education and Care in Economically Advanced Countries' (Card 8, Innocenti Research Centre (UNICEF), 2008).

United Nations, *Declarations, Reservations, Objections and Notifications of Withdrawal of Reservations Relating to the Convention on the Elimination of All Forms of Discrimination against Women*: Meeting of the States Parties to the Convention CEDAW, 14th mtg, 23 June 2006, Item 6 of the Provisional Agenda, UN Doc CEDAW/SP/2006/2 (10 April 2006).

United Nations, *Report of the Committee on the Elimination of Discrimination against Women* 13th sess, UN GAOR 49th sess, supp no 38, UN Doc No A/49/38 (12 April 1994).

United Nations, UN GAOR 27th special sess, 5th mtg, UN Doc A/S-27/PV.5 (10 May 2002).

United Nations Committee on the Elimination of Discrimination against Women, *Concluding Observations of the Committee on the Elimination of Discrimination against Women: Libyan Arab Jamahiriya*, UN Doc A/49/38 (2 April 1994).

United Nations Committee on the Elimination of Discrimination against Women, *Concluding Observations of the Committee on the Elimination of Discrimination against Women: Libyan Arab Jamahiriya*, 43rd sess (19 January–6 February 2009) UN Doc CEDAW C/LBY/CO/5 (6 February 2009).

United Nations Committee on the Elimination of Discrimination against Women, *Consideration of Reports Submitted by States Parties under Article 18 of the Convention Initial Reports of States Parties – Libyan Arab Jamahiriya*, UN Doc CEDAW/C/LIB/1 (18 February 1991).

United Nations Committee on the Elimination of Discrimination against Women, *Consideration of Reports Submitted by States Parties Under Article 18 of the Convention on the Elimination of All Forms of Discrimination against Women: Second Periodic Reports by States Parties – Libyan Arab Jamahiriya*, UN Doc CEDAW/C/LBY/2 (15 March 1999).

United Nations Committee on the Elimination of Discrimination against Women, *Consideration of Reports Submitted by States Parties under Article 18 of the Convention on the Elimination of All Forms of Discrimination against Women: Combined 2nd, 3rd, 4th and 5th Periodic Reports of States Parties – Libyan Arab Jamahiriya* UN Doc CEDAW/C/LBY/5 (4 December 2008).

United Nations Committee on the Elimination of Discrimination against Women, *Consideration of Reports Submitted by States Parties under Article 44 of the Convention: Second Periodic Reports of States Parties Due in 2000*, UN Doc CRC/C/93/Add.1 (19 September 2002).

United Nations Committee on the Elimination of Discrimination against Women, *List of Issues and Questions with Regard to the Consideration of Periodic Reports: The Pre-Session Working Group Considered the Second Periodic Report of the Libyan Arab Jamahiriya*, 43rd sess (19 January–6 February 2009) UN Doc CEDAW/C/LBY/Q/2 (12 August 2008).

United Nations Committee on the Elimination of Discrimination against Women, *Responses to the List of Issues and Questions with Regard to the Consideration of the Second Report Libyan Arab Jamahiriya: Pre-session Working Grou*p, 43rd sess (19 January–6 February 2009) UN Doc CEDAW/C/LBY/Q/2/Add.1 (9 January 2009).

United Nations Committee on the Elimination of Discrimination against Women, *Ways and Means of Expediting the Work of the Committee Report of the Secretariat* (29th sess 30 June–18 July 2003) Annex II, Item 6b of the *Provisional Agenda*, UN Doc CEDAW/C/2003/II/4 (14 May 2003).

United Nations Committee on the Rights of the Child, *Consideration of Reports Submitted by States Parties under Article 44 of the Convention: Concluding Observations of the Committee on the Rights of the Child: Libyan Arab Jamahiriya Initial Report*, 17th sess, UN Doc CRC/C/15/Add.84 (4 February 1998).

United Nations Committee on the Rights of the Child, *Consideration of Reports Submitted by States Parties under Article 44 of the Convention: Concluding Observations: Libyan Arab Jamahiriya Second Report*, 33rd sess, UN Doc CRC/C/15/Add.209 (4 July 2003).

United Nations Committee on the Rights of the Child, *Consideration of Reports Submitted by States Parties under Article 44 of the Convention: Initial Reports of States Parties Due in 1995 Addendum – Libyan Arab Jamahiriya* (23 May 1996) UN Doc CRC/C/28/Add.6 (26 September 1996).

United Nations Committee on the Rights of the Child, *Consideration of Reports Submitted by States Parties under Article 44 of the Convention: Third and Fourth Periodic Reports of States Parties Due in 2005 – Libyan Arab Jamahiriya (1 September 2009)*, UN Doc CRC/C/LBY/3–4 (2 June 2010).

United Nations Committee on the Rights of the Child, *Treaty-Specific Guidelines Regarding the Form and Content of Periodic Reports to be Submitted by States Parties under Article 44, Paragraph 1(b), of the Convention on the Rights of the Child*, 55th sess UN Doc CRC/C/58/Rev.2 (23 November 2010).

United Nations Economic Commission for Africa, *Economic and Social Conditions in North Africa Part III: The Economic Participation of Women in North Africa*, 20th mtg of the Intergovernmental Committee of Experts (Tangier, Morocco 13–15 April 2005) UN Doc ECA-NA/TNG/ICE/XX/3/III/Rev.1 (March 2005).

United Nations Economic and Social Commission for Western Asia, *The Millennium Development Goals in the Arab Region 2007: A Youth Lens*, UN Doc E/ESCWA/EAD/2007/3 (UN-ESCWA, 2007).

United Nations Human Rights Committee (HRC), *Consideration of Reports Submitted by States Parties under Article 40 of the Covenant, Fourth Periodic Reports of States Parties: Libyan Arab Jamahiriya*, UN Doc CCPR/C/LBY/4 (10 May 2007).

United Nations Secretary General (Kofi Annan), *Secretary General Says It is Duty of All to be 'Vigilant and Articulate Custodians' of Women's Anti-Discrimination Conventio*n, UN Doc SG/SM/7258, WOM/1152 (Press Release, 10 December 1999).

World Economic Forum, *Global Competitiveness Report 2008–2009* (WEF, Geneva, 2008).
World Economic Forum, *Global Competitiveness Report 2009–2010* (WEF, Geneva, 2009).
World Economic Forum, *Global Competitiveness Report 2010–2011* (WEF, Geneva, 2010).
World Health Organization, 'Country Cooperation Strategy for WHO and the Libyan Arab Jamahiriya 2005–2009' (EM/ARD/009/E/R, Regional Office for the Eastern Mediterranean, WHO, 2006).

Theses

Abdul Qadir, Hussein *Tawazun Al-Sulth fi Al-Dimuqratiyyh Al-Sh'biyh* (LLM Thesis, Jami't Qarywnis, 2002) [Trans: *The Balance of Government in Libya* (Garyounis University)].
Barber, Amee, *Independent Escort Work and Motherhood: Case Studies of Toronto and Edmonton* (MA Thesis, Queen's University (Canada), 2008).
Begum, Afroza, *Protection of Women's Rights in Bangladesh: A Legal Study in an International and Comparative Perspective* (PhD Thesis, University of Wollongong, 2004).
Bespinar-Ekici, Fatma Umut, *To Work or Not to Work: Women's Experiences in Mexico and Turkey* (PhD Thesis, University of Texas at Austin, 2007).
Cooper, Hilary Weiss, *The Transformation of a Woman's Sense of Self After the Birth of Her First Child* (PhD Thesis, City University of New York, 2007).
Delyser, Gail, *Experiences at Midlife of Intentionally Childfree Women* (PhD Thesis, Institute for Clinical Social Work, Chicago, 2007).
Drayton, Kandra, *Motherhood: How it Affects Women Journalists' Experiences* (LLM Thesis, University of Florida, 2004).
Mesrati, Ali Omar Ali, *The Best Interests of the Child: International Child Law as Interpreted in the Libyan High Court Jurisdiction* (PhD Thesis, University of Wollongong, 2009).
Mishtal, Joanna Z, *Contradictions of Democratization: The Politics of Reproductive Rights and Policies in Postsocialist Poland* (PhD Thesis, University of Colorado at Boulder, 2006).
Nizalova, Olena, *The Economic and Social Consequences of Maternity Protection: A Cross-Country Analysis* (LLM Thesis, National University: Kiev-Mohyla Academy, 1999–2000).
Paul-Odouard, Reshmi, *Emotional Intelligence, Social Problem Solving, and Demographics as Predictors of Well-being in Women with Multiple Roles* (PhD Thesis, Adelphi University, 2006).
Sharp, Cassandra E, *Becoming a Lawyer: The Transformation of Student Identity through Stories* (PhD Thesis, University of Wollongong, 2006).
Skupas, Danielle P, *Contesting Francoist Domestic Ideology: Carmen de Lcaza's Mothers and Daughters* (PhD Thesis, University of Wisconsin – Madison, 2007).
Supple, Brooke Lecky, *'Life as a Gyroscope': Creating a Grounded Theory Model for Full-time Working Mothers in Higher Education Administration Developing and Maintaining a Fulfilling, Balanced Life* (PhD Thesis, University of Maryland, College Park, 2007).

Conferences

Abu Alsyd, Fwzyih Muhmmd, 'Mu'wiqat Aml Al-Mr'ah wa Turuq Muwjhtaha' (Paper presented at the Aqtsadiat T'liym wa Aml Al-Mr'ah Fi Aljmahyriyh Al-Ozma, Bnghazy (Libya) Jami't Qarywnis, 10–12 March 1997) [Trans: 'Women's Employment in Libya: Obstacles and Solutions' (Paper presented at Women's Education and Employment in Libya: An Economic Perspective, Benghazi)].

Al-Adly, Mahmud Salih, 'Al-Bu'd Al-Ensany Lihq Al-Mr'ah fi Al-Aml wa Al-T'liym wa Mrdwduh Al-Eqtisady' (Paper presented at the Aqtsadiat T'liym wa Aml Al-Mr'ah fi Aljmahyriyh Al-Ozma, Bnghazy (Libya) Jami't Qarywnis, 10–12 March 1997) [Trans: 'The Human Factor for Libyan's Women Education and Employment and its Economic Return' (Paper presented at Women's Education and Employment in Libya: An Economic Perspective, Benghazi)].

Al-B'jh, Fathi Muhmmd, 'Malm Yntbih Elyh Tqwym Al-Tnafusyh Fi Al-Jmahyriyh: Nzrh Fi Al-Hkmaniyh wa Siyasat Al-Tmkyn' (Paper presented at the Al-Siyasat Al-Ammh, Bnghazy (Libya), 12–14 June 2007) [Trans: 'What Has Not Been Considered by the Competitiveness Calendar in Libya: An Insight into Governance and Empowerment Politics' (Paper presented at Public Policies, Benghazi)].

Al-Jrwshi, Jibryl, Mnswr Al-Zghynyn and Raby'h Al-Zydani, 'Al-Mr'ah Byn Al-Kullyh wa Al-Byt Fi Msratah' (Paper presented at the Aqtsadiat T'liym wa Aml Al-Mr'ah Fi Aljmahyriyh Al-Ozma, Bnghazy (Libya) Jami't Qarywnis, 10–12 March 1997) [Trans: 'Women Between College and Home in Mesrta' (Paper presented at Women's Education and Employment in Libya: An Economic Perspective, Benghazi)].

Al-Zaquzi, Mufidh, 'Al-Mr'ah wa Al-Aml wa Ta'dud Al-Awar wa Tadarubha' (Paper presented at the Aqtsadiat T'liym wa Aml Al-Mr'ah Fi Aljmahyriyh Al-Ozma, Bnghazy (Libya) Jami't Qarywnis, 10–12 March 1997) [Trans: 'The Woman and Work: A Conflict of Multiple Roles' (Paper presented at Public Policies, Benghazi, published 12–14 June 2007)].

Al-Zwy, Salih Muftah, 'Dawr Al-Qanwn fi Tnfydh Al-Siyasat Al-Amm' (Paper presented at the Alsiyasat Al-'Ammh, Bnghazy (Libya), 12–14 June 2007) [Trans: 'The Role of Law in Executing Public Policies' (Paper presented at Public Policies, Benghazi)].

Ba'yrh, Abu-Bkr Mustfa, 'Al-Siyast Al-Ammh Lltnmiyh Al-Edariyh' (Paper presented at the Al-Siyasat Al-Ammh, Bnghazy (Libya), 12–14 June 2007) [Trans: 'Public Policies for Administrative Development' (Paper presented at Public Policies, Benghazi)].

Bu Z'kwk, Muhmmd Ramadan and Muhmmd Kaybh, 'Al-T'liym wa Msahmat Al-Mr'ah Al-Lybyh fi Suwq Al-Aml' (Paper presented at the Aqtsadiat T'liym wa Aml Al-Mr'ah fi Aljmahyriyh Al-Ozma, Bnghazy (Libya) Jami't Qarywnis, 10–12 March 1997) [Trans: 'Education and the Contribution of Libyan Women in the Labour Market' (Paper presented at Women's Education and Employment in Libya: An Economic Perspective, Benghazi)].

Committee on the Elimination of Discrimination against Women, 'Progress Achieved in the Implementation of the Convention on the Elimination of All Forms of Discrimination against Women' (Paper presented at the Fourth World Conference on Women UN Doc A/CONF.177/7, Beijing, 4–15 September 1995).

Hasn, Abudl Hameed Sa'eed, 'Etijahat Al-Mr'ah Al-Libyyh Al-Amilh fi Al-Aml' (Paper presented at the Aqtsadiat T'liym wa Aml Al-Mr'ah fi Aljmahyriyh Al-Ozma, Bnghazy (Libya) Jami't Qarywnis, 10–12 March 1997) [Trans: 'The Directions of the Working Women in Libya' (Paper presented at Women's Education and Employment in Libya: An Economic Perspective, Benghazi)].

International Labour Office, 'ILO Conference to Debate Key Issues: Child Labour, Maternity Rights on Agenda' *World of Work*, No 29, Geneva, April–May 1999, 7.

Mahfwz, Majidh, 'Musharkt Al-Mr'ah fi Al-Aml wa Al-Entaj' (Paper presented at the Aqtsadiat T'liym wa Aml Al-Mr'ah fi Aljmahyriyh Al-Ozma, Bnghazy (Libya) Jami't Qarywnis, 10–12 March 1997) [Trans: 'Participation of Women in Work and Production' (Paper presented at Women's Education and Employment in Libya: An Economic Perspective, Benghazi)].

Mashat, Adel Abdulhamid et al, 'The Social Role of Accounting: Views and Perceptions of the Accounting Community in Libya towards Corporate Social Responsibility and Accountability' (Paper presented at Social Responsibility Research, Leeds, 4–6 September 2005).
Obeidi, Amal, 'Bawadir Al-Eslah Al-Siyasi wa Athruh Ala Siyasat Tmkyn Al-Mr'ah fi libya: Dirash Estkshafih' (Paper presented at the Al-Siyasat Al-Ammh, Bnghazy (Libya), 12–14 June 2007) [Trans: 'Political Reform in Libya and its Impact on Women: A Discovering Study' (Paper presented at Public Policies, Benghazi)].
Sanqr, Saliha, 'Ghyab Al-Bhth Al-'Elmy An Qadaya Al-Mr'ah' (Paper presented at the Al-Mr'ah Fi Al-Mujtm' Al-Arabi, Bnghazy (Libya) Jami't Qarywnis, 28–31 March 1989) [Trans: 'The Absence of Scientific Research Concerning Women's Issues' (Paper presented at Women in Arab Society, Benghazi)].
Shin, Heisoo, 'CEDAW and Women's Human Rights: Achievements and Obstacles' (Paper presented at Human Rights 2004: The Year in Review, Castan Centre for Human Rights Law Annual Conference, 3 December 2004).

Other Sources

Azeem, Sherif Abdel, *Women in Islam Versus Women in the Judaeo-Christian Tradition: The Myth and the Reality* (essay originally published by the World Assembly of Muslim Youth, 1995).
Byrnes, Andrew, Maria Herminia Graterol and Renee Chartres, 'State Obligation and the Convention on the Elimination of All Forms of Discrimination against Women' (Paper 48, University of New South Wales Faculty of Law Research Series, 2007).
Cai, Lixin, 'Work Choices of Married Women: Drivers of Change' (Visiting Research Paper, Productivity Commission, Canberra, July 2010).
Dobrovetsky, Diana, 'Libya's Reconciliation with the West: Implications for U.S. Foreign Policy' (University of Illinois at Chicago, 2004).
Golden, Marissa Martino, 'Women in the Administrative State: The Impact of Motherhood and Family-Friendly Policies on Women's Career Paths in the Federal Civil Service' (Working Paper No 29, University of California, 2006).
International Labour Organization, *ILO Conference to Debate Maternity Protection Health and Safety in Agriculture* (ILO Media Release, Geneva, 29 May 2000).
James Martin Center for Nonproliferation Studies, *Inventory of International Nonproliferation Organizations and Regimes: African Union (AU)* (,2011) <http://cns.miis.edu/inventory/pdfs/au.pdf>.
Nagengast, Carole, 'Women, Individual Rights and Cultural Relativity: Power and Difference in Human Rights Debates' (266, University of New Mexico, 1998).
National Women's Justice Coalition (Australia), 'Submission to the International Labour Conference 87th Session, 1999, Revision of the ILO Maternity Protection Convention (Revised) 1952 (No 103) and Recommendation 1952 (No 95)'.
Šabič, Zlatko, 'Foreign Policy Profile of Libya' (Karina Kuster 4.l. POL–MO, 21040499, Univerza V Ljubljani, Fakulteta Za Družbene Vede, 2007).
Weiwei, Li, 'Equality and Non-Discrimination under International Human Rights Law' (Norwegian Centre for Human Rights, University of Oslo, 2004).

Web Pages

Al Jazeera, *Profile: Muammar Gaddafi* (22 August 2011) <http://www.aljazeera.com/indepth/2011/02/201122117565923629.html>.

Al-Masraf Al-markzy Al-Lybya, *Al-Namw Baswal Al-Bonwk Al-TJarea Al-Lybya fy Al-Rba Al-Thany* (4 June 2011) <http://www.moheet.com/show_news.aspx?nid=301056&pg=3> [Trans: Central Bank of Libya, *Economic Bulletin for the Second Quarter of the Year 2009*].

Amnesty International, *A Fact Sheet on CEDAW: Treaty for the Rights of Women* (25 August 2005) <http://www.amnestyusa.org/women/pdf/cedaw.pdf>.

Arab Human Rights Index, *Libya: Human Rights Profile. International Conventions (undated)* (17 March 2011) <http://www.arabhumanrights.org/en/countries/country.aspx?cid=10>.

Arabic German Consulting, *The Arab League: The League of Arab States* (18 April 2011) <http://www.arab.de/arabinfo/league.htm>.

ASEAN Social Security Association, *Social Security Country Profiles: Vietnam* (5 December 2010) <http://www.asean-ssa.org/CP_Vietnam.pdf>.

Association of Professional Engineers, Scientists and Managers, Australia, *Work and Family (Access to Part-Time Work)* (30 October 2009) <http://www.apesma.asn.au/women/work_and_family.asp>.

Association of Professional Engineers, Scientists and Managers, Australia: Professional Women's Network, *Work and Family (Access to Part-Time Work)* (24 June 2011) <http://www.apesma.asn.au/women/work_and_family.asp>.

Australian Government and Australian Institute of Health and Welfare, *Health Expenditure Australia 2008–09* (10 October 2011) <http://www.aihw.gov.au/publication-detail/?id=6442472450&libID=6442472431>.

Australian Government, Department of Foreign Affairs and Trade, *About Australia: Women – Towards Equality* (2 November 2011) <http://www.dfat.gov.au/facts/women.html>.

Australian Government, Department of Foreign Affairs and Trade, *Travel Advice: Libya* (9 June 2011) <http://www.smartraveller.gov.au/zw-cgi/view/Advice/Libya>.

Australian Government, Family Assistance Office, *Family Tax Benefit Part B* (9 June 2011) <http://www.familyassist.gov.au/payments/family-assistance-payments/family-tax-benefit/family-tax-benefit-part-b/>.

Australian Human Rights Commission, *International Review of Indigenous Issues in 2000: Australia* (1 June 2011) <http://www.hreoc.gov.au/social_Justice/native_title_issues/fight.html>.

Buffalo News, *Walking the Tightrope between Motherhood and a Career Will Never Be Easy, But for Thousands of Western New York's Working Moms Things are Slightly More in Balance Thanks to the Efforts of their Employers. Column: HSBC Lauded for Helping Working Mothers* (21 May 2011) <http://www.highbeam.com/doc/1G1–152211225.html#mlt>.

Bureau of Near Eastern Affairs, *Background Note: Libya* (US Department of State, 16 June, 7 July 2011) <http://www.state.gov/r/pa/ei/bgn/5425.htm>.

Businessweek, *Covering the Mommy Wars* (21 May 2011) <http://www.businessweek.com/magazine/content/06_11/b3975114.htm>.

Caskey, Christopher, *X-Press Yourself: Modesto Woman is Busy, Busy, Busy: Leilani Perillo Maintains Sense of Humor about the Stress of Motherhood* (21 May 2011) <http://proquest.umi.com/pqdweb?did=1085780431&Fmt=7&clientId=20901&RQT=309&VName=PQD>.

CEDAW, *Convention on the Elimination of All Forms of Discrimination against Women, 14th mtg, 23 June 2005* (20 October 2011) <http://www.un.org/womenwatch/daw/cedaw/statesmeeting/fourteenth.htm>.

Central Intelligence Agency, *The World Factbook: Population* (10 May 2011) <http://www.nationsencyclopedia.com/WorldStats/CIA-World-Factbook-Population.html>.

CoinMill.com, *The Currency Converter* (23 October 2009) <http://coinmill.com/AUD-LYD.html>.

Division for the Advancement of Women, Department of Economic and Social Affairs, *Convention on the Elimination of All Forms of Discrimination against Women: Country Reports* (26 May 2011) <http://www.un.org/womenwatch/daw/cedaw/reports.htm>.

Draft Constitutional Charter for the Transitional Stage (23 October 2011) <http://www.al-bab.com/arab/docs/libya/Libya-Draft-Constitutional-Charter-for-the-Transitional-Stage.pdf>.

Esterik, Penny Van, *Breastfeeding: A Feminist Issue (WABA Activity Sheet 4)* (19 May 2011) <http://www.waba.org.my/resources/activitysheet/acsh4.htm>.

Exchange Rates for Kuwaiti Dinar, *Convert Kuwaiti Dinar to Australian Dollar* (2 November 2011) <http://themoneyconverter.com/KWD/AUD.aspx>.

Exchange Rate: Currency Information Libyan Dinar (25 October 2011) <http://www.exchangerate.com/currency-information/libyan-dinar.html>.

Exchange-Rates (15 October 2011) <http://www.exchange-rates.org>.

Family Assistance Office, Australian Government, *Can I Get Family Tax Benefit Part B?* (20 October 2010) <http://www.familyassist.gov.au/payments/family-assistance-payments/family-tax-benefit/family-tax-benefit-part-b/>.

Ghandour, Fatma, *Women's Status in Libya: Breaking the Cultural Shackles* (11 November 2009) <http://www.alarabonline.org/english/print.asp?fname=2008/07/07–17/zfeaturez/971.htm>.

Government of the United Kingdom, *Adoption Leave and Pay* (13 November 2009) <http://www.direct.gov.uk/en/Parents/Moneyandworkentitlements/WorkAndFamilies/Adoptionrightsintheworkplace/DG_10029406>.

Human Rights Watch, *Libya: Arrests, Assaults in Advance of Planned Protests*, 17 February 2011 <http://www.hrw.org/news/2011/02/16/libya-arrests-assaults-advance-planned-protests>.

ILOLEX, *Database of International Standards: Ratifications: Convention C111* (11 May 2011) <http://www.ilo.org/ilolex/english/newratframeE.htm>.

Index Mundi, *Libyan Inflation Rate (Consumer Prices)* (23 May 2011) <http://www.indexmundi.com/libya/inflation_rate_(consumer_prices).html>.

International Labour Office, *Conditions of Work and Employment Programme (TRAVAIL)* (26 May 2011) <http://www.ilo.org/travail/lang--en/index.htm>.

International Labour Organization, *Alphabetical List of ILO Member Countries* (14 July 2011) <http://www.ilo.org/public/english/standards/relm/country.htm>.

International Labour Organization, *Convention No C111* (2 July 2011) <http://www.ilo.org/ilolex/cgi-lex/ratifce.pl?C111>.

International Labour Organization, *Country Ratification the Maternity Protection Convention, 1919 C3* (14 September 2011) <http://www.ilo.org/ilolex/cgi-lex/ratifce.pl?C003>.

International Labour Organization, *Country Ratification the Maternity Protection Convention, (Revised) 1952 C103* (14 September 2011) <http://www.ilo.org/ilolex/cgi-lex/ratifce.pl?C103>.

International Labour Organization, *Country Ratification the Maternity Protection Convention, 2000 C183* (14 September 2011) <http://www.ilo.org/ilolex/cgi-lex/ratifce.pl?C183>.

International Labour Organization, *C3 Maternity Protection Convention, 1919: Ratified by Libyan Arab Jamahiriya on 27:05:1971* (24 September 2011) <http://www.ilo.org/ilolex>.

International Labour Organization, *C103 Maternity Protection Convention (Revised), 1952: Ratified by Libyan Arab Jamahiriya on 19:06:1975* (24 September 2011) <http://www.ilo.org/ilolex>.

International Labour Organization, *List of Ratifications of International Labour Conventions Libyan Arab Jamahiriya* (7 April 2011) <http://webfusion.ilo.org/public/applis/appl-byCtry.cfm?lang=EN&CTYCHOICE=1520>.

International Labour Organization, *Maternity Protection* (30 October 2009) <http://www.ilo.org/travaildatabase/servlet/maternityprotection>.

International Labour Organization, *States Parties* (28 October 2008) <http://www.ilo.org/ilolex/cgi-lex/ratifce.pl?C183>.

Inter-Parliamentary Union, *Women in National Parliaments* (11 November 2009) <http://www.ipu.org/wmn-e/classif.htm>.

Kakchi, Suvendrini, *Japan: New Rules to Promote Motherhood and Let Women Keep* (23 May 2011) *Global Information Network* <http://proquest.umi.com/pqdweb?did=1130043161&Fmt=7&clientId=20901&RQT=309&VName=PQD>.

Lerner, Sharon, 'The Motherhood Experiment' (23 May 2011) *New York Times Magazine* <http://proquest.umi.com/pqdweb?did=1227563021&Fmt=7&clientId=20901&RQT=309&VName=PQD>.

Lewis, Paul M (ed), *Ethnologue: Languages of the World* (9 June 2011) SIL International <http://www.ethnologue.com/show_country.asp?name=libya>.

Libyan Mission, *Libya at the UN* (12 November 2008) <http://www.libyanmission-un-org/welcome.htm>.

Linnecar, Alison and Virginia Yee, *Maternity Legislation: Protecting Women's Rights to Breastfeed (WABA Activity Sheet 6)* (19 May 2011) <http://www.waba.org.my/resources/activitysheet/acsh6.htm>.

NationMaster.com, *Labor Statistics (Libya)* (11 October 2008) <http://www.nationmaster.com/time.php?stat=lab_for_fem_of_tot_lab_for&country=ly>.

New South Wales Teachers Federation, *Adoption Leave* (26 May 2011) <http://www.nswtf.org.au/TemporaryTeachers/adoption.html>.

News 24, *Libya to Get New Constitution* (21 June 2011) <http://www.news24.com/Africa/News/Libya-to-get-new-constitution-20070821>.

Obeidi, Amal, *Al-Mrah wa Al-Bhth Al-Almy fy Aljmalt Allybya: Drash Thlylyh Letjahat Alrsal Alalmyh fy Klyt Algtzad (1990–2009)* (15 November 2011) <www.finstonconsulting.com/ … /Arabic%20Paper%20by%20Amal%20Obeidi.pdf> [Trans: *Women and Scientific Research in Libyan Universities: Analysis of Trends in School* for Thesis in the Faculty of Economics Garyounis University (1990–2009)].

Office of the United Nations High Commissioner for Human Rights, *Committee on the Elimination of Discrimination against Women: Sessions* (15 October 2011) <http://www2.ohchr.org/english/bodies/cedaw/sessions.htm>.

Office of the United Nations High Commissioner for Human Rights, *Committee on the Rights of the Child* (15 August 2011) <http://www2.ohchr.org/english/bodies/crc/>.

Office of the United Nations High Commissioner for Human Rights, *Fact Sheet No 22, Discrimination against Women: The Convention and the Committee* (9 July 2011) <http://www.unhcr.org/refworld/docid/47947740d.html>.

Philadelphia Inquirer, *Editorial: Parents Stretched Thin: Moms Need More Than a Day* (21 May 2011) <http://www.highbeam.com/doc/1G1–163287696.html>.

Programme on Governance in the Arab Region (POGAR), *Libya in Brief* (4 November 2009) <http://gender.pogar.org/countries/theme.aspx?t=4&cid=10>.

Robbins, McLean, *Less is More: More Mothers Desire Part-time Work Options, Study Finds* (23 May 2011) <http://proquest.umi.com/pqdweb?did=1383313591&Fmt=7&clientId=20901&RQT=309&VName=PQD>.

Simpkins, John L S, *Libya's Legal System and Legal Research* (16 June 2011) <http://www.nyulawglobal.org/globalex/libya.htm>.

Trading Economics, *Labor Force: Female (% of Total Labor Force) in Libya* (24 June 2011) <http://www.tradingeconomics.com/libya/labor-force-female-per cent-of-total-labor-force-wb-data.html>.

United Nations, *Great Socialist People's Libyan Arab Jamahiriya: Public Administration Country Profile* (4 October 2010) <http://unpan1.un.org/intradoc/groups/public/documents/UN/UNPAN023273.pdf>.

United Nations, *List of 24 Multilateral Treaties on the Protection of Civilians* (9 June 2011) <http://treaties.un.org/doc/source/events/2004/list.pdf>.

United Nations, *Treaty Collection: Convention on the Elimination of All Forms of Discrimination against Women* (5 September 2011) <http://treaties.un.org/Pages/ViewDetails.aspx?src=TREATY&mtdsg_no=IV-8&chapter=4&lang=en>.

United Nations, *Treaty Collection: Convention on the Rights of the Child* (29 August 2011) <http://treaties.un.org/pages/ViewDetails.aspx?src=TREATY&mtdsg_no=IV-11&chapter=4&lang=en>.

United Nations, *Treaty Collection: Optional Protocol to the Convention on the Elimination of All Forms of Discrimination against Women* (6 September 2011) <http://treaties.un.org/Pages/ViewDetails.aspx?src=TREATY&mtdsg_no=IV-8-b&chapter=4&lang=en>.

United Nations Development Programme, *Human Rights Profiles: Libya* (12 May 2011) <http://www.arabhumanrights.org/en/countries/country.aspx?cid=10>.

United Nations Development Programme, *Libya: Labor Force, Female (% of Total Labor Force)* (5 November 2008) <http://www.undp-pogar.org/countries/morestats.asp?cid=10&ind+188>.

United Nations Development Programme: Arab Human Rights (AHR), *Libya: Country Reports: Convention on the Elimination of All Forms of Discrimination against Women* (15 October 2011) <http://www.arabhumanrights.org/en/countries/convreports.aspx?cid=10&cnv=6>.

United Nations Division for the Advancement of Women/Department of Economic and Social Affairs, *Convention on the Elimination of All Forms of Discrimination against Women: States Parties* (10 May 2011) <http://www.un.org/womenwatch/daw/cedaw/states.htm>.

United Nations Economic and Social Affairs, United Nations Statistics Division (15 November 2008) *Demographic Yearbook 2003* <http://unstats.un.org/unsd/demographic/products/dyb/2000-round.htm>.

United Nations Educational, Scientific and Cultural Organization (UNESCO), *World Data on Education: The Socialist People's Libyan Arab Jamahiriya* (27 October 2010) <http://www.ibe.unesco.org/Countries/WDE/2006/index.html>.

United Nations High Commissioner for Refugees (UNHCR), *Lack of Funds Threatening UNHCR's Work in Libya, Neighbouring Countries* (9 June 2011) <http://www.unhcr.org/4da81fcd9.html>.

UN Women, *Convention on the Elimination of All Forms of Discrimination against Women: Declarations, Reservations and Objections to CEDAW* (22 October 2011) <http://www.un.org/womenwatch/daw/cedaw/reservations-country.htm>.

UN Women, *How We Work* (15 November 2011) <http://www.unwomen.org/>.

Vickers, Melissa, *Breastfeeding: Providing Food Security and Security through Feeding* (19 May 2011) <http://www.llli.org/docs/WorldFoodDay.pdf>.

Voice of Libyan Women (30 June 2012) <http://www.vlwlibya.org/>.

World Alliance for Breastfeeding Action (WABA), *Breastfeeding and HIV: Protecting Babies, Empowering Mothers* (19 May 2011) <http://www.waba.org.my/whatwedo/hiv/index.htm>.
World Alliance for Breastfeeding Action (WABA), *Health Care Practices* (19 May 2011) <http://www.waba.org.my/whatwedo/healthcarepractices.htm>.
World Alliance for Breastfeeding Action (WABA), *Women and Work* (19 May 2011) <http://www.waba.org.my/whatwedo/womenandwork/index.htm>

Index

For Product Safety Concerns and Information please contact our EU representative GPSR@taylorandfrancis.com Taylor & Francis Verlag GmbH, Kaufingerstraße 24, 80331 München, Germany

Batch number: 10726294

Printed by Printforce, the Netherlands